GULAG
REMNANTS OF WAR

**memoir of
an American
in Hitler's army
and in Stalin's gulag**

Peter Schwarzlose

The major stations in the book

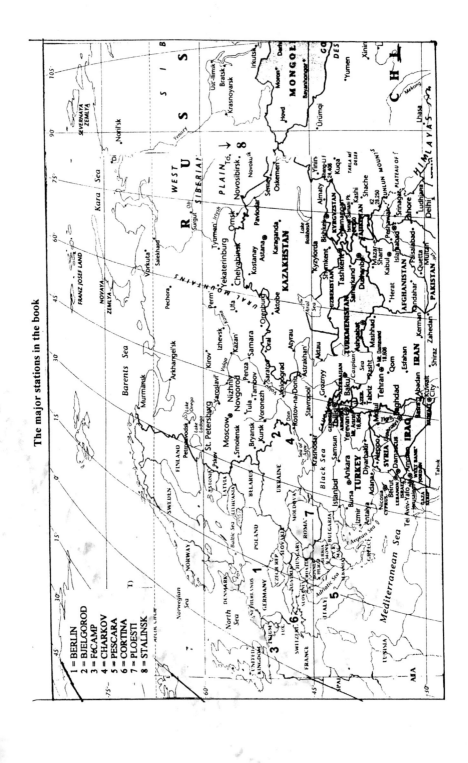

1 = BERLIN
2 = BJELGOROD
3 = FeCAMP
4 = CHARKOV
5 = PESCARA
6 = CORTINA
7 = PLOESTI
8 = STALINSK

GULAG
REMNANTS OF WAR

Published by Monika Press
22 Lighthouse Road #493
Hilton Head Island, SC 29928
843-671-2247
www.gulagmemoirs.com

ISBN 0-9776995-0-1

LCCN 2005938078

First Edition

Printed in the United States of America
By BookMasters, Inc.

Testimonials

I finished your book with fascination.... It seems that you were doomed at every turn....everybody interested in history and the events of that time MUST read your book."

Cyril Geacintov, New York

"Every actor in Hollywood would lick his fingers to play the lead in this movie."

David Smith, Sea Pines, Hilton Head

"Fabulously written, truthful, precise and mind boggling..."

Herwig Zahm, Munich Germany

"I couldn't put it down until I turned the last page. Exciting and absolutely wonderful..."

Melvin Davis, Hilton Head Island

"I just finished your book, thank you for sharing your exciting experiences with me."

Sam Nixon, Christiansburg, VA

"I enjoy reading about your adventures...my parents remember meeting you in 1950 at a family reunion."

John Schwarzlose, CEO Betty Ford Center

"Phenomenal.... couldn't put it down. What a story of your life experiences and your time in the GULAG... passed it on to a friend who felt the same."

Philip Thornton, Hilton Head

"...the most realistic, detailed writing on the fighting part of a war I have ever read or heard....an incredible story...and then reduced to servitude in Russia for 4 years."

John Kerr, Tide Point, Hilton Head

"WOW! An incredible ride. The details about everything are fantastic! Surviving the dragon's teeth only to live in its Siberian belly and to live to tell an unforgettable story. What a painful, torturous involuntary education for a young man! I am truly grateful to know you and this book has been an enlightenment for me."

Chadwick Golden, DMD

"It is very difficult for me to find one word that might describe you book, GULAG. So I'll try 'fascinating'. It is so unusual that a gifted novelist would have a difficult time writing a book that devised the depth, the circumstances, and the many characteristics of the story's central personality.... It's a corner piece for a movie of your incredible experiences...."

Lt. Gen. "Fly" Flanagan, ret.

Siberia 1945—1949

If you ever forget how good you have it,
look at me. Four years and four months
prison and 4731 times, sauerkraut soup
in a row, that's what I represent.

(The mess kit displayed on the cover was made
by Peter when he arrived in the camp in
Stanlinsk in 1945. After his return from Siberia
he applied this reminder to the front side.)

Dedication

This story pays tribute to millions of nameless people, civilians, soldiers—Baltic, Bulgarian, German, Hungarian, Italian, Japanese, Polish, Russians and members of many other nations—who suffered or disappeared in the Russian Gulag. Millions are buried all over Russia with neither a name on their shallow graves nor a cross to mark it. They died without hope, without the support of their countries and their families who to this very date are unaware of their fate.

The government of Nazi Germany should be remembered, because if we would forget only *one* of the atrocities committed during its reign we would do the gravest injustice to the victims who vanished without trace. It is an historical fact that the government of Nazi Germany consisted of the worst criminals the world has ever seen. These monsters in power were oblivious to the rights of human beings. For us, who have survived by the grace of God, it is our everlasting duty never to permit the reappearance of such a regime anywhere in this world, or to condone political blunders and individual or collective cowardice that made its creation and deeds possible.

I never would have been able to write this book, if it were not for my friend, Arthur Otto. During those difficult fifty-four months we spent as prisoners in the Gulag, he kept my spirit and my resilience alive with his never failing confidence, his unfaltering friendship and his selfless support. He will live in my memory forever.

My mother, Olga, was a shining and guiding example not only for me, but also for others she met during her long life. Whether it was in Berlin, during the First World War, or in the Second World War when faithful friends protected her from the Nazis, she always prevailed, even in the most difficult circumstances and survived by the strength of her personality, her resourcefulness, and her never failing trustworthiness. For me she was not only my beloved mother but my heroine as well. Her example guides me and encourages me every day of my life and will continue to do so until my dying day.

Contents

Preface

Sometimes non-fiction books are written because the author loves to write. Other times the author has lived under exceptional circumstances and wants to keep his experiences alive for posterity. In my case I decided to write for the latter reason. This is my memoir in the form of a novel as a narrative of a crucial time in my life.

I have waited fifty-six years to put everything on paper. This is the first I have written about these times. It was difficult for me to start, because the events I am about to describe are painful for me to remember. They continue to wake me up at night when I think about them.

After I returned from Siberia at the end of 1949 I began to compile notes with the intent of writing this story. But I could not do it while everything was fresh in my mind. Many years later I started to put the story together. Friends, to whom I told bits and pieces of what I am about to tell you, convinced me that I should share my experiences.

Of course, the hardest part is to put personal experiences on paper and describe them in a way that enables readers to see everything vividly. The reader should be able to relive the events without being bored by historical or personal detail.

The driving force behind this endeavor was my mother, Olga. While she was still alive, I spoke to her often about my adventures, and she related hers to me. She had many stories to tell many of which I didn't know.

I intend history to be the skeletal foundation for my story. Of course, not every quoted word here is stated verbatim because I cannot remember exactly what people said. But I do remember the essence of what they said.

Did my mother and I really live the lives I describe? Yes, we did. Even though today I am eighty-one years old and my family and my friends who appear on these pages are no longer alive, I am reporting to you truthfully that what I write happened to these people, to Olga, to me, and to my friends, Arthur, Karl, and Galina Dimitrewna Xerimnik.

The events, which cover two world wars, are worth telling if for no other reason than as a description of the first half of the last century. I hope I will convince younger readers that life was exceptional during that time and readers of the older generation that they were fortunate to skip the bad parts.

Life can be much worse, or much better, than illusions are portrayed in movies. Furthermore, I am not reporting tragedies and hardships to create a dramatic effect but simply to describe my life as it was. I hope it will make exciting reading for you.

Let me emphasize that to my mind no matter where life takes you, or how difficult it might be, you can make the best of it.

Peter Schwarzlose,
August 2005,
six years after my friend Arthur died

Prologue

Today, as I look back to the years I spent in Hitler's army, to many horrors of war, to seven times I was wounded, to four and one half years in the Siberian gulag, almost starving to death and experiencing the present, living as retiree on Hilton Head Island, South Carolina, playing golf in a paradise, I consider myself with sincere conviction the luckiest man alive. A few explanations are in order to understand why World War II and its aftermath turned my life upside down.

My mother, Olga Dalzell, was born in Brooklyn, New York, in 1883. Her mother, Maria Tiana, had arrived in 1869 from Milan, Italy, with her parents, on a three-mast schooner. Her father, Augustus Dalzell, originated from Scotland. His ancestors had come to America around 1750. Both of her parents died early. She became an orphan and was adopted by her father's sister-in-law. She spent her last school years in Cincinnati, Ohio, in a boarding school. During a visit from school to her home in Brooklyn, my mother went to a concert with her stepmother and was introduced to the star of the evening, a young, dashing pianist. They fell in love and the young man asked Olga's stepmother for her hand in marriage. They married in 1913 and left for Europe in the spring of 1914 on a concert tour through Europe.

Egon Pütz was of German-Spanish extraction. In Europe, Olga stayed with her husband's mother in Berlin while he performed in London. The beginning of World War I in August 1914, surprised Egon there and did not permit him to return to Germany to fetch his wife.

He wrote a short letter to Olga telling her that he would have to return to the USA to earn money. Olga was stranded in Berlin for the remainder of the war. The letter was the last she ever heard from her husband who disappeared without a trace.

At the end of World War I, without funds, stranded in Berlin and living with her mother-in-law, Olga started to work in the newly created moving pictures industry in *Berlin-Babelsberg* in minor acting jobs. As soon as the US embassy was reopened she obtained a divorce. During that time she met a wealthy German, my father, whom she married in April of 1920.

My father, Kurt Schwarzlose, came from a well-known family in Berlin. His father had founded a cosmetic company in 1865, which manufactured mainly perfumes and Eau de Colognes and also operated a chain of cosmetic shops. Kurt had chosen not to follow in his father's footsteps becoming a merchant but rather opted to be an officer in the Emperor's army. Losing World War I ended that career.

Olga and Kurt's marriage didn't start out on a happy footing. When I was born in 1924, my father was vacationing with his girlfriend in *Binz* on the Baltic Sea. Though my father was happy to have an heir for his company, he could not stop his philandering.

In 1926, my mother planned a trip to the USA to find out whether or not she could make it in New York on her own. She took me along on this trip, but not before going to the US Consulate to put my baby picture in her passport. An official seal embellished it. Somehow she was convinced that this procedure made me a US citizen.

After checking out her economic viabilities in New York, without vocation or a finished education, she realized she had to return to Berlin and try to live with her husband. These were years of economic upheaval, the 100% inflation of the currency in 1923 and the crash in 1929, which affected the German economy as badly, if not worse, as the American, and the years when political extremist from the right and the left tried to take over Germany. The young Democracy was rather helpless—dealing with the Free Corps, the Communists and the Nazis.

In 1936 however, three years after Hitler came to power, Olga finally obtained a divorce. A separation agreement stipulated that my father had visitation rights to see me each year during summer recess. My mother and I left for Long Island, New York, where I went to school. From then on, I spent the summers with my mother in Germany, visiting my father, until the fateful summer of 1939.

My mother Olga in Brooklyn, 1913

My father Kurt as a young lieutenant in the emperor's army, 1913

My mother (in leather) with American flyers in Berlin, 1919

1

AND THEN THERE WAS WAR

It was August 5, 1939; I just had my fifteenth birthday. We would stay another month in Germany before summer vacation was over and my mother and I would return to the USA. My time with forester Laurenz in Pomerania was cut short because my father made plans for me to spend some time with him. I wondered.

In the end it turned out to be enjoyable. My father and Marcella, his second wife and my so-called stepmother, took me to Heiligendamm, a fashionable resort at the Baltic Sea. For a change, all three of us were getting along fabulously. We spent time on the beach and played golf almost every day.

My father was a late-in-life golfer. He had a terrible swing but was ambitious with his game. His handicap, 23, was an embarrassment, but we had fun on the golf course. Marcella's handicap was 12, not bad for a woman. I played a 10 by now and showed off my skills, acquired with a lot of practicing. Marcella and I gave my father 13 and 11 strokes respectively, which made it difficult for us to gain the upper hand. As a golfer he should have noticed that my handicap couldn't have dropped from 19 to 10 without extensive work on the golf course, but he didn't.

Most evenings I was permitted to stay up late for dinner in the swanky hotel ballroom. The hotel had a beach-like look, all white in turn-of-the-century-style architecture with lots of windows overlooking the sea. On the front terrace was a modern big band playing the latest hits, which enabled me to try my dancing skills with Marcella. She was fun to dance with, a good-looking blond, slender and well-proportioned.

Wilhelm II, the last German emperor, had built this resort for himself, his family, and their entourage, a luxury hotel and six large bed-and-breakfast villas named after his children. The villas were built in identical neo-baroque style, or so the hotel brochures claimed. They were always freshly painted white, kept spotlessly clean to look impressive to foreign visitors who came every year. To me the architecture looked awful, *kitsch.* The villas seemed more like decorated wedding cakes than bed and breakfast places.

Heiligendamm had been the resort of choice for the Emperor's family and his entourage before the World War I. It was not too far from Berlin and could be reached by train in only two hours. People who came to *Heiligendamm* when I was there were wealthy, or influential, or both. The mixture was odd and astounding. The Queen of Holland and her daughter Juliana, the King of Norway with his crowd, all mixed nicely with upper class Nazis from Berlin. Goebbels, the limping propaganda minister of the Third Reich, was there with his wife, Magda, and their children. The Archduke of Mecklenburg of the old German royalty was there too.

For an inquisitive boy of sixteen it was exciting to watch these celebrities surrounded by servants and lackeys but otherwise behaving and looking like normal, everyday people. Except for those excitements, it would have been a dull and boring place for a young vacationer like me.

Left undisturbed, the beach consisted of nothing but pebble stones. Every year it was replenished with truckloads of pure white sand from neighboring beaches several miles away to turn the area into a *real* beach. Only wealthy people who came here in the summers to enjoy the exclusivity, and paid for it, made it possible to have this semblance of a beach. The whole beach, even after all the sand had been carted in, was only 500 yards long, just enough to accommodate the few hundred visitors from the hotel and the bed-and-breakfast establishments. During the winters, the sea washed most of the sand away. Before the next summer season the sand replacement process had to be repeated.

Everybody who visits beaches on the Baltic or North Sea comes equipped with shovels because you have to build a 'castle' to assure your privacy and to stake a claim to your spot on the beach for the rest of the vacation. When I started to build our castle, a two-foot high wall of sand surrounding one of the famous wicker beach chairs, I sorted out thousands of pebble stones.

Heiligendamm, August 1939
Father, Stepmother, fox terrier Curry and me

My father and his wife sat in one of these comfortable beach chairs enjoying the sun and the view of the sea while I shoveled sand, sweat dripping from my forehead, to complete the castle. It was a lot of work. Once I had finished I went to collect shells of various sizes and shapes from the edge of the water and stuck them to the sand walls, creating the outline of a whale with my initials in the middle— PKS. That took me the better part of the day and kept me busy while getting a tan. In the evening I felt I had earned my dinner.

The only other attraction around *Heiligendamm* was a small steam engine with four old-fashioned passenger cars attached. They rode on a narrow-gauge railroad track and transported passengers and sightseers to *Doberan,* the nearest small town. The excitement in *Doberan* came from the racetrack. Once a week some beat-up old horses from surrounding farms ran around the track pretending to be racing. Big deal!

From all I could observe the entertainment value of these races was limited. Few people ventured all the way to *Doberan* to see the horses, and if they did, it was mostly for the fun of riding on the small train. The train stopped here and there, permitting people to get off to pick flowers or have a picnic. They waited at the same spot to be picked up again on its return passage. If we young people behaved nicely and showed real interest in the small but bully looking steam engine, the engineer would permit us to step up into his cabin to watch him handle the controls. Today, 66 years and two political systems later, the train is still running—same engine, same cars, and same routine—as when I was there as a boy 66 years ago.

"What are you going to do about playing golf when you're back on Long Island?" my father asked one evening at dinner while I devoured my second dish of ice cream. He always used these opportunities of luxurious relaxation to imply life with him was better than with my mother, with many more perks and better entertainment than she was able to afford in the USA. Regularly and routinely he would lash out at the Americans. I knew what was coming next.

"And what are your friends at school going to say about your stay in Germany? Do you ever discuss the success Germany enjoys in the world now? Just look at the people here and you know what I am talking about," he declared.

What was I going to reply without annoying him and his wife, my stepmother, and without ruining my vacation? And furthermore, how could I explain to a proud former officer of his Majesty's army what my American friends thought about Herr Hitler and his goons?

I simply followed my mother's instructions and kept the controversy out of play. "Papi, if there's one thing we don't discuss in school, it's politics. We talk about sports, mostly about baseball but also about American football and basketball. You know, I have tried to explain these sports to you, but it's difficult for me to make sense and describe the rules accurately to you without you being present and observing a game."

He agreed on that score; we had gone through that before. I could not possibly have related to him the remarks made in school about goose-stepping Nazis and land-grabbing Germans who had marched into Austria and had occupied the Sudetenland. And I couldn't tell him about the harassment I endured from some of my classmates to whom I was the German kid, the little Nazi, much less tell him how much I liked my Jewish friend, Bert Larson, and his family, or tell him about the many golfing tips I had received from Mr. Larson. That would have really opened up a can of worms.

My mother had sworn me on my Boy Scout's honor never, but never, to be drawn into a discussion about politics with anybody, not even, especially not, with my father. It was easy for me to obey this oath because politics did not interest me one bit, even though I was in Germany where I was constantly surrounded by politics. Now, on the terrace of this beautiful hotel, I was trying to change the subject.

"Aren't we going to play golf tomorrow, and who is going to play with whom?" I asked, trying to be very clever but not fooling anybody.

I didn't know whether Marcella read my thoughts or whether she also wanted to drop politics and talk about golf. Anyway she chimed in, "Yes, let's discuss our game tomorrow. I'll play with the Archduke of Mecklenburg. His 24 handicap will give the two of us three strokes against your combined handicap of 33. You, Peter, will play with your father."

"Wonderful. Papi, his title won't help him if we play up to our natural talents. Marcella can't carry him alone."

My father laughed proudly because I had alluded to his talents in playing golf. Our vacation ended on an especially happy note after we beat our opponents 5 and 3 the next day.

I returned from Heiligendamm. My mother, who had stayed in Berlin with her friends from the American Women's Club, was trying to do something to make me happy. It was my sixteenth birthday. She organized a fabulous party for me.

It was supposed to be a surprise, but the only surprise was that Marianne, my one and only love, was there. At that time I was positive I would never love any girl but her. She was tall and blond, and she had beautiful blue eyes. Her hair had an inside roll as the latest fashion dictated. Her make-up was smashing, crowned by a light pink lipstick on the lips I longed to kiss.

There was one hitch, an almost insurmountable one—she was two-and-a-half years older than I. At sixteen, that was an eternity. Girls that much older wouldn't even look at you. And now she had come to my party. I tried to figure it out. The only explanation I could fathom was that she was the daughter of a friend of my mother's; that was the reason she had accepted the invitation.

Not by the wildest stretch of my imagination did I think she had arrived because of me. Now, honestly, no girl her age would stoop so low as to come to the birthday party of a mere child. But here she was.

She appeared gorgeous and beautiful. I would be damned if I would not do something to stake my claim right then and there. When I couldn't wait any longer, because the party was about to be over, I approached Marianne and took my heart into both of my hands (a nice old German saying: *Ich hab' mein Herz in beide Hände genommen*). "Hi, Janne, it was nice of you to come to my party. What an exciting surprise it was for me. So many of my old friends came, and I didn't find much time to talk to you. How about going to a movie tomorrow? I know just the one you'd like to see and it's going to be my treat."

I was sure she would raise her eyebrows, wrinkle her nose, smile a little condescending smile that I had noticed repeatedly crossing her face, and turn me down. In my imagination I had already heard her ironic laugh and her blasé reply. I cringed.

Surprise, surprise. "That's a great idea," she replied. "I'd love to go to the movies with you, Peter. Give me a call and tell me where we'll meet. I've got to run now. My parents are waiting, and I don't want to disappoint them."

Off she went, leaving a totally surprised and happy *me* behind.

A while ago my father had explained to me jokingly: "When you choose a girlfriend, pick an older one. She will be more rewarding; young girls just giggle a lot."

I didn't quite understand what he meant at the time, but during my formative years I tried to listen to him. I must say, as you will see later on, I was not without success. On my first attempt to follow his advice he had been proven right. Janne's friendship was a boost to my ego, and the remainder of the vacation was heaven.

On Sept 1, 1939, Hitler's troops invaded Poland. Two days later Great Britain issued an ultimatum, which historians later said surprised "Mr. Hitler" and which he failed to acknowledge. The Second World War was under way.

This happened at the end of my summer vacation, the most inopportune time for my mother and me. I wonder sometimes when I lie awake at night what would have been the course of my life if the war had started a week later. My life would have been far different. But let us return to my story.

Our ship was supposed to leave Germany on September 3. Hitler had started his war just two days before my mother and I were to embark for New York.

The radio broadcast of his speech, screeching and bellowing, ranting and raving, still rings in my ears. He explained to the German public, no, he yelled at his listeners, that he could no longer tolerate the brazen and outrageous violations of Germany's borders by the Poles in Upper Silesia. Of course, he knew very well what he was doing. He had trumped up a fabricated incident in Upper Silesia, near the city of Oppeln, to justify the invasion of Germany's peaceful neighbor.

British Chancellor Neville Chamberlain's appeasement policy went to hell in a hand basket. Not too long ago Chamberlain had proudly waved a piece of paper in front of the waiting reporters as he stepped off the plane upon returning to London from his negotiations with the Führer. "Peace in our time," Chamberlain proclaimed after he had agreed to Hitler's annexation of Czechoslovakia. That was not the way Hitler saw it.

My mother told me later that the reception of the declaration of war by the German people was in dramatic contrast to what she observed in 1914. Then the people had been singing in the streets, placing flowers under the helmets of the marching soldiers. This time everybody in the streets seemed to be subdued, as if they felt the arrival of an impending disaster.

My parents got together immediately, which they seldom did for any reason, to discuss what to do in this situation.

That's probably what children understand the least, this total lack of communication between two people who put us into this treacherous world and then divorce each other. But here was a reason to talk that they could not wish away, no matter how hard they might have tried.

After the trumped-up incident in Upper Silesia all German borders with Poland had been closed immediately. The Hamburg-American Line, when my mother contacted it, informed her that the planned departure of the *Bremen* had been delayed for the duration of the hostilities.

According to the German political commentators the 'conflict' would undoubtedly not last longer than six weeks. Considering the results of the Czechoslovakian skirmish, the strength of the German army vis-à-vis the Polish army, and the inability of the so-called Allies to make up their minds, it would be over soon.

But this time the German propaganda machine had overestimated the patience and gullibility of the Allied countries. Hitler had lied once too often. The Allies were fed up with his shenanigans. They had obligations too that they could not ignore any longer. England and France declared war on Germany to abide by the terms of their mutual assistance pact with Poland.

Historians, when they were able to search the German archives six years later, discovered that Hitler was totally aghast, consternated and surprised, throwing one of his famous fits, tearing down the curtains at the Chancellery, and screaming his head off. He could not believe that England had finally faced up to the fact that he was a mendacious liar. England had decided that the monster could not be pacified. He had to be confronted and destroyed.

For my mother and me the war meant that our to return to the USA would be delayed indefinitely. My parents came to the conclusion that we should wait until the war was over. We should not cross the Atlantic while German U-boats were trying to torpedo every ship in sight.

My mother, still remembering her ordeal during the first war, did not want to remain in Berlin. She decided that after getting me situated she would go to Switzerland to stay with the Wiedmers, her old and dear American friends, who resided in Zurich.

Both my father and my mother thought it best for me to go to a boarding school to keep up my education. They registered me at a small school in the northern part of Brandenburg, the province north of Berlin. It was my father's choice and was called the Landschulheim Lychen. Of course, nobody asked me my opinion. My pleading with my mother to take me with her to Switzerland helped me not one iota. With the worries the grown-ups had at this juncture I was just in everybody's way.

"Listen Peter," my mother tried to pacify me, "I don't believe this war will last too long. The Germans are too strong for the Poles, and if it is true what everybody is saying, the French and the English don't want to fight another big war. They still have had enough from the last one. Your father is of the opinion that a little bit of discipline will do you good. I tend to agree with him. I inquired about the school and have obtained excellent recommendations. Be a good sport, don't put up a fuss, and go there for half a year or so. Then this episode will be over, and we'll go back to New York together, I promise."

I was totally disappointed and almost hysterical when I heard her response. I made one final and, for a young boy of my age, rather dramatic statement. "Mom, I realize that this is a difficult time for everybody, but I think you're deserting me when I need you most," I said very seriously while looking straight into her eyes. "I'm afraid about what's going to happen to all of us and particularly to me. What are your plans if this war takes longer than you anticipate, can you tell me that?"

The outcome of our discussion and her answer were predictable. What could I do against the opinion of the grown ups, my parents?

A couple of days later my mother took me to a school in this God forsaken little town of *Lychen* where I met my new school buddies. *Lychen* is located six miles east of *Fürstenberg,* which is 60 miles north of Berlin, surrounded by a lace work of medium-to-large lakes in an agrarian environment with small farms, lots of forests, but no manufacturing industry of any kind. It presented itself as a beautiful countryside. At least that's what my mother pointed out to me eagerly, trying to improve my spirits.

What was obvious was that the entire exercise was conducted at my expense. What the heck, I thought, trying to pacify my own negative premonitions, six months is not an eternity. I promised to give it a try.

Later I wrote a long letter to my friend Bert back in New York. I hoped it would make it to the United States if my mother mailed it from Switzerland, which she promised to do.

The problems in school arose almost immediately. After only a week the principal called me into his office and announced pompously, "I'll have to register you with the local Hitler Youth organization. Tell me the number of your HJ (*Hitler Jugend*) unit, and your member number in Berlin."

I thought I would drop dead right then and there. What was the man talking about? I was aghast and protested strenuously that I had never been in any Hitler Youth organization in my entire life, and I didn't intend to join one now.

"I'm a member of the Boy Scouts in America, and that's all." I reiterated again and again that I had spent my summer vacation in Germany to live up to the divorce agreement between my parents. During the rest of the year I lived and went to school on Long Island in the USA. I tried to convince him I was an American, and that I never had been and never intended to be a member in any German party organization, Hitler Youth, or any other. I felt helpless in the principal's office like any sixteen-year-old would in a similar situation.

The Boss—that's what everybody called the headmaster—was very surprised by my statements. He told me he would have to check everything I said with my father in Berlin.

The next day he called me again into his office and informed me that my father had totally disagreed with my description of the situation. My father had told him that although I had traveled back and forth to the United States with my mother, my picture had been entered into her passport *for convenience sake only.* That didn't make me an American, he said, since he was my father and he was German. I had been born in Berlin as his son and, therefore, I was a German citizen.

There was no way I could contact my mother in Zurich. A war was going on and most connections had been interrupted. Even if they had not been, how could I have managed to contact her from a school in the middle of nowhere with the only available telephone in the headmaster's office?

When I finally managed to get my father on the phone, he got angry and scolded me. "I'm in the middle of a very important business discussion. Don't bother me with such petty things. Do your work at school and be a credit to your family. It's an honor to be a German. You should try to live up to your heritage instead of masquerading as an American." Then he hung up the phone on me, just like that. He had deserted me. I never forgave him for that.

I told the Boss that I was not going to any Hitler Youth meetings no matter what my father had said. As unwavering as possible, I stuck with that decision for the next three years of my life.

Considering the omnipresence of the Nazi party in Germany and in every German's life, my obstinacy was only possible in this little school in the middle of nowhere. I would have run up against a brick wall with my continual display of passive protest if I had tried my shenanigans in Berlin.

Many of my new friends at school, most of them from divorced parents, supported my position, but they were afraid to do so openly. In the end I took part in Hitler Youth glider classes. I did it after much bullying and attempts at intimidation by the Boss and the *Ortsgruppenleiter* (local party official). They threatened me that I would never be admitted to any university in Germany without a membership in the Hitler Youth. The glider classes were not laced with as much political indoctrination as other branches of the Nazi organization. I made believe in my own mind that I had struck a compromise I could live with without giving up my principles.

Like any boy my age, I loved the activity with the gliders and the flying. After many hours of practice I turned out to be an accomplished glider pilot.

The type of glider plane used by us beginners had a single wing across the top of an upright wooden frame with a small seat in front, a wooden plank, for only one person. We spent a lot of time sitting on this wooden plank while the plane was resting motionless on the ground. We practiced handling the joystick to guide the plane. With both our feet placed on the side rudder pedals, we handled the stick carefully. We moved it up or down and sideways, left or right between our legs. We held the stick in our hand, trying to keep the plane balanced. We tried to keep it totally steady with the help of only the wind so its wings would not tip to either side and touch ground.

It was not easy, but it was a perfect exercise to develop a feeling for what the glider would do in the air. Our practice taught us how little movement the joystick really needed to affect the plane's behavior in the air. After many hours we did it right. The instructor finally informed us that we were going to take turns for our first solo flight.

Together we pulled the plane to the top of a small hill while it rested on a small cart with two rubber wheels. The first guy—to my great disappointment it was not I—sat down on the seat with a leather helmet strapped to his head for protection. The instructor commandeered six of us to huddle in the sand in the back of the plane. One sat behind the other, the first one holding onto the plane's tail and the next one holding on to the guy in front, everybody digging in with his heels.

Under the pilot's seat, on the bottom of the upright frame, was a large iron hook. The instructor told ten students to grab a 90-foot-long rope made of rubber and linen fiber. It would propel the glider into the air if it were stretched tight enough. The ten guys were told to position the rope around the hook under the nose of the plane, then align themselves, five on each side of the rope in front of the glider, to be ready on his command. On the count of three they ran downhill, holding tightly onto the rope. We sat in the back holding the glider in place until the tension of the rubber rope, became impossible to resist.

The guys ran down the hill, and the rope became tighter and tighter. Finally, we couldn't hold on any longer and let go. The glider, propelled by the tension of the rubber rope, shot into the air like from a catapult. We all cheered happily about our accomplishment.

The glider flew straight down the hill holding its elevation until its velocity diminished gradually. Its nose came down slowly and touched the ground. After skidding about 20 yards through the sand it came to a stop. We all ran down the hill and congratulated our comrade, the first pilot. The instructor was satisfied, most likely because nothing had gone wrong.

My turn came on the third try and I discovered that flying a glider was an exhilarating experience. I hoped I would experience this feeling many more times.

As the time of winter vacation approached I was looking forward to an honest-to-goodness talk with my mother. I spent the vacation at my father's home. My mother was scheduled to arrive from Zurich by train. I prepared myself for our discussion and was determined not to give in this time.

When I picked her up at the main station she was as happy to see me, as I was to see her. We both cried a lot.

In her home I confronted her with well-prepared arguments, which I intended her to use in turn with my father. All this nonsense of the Hitler Youth, my being German, and all the other idiotic, false information had to be corrected. After a long discussion back and forth with many subterfuges on her part, she admitted to me that she was helpless. She depended upon my father for her—our—financial support. She didn't want, and couldn't afford, to anger him.

"Holy Moses, do you realize what's going to happen to me now?" I exclaimed in total consternation. "If this war continues for a few years—and I don't see an end to it now that England and France have gotten into it—everybody in school says we will be old enough to be drafted into the army. That's the last place I want to be. You have got to do something, Mom."

My mother was distraught but unable to help me. She tried to convince me I was seeing things much too bleakly. She promised to go to the American consul general in Zurich as soon as she got back and explained to me that she didn't want to be seen entering the American consulate in Berlin. The world was really going crazier and crazier by the minute.

Six months later when I saw her again, she hadn't made any progress. The American consulate in Zurich didn't have my records;

couldn't confirm my citizenship. They told her to start her inquiry in Berlin where the consulate had put my baby picture into her passport many years ago.

Apparently at the time of my birth in August 1924—and later before traveling to the United Sates when everything was hunky-dory with the picture of her baby in her passport—she had not bothered to register me as a US citizen at the Berlin consulate. She had thought the vice consul would do that for her, or she had forgotten to get copies of the papers. That was just as bad. It had been the same problem then as now; she didn't want to face any problems with my father. When her marital troubles worsened and when she wanted to take me with her to the United States, she continued her illusion that my baby picture in her passport would be good enough. That was true until our last trip. She procrastinated the confirmation of my status until I no longer looked like a baby. I was too old and it was too late.

Legally, she explained to me sadly, she had goofed and the bureaucrats had goofed too. My baby picture in her passport wasn't enough to support my claim to be a US citizen. With the support of the German government officials my father claimed otherwise. In such a minor matter nobody at the US consulate was going to risk a confrontation to set the record straight.

I was petrified. I knew what this would mean if the war were not over soon. In a worse scenario I knew what this would mean to my future if the Germans were not going to lose the war.

"Mutti, please keep your fingers crossed and pray for me. Don't give up trying because I don't believe this war is going to be over soon," I pleaded.

She was in tears, wringing her hands in desperation.

"Oh, Peter, I promise, I will not leave you alone in this, no matter what happens. I will keep trying to convince somebody at the consulate in Zurich to change the documents the way they are supposed to be."

Fat chance!

By this time I was almost fifteen-and-a-half years old. The future looked bleak to me. Up to this point the Germans were winning their war all over the map. There was only a slight chance the war would end before I turned eighteen. I feared I would be drafted into this mess.

At school I found out quickly that it did me considerable harm to talk about America and describe to others my experiences with my friends over there. I kept my mouth shut. Most people quickly forgot about my special situation anyway. The fellows in my room—we always were four to a room—were okay and gradually my life became normal, or as normal as it could have been.

The German armies were having an easy time wherever they went, not only in Poland, which they finished in sixteen days, but also a year later in France as well. The Italians joined the fracas thinking to participate in the spoils. The saga of the blitzkrieg was born.

In the summer of 1940 the war in France became serious, but it didn't last more than a few weeks. The British, trying to help their French allies, sent an expeditionary force to the Continent. It almost got trapped near Dunkirk on the French side of the British Channel but was successfully extracted with the help of many private British citizens. They crossed the Channel to bring their soldiers home to safety with every conceivable floating vehicle that could be called a boat. To let the British get away was the biggest mistake Hitler made in his pursuit of victory. The *Führer* had blinked. It was a turning point in the war.

We, in our little school in the hinterland of Germany, had to listen every day to the German victory celebrations on the radio. The success stories of the U-boats were broadcast with special fanfare announcing how much tonnage had been demolished. The bombing raids by the Luftwaffe were announced with another fanfare, marching music, and interruptions of the regular program. Fanfare also preceded announcements of the progress of the army as one town after another in France fell to the invading Germans racing from victory to victory.

In my class at school I met a nice fellow named Hans Werner who was about a year older than I. His divorced mother was involved in a relationship with an American businessman in Berlin. One day she called and informed the Boss that she had married the American and was leaving Europe. She instructed him that her son should be sent to Copenhagen. Hans and I had spent some time together talking about New York, not knowing at the time how soon he would be going there.

Detailed instructions by his mother and a ticket to Copenhagen followed a few days later. I gave him names of friends on Long Island in case he went there. He didn't know where his new stepfather in America lived. His mother had only told him what he needed to know to leave school.

I never heard from Hans again except that after the war I found out that he went to Boston. When he was nineteen years old he joined the US Air Force as a volunteer. In late 1944, he was shot down during a bombing mission over Berlin.

We didn't see much of the war in our little town even though it was only 60 miles north of Berlin. There was nothing of strategic value nearby, and the Allied bombers had no interest in wasting their precious bombs.

French prisoners appeared as work gangs after the fighting in France was over. Since by now most able German men had been drafted and were serving in the army, the Frenchmen were doing road repairs. We tried to talk to them and asked them, in our best French, where they came from. They explained they had been captured near Reims. With a food scarcity for Germans, under the prevailing rationing system, food for the prisoners was very limited. The poor guys were constantly hungry. We offered them our lunch sandwiches and improved our conversational French. This was okay until some German guards observed what we were doing and chased us away.

The French soldiers remained in our area for only a short time. After the French armistice was concluded they were sent home to work in ammunition factories and to help construct the West Wall, the fortification the Germans were building along the British Channel. The West Wall was a collection of gigantic concrete bunkers and casemates, which would ultimately be equipped with light and heavy weapons. The German propaganda said Germany wanted to avert an invasion of the mainland by Allied forces should they ever be so foolish to try.

German He-111 bombers began dropping bombs on English cities, killing innocent civilians. The war was getting ugly. It was the beginning of the Battle of Britain with British Spitfire fighter aircraft doing a hell of a job destroying the attackers.

While the German air force bombed helpless Poland, Belgium, and Holland, this time they picked on a country that could and would fight back. The Royal Air Force reciprocated by slaughtering the attacking German bombers and their protecting fighter aircraft. The Spitfires were superior to the Messerschmidt 109s and dominated the skies.

To retaliate for the bombing of their own cities, the RAF flew over Germany with a few of their planes. A pompous General Field Marshall Hermann Göring, commander-in-chief of the German air force, had earlier proclaimed audaciously, "If only one British plane should show up over Berlin, you can call me Meier."

British reconnaissance planes appeared almost every night over Germany. The resulting air raid alarms chased us into the cellars. We called the planes Mosquitoes because of the high-pitched sounds of their engines. Nobody knew if they carried bombs or not. But whether they did or not, the fact that they could violate German air space at will was bad enough for the morale of the civilians.

At night when the air raid sirens went off we had to climb sleepily into the skimpy cellar of our dormitory building and slept uncomfortably on wooden bunk beds. Maybe the Boss knew as well as we did that no bomber would ever waste a precious bomb on a small school building tucked away in the woods. But he was responsible for our lives, and he wanted to be safe rather than sorry.

If a bomb had struck our building it would have afforded little protection. The cellar wasn't built to be strong enough. After many nights the cellar became a real bore. We couldn't sleep on the narrow bunk beds and our performance at school suffered. Half awake and grumpy most of the night, we teased each other mercilessly about everything we could think of—girls, our clothes, families, and our grades.

Everything one experiences in life, no matter how bad it might look at first sight, has a positive side. During those endless nights in the air raid cellar I, for instance, learned how to debate and how to be quick with my tongue. I learned one more thing—children and young people can be awfully cynical and brutal with each other with observations and remarks. Many times I had to hold my tongue to avoid making derogatory comments about the Nazis and their pompous behavior.

Especially one guy in the governmental clique got it on the nose—Hermann Göring, the creator of the German air force. He was the target of many jokes. He most certainly had earned the name Meier for himself.

Soon British planes made their first bombing runs over Berlin. The spell of the invincible Nazi war machine was broken.

As time wore on more and more countries entered the war against Germany. Unfortunately for my way of thinking, the USA was still on the sidelines. No matter how much Winston Churchill cajoled President Roosevelt to enter the war, the US public was not ready for it.

After previously signing an elaborate peace agreement of friendship and mutual assistance with the Soviet Union—at the end of the Polish war in 1939—Hitler attacked Russia on June 22, 1941.

Six months later the ruthless Nazis gave the secret order for the 'final solution' of the Jewish question.

The whole nation was in shock over the beginning of the war with Russia. No matter how much the *Führer* screamed and yelled in his radio addresses, presenting exaggerated claims about the superiority of his weapons and the victorious German soldiers. He had vowed for years never to fight a war on two fronts. The casualties were mounting. The German armies quickly won the upper hand wherever they went, but too many women on the streets of every German town were clad in black.

A famous opening line in Hitler's speeches referred to the staggering losses during the First World War and the pain they had caused. From the beginning of his regime in January 1933 until the beginning of the war with Poland in 1939 he had pronounced, "Never again will a German mother cry for her son."

It was added to the growing number of lies he had uttered to the nation over the years. Hitler completely surprised Stalin with his attack. Stalin, the dictator, had not listened to his generals and their warnings. Dictators seldom do.

German Panzer divisions stormed through western Russia, taking hundreds of thousands of prisoners. In one battle alone, near

Kiev, they captured 400,000 men. They raced towards Moscow where Stalin was desperately trying to build a last line of defense.

And then "General Winter" came. First torrents of rain fell during the early weeks of October 1941. The rain turned the prevailing dirt roads into rivers of mud. Nothing could be moved any more. All supplies stopped. Even the famous German Panzer couldn't move, and the horses couldn't pull their heavy loads of supplies. Hitler was reported to be fuming at his generals, but there was nothing anybody could do. It was his fault.

Before starting the war with Russia, Hitler had tried to subdue a revolt in Yugoslavia. His general staff had advised against it. The Germans had met more resistance than anticipated, and the suppression of the revolt took too long. Consequently the war with Russia started two months too late in the season.

Now, in September and October 1941, the entire German army was immovably stuck in the mud. Then the thermometer plunged to below zero Fahrenheit and the soldiers in their summer outfits began freezing to death. Horrendous casualties from frostbite decimated the infantry. To top it all off, it started to snow heavily. The weapons couldn't function any more and many soldiers froze to death.

At the end of 1941, the majority of the German army was stuck and incapacitated in sight of the towers of the Kremlin only thirty miles west of Moscow. The attack stopped dead in its tracks. Not even the promise of warm food and dry quarters a few miles down the road in Moscow could propel the tired troops any further.

It was time for the Soviets to retaliate. The Russian army, humiliated for so long by the superior equipment of the German army, counterattacked. German intelligence under the leadership of Admiral Canaris had warned for weeks that the increase of short wave communication coming from behind the Russian front indicated the arrival of a whole new army of over 30 divisions. Hitler didn't want to believe the truth. He called his spymaster a traitor and a coward.

For Germany there was another surprise in the making. The Japanese, obsessed with American embargoes on oil and other vital materials, as well as the buildup of American naval power in the Pacific, attacked Pearl Harbor on December 7, 1941.

"A day that will live in infamy" was the way President
Roosevelt called it in a radio address to the nation. Hitler actually
was doing Roosevelt, and definitely Churchill, a favor when he declared war on the USA. The industrial might of the United States of
America came to the help of the Allies.

On the morning of December 8th, I was called to the phone in
the office of the headmaster. My father was on the line. I could hear
from the tone of his voice that he was terribly upset.

"Peter did you hear the news? Isn't that terrible? That's the end.
I feel so awful and I would like to tell you how sorry I am, do you
hear?"

I didn't answer. After a few seconds of silence I hung up the re-
ceiver and cried.

It was going to be my turn just as I had anticipated in my discussions with my mother. In the summer of 1942, six months after
Germany entered the war with America, I was just getting ready to
celebrate my 18th birthday, when the local Nazi party official of our
little town in Brandenburg called upon the Boss at the school to give
him a list of names. After the end of the school year in July all pupils
on this list would be inducted into the RAD.

The *Reichsarbeitsdienst* (National Work Service) was established in the early days of the Nazi regime as an auxiliary working
organization to get the unemployed off the streets. They had built
various public projects, most notably the famous Autobahn. By
1942 the RAD was serving as a honest-to-goodness paramilitary organization. It was engaged in constructing fortifications near the
front lines and in performing other services in the occupied Russian territories. To keep the partisans under control, for instance. The
RAD also escorted many thousands of prisoners to their camps in
Germany. It provided basic military training for young Germans in
preparation for their induction into the military service.

I was supposed to report to the RAD recruiting office on August 15, 1942. The inductees from our school had been ordered to report to a variety of different locations. Mine was in Eberswalde, a
medium-sized town 70 miles northeast of Berlin.

I made several attempts to call my mother but couldn't reach her. Telephone connections to Switzerland took many hours and sometimes days of waiting. I was so upset and demoralized that I only wanted to hear her voice and to tell her, "It's too late now."

My mother had had a very good life in Switzerland. She experienced peace in a free country without political harassment. Although everybody talked a lot about the possible involvement of the country in the war, it was at peace nevertheless. The people seemed to be in constant anticipation of what Mr. Hitler, as the Swiss called him, might do to attack the small neutral country as he had done with others before. They discussed what Switzerland should do, or could do, to maintain its independence. The Swiss were a thorn in the dictator's side, which they knew very well. On the other hand, he needed them as a diplomatic go-between with the rest of the world.

Olga's friends, Monica and Bill Widmer, were Olga's age. They had known each other for over twenty years, living together in Berlin, enjoying mutual friendships at the American women's club, the bridge playing, the cosmopolitan, international life, and the many cultural advantages Berlin had offered during the '20s and '30s. Those years after the first war had been fabulous. The devastating inflation was over and the people of Berlin had tried to forget the first big war.

Bill had worked out of his office in his home in Berlin with his European customers. He had moved to Switzerland because of the deterioration in the political climate and the encumbrances put on his travel by the Nazi authorities. Crossing German borders with existing restrictions and currency regulations became too much for him.

Olga was at ease with these two, living with them in their beautiful home in the suburb of Zollikon high on the hill overlooking Lake Zurich. She would have been totally happy with one exception—she missed her son. By now she had been in their house for many months, which made her feel that she was imposing on them. But Monica, who knew Olga well, alleviated her worries.

"Olga, what would I do without you? Bill is on business trips most of the time. What would I do in this big house all by myself?

Be a good sport and stay with me. We have fun and you have found many new friends. Zurich, in spite of its provincialism, isn't such a bad town. Granted the war has left its mark. I know you are missing Peter, but I doubt that you can do anything for him now that he has been called into the RAD."

My fate in Germany was a terrible worry to my mother, no matter how much Monica tried to ease her anxieties. She knew she was responsible for my predicament. Nobody can convince a mother she can't do anything to help her son. Olga feared more than ever that my premonition to be inducted into the German army might become a reality.

When she received information from friends in Berlin that I, barely eighteen, was on my way to the occupied Polish territory, she decided to return to Berlin at once to be with me or at least near me, in case I needed her.

Everybody in Zurich warned her of the danger to her personal safety from the Nazis and from the constant bombing by the Allies. They tried to convince her of the futility of her efforts on behalf of her son. What would she be able to do for me anyway? She would be in Berlin and I was somewhere in Poland.

"Don't be foolish," Bill said to her. "Stay with us in Switzerland. When the time comes that Peter needs you, you'll be able to help him much more effectively from here, the haven of neutrality, than in Berlin."

"That's your opinion, Bill, and I appreciate your advice. But do you know what my boy will think of me if I stay here as if nothing has happened, when I know full well he is in grave danger because of my foolishness?" Olga replied. "Don't you think the situation is bad enough? I feel guilty that I couldn't help him when he needed me. Had I possessed one ounce of reason I would have seen the signs on the wall in 1939 before I left for Europe. All my New York friends warned me, begged me that we should not go on this stupid trip. We should never have gone to Germany. What would you do, Bill, if Peter were your son? I still have a number of friends in high places in Berlin. I don't think anything is going to happen to me. And bombs? I don't fear bombs. The good Lord knows when my time will be up. I have a sneaking suspicion that my name and number will not be on his calendar for a long time. This is my boy, the only one I have, and he is not going to go through this without me, no matter what."

She had made up her mind and that was that.

Upon arriving in Berlin, my mother found that her small apartment was still intact. She waited to hear from me.

My father, her ex-husband, was of little help with her worries about me. He was proud to see his son in the RAD. But he didn't know any more about my whereabouts than my mother did.

"Don't worry about Peter," he said to her. "He'll be a good worker and an honor to his country. I hope that he won't have to fight this war."

"Your regrets are too late, Blacky," she used the nickname she'd given him during their early courtship, "and as I have said to you before on countless occasions, I know Peter is an American, just as he knows he is an American. You shouldn't have turned him over to those brutal, power-hungry Nazis. Why did you do it? Can you tell me, please? What happened to your aversion to the brown shirts? There'll be no glory for Germany in this war, only suffering and millions of dead people. She'll lose another war and this time it will be a lot worse. Don't you remember when you came home from the last disaster, only 24 years ago, and had lost everything? And now we have the next catastrophe. Your memory seems to be very short. Germany is totally surrounded by enemies. Just like the last time. She'll be outgunned and out-manned just as before, and I repeat, she'll loose again. You had to put our son in the middle of it? This will be on your conscience for the rest of your life. And if you should ever forget it I'll remind you, I promise."

She was angry and berated him. But at the same time she was drained and exhausted, as she had often been after confrontations with her ex-husband. As always, the discussion ended in no-man's land.

I had left Berlin shortly before she arrived. The mail service from Germany to Poland was in bad shape. I had informed everybody in the family that they could get in contact with me by mail once we received our military postal numbers, but that had not helped. They didn't have the postal numbers. It would finally take two months before the first mail found me.

My time in the induction camp was brief. The camp had been only intended as a staging area to assemble the inductees and send them on to their final destinations. We were almost immediately transported to Posen in the western part of Poland (called Poznan today).

After the transport arrived at the main station and we disembarked from the train, we marched through the city past its outer limits until we arrived outside a dense forest. The road led us deep into the woods. There it was, the camp. Watchtowers were all around it. A triple barbed wire fence connected the towers to form an impenetrable protection.

"What's the matter? What do these fortifications mean? Are they intended to guard us or protect us?" I murmured to the guy next to me.

"That's a valid question," was the quiet and equally anxious reply.

We marched through the gate. It was a terrifying situation for all of us. Some of the guys, almost panic-stricken, feared that we had arrived as prisoners in some kind of a political camp, a KZ (concentration camp). We discovered the next day that the barbed wire was for our protection. Apparently Polish partisans were everywhere.

While listening to comments, concerns, and verbal exchanges of the other men around me, I realized I had an advantage over most of them. This was not the first time I had been away from home. I had already experienced during my years at boarding school how it felt to be away from the comforts of home. I had learned first hand the invaluable exercise of thinking on my own feet.

Still, even for me it was difficult to adjust. The camp was not so civilized and sheltered as my boarding school. The *Arbeitsdienst-führer* were not as compassionate and understanding as my teachers had been. It was the *Arbeitsdienst,* a paramilitary camp and a lousy one at that.

The camp covered ten acres inside the barbed wire fence. Ten single-story wooden barracks were arranged in two rows on each side of a field, which looked like an old soccer practice area. Eight barracks were designated for us as sleeping quarters. Seventy-five men moved into a barrack. A larger barrack was designated as a mess hall. The tenth one was reserved for the administration and the *Mittlere Führer,* a term used for the officers in the *Arbeitsdienst.*

We discovered that the field was ideal for exercising, at least in the minds of the drill sergeants. The primary rationale for this camp was to get us under control and instill a sense of total obedience, a boot camp period.

The food was wholesome but plain—very plain. The scarcity of food throughout the German realm and the ration card system of the homeland seemed to reach all the way to Poland. Three times a week we ate hot yellow pea soup for lunch with a few small pieces of salty, smoked pork swimming around. On other days it was 'delicious' white cabbage with potatoes, simply boiled in water. Breakfast was enriched by light brown water, called coffee, and dry bread covered with transparent, sweet turnip marmalade. For me the quality of the marmalade was nothing new. I had eaten that stuff in boarding school, but it was a rude awakening for the other men who came straight from mother's home cooking, or even better, from a farm. When the guys stirred their grub in their mess kits the comments were crass and appalling.

For dinner we got another piece of bread and a small slice of sausage. Every other day the evening meal consisted of an indefinable vegetable soup. Once a week everybody got a piece of butter and a half-pound of artificial honey. This stuff, which they called honey, must have been an invention of the German war machine and of creative minds in the ministry of propaganda. It had very little to do with real honey. The German bees were probably all on strike. Somebody mixed sugar and emulsifier together with honey aroma. Bingo, it was supposed to be honey. At least the paste was sweet. Young men will eat anything when they have to do physical exercise all day long.

Our daily schedule was military, and the RAD *Führer* were tough. We were thrown out of bed at 5:00 A.M. every morning, followed by aggressive exercising in front of our barracks with a spade until our hands were blistered. To top it all off we hit the dirt every time a sergeant barked his orders, "Down on the double, up on the double, and down again."

It was strenuous and monotonous. If we could have we would have let the sergeant do a little jumping himself.

Oh, yes, I have failed to mention that right after our arrival at the camp, we were issued a full set of gear—a standard uniform of the *Arbeitsdienst,* underwear, and all kind of things a man needs. Aside from the brownish-gray uniform with swastikas on all buttons and on the band around the left arm, basic equipment was a spade instead of a carbine. Mind you, this was not an ordinary, normal spade used for digging holes. No, it was a special spade designed only for *exercising.* This spade had a thin layer of chrome looking very glossy. Tired and beat as we were, we had to polish the darn things every evening.

When we finally turned in at night, we were so tired we went out cold. Most of us were barely 18 years old and even under normal circumstances we would have needed lots of sleep. Many a night I heard some of the fellows crying into their pillows either from homesickness or from exhaustion.

The *Truppführer* in charge of our barrack had a room at the end of the building. Our bunk beds were doubled up one on top of the other. They were made of wrought-iron rods with four wooden boards lying across the rods on the bottom. A rough linen sack filled with straw lay on top. Another linen sheet was supplied as a cover and a pillow of the same material. Most nights we were too tired to notice where we slept, or what we slept on. We fell asleep as soon as our heads hit the pillow. Some guys didn't even eat before they started snoring.

After we had settled in the guy above me introduced himself as Helmut, while his feet were dangling from the upper bed into my face. Helmut came from Stettin, a large city with a harbor where the Oder River meets the Baltic Sea. At first Helmut constantly wanted to demonstrate his expertise in Jujitsu to everybody. After a few days of exercising he was too tired to show off. Nobody was interested in his display of the art of self-defense.

As time went by Helmut proved to be all right. He and I became friends. We talked about our homes, families, and schools, but I never dared to discuss my American mother and my wrangled citizenship with him. Something told me to keep my mouth shut.

After Helmut and I discovered we liked each other, we decided to stick together, to keep our backs against the wall, so to speak. We both realized that under the circumstances we had to have a friend in whom to confide every once in a while. The going was tough and was getting tougher. None of us could make it alone.

It was indicative of how young we were that in our spare time our favorite subject of conversation was school. Helmut's school had been in Stettin where he was born and had lived all his life. He was curious to find out more about my boarding school, its regimen, and its curriculum. He was surprised that I had been drafted into the RAD without a chance to finish the Abitur (high-school curriculum to enter college).

Helmut was a year older than I. He had finished his Abitur before joining the RAD. This put him at an advantage if he wanted to attend a university later on. The *Ortsgruppenleiter* had pulled me out of school prematurely. It had been his special chicanery. Attendance at a university after the war, at least in Germany, would be difficult and highly unlikely for me without going back to school to start where I had left off and to finish the Abitur.

Helmut's school had placed a higher emphasis on Latin than mine, which would make it easier for him to attend medical or law school. My school had favored modern languages like French and English. Our discussions about school took our minds off the monotonous daily drills and helped us keep our sanity.

The RAD drill *Truppführer* and *Obertruppführer* were guys in their mid-thirties, indifferent and unfriendly. Their only goal was to preserve their relative position of safety as instructors, as far away as possible from the Russian front lines and the actual fighting.

In the summer of 1941, at the beginning of the war with Russia, most of them had been with the first RAD units. They followed the regular army into Russia to do construction work. It was mainly to change the gauge of the railroads to the German standard width to accommodate their own rail stock. The railroads were needed to feed the hungry army and to supply it with ammunition. Later on the RAD were escorting tens of thousands of Russian prisoners, during endless marches from the front lines to their final destinations. The prison camps were located in occupied territories or in Germany. As the war wore on, construction of fortifications would become a typical engagement for its members who were getting younger and younger.

Our *Truppführer,* an old hand with the RAD, was a particularly disagreeable and repulsive character. I would say that he was a small man without going so far as to call him a dwarf. His arms were much too long for his body, which made him look like an orangutan. I don't mean to insult these graceful animals by this comparison. His hair was thin and reddish on the orange side, the same color as an orangutan. Most of the time he looked unkempt, as if he had slept in his uniform, which he probably had.

Unobserved by the *Truppführer* or any of his buddies the men copied his walk when he was not present in the barracks. Helmut was the best with his imitation, grunting and slouching forward with the back of his hands dragging on the floor, like an ape in the zoo. We decided amongst ourselves that the *Truppführer* had a face only a mother could love. His speech was high-pitched and slurred. His choice of words was limited. His IQ must have been that of a Mongoloid ant. My guess was he had remained in the *Arbeitsdienst* all this time only because the army recruiters had shared our opinion and rejected him—probably for more reasons than we could think of.

The worst display of his character cropped up when he started to brag, often in vivid and extensive detail, about how he had executed Russian prisoners of war during his convoy activities. These unfortunate POW's had to march for days without food and almost without any water after being captured. Because they had become too weak to go on they often fell exhausted by the wayside, ready to die. He proudly detailed and portrayed to us how he had shot them, executed them, just like that.

According to *Truppführer* Werner—the name of this son of a bitch—these quasi-executions happened frequently during the march into captivity. "You should have seen how the scum squirmed and begged," he bragged disgustingly. "I was glad for every one we didn't have to guard anymore. They're subhuman anyway, that's what our propaganda says all the time. Bang, one bullet, and that was it. We just left them where they fell. We had no time for burials anyway, and enough wild, hungry dogs were roaming the countryside," he related to us with his sweaty, shining red face gloating, void of any feeling for what he had done.

Some of the young men were laughing, encouraging him to tell more about his brutal and unmerciful experiences, but others were not. Helmut and I just looked at each other and were very quiet.

"What's the matter with you two?" He addressed us when he noticed our obvious lack of interest and enthusiasm.

"Don't you like to hear about my experiences, or don't you believe me?" *Truppführer* Werner, the imbecile, had noticed that we were not cheering him on like some of the others.

I had to answer. After all, he was our superior. I said, *"Truppführer,* I just don't feel like laughing when I hear how those Russian prisoners of war had to die helplessly and without reason. The Geneva Convention guarantees all prisoners their lives, food, and shelter after they surrender and put their weapons down. At least that's what the *Feldmeister* (Lieutenant) explained to all of us yesterday during class. Germany is a member of the Geneva Convention, isn't it?"

We had classes every second day about the rules of conduct of the German army and of the members of the RAD in occupied territories. They were about the Geneva Convention, and all kinds of political subjects. Mostly about how Germany would govern the 'new' provinces and exploit their resources.

"I see," said the *Truppführer,* dragging out his exclamation, his bloodshot, ugly eyes bulging while he wrinkled his narrow forehead in mock concentration.

"You are two wise guys! Well, we will have to pay special attention to you two, won't we, so that you won't have so much time to be critical about the war experiences of your superiors?"

During the next few weeks he tried everything in his power to live up to his threat. It was a little harder on us to live with the stress and the exertions of basic training, and with his chicanery on top, but, *Truppführer* Werner could kiss our asses, as far as the two of us were concerned.

We couldn't wait to be transferred to an active engagement where we would find a different climate—so we anticipated—and would be able, we hoped, to repay him in kind. I must report that there were others in our barrack that felt the same as Helmut and I did. They told us so after dark when the barracks were quiet and most men were asleep.

It was a weird situation. We were raw recruits to put it mildly, young, barely grown up, badly in need of experience on how to conduct ourselves in the grown-up world without being exposed to subhuman criminals like *Truppführer* Werner. We knew instinctively, however, that it would have been useless, even suicidal, to complain to an officer. We kept our mouths shut, obeyed his orders, cleaned the latrines, spent our nights on extra guard duty, and hoped we would be moved to active duty real soon.

Our extra guard duty at night turned out to have its special rewards. One night as we were patrolling the perimeter of the camp and its encircling barbed-wire fences, we met some young Polish girls. They were standing on the other side of the fence, waving at us and calling out to us in halting German. Of course, while being on guard duty we couldn't respond without violating the military code and that of the *Arbeitsdienst,* facing serious consequences. We called back to them quietly that we would come back the following night, same place, same time, to which they joyously agreed.

The girls were very young, full of laughter, and just as curious as we were to find out what life was all about. The barbed wire fence, which separated us, was a limiting factor. We kissed and fondled and touched and commiserated, with the proper precaution to avoid the sharp thorns of the wire fence, but otherwise it was a harmless encounter. All participants remained as virginal as they had been before.

Early one morning at the end of September, after four weeks of constant drills and exercises, the alarm sirens pierced throughout the camp. We were ordered to pack our belongings and equipment immediately. We returned the polished spades and received carbines instead.

Marching to the railroad station in Posen, we sang boisterous military songs we had learned during the past weeks. At the station we climbed into boxcars of a waiting train. Twenty-five men were assigned to a 20-ton car. On the floor of the cars was straw to sleep on, nothing else. The train immediately took off, eastward, in the general direction of the Soviet Union and the war. It soon crossed the border into the former Soviet territory, now occupied by the Germans.

None of us had ever been that far to the east, neither to Poland nor to Russia. It was late in September and the weather was still warm. All doors of the boxcars were open wide to get fresh air, enabling us to watch the countryside.

The fields on both sides were cultivated and farmers were working everywhere as long as we passed through Poland. As soon as we entered the USSR we could see nothing but dense woods and underbrush. When the train stopped we discovered that the underbrush were hazelnut bushes as far as the eye could see. We could see few farming activities.

Helmut and I were standing at the open door making our observations. "If you compare this to the countryside in Germany or Poland it looks like a wilderness. So little of the land appears to be cultivated. Either they grow their grain and corn somewhere else or they have very little to eat," he said quietly.

"Everybody who has traveled to the USSR says it's quite different further to the south in the Ukraine where the climate is warmer and the crops can be planted earlier and grow longer. In 1939 after Germany and the USSR divided Poland between themselves, and Hitler had concluded his deal with Stalin, Germany received millions of tons of grain from the Ukraine every year. Of course, it wasn't enough for our greedy supreme commander," I replied sarcastically. "He wanted to have it all."

"Peter, how many times have I told you to keep your mouth shut," Helmut whispered urgently into my ear. "People might overhear our conversation. You'll lose your head one of these days if you talk like that, and I'll lose mine for listening. You can think whatever you want, but keep your lips sealed. You know I won't rat on you, but we are surrounded by big ears."

"Yes, I am sorry, Helmut, you're right," I replied contritely. "I will try to follow your advice. It's just a relief to confide in a friend."

Helmut had stopped my outspoken talk before during our time at camp, as he was doing now. "Me and my big mouth," I thought to myself.

He meant well. I resolved to listen to him and not voice my criticism of the system and our "beloved *Führer*" in the future in public.

The entire camp of 600 men had been loaded onto the train. I counted the cars behind the locomotive when we were able to get out of our boxcar for the first time to stretch our legs. I counted twenty-four boxcars altogether with twenty-five men each.

Our transport stopped frequently at small stations to take on water for the locomotive. That gave everybody time to relieve themselves, get food from the front of the train where the kitchen-car was, drink some water, and move our stiff legs.

As we were watering the hazelnut bushes I said to Helmut, "Man oh man, sometimes I have to pinch myself. Can you believe what is happening to us? We are probably on our way to meet Ivan. What do you say, Helmut? I could have lived without this experience."

"You're reading my thoughts exactly," was his subdued reply. "I feel green and young. I hate to admit it but I'm scared."

The train whistle, blowing twice, interrupted us. We hurried back to climb into our boxcar. Whoever commanded the train was in a big hurry to get us to wherever we were going. Most of the time the train went as fast as the engine could pull it.

On the third day of our journey we saw the first legible sign on a station house as the train passed by. It was spelled in Latin letters instead Cyrillic ones. Most likely the German army had replaced it. It read Bjelgorod. After consulting a map, we found that this town was located in the middle of the Ukraine between Kursk to the north and Charkov to the south.

The train continued further east, past Starobjelsk and towards Millerovo. Only a few miles further it stopped and everybody was ordered out. We assembled in groups of 100 men around the boxcar where the *Mittlere Führer* had been. A major of the army was standing now higher up in the doorway of the boxcar so everybody could hear him better.

We listened to what this superior wanted to tell us. We discovered to our total surprise for the first time that most of our *Arbeitsdienst Führer* and instructors from the training camp, including *Truppführer* Werner, were gone. Only a few remained.

We thought this new group of officers must be coordinators with the army. They were real army personnel according to the uniforms they were wearing and must have joined us during the middle of the night on our last stop. A major and several lieutenants and sergeants were facing us now. "Pay attention everybody," the major addressed us. "Let me give you a short summation of the situation. We are on our way to the immediate rear of the front lines, north of Stalingrad along the Don River's southern bank. We'll be close to the front lines and the fighting. I've been assigned to lead you for the time being, because you're going to work for the army. The other men with me are experienced and will give you the proper instructions. We're proud to have you and to be here with you."

Bullshit! How phony could it get? I thought.

"During the following days we'll instruct you in the use of carbines and hand grenades and you'll also have extensive target practice. A little practice might come in handy this close to the fighting. One never knows what will happen. Of course, you'll receive live ammunition."

Helmut and I looked at each other with open mouths, stunned. The major was not finished and continued.

"A unit of Italian troops is positioned north of the area where we are going. They are helping Germany," his very words, "in her struggle to defeat the Bolsheviks. You, the proud members of the RAD, will be responsible for building trenches and fortifications to the rear of the Italian division just in case they are needed as backup defensive positions. It goes without saying that we've got to protect ourselves at all times."

Since we were not standing at attention, the men remarked about this new surprising development and uttered sarcastically disparaging comments about our Italian brothers in arms.

Everybody remembered how the Italian army had fared in Abyssinia during the colonial conflict of 1936–38 when Italy tried to annex the backward kingdom as a colony. They fought for several years without gaining any advantage before making peace with the Ethiopian Emperor Haile Selassie. The same had happened to them at the beginning of this war in the small country of Albania. It is across the Adriatic Sea from Italy's mainland. Consequently, our respect for Italians as soldiers was low.

The major ordered us to quiet down and to accept our assignment with the respect and enthusiasm it deserved and also with the unwavering obedience and devotion of true *Deutsche Arbeitsdienstmänner.*

The summer was not over, he said, but the high command wanted to create defensive positions for the coming winter along the entire front. The plan of the German army was to push aggressively further to the south. It wanted to surround Stalingrad, break through the Russian lines and then turn north in a gigantic pincer movement to encircle the opposing forces and destroy them once and for all.

"To support and protect the flanks of this movement to the north, we must give the Italians a solid base so they can defend the line at the Don and hold their present position against the Russians forces at the onset of the dreaded Russian winter," he detailed.

Helmut and I and the men around us were shocked. These were candid remarks. What was this supposed to mean? Normally it was not the kind of information an officer would give to young recruits, and that's what we were.

The two of us were now standing next to each other. "Why does he give us this army talk, as if we knew what it meant to encircle the Russians from the south to the north?" he whispered into my ear. "I can't believe that we've got to know all that. Or why anybody of importance cares whether we know. Why does he want to tell us what the intention of the German high command is? The guy is almost as nervous as we are. What do you think?"

Helmut smelled a rat. I was wondering too what these explanations could really mean, but I held a finger over my lips indicating to keep his mouth shut and wait until the major had finished his announcement.

"Of course, we'll not get involved in the actual fighting, if we can help it," he said. Then he went on to tell us in an unsuccessful attempt to calm our nerves, "You haven't been properly trained so far, and with your present level of preparation I wouldn't want to be the one who leads you into battle."

As he stood there in front of us we could see that he wore on the left side of his tunic an Iron Cross First Class medal, an Iron Cross Second-Class ribbon, the infantry attack medal in bronze, a black purple heart, and the 'frozen meat ribbon.' He wasn't a novice but a seasoned veteran of the Russian campaign.

The last mentioned medal—actually only a ribbon—had been given its cynical name by the common soldiers from experiences in the previous winter of 1941 when the German army almost disintegrated in the terrible cold near Moscow. Every soldier participating in that battle had received this medal like a campaign ribbon. Many soldiers had lost a finger, a toe, or an ear, frozen off by the hideous cold temperatures, without adequate winter clothing to protect them. The German army had been totally unprepared. The major had been there and seemed to know what he was talking about.

"One never knows what can happen when you're close to the front lines," he continued. "My officers and I believe it's better for you to be able to defend yourselves. That's why we will train you in basic infantry procedures and weapons. We commence early tomorrow morning. Of course, you will receive the necessary tools to dig trenches and equipment to roll out barbed wire in front of the trenches, because that will be your job. We will arrive at our designated location by tomorrow. Now, get back into the boxcars and have a good night's sleep. You won't sleep so comfortably again for a long time. Dismissed!"

As we stumbled back to the boxcars I remarked, "Can you imagine what the situation must be out there? Something must have gone terribly wrong. Just picture what may have happened to the Italians if our army feels the need to rush us out here in such a hurry? Who could be more unqualified than we are? Ever since the alarm sounded at the camp a few days ago we have been in a hurry. My God, we are only young men of the *Arbeitsdienst* with no formal military training."

My mind began to race. "Just two or three days of minimal instructions? If they teach us how to handle the carbines and hand grenades that will not be enough to make a fighting force of us. It won't give us resilience to repulse an enemy attack. We're only supposed to serve for three months in this glorious work service. It looks like it'll take a little longer. Helmut, we'd better take good care of ourselves, or our goose is cooked for sure."

He didn't answer. I tried to go to sleep. Though I cannot speak for all the others, I was dreadfully afraid. Yes, I was afraid for my life. I didn't sleep a wink all night.

The next morning we left the train. We assumed that it returned to Poland where it had come from. We had a full day's march ahead of us, about thirty miles, until we arrived at a small village in the middle of nowhere. From all appearances the civilian population of the village had deserted it. There was absolutely nobody in sight. The terrain was flat as far as the eye could see. In the distance the fields were slightly undulated, but with no trees anywhere. About twenty to thirty houses comprised the whole village. They had thatched roofs, small windows and hardened mud walls painted with white paint on the outside. The houses were deserted, totally empty. Not even a lonely chicken was running around anywhere, their owners apparently had vacated them a long time ago.

In the falling dusk we gathered some putrid smelling old straw from open storage areas behind the houses. It helped us to create a semblance of a sleeping surface and was better than nothing. At least the army officers acted as if they knew what they were doing, which gave us some badly needed confidence. The last thing we did was to pick up spades from a supply wagon—spades again—which stood in the middle of the village, for digging foxholes and trenches.

Next, he had said, we'll begin with weapons training, starting early in the morning, exercising, target practice with live ammunition and concurrently receiving instructions in the use of hand grenades. For the time being nobody seemed to be in too much of a hurry to let us dig trenches or erect barbed wire fences, and they'd professed only a short while ago that would be our main area of activities? All of this made us even more suspicious what was really going on.

For our weapons training we were split up into platoons of fifteen men each. Every platoon was under the tutorship of a sergeant as instructor. Our sergeant seemed to be an easygoing guy, but the worrying type. He was deadly afraid we would be too dumb to handle hand-grenades and would blow him and us to smithereens unintentionally.

"Don't ever forget to throw the grenade away after you pull the pin," he warned. "First you make up your mind where you want to throw the grenade, unscrew the cap, pull out the pin with a quick jerk, count to three and throw the damned thing away immediately. Don't wait. Don't change your mind. Just throw it in the direction of the enemy," he emphasized repeatedly and forcefully.

Our instructors had prepared a few decoy grenades without gunpowder, to let us practice what to do, to let us get "hands-on" experience without endangering anybody. Every one of us took his turn several times going through the motions with the decoys. We unscrewed the caps, pulled the pins and threw them at an imagined enemy. We did this for about half a day until the sergeant was satisfied with our performance. It is hard to imagine how stupidly some of the men were acting. One guy pulled the pin, counted to three and then looked at the instructor with the grenade in his hand:

"Which direction is the enemy, Sergeant?"

My God! Fortunately the sergeant had enough experience with dumb recruits.

At noontime we went to the field kitchen and got some hot pea soup. It was delicious. As we were eating, several soldiers passed about fifty yards from where we were sitting without saying as much as a word, or without even looking in our direction. They were clad in what looked like Italian uniforms and made a rather befuddled impression.

"God, do they look dense", one of us remarked. "Lieutenant, did you notice that none of them had any weapons or any other gear?"

The lieutenant, Max was his name, lieutenant Walter Max, looked younger than we were. The decorations displayed on his chest proved he was a seasoned veteran. He looked up and saw what we had seen. He made a face as if he was not only very surprised, but upset and angry as well. This continued for half an hour, as we sat there eating. The Italians were hurrying down the road in groups of five or ten, obviously eager not to get in contact with anybody.

"Their appearance without weapons and equipment is totally out of place. Here in Russia, deep in enemy territory, one should never walk around without a weapon, not even if you are an Italian," Lieutenant Max mumbled more to himself than to us.

"Sergeant, you continue what you were doing after the break. I will investigate with Headquarters to find out what this is all about," he ordered. He jumped to his feet and disappeared.

None of us realized immediately that we were witnessing, no, participating in a catastrophic development. To us the world looked very peaceful on an early afternoon of a beautiful day. Really, where was the enemy?

For the past few weeks the front line on the Don River, to the north of our little village had been occupied by Italian forces, which evidently had begun to disintegrate. Maybe the infantry units were still holding their positions but some of the support units were surely deserting them.

The lieutenant came back after less than an hour. He immediately went to see the major, who called the officers and sergeants for a meeting, on the double. They stuck their heads together to debate the situation. Helmut, like the rest of us, had observed everything. He walked over to me, bringing another guy with him who was assigned to our group of fifteen. It was Hans Labuske. Hans smiled at me.

"Hello, I am Hans, we know each other from the camp. Helmut has told me all about you, Peter. Do you mind if I join you two? Quoting *Friedrich von Schiller* appropriately: *Drum sei ich, gewährt mir die Bitte, in Eurem Bunde der Dritte.*" (Let me be, permit my request, the third one in your midst.)

We laughed at this brief reminder of our school experiences and empathized about our fate. Only a few weeks ago his quotation might have been appropriate during a literary exercise at school with our German teacher. In our present circumstances it just sounded funny and from another time.

"Oh, don't be silly Hans, of course, join us. We'll soon need to support each other anyway. The way I judge the situation, we're going in one hell of a mess in no time at all," I answered with a laugh.

"I couldn't agree more, Peter," was Helmut's comment. "We'll know in a few minutes what the lieutenant has discovered about the Italians. And I'll bet you it's not going to be pleasant. We're not exactly military experts but I can't imagine that soldiers of any nation should run around like these Italians do."

"But, think of it," Hans interjected, "if worse comes to worst what are we going to do? And let's assume the Italians holding the combat line in front of us are starting to desert. The '98k' carbines and hand grenades, which we are learning to handle, are not adequate to stop an advancing Russian force. The officers better think fast; otherwise we have to run too, and I mean faster than the Italians."

The three of us, schoolboys and hardly four weeks in uniform were making tactical plans. We were scared out of our wits. What a joke that was! Of course, we had good reasons to be scared. It didn't take long for us to find out.

The lieutenant came back to where we were still exercising, and practicing with our weapons. We hurried to meet him and waited anxiously what he would say.

"Listen everybody and listen good. I won't have enough time to give longwinded explanations. From what I've seen about you, you're quick on your feet and in your heads." That didn't sound good at all.

"The major was unable to establish communications with our Italian allies. The headquarters of the German division doesn't know anything either. Therefore, I have arranged that at nightfall, in about two hour's time, we'll receive more sophisticated infantry weapons. We'll get MG 34 and 42's. That's what is available at this moment, of course, together with the necessary ammunition. We'll commence training immediately and continue on throughout the night. Over there," he pointed to an area about 300 hundred feet away, "is the collection point for spades and fortification equipment. Deliver all your material promptly. For the time being you won't need it any more. After you've received your weapons and ammunition, we'll occupy a defense perimeter to the north of this village. We'll dig foxholes and wait for Ivan, I mean the Russians. I'll tell you more about what we're going to do when you've all your weapons."

Wow, this was a mouth full. What did we know about a shooting war? Only a few of us had ever used, or practiced, with a carbine, much less an MG 34 or 42, and that's what we were going to get now? How were the instructors going to teach us, literally overnight, to handle these sophisticated weapons and how to conduct ourselves in case of an attack?

"Helmut, Hans, let's get together right now," I called out waving at them. We separated from the rest of the guys, to hold a "war council"—good choice of words.

"As soon as the weapons arrive we'll try to get an MG with enough ammunition and as many hand grenades as we can carry. Then we'll work together as a team. I don't think we want to stand around with carbines 98k and 60 rounds of ammunition, firing single shots at the enemy, while the Russians attack us. Then we only have to wait until they make mince meat out of us. We should be better equipped to hold the bastards off. And one more thing, I think we should try to get a *Hohlhaftladung* (magnetic anti-tank weapon) or several of them, if they bring any."

"Hold it buddy, hold it." Helmut raised his voice and his hand, interrupting me angrily in mid-sentence. "I don't think I'm hearing right? What do you want us to be—local war heroes? Chasing decorations, or what? I've absolutely no intentions whatsoever to be a hero. I just want to survive my three-month *Arbeitsdienst*. Hopefully I will find a way to weather the rest of the war. Count me out of your glorious efforts to defend the Fatherland."

"Oh yes?" I retorted, equally angrily and upset, getting myself hot under the collar. "How do you want to survive the next few days? Tell me that. Mind you, I'm not talking about the next three months you're talking about, just the next three days. Do you think the Ivan will stop long enough to ask us about our preferences of survival, and whether or not you want to be a hero or not? Do you really think I want to be a war hero, or that I'm craving for somebody to pin decorations on my chest? I've told you where I'm coming from, and how I got here. This is not *my* Fatherland and not my army. I've the least incentive of all of us to fight this war. But that does not mean that I don't want to survive and stay alive, to live for whatever life has to offer if we get through this mess. We all know very little about life anyway, do you want to lie down now and play dead or stupid? The only way I can visualize to reach my goal is to defend myself right now as best as I am able to and as vigorously as possible. In order to do that we cannot let any Russians come near us, we need weapons. If you call that false heroism, Helmut, good bye, Hans and I'll look for somebody else in this little group who'll be sharing our thoughts."

I was fighting mad. Who the hell did this idiot think he was?

"He is right," Hans cut in quickly, supporting my position, and at the same time trying to calm us down. "We don't know what's going to happen, but we certainly have to try everything we can to get us out of this mess alive. Our instructors are uptight and almost panic-stricken. They don't seem to know exactly what to do either, and we're panic-stricken too. We've not much time any more, we've got to stick together, develop some initiative and fight now, or we are lost."

Hans was trying his best to be persuasive, adding a few thoughts of wisdom of his own in the same context as I'd done in my outburst. Helmut seemed to regret his earlier heated response. He looked at us like a dog with his tail between his legs and mumbled, "I am sorry, Peter, Hans, I didn't think this through before opening my mouth. This is a damned situation, and, fuck, shit, who got us into it, damn, kiss my ass everybody." He was cursing to let off some steam. He tried to regain his composure and asked, "What shall we do? How can we help ourselves? We know nothing, and we're nothing but cannon fodder? Yes, Peter, I have to admit. You're right. We have to get our act together, get organized, grab the best weapons we can and learn how to use them. I'm a good thrower. I was always the best at school throwing balls further than anybody. I'll get the hand grenades. Peter and you Hans should train at the machine gun 34 or 42, whichever they'll supply. Let's see the lieutenant or the sergeant and talk to them about it. I'll bet they'll be delirious to see some of us take an initiative."

It's amazing what a bunch of eighteen-year-olds can come up with when their lives are in danger.

Helmut was certainly changing his tune, to say the least. For me it was no time to carry a grudge or to rub it in.

Two of the best weapons in Germany's arsenal of infantry armament were machine guns of the type MG 34 and 42. They were named according to the year they'd been entered into service. The MGs were the best the infantry had; especially in 1942 when the army was equipped with very few "easy to handle" machine pistols. The Russians Kalaschnikovs had a 35-bullet ammunition drum and were effective, dependable, fine weapons. The MG 34 spit out 300 bullets per minute. As far as speed of fire goes, this was fast enough. The bad part was that the 34s were susceptible to dirt. If the tiniest speck of dirt came close to its chamber, it would jam up immediately. You don't want that to happen, especially when you're in a tight combat situation, and the enemy is rushing your position. When the MG 34 jammed up it had to be taken apart and thoroughly cleaned so that it was working again. The enemy seldom waited long enough for this procedure to be completed. The good thing was that the early versions of the Soviet Kalaschnikov also jammed up easily, though for a different reason.

A newer and vastly improved MG 42 was not only faster than the MG 34. It was also less susceptible to dirt. You could literally bury it in the mud and it would continue to be operational. Its disadvantage was an enormous consumption of ammo. With an MG 42 one couldn't possibly keep enough ammunition on hand. To hold it steady at that speed of fire and to aim it and fire it at the advancing enemy with any accuracy was impossible. It was a different story if it was mounted. The MG 42 on a gun carriage became a so-called 'heavy' MG. Then it was a very reliable, accurate, fast and an extremely deadly weapon. Both weapons, the MG 34 and 42, were not easy to handle for untrained soldiers, especially for greenhorns like us without any weapons training.

I told Helmut and Hans to come with me, and we approached Lieutenant Max, as soon as he reappeared again.

The lieutenant had been very productive indeed. Following him was a supply wagon pulled by two horses. The wagon was filled to the brim with weapons and plenty of ammunition boxes.

Yes, that's right. We discovered that the famous German army was not as motorized as it was demonstrated during the weekly newsreels in the movie theatres at home. In reality the army conducted its war in Russia supported mostly by a horse and buggy operation. Of course, the army had some tanks—*Panzer*—and chain-driven personnel carriers, but these were only available to the elite SS and *Panzer-Grenadier* divisions. The normal infantry divisions relied on horses and nothing else for the supply of food, ammunition and other things. This, as I said, was in total contrast to what was shown in newsreels back home. Consequently the sight of the horse-drawn wagon was a big surprise, coming recently from the home front. It prompted Hans to ask the officer, "Lieutenant, sir, wouldn't it have been faster to bring all this on a truck?" He blurted this out without hesitation or second thoughts.

"Listen, *Arbeitsdienstmann Labuske,*" the lieutenant barked angrily, "if I need any advice from you on how to do my job I'll solicit it immediately. Do you understand? My job is to get you nincompoops into some kind of a fighting shape. This'll be difficult enough, or let me phrase it more succinctly; *it's almost impossible.* I'll try, not only for your protection, but also for my own. What I need from you is your unconditional cooperation and uninterrupted attention. I don't want to hear any dumb remarks, and I expect an immediate execution of all my orders. Do you understand?"

"*Jawohl, Herr Leutnant,*" all three of us answered with one voice.

"Could the three of us volunteer to be in a MG crew, equipped with an MG 34 or 42 to make ourselves useful, sir?"

This came from Helmut, without catching a breath and taking the lieutenant—and us too—by surprise. A minute ago Helmut had tried to accuse me of senseless heroism, and now he was upping the ante—"To make ourselves useful, sir."

The situation was deadly serious; otherwise I would have burst out laughing. People are hypocritical and often disoriented especially when their sphincter is palpitating faster than their heart is beating.

"You're an interesting group, you three," the lieutenant chuckled. "But you're just what I need right now. You'll get your wish. Sergeant Arthur will introduce you to the MG 34. We brought three of them with us. Be quick to learn. I don't give us more than two days before *"die Scheisse kniehoch wird."* (the shit gets up to our knees). Be sure that you can handle the MG by tomorrow afternoon. I'll need an expert demonstration, do you understand? Assemble the weapon, disassemble the weapon, hit targets at 300 feet and do it fast, very fast, if you care to stay alive."

"Lieutenant, I assure you that we want to stay alive and we won't disappoint you," I shot back.

Sergeant Arthur appeared at the lieutenant's command, and our training on the MG 34 commenced immediately. We were separated from the rest of the guys who continued their instructions with carbines and hand grenades. To be something special and to be especially well equipped—that's what we had wanted and that's what we got.

The sergeant was a pragmatic guy, a little older than the rest of the instructors and very much aware of the awkwardness of the situation. He also was a good teacher.

"Listen, young fellows, I won't make any big speeches, let's get going, okay?" That was it. He started our education by taking the MG apart, on a square piece of tent cloth lying in front of us, and putting it together again, very slowly, talking and describing what he was doing with every single part of the weapon while his fingers worked expertly, fast and meticulously.

"Any questions?" He looked at us expectantly.

"Yes, sergeant," Hans said, "could you repeat the whole process once more and then I'll try it, okay?"

"Okay, Hans, and you guys too, I'll call all you by your first names. Let's go! Show me if you have a good perception of weapons."

He disassembled and reassembled the weapon once more, and then handed it to Hans. Hans took the weapon, and with a little coaching from the sergeant here and there, he managed to take the MG apart, and to put it together again.

"Great going," I said. "Now let me try!"

Doing as best as I could, I managed to do the job, and Helmut, who followed me, was just as good or even better. The sergeant was pleased, more than pleased.

"Great, you guys are really more than I'd expected, now let's do it a few more times, just to get to know every little part of the MG and where it belongs and then we'll commence target practice."

We practiced and practiced, and after a few more times we were fast and precise. It's surprising what one can do with the proper incentive; and man, did we have an incentive to handle the MG properly.

At noontime, and after lots more practicing, we proceeded to a makeshift range for target practice. The sergeant, lying down, settled behind the MG, rested it on its tripod and inserted the ammunition belt.

"Now, soldiers, these MGs are eating ammunition at a frightening rate. To stop the MG from using up too much ammunition, even though your finger is still wrapped tightly around the trigger, you'll pull every sixth bullet out of the ammunition belt. This way the MG will detect a blank and stop after five bullets, you pull the lever to load the next round into the chamber, then you aim again and squeeze the trigger for another burst of five bullets. Let's try it."

He pointed to a stake in the distance where he had pinned a paper sheet as target.

"That piece of paper is my target. We'll see how many of the first five bullets hit the paper. Hans you are next after me and then Peter and Helmut."

He aimed the MG, settled the weapon into his shoulder and pulled the trigger. One short burst, the five bullets were gone, and only a few shreds of paper were still where a whole piece was a second ago. We were impressed. This was a marksman, fantastic indeed.

"My God, tremendous! How'd you do it, with the MG jumping like a rabbit? " I said.

"Hans, it's your turn now," said Sergeant Arthur.

Hans positioned the MG aiming at the paper, which the sergeant had replaced with a new sheet, put the tripod in the sand, checked the five bullets, aimed, and squeezed the trigger. The gun jumped high into the air and the bullets went all over the place but not anywhere close to the target area. We were flabbergasted, and the sergeant laughed.

"You see, it's not as easy as it looks. The MG has substantial recoil, much more noticeable than a carbine. After all, remember, five bullets instead of one leave the nozzle almost at once. You have to settle the shaft firmly into your shoulder, and then, as you pull the trigger with the index finger of your right hand, you steady the MG with your left. Here, I'll show you again."

He fired another burst with the same results.

"I've done it so often, that it's difficult to explain. The main thing is that you are fully aware, and be expectant, of what's going to happen to the MG when you pull the trigger."

One after the other we tried, and after a while we became better and better. Even though we were far from being as good as the sergeant, we were able to hit the paper with at least two or three bullets of each burst.

"Let's not screw this up," I grumbled, "Either we'll hit them, or they'll hit us." I couldn't have put it any more accurately.

"Let's go and get something to eat; I heard the field kitchen has cooked some deliciously tasting pea soup with beef in it," the sergeant tempted us.

Food was important, and you may not believe it, for the first time since joining the *RAD,* we had forgotten all about it. After the sergeant's reminder we felt the grumbling in our stomachs, and the hunger came back to us with a vengeance. We trotted to the field kitchen, and our mess kits were filled with a thick, wonderful smelling pea soup. We got some black bread, and settled on a tree trunk near our shooting range together with the sergeant.

"Sergeant, can you also teach us how to attach and use the magnetic anti-tank charge? I've noticed that a few were on the wagon with the other weapons."

I was eager to get all the learning I could get as long as there was time.

"Of course," he replied. "It's really similar to using a hand grenade. You unscrew the cap of the handle and stick the three magnetic prongs at the end of the charge to the metal of the tank. Before starting your attack watch out that you first locate and pinpoint a flat surface area on the side of the vehicle where the magnets will cling firmly to then, but only then, pull the pin. After that move away fast, you have five seconds to reach a safe spot before the charge explodes. It's almost the same reaction time as a hand grenade. Frankly, I have never done it myself. It takes a lot of courage to get close to a T 34 (Russian model tank). The chains of the vehicle are churning, most of the times there's infantry all around the tank, the crew shoots through slits on the vehicle, and you have to make damned sure that you get away from it after you pull the pin. I imagine when my life is at stake I could do it. One never knows what one will do when it's a question of life or death. But, as I said, I've never done it, never been forced to so far. I'll get one of these magnetic charges at nightfall, and I'll show you how to handle it, okay?"

The darkness settled, and for the first time in our lives we were scheduled for guard duty while facing the enemy. The code word for the night was *Freiheit* (freedom), which I thought was rather inappropriate, but what the heck.

From 1 A.M. till 2 A.M. Helmut and I were to patrol our side of the village. Hans, together with another guy, woke us up. He had a hard time to get us to respond. Young people always can sleep, and I was the champion of all sleepers.

We walked 200 yards back and forth, constantly whispering to each other. "What the young Polish girls might be doing right now, probably getting hold of the next set of recruits," I said. "I really would've liked to have had a tumble in the hay with that cute one with the black hair and the upturned nose. It would've been my first time, you know. Now I am learning how to kill people and still have to wait for my first fuck."

"Don't be so crass," Helmut was blunt in his response. "I have to be in love with a girl before sleeping with her. Just sticking my dick into somebody wouldn't work. Ideally the first woman in my life should also be the mother of my children."

"Holy smokes, Helmut, I never would've guessed that you are such a prick. If you keep that up, you'll be a virgin by the time this war is over." We both laughed, but then he got serious.

"No, honestly, when I left *Stettin,* I made a vow to my girl friend, and she made one to me. We promised each other that we'd remain faithful, until we'll see each other again."

"Well, all right, then you already nibbled a little bit on the edges, but so far I've done absolutely nothing, and I'd kick myself for being so stupid and so timid and so infantile. I can only imagine how Marianne, my girlfriend in Berlin, felt about my childish behavior."

Helmut was upset. "What are you implying? Are you crazy? My girl and I have kissed, but otherwise we've never gone any further. This stuff near the fence of the camp with the Polish girls was more than I've ever gone before. I must admit it was fun, those hard tits and their firm butts felt wonderful. I'm dreaming about them quite often."

"Thank goodness, for a minute I thought you were queer," I replied. "Psst! Did you hear that? It sounded like somebody coughing. Let's stand here behind the corner and wait for a minute to see what it was."

Nobody appeared, nobody coughed, and after a few minutes we continued on our rounds. We were silent, caught up in our thoughts about girls, missed opportunities and the desperate loneliness of our situation. After our guard duty it was a short night. We woke up the next morning with more anxieties than we had taken to bed the night before. The sergeant had slept with us in our little hut. He was anxious to assemble the platoon immediately. He wanted to prevent any scuttle but from reaching us and to upset our apprehensive minds. It was enough for him that we were exposed to wild speculations when we went to the kitchen to pick up our breakfast.

The cook had brewed some weak, but at least hot, coffee and everybody received dry bread and marmalade. The next training session with our weapons started only ten minutes later.

We detected some grumbling in the far distance every once in awhile. It was probably a thunderstorm. But the sergeant added some wisdom to our inexperienced young minds and ears.

"Guns," he said. "Big guns, about twenty miles to the east, where the Don is. It is at least a 6-inch caliber, field howitzers or even Stalin-organs. Must be near the Don, just about the area where the Italians are.

That doesn't have to mean a thing it could be a routine bombardment. On the other hand it could mean trouble. Now, let me tell you something positive. The lieutenant has told me, that we have established contact with one of our grenadier battalions on our left side to the north. That's good. We have another group of RAD men on our right flank to the south. You'd be the judge, whether that's good or bad. It will depend on what type of Russian troops we are facing. I hope that they're as new to the game as you are. If you, and the RAD on our right side, are hit by battle-hardened units . . . God be with us. We also have received news that a company of infantry from the 32d division is on its way to relieve you."

Of course, the sergeant was worried, but his anxieties were not very helpful for our already low morale. *'Battle-hardened Russian troops'* was all we needed with our four-day instruction in modern warfare.

Lieutenant Max went from platoon to platoon, making his rounds of inspections to give detailed instructions to the supervising sergeants about the areas each platoon was supposed to defend. The defensive line he was trying to compose at the edge of the village was a thin line indeed. One MG every fourth house, about 300 feet apart in between the foxholes occupied with 17- to 18-year-old RAD men with carbines and hand grenades.

"Let's all move thirty yards away from the houses toward the open field and then dig in. Foxholes are the best protection against artillery shells. A house is a more obvious target and easier to hit than a foxhole in the ground. They'll most likely assume that we'll stay within the protection of the houses. Sergeant, show the guys how to do it. Don't dig them too shallow. Every hole at least six feet deep, you'll need full cover when the shells explode.

"By the way, how's our group of young men performing with the MG? Are they as good as their mouths are loud?"

"Yes, sir, everybody is doing great, they're real talents. I believe they'll hold their own," answered the sergeant.

The lieutenant left and the sergeant showed us how to dig foxholes. After two hours of excavating and sweating we were finished.

As the afternoon progressed the grumbling of the artillery came nearer and the sergeants around their young charges became more and more agitated.

"Don't shoot at the first Russian you'll see. They'll be 400 or 500 yards away, and you'll only waste ammunition. Wait 'til they are closer, about 150 yards, and then *"haut sie um"* (knock them off).

"Sergeant, so far the Italians are still in front of us, aren't they?" one of the guys blurted out. "I mean they just can't disappear. That would be desertion, wouldn't it?"

"You're right, but I am afraid that our Italian friends see it differently. Most likely they're already on the run and don't care. Otherwise I doubt that our higher ups would have put you, the *RAD*, into this position. It's almost is an exercise in futility, really, creating a *HKL (Hauptkampflinie* or main battle line) with raw recruits. But I'm confident you'll surprise yourselves and us as well."

We continued to deepen our foxholes and asked the sergeant whether we should fall back towards the houses in case and if he would give orders to do so.

"Hans, Peter, Helmut—you are formidable young men. I've known you only a few hours, but I'm proud of you. I'm sure you'll handle our predicament all right and do the right thing when the time comes."

Sergeant Arthur was trying to motivate us and to straighten our backs while scaring us even more. He probably was being scared himself.

We saw the first Italian soldiers coming towards us across the field. It was shortly before nightfall and dusk was settling making the details even more difficult to detect. But we recognized them as Italians, because of the light green uniforms they were wearing. The Russian uniform was light brown in comparison. Our sergeant had explained this much to us.

"Nicht schiessen, don't shoot, don't shoot!" They were yelling in halting German. We tried to stop some as they rushed by, or at least one of them, with little success, until our sergeant fired a warning volley into the air.

He commanded one of the RAD men, who said he had learned Italian at school, to shout at the Italians to stop or he would kill them. A few of them finally listened. We surrounded them with our weapons drawn to frighten them even further. Prompted by our sergeant, our interpreter questioned them.

"Why are you deserting your position? What's going on near the Don? Are the Russians crossing the river? Where're your weapons and your officers?"

The Italians soldiers looked as young as we and were visibly shaken. We didn't project a very peaceful attitude. I'm sure they were expecting any minute to be killed or beaten up by us.

The answers given by one of them with a few stripes on his epaulettes turned out to be discouraging. The officers had already disappeared on a truck two days ago. The soldiers hadn't received any supplies, neither food nor ammunition, for quite some time. The weapons they were brandishing were antiques. The carbines they displayed were of a small caliber with an extremely short barrel, only effective at 80 to 100 yards, maximum. The minute the first Russians had crossed the Don they had turned and run away to save their lives.

Our men got a little unruly and shouted at the interpreter.

"Ask them were the Ivan is, for Christ's sake."

"Let's find out what's going to happen next."

"Does the Ivan have any tanks?"

"Was the artillery we heard from field howitzers or from rocket belching Stalin-organs?"

Questions came from all sides and from everybody at the same time. Tension and fear were conspicuously present. The sergeant ordered everybody to calm down. Our interpreter was finally able to get us some answers, after sorting out all our questions.

According to the Italians the Ivan was busy crossing the Don. They're placing more and bigger pontoons on the river to bring heavy equipment across. The artillery fire had come from howitzers and Stalin-organs. They hadn't seen any tanks but had heard chain-driven vehicles on the other side of the river, which could've been anything from personnel carriers to T 34's.

Okay. Now we knew a little more, though the information didn't help us any and wasn't comforting. Some guys were running to the latrine with their pants full, and I was feeling some conspicuous rumbling in my lower intestines.

Lieutenant Max came and calmed us down.

"Don't worry about anything tonight. According to my experience, and the sergeant will bear me out, the Ivan hates the dark and seldom starts an attack after sundown."

Sergeant Arthur nodded vehemently.

"Let's leave the Italians alone," the lieutenant ordered. "Don't even think about them. They aren't worth anything in their present condition and only represent a liability if we try to integrate them into our defensive position. Tell them to go." He motioned to the interpreter to relate this to the Italians.

Man, oh man, I'm telling you, I've never seen a bunch of guys disappearing so fast, and being obviously relieved about it. Before you could count to three they had gone out of sight.

A half an hour earlier a communications unit from an infantry regiment had arrived with a DORA unit on their backs. The DORA was the most modern UKW communications equipment the German infantry had in its arsenal. Now we would at least know what was going on "in the rest of the world." Our officers were visibly relieved. They told us that an infantry company would be arriving at our location sometime the next day. That was the first thing they ascertained with the help of the DORA. This infantry company was part of the strategic reserve in the area between Stalingrad and the Don.

There was a high degree of nervous anticipation in the air. While our officers didn't know whether they could rely on us or not, we didn't know how reliable our officers were and how much we could trust their leadership.

They probably thought, "Will they run after the first shells explode like the Italians did, or will they stay and fight?"

And to us the big question was will they provide the leadership we expect from them?

In the opinion of regular army men we had not been properly trained and browbeaten enough into a kind of unwavering discipline, which every army professional in the world considers essential for combat troops.

The most surprising thing, considering what was coming our way, was the *RAD's* men were the calmest of the lot. Sometimes ignorance is a blessing.

Helmut, Hans and I crawled into our hut. We worked on our MG, taking it apart, putting it together again and jabbering away like people tend to do when they're scared shitless. The sergeant organized the night watch and gave special instructions to wake him at the slightest disturbance. The Password for the night was *"Tapfer"* (courageous).

Our adrenaline was pumping, and I don't think we slept more than a few minutes at a time. Shortly after falling asleep I woke up and noticed that Helmut was awake also.

"You know," I whispered, "today we're exactly six weeks in this outfit. You can call us old-timers now, if that ever is a laugh. In another six weeks we'll be going back to our home towns, and everything will feel like a bad dream."

"You better hope and pray, my friend, that your head is still in a place where it can experience dreams," was his reply. "If I only think for one minute what is going to happen tomorrow, I have to run outside and relieve my bowels." He jumped up, and ran outside.

A red glimmer was rising over the horizon in the east announcing a new day when he came back.

"Let's go outside and be prepared for whatever will happen. Remember what the lieutenant said. The Ivan likes to attack in the early morning hours."

We got up from the stinking straw, fully dressed as we'd been for the last four days, grabbed our MG and ammunition boxes, and went outside. The sergeant arrived with more metal boxes filled with ammunition as extra reserves.

"Here, present for you! When the fracas starts you can never have enough of these. The ammo is gone in no time at all. Let's go outside, and you show me how to disassemble and reassemble the MG in twenty seconds. Okay, lets go."

We ran towards our foxhole, jumped in, positioned the MG and did what the sergeant had told us in eighteen seconds flat.

"You are good, my young friends; you're going to survive, I'll bet."

I was wondering who'd be able to collect on the bet when this was over.

We settled in our foxhole as comfortably as we could, enlarged it a little here and there and waited. To the left and to the right it was eerily quiet. We saw only very little movement on the field in front of us.

About fifteen minutes went by, the sky was getting lighter, and the sun in the far distance crept higher ever so slowly. The visibility by now was 300 to 500 yards. We were staring and staring trying to make out any movement on the flat expanse until our eyes started to water.

"There they are." Our sergeant shouted and alerted the guys to the right and the left. "Don't shoot yet, I'll fire the first shot when they get close enough, and then it's your turn."

It could've been a beautiful September morning indeed if it hadn't been for the circumstances we were in. As the sun was rising over the horizon we could see pink clouds gliding across the sky and the birds in the field were starting to sing happily about the arrival of a new day. A lonely hare hobbled across the field nibbling at pieces of something here or there. He was totally unaware of the armed men staring at him, or of the multiple killing-power facing in his direction.

The advancing Russian soldiers didn't seem to suspect anything. They knew that their adversaries had fled the day before. Now they were advancing leisurely over the flat, harvested field, the ubiquitous *Kalashnikovs* hanging loosely in the crook of their arms. The morning silence was only broken by muffled pieces of their conversation drifting across to where we were. So far we had not heard any engines, no tanks, no armored cars, no trucks, nothing.

Slowly they came closer and closer and more clearly visible to us standing deep down in our foxholes with limited visibility. Every one of them carried a knapsack on the back for the provisions with a helmet tied on top of it.

How long was the sergeant going to wait?

Bang, he had fired his carbine: "Got him," he yelled.

We had already aimed our MG at the advancing figures, which by now could be clearly seen at 150 yards distance. Helmut squeezed the trigger for the first time (he had been the best shot during our trials), reloading the chamber immediately for the next burst. We saw a few Russians fall, not only from our MG fire but also from the bullets of the rest of the men. There was confusion on the enemy side. They hadn't expected any opposition and were retreating quickly. Our sergeant yelled with relief. "They're new at this too otherwise they'd have just spread out and had continued coming at us."

Several minutes later the enemy's artillery started to respond for the first time. We could hear the howling of grenades through the air high above us. Ten to fifteen shells fell into the village to the rear of our foxholes. Nothing more happened for a while. To better observe the area in front of us some guys started to climb out of the foxholes.

"Stay down, damned, you mother-fucking fools," the sergeant yelled angrily and the other military men chimed in, cursing and yelling.

"So far the Russians have no idea where our positions are. You are almost invisible to them in your foxholes and against the background of the village. You saw how far the artillery shells were off target; they think you are sitting in the houses. For God's sake stay down, or you'll give our position away. Once they have discovered where you are the mortar or the artillery will be able to get you."

But there is a smart aleck in every group. To our left a guy got up, climbed out of his hole, yelled and waved his carbine in the direction of the enemy:

"No Italians any more, now you're facing the real thing, and we're going to . . ."

Bang. He fell where he'd stood, flat on his face. His forehead neatly punctured by a sharp shooters bullet.

A groan went through the group near us. We didn't know the guy, but he was the first casualty we'd ever seen.

"Did you see it? Bang, right through the middle of his forehead." Hans started to whimper and to cry: "What did he do, and what did we do to be in this mess?"

I thought that sounded rather superfluous from my learned friend, who had used a sophisticated Schiller quotation only a little while ago. What were *we* doing in Russia? They certainly didn't invite us. But here he was as a member of the aggressors, deep into mother Russia's territory.

Helmut and I calmed him down having a hard time not to join him in his hapless fear. The sergeant was really upset about this idiot's arrogance, gross disobedience and mad as hell at the same time.

"What a damn fool, don't anyone of *you* do anything stupid like that, I'm telling you. Now you know the guys in front of us know what they're doing. They have sharp shooters to pick off any careless idiot who wants to be a hero. Watch out, here they come again."

Sure enough another wave of brown clad Russians, jumping, ducking and weaving for protection came running towards us. This time they were more careful, they knew there was opposition ahead. We were using our MG deliberately, as we had been taught and were effective enough. The Russians casualties must've been substantial. They withdrew again and reassembled at a safe distance from our fire.

"If we only had some mortars," we heard the Sergeant mumble under his breath. "It would be foolish to waste our ammo at this distance."

We saw some army medics, each with clearly visible Red Cross armbands on the left arm, hurrying about, which indicated to us that our side had some casualties as well. They were carrying wounded men away on stretchers.

"Did you see a first aid station?" I asked the sergeant, when he came by.

"Where did the medics come from, we certainly didn't see any before."

"More and more segments of the infantry must have been arriving. I see a lot of activity behind us in the village," he explained. "Be happy that we're not alone any more."

We even had time to eat something. In the heat of the battle we didn't notice that almost five hours had passed, by now it was noontime. Hans had calmed down and felt bad about his earlier tears, and his breakdown. Both of us told him not to worry.

"We're probably as close to crying as you were, Hans. Don't worry. I only hope I'm not going to shit in my pants when the first artillery shells are falling near us," I said.

"I'm glad I found you two," Hans lamented. "I'm going to write to my mother, the first chance I get. I'll tell her all about you two, and how great you are, and what a support you are. I don't know what I would do without you."

He was still upset, trying to reassure himself with thoughts of home, and his loved ones. Poor bastard, nobody could help him. We had enough problems to keep our own sanity. The fighting had begun; only the real thing was yet to come.

The Russians were not going to squander more men without support by tanks or heavy weapons. First, they were going to soften us up with some serious artillery fire. We could hear rumbling in the distance, engines of trucks and also of chain-driven vehicles. The sergeant guessed out loud, "T 34, also some other trucks, I wonder what kind of weapons they carry?"

The distance was too great to make out anything. Handicapped by a glittering sun it looked to us as if a deep gorge was cutting across the terrain 600 to 700 yards to the north of our position. The gorge was hiding the movements of the enemy effectively. The field in front of us was void of any crops. We were standing six-foot deep in our foxholes, consequently the horizon was very low, and we could only guess where the gorge was located. We'd become aware that the retreating Russians had suddenly disappeared, as if they'd been swallowed up by thin air. The location of the gorge must have been exactly in the area where they'd vanished.

During the lull in the fighting we left our foxholes, went toward the houses of the village and took turns napping. I was dreaming wildly about home, school and Polish girls, but not for long. As soon as we awoke we started cleaning our MG 34, getting ready for the next attack.

Later I found a nice spot in the warm sun on the western side of the house well protected from enemy view and any stray bullets and was leaning against the wall, daydreaming, thinking about my mother and where she might be at this moment.

Strangely enough, I almost totally forgot about school. Only a thought, kept ticking in the back of my mind every once in a while,

as a reminder of the boss and the son of a bitch *Ortsgruppenleiter.*
He was the S.O.B. responsible for the mess I was in. I was positive
that these two bastards had been in cahoots with each other. They had
initiated my early induction into the working service. The *OGL* was
the party official I detested the most. Watching him go by in his shit
brown uniform with the swastika armband, his short cropped hair
and his constant *"Heil Hitler"* (Hail Hitler) with a straight, raised
right arm wherever he met people on the street of the village or elsewhere. I wished that both of them were with us now. I would have
liked to watch their sphincters palpitating.

Since I hadn't received any mail from my mother I didn't know
anything of her whereabouts. I hadn't heard from my father, my girl
friend or any of my relatives either. I believed my mother to be in
Zurich, well-protected and far away from the Nazis. At least one
member of the family was in the safety of a neutral country, so I
hoped. Little did I know where she really was? Of course I was frustrated. Couldn't anybody write to me? Mail would have been the one
thing to shore up my morals but none of the other *RAD* men had received any mail either. I was sitting there, brooding, angry with myself with life in general and scared about the outcome of the battle
we were facing.

Helmut came around the corner of the house looking for me.

"There you are, don't sit around here in the sun as if you are on
vacation. We see lots of activities to the north; maybe you'd better
come back to our hole. We can see vehicles moving around near the
gorge. We should be in our foxholes when they start to attack."

"I am coming; I'll be ready, don't worry," I replied. I could see
that he was trying to give me a guilty conscience, but I followed him
back to our foxholes anyway. Soon afterward the lieutenant showed
up to check on our preparedness. He spoke to us of the things to come
and tried to keep us quiet. I wondered how he was feeling.

In retrospect, I must admit—that the professional soldiers treated
us well, extremely well and they were patient. They listened to many
stupid and fearful questions from the young men. They were concerned about us. Whether the concern was real or pretended I don't
know, but we appreciated it. After all, we were no battle-hardened sol-

diers. We looked up at them like we would have looked up at our favorite teachers in school.

The Russians took care that our sentimentalities were not carried too far. Suddenly we heard a frightening, howling noise rising from the area where we suspected the gorge. It repeated itself about twenty times in rapid succession while a large cloud of smoke rose into the air above the plain.

"Stalin Organ." The Sergeant shouted, "Stay in your holes don't leave them and don't raise your heads, whatever you do, stay put."

We were so scared that all our curiosity had left us—anyway we were not going to move. The terrifying, dreadful noise grew louder and louder. As the screeching, gurgling and howling accelerated to a deafening crescendo we huddled with our heads between our knees as deep down in our foxhole as we could.

Tremendous explosions erupted all around in the village behind us, throwing fountains of dirt high in the air. Several men lost their nerve and started screaming, jumping out of their foxholes and running away. We were scared out of our wits too, but our pants were too full to even think of climbing out of our hole, much less of running away.

The smoke, the dust and the dirt had hardly settled when the second salvo left the rocket launchers. It caused even more havoc on impact. The sergeants and officers, shouting obscenities and firing their pistols in the air had driven the men back into their foxholes.

"You fucking cowards, you imbeciles, do you want to desert like the Italians and be killed in the open? Protect yourselves and stay down, or we'll shoot you before the Russians get to you. Take your guns and use them the way you've learned, or your life isn't worth a damn."

As the noise of yet another salvo of rockets from the *Stalin Organ* came closer and their impacts became imminent, the young *RAD* men jumped back into their foxholes. Some were crying— some were holding the back of their pants.

"Down, everybody down, stay down, for God's sake," the sergeant yelled one more time. Now, the Russians had seen where the enemy's position was located and adjusted their aim. The explosions of the rocket shells were all around us. They were earth shattering. Their impact was very close and truly mind-boggling. The foxhole next to us was hit smack in the middle. All were ripped to shreds.

"Hurraeh, hurraeh," the yelling from the Russian infantry sounded across the plain—that was not the only thing. The rumblings of tanks slowly rolling across the field became louder and louder. Soon the monsters became visible and crawled closer.

With their own soldiers within range, the Russians stopped firing the Stalin Organ, and we dared to stick our heads over the edge of our foxholes. The enemy's soldiers were hardly 150 yards away and came running towards us.

"Helmut, Hans, get your MG going and give them a hot reception," I yelled. We proved to be a good team and demonstrated what we had learned only a day ago. Helmut was working the MG in sporadic bursts and the results were visible. The men to the right and left responded also, and the casualties of the Russian infantry were heavy. But they kept coming anyway, jumping up and down, weaving from side to side like a well-trained infantry should. They came nearer and nearer until the closest Russians were only 60 yards away.

"Let's forget the five shot intervals," Helmut shouted. "Give me the full belt don't pull any bullets, to hell with the ammo."

Hans, who had prepared and fed the ammunition into the MG, did what he was told and I readied the next box of ammo without pulling any bullets from the belt. Helmut did a fantastic job keeping the MG under control. I remembered our hand grenades and pulled several out of a box unscrewing the caps to be ready to pull the fuse and throw them towards the approaching enemy. The tanks stopped their relentless path, and the attackers were backing off visibly shaken, giving us a breather. We seemed to have averted the worst at the last minute.

"What are we going to do during the next attack?" I yelled over the din all around us. "We seem to have casualties our defenses are getting mighty thin. Lets fall back toward the house; the walls will give us more protection."

"Okay," Helmut yelled back. "You'll say the word and we'll jump. I'll take the MG and you two bring the rest of the ammunition, hand grenades and anti-tank charges."

Hans nodded with tears in his eyes. We heard and saw the next salvo exiting the *Stalin Organ*. The rockets exploded around us. The damage to the little huts in the village and also to our defensive positions was devastating. Cries for the medics came from everywhere. And now we could not only hear the tanks; we could see them. Three, four or more of these ugly monsters were rolling stubbornly and with undeterred determination toward our position. The lead tank was pointing its turret and its 4-inch gun directly at us.

I had heard and read many war stories, stories about the First World War and how intimidating and terror inspiring a tank attack was for the defending infantry. All stories I'd read, and all movies I'd seen were nothing compared to the real thing. These steel monsters were moving ahead relentlessly, firing canons from their turrets and MG's from several openings in the armor. I was feeling the urge to jump and run too. These menacing, bullet-spitting steel monsters were slowly rolling towards us. I was sure that we were all going to be mowed down and die. The only thought in my mind was to run away from these killing machines. The treads were going to maul us, bury us, and kill us.

Helmut looked at me, the expression of pure fright on his face told me everything, and mirrored what I was feeling. On the right side of us *RAD* men were breaking away and the officers were yelling and cursing. The situation seemed hopeless. "Seemed" is not the right word, it was hopeless.

The nearer the T 34s came, surrounded and shielded by infantry, the more ridiculous the protection of our little house looked to me. From what I could imagine, the T 34 would just roll over it, bury it, squash it and us under it, period.

"Helmut, let's jump toward the house now. You can take better care of the infantry with the MG from there. If they come near the house we're all dead. Hans, watch out for any hand grenades tossed in our direction or through any of the windows. The first grenade that flies into the house—throw it back immediately. And be quick about it. I'll get busy with the magnetic charge, may be we'll get a chance to finish off the nearest tank before it finishes us." I was yelling. I had a hard time running toward the little house with a load in my pants.

All this was a fearful reaction on my part. I was simply too scared for my life to do nothing, to wait until the monster would bury us alive. As soon we had reached the house Helmut started firing with the MG through a narrow window at the rapidly advancing infantry while Hans fed him the ammunition belt that raced unimpedded through the MG's chamber. Hans yelled at me that he was going to watch for hand grenades.

As the first grenade sailed through the window, he picked it up instantly, and threw it back. It was marvelous how fast his reaction had been. Just outside the window the grenade exploded taking a few Russians down.

"Let's throw some of our grenades at them," I yelled as the engine noise of the tank and its churning treads came nearer and grew more terrifying and ear-splitting by the second.

"Helmut, come over here with the MG. I'll open the door. The T 34 must be right in front of the house." I screamed almost hysterical with fear, "Fire at anything that moves around the tank."

I pushed the door open, only to be confronted with the broad side of the monster hardly six feet away from me with soldiers huddling not far behind it. Helmut fired at them, and I jumped out of the door with my tank charge and stuck it on a flat metal surface on the side between its wheels. The charge stuck, I pulled the fuse and hurled myself back through the door falling onto the floor inside.

First I heard a small explosion—that of the magnetic charge—immediately followed by a huge explosion inside the tank. The back of our little house collapsed as the tanks turret fell on it after being hurtled through the air. The force of the exploding ammunition supply inside the vehicle had blown off the turret. The anti-tank charge must have penetrated the tank at a vulnerable spot.

I felt a sharp pain in the calf of my right leg. As I looked around I saw a long piece of shrapnel sticking out of my boot. The sight of it almost made me faint. Surprisingly I felt no pain.

Outside, the enemy retreated panicky and disorderly down the field from where they had come, totally confused by the destruction of the tank and our violent resistance, which they had not expected.

The noise of small arms weapons from our side increased. Hand grenades were exploding everywhere. We had been saved at the last minute by the arrival of the infantry. As soon as it was clear that we were not in immediate danger any more, I yelled, "Helmut, come over here. Cut my boot off and pull the shrapnel out of my leg. Come on now. Move! Do it quickly! The blood is running into my shoe and it's starting to hurt badly."

Helmut hesitated. He was horrified as he stared down at the shrapnel that was sticking out of my leg. Finally he pulled out a knife, cut the boot shaft carefully from the top down, and peeled it away. My pants, my socks, everything was soaked in blood. He was very careful and slow but could not avoid touching the piece of metal embedded in my calf. Excruciating pain started to hit me. The pants were sticking to my leg as he tried to pull them away. Carefully he pulled the cloth off until we could see the extent of the damage. The wound didn't look very big, but nevertheless the shrapnel stuck straight out of the muscle of my calf and it was bleeding.

"Let me call the medic before I do any damage to your leg," Helmut insisted.

"Go on, hurry up," I shouted. "This thing does not tickle; it hurts."

He rushed outside, while Hans gave me a sip of water. The sergeant came in and knelt down next to me, trying to comfort me. He was absolutely glowing.

"Don't worry, Peter, your leg will be all-right, my courageous *Arbeits dienstmann.* You saved all of us. The Russians would've been all over us if you hadn't blown up the T 34 and our infantry would've been too late. The lieutenant will write a report about the whole action, you can be sure of it. Now let's see that we'll get you to a field hospital and then home."

Helmut came back with a medic who took one look, pulled out a syringe and an ampule of tetanus serum and injected it quickly into my thigh.

"We don't want you to get an infection or worse, my friend," he explained. "We'll carry you to our field hospital, and I'll try to pull out this shrapnel by myself."

He carefully tried to wiggle and to pull out the shrapnel several times. It seemed to be stuck in the muscle, and he didn't want to make an incision. I looked on as he was moving the thing trying to remove it, biting my teeth not to scream.

"I don't want to rupture the muscle," he explained. "Come on, try to stand up, we'll support you on both sides and walk you to one of those horse and buggy carts. It'll transport you to the first available field hospital."

That's what we did. Helmut and Hans grabbed and supported me from the right and the left. I hobbled to the cart, and we said good-bye.

These two had been wonderful buddies and friends. Without their courageous commitment none of us would have survived.

"Watch out for yourselves," I said. "If they discharge you in time, maybe we'll see each other in *Eberswalde.*"

I would have pulled the shrapnel out of the leg by myself and walked, had I realized at that moment what I would have to endure on the shaking and rattling horse drawn buggy. Two other wounded men were put on the wagon with me. Their wounds were more severe than mine. One had his entire left foot missing. His lower thigh was tied up with a tourniquet to prevent the blood from flowing out of the stump. The other guy had been shot into the abdomen, and was in severe pain. Both were chalk white and were groaning continuously. At first, after they had been struck, they'd felt nothing as one guy whispered to me. I had experienced the same, but now the initial shock was wearing off, and excruciating pain was swallowing them and me too.

After an endless time the buggy slowly descended into a valley. I could see huge tents with Red Cross emblems on top and all sides. A hundred yards further away I saw the most beautiful sight I've ever seen, a JU 52-transport plane. It had Red Crosses painted all over its body and was ready to take off. Medics lifted us off the buggy and a doctor quickly inspected all our injuries.

"Take these two to the operating room," he said. "And put him onto the table over there," pointing at me. " I'll just make a small incision where the shrapnel has penetrated and pull it out before it develops any gangrene."

That's what he did. I felt a great relief when he held the twelve-inch long shrapnel in front of my face to let me look at it. After an injection the penetrating pain miraculously disappeared.

"No serious damage to your leg. You'll be like new in a little while. Let's put you on the plane right away. I assure you that flying won't cause any more damage to your leg." The doctor smiled at me, and left to take care of the next casualty.

Before I knew it, the medics loaded me onto the JU 52. The plane took off rumbling and skipping over the barely level field, which had never been intended to be a runway.

That was the *Tante Ju* (Aunt JU), as all soldiers called her affectionately. It was the only diesel engine driven plane in the world, sturdy as an ox and capable of taking off from any level field of dirt or grass.

We flew for about a half hour until the plane touched down on a field similar to the one from which we departed. The locomotive of a train was already waiting for us. In front of us stood another JU 52, which had landed before us. They were unloading wounded men. We were carried onto the train by Red Cross personnel and cleaned up by some young nurses.

This was terribly embarrassing for me. I had messed my pants. We were put down on narrow, clean beds covered with clean white linen. What a feeling! The beds in the former passenger wagon were arranged alongside the windows to the right and left side of the wagon. A narrow aisle for the nurses was in the middle. They walked back and forth, while taking care of the wounded men. Three beds were on top of each other. Several nurses were busy making us comfortable taking a first look at our injuries. Outside, the JU 52 had taken off for another load of wounded men. The train started to move.

"Where are we heading?" I asked the nurse as she came by.

"You'll be on this train for quite a while, son. Here, take this pill with a little water and try to sleep. You'll need a rest."

I took the pill and fell asleep almost instantly. Peter, the wounded *Arbeitsdienstmann,* was on his way home.

The train was superbly equipped from a medical point of view and included a small operating room with all necessary gear to perform emergency operations. After three days we arrived at Frankfurt/Oder. Whenever the train stopped, which on account of attacking enemy planes was rather frequently, the operating room was busy handling the most urgent emergencies. Except for the enemy planes there was no reason why it took the train as long as it did. The Russian air force was hunting for German trains, and the German air force, after their heavy losses over England, was unable to protect the transports. A great number of bridges and tracks were down or under repair. One detour after another delayed us time and again.

Miraculously my injured leg healed quickly. I discovered for the first time in my life that the heeling mechanism of my skin surprised most doctors and nurses. Nurse Emma, who was an absolute angel to the forty-two men in her car, marveled about it every time she changed my bandages.

"And you didn't get an infection? You're the luckiest man alive! You know? Especially with shrapnel wounds infections are extremely common," she explained as she changed the bandage and cleaned my wound. "I am telling you, by the time we arrive in Germany this 'little' hole in your leg will be almost closed. I can't detect any damage to the muscle and the doctors will wonder why you were on this train in the first place," she said jokingly.

I could understand her appraisal of my injuries because the problems of the other men were different. Many of the soldiers had severe injuries. They were hurting so much that I couldn't sleep because of moaning and cries for help, which were interrupting the night. She was a heavenly blessing for everybody, helping the badly wounded with pain medication. She listened to the worries of some of the more seriously injured men about how to continue life with an amputated leg or arm. She commiserated with the worries whether the girl friends and wives would leave, or stick it out with them—now that a cripple was coming home instead of a healthy, vigorous man whom they had married not too long ago.

She cuddled them, wept with them, and was a mother confessor to all.

She almost had a fit when she found out that I wasn't even a soldier, but only with the RAD, and how I and the other youngsters had been dragged into action at the front line. She complained about the bad organization, the inept high command and the war in general. But, like everybody else in Germany, she felt that the *Führer* would fix all problems and that his wisdom and genius would save Germany. It was sickening to listen to this wonderful woman repeating the nonsense from *Dr. Goebbels* propaganda machine. I kept my mouth shut. It would have been suicidal to talk to her about my own feelings about our wonderful *"Führer."* Nevertheless, I adored her—as did all the others.

The train's final destination was Frankfurt/Oder on the Polish border, the easternmost city of the German *Reich* before the war with Poland. Upon arrival we were taken off the train and moved into a very, very old hospital in the city, which was totally unprepared for a transport of this size.

Nurse Emma had been correct with her assumption. The doctors wondered how I got onto this transport together with severely injured men. They changed my bandages for a few days and then transferred me to my reserve unit in *Eberswalde.*

Before all that happened I managed to call my father from the hospital to find out how he was and to tell him briefly what had happened to me, and where I was. He was happy to hear from me, and that I'd made it all in one piece.

Lo and behold, two days later I was called to the main gate, because I had a visitor. It was my mother! We fell into each other's arms and were busy telling each other stories of our adventures during the past several months.

"When and why did you come back to Germany, for heaven's sake?" I scolded her. "You were in a haven of peace and here you are in the worst possible place on earth? Why for heaven's sake did you do it?"

Of course, I knew why she'd done it, but she didn't admit it. She rather invented some transparent subterfuges about friends and obligations and other fairy tales. It made me deliriously happy to see her, and I told her so, which made her cry and telling me for the hundredth time how she wished we'd stayed in America.

She berated me about my activities with all these weapons and getting involved with the tank. I should be more careful in the future and uttered all those nonsensical things mothers talk about being worried and not understanding a thing. Of course, I promised to be more careful in the future. What could I have said?

"We should never have made this trip across the ocean in the summer of 1939." She sobbed. "I should have listened to my friends."

Well, here we go again: In 1942, all of this was 20/20 hindsight and I had heard it a hundred times. If my aunt had balls she'd be my uncle.

She checked into a small pension in the vicinity of the barracks, and we saw each other daily while my discharge procedure was slowly processed. Wounded or not wounded, we were in Prussia and the exacting Prussians were going to keep me until I had completed my three-month *RAD* service to the day.

While I was waiting for my discharge, passing the time with totally useless activities, I had some unexpected and happy surprises. Three weeks after I made it back to *Eberswalde* a transport of RAD men arrived with men who were going to be discharged at the same time as I. Guess what? Helmut and Hans were on the transport. We embraced and slapped our shoulders so hard that I felt I had been wounded again. Everybody was happy to see each other unscathed. We opened a bottle to celebrate the occasion, and I told them about my mother's visit. In the evening I introduced both to her properly and to reminisce in gory details about "our battle on the Don." My mother sat there without saying a word, rather upset and terrified to hear the specifics of what we'd been going through.

Of course, I wanted to know all the particulars of what had taken place after I left. These two friends told me that the Russians had not attacked again before they left. They had only remained at the *HKL* (*Hauptkampflinie* = main line of battle) for two more days.

All *RAD* men had been withdrawn immediately after regular troops arrived. Nobody felt comfortable with young men around without adequate training, so they said. It would be better for them to go back to Germany to be properly prepared before fighting in a war.

"They should've thought about that before, I was scared out of my wits," Hans remarked. By now we completed our three months of service in the RAD.

A few days later I was called to the office of the RAD commander, together with my two friends. The administrative personnel of the RAD barracks were also present. The commander made a little patriotic speech about the invaluable services of the RAD in the defense of the *Vaterland,* and presented me with a black *Verwundetenabzeichen* (Purple Heart) and the Iron Cross II class for exceptional valor in the face of the enemy. Helmut and Hans also received the Iron Cross II class for their bravery in battle.

The camp commander turned out to be one of these arrogant Nazi big wigs I hated so much. He expressed haughtily he would never have expected *me* to 'ever' receive such high honors for "exceptional valor."

"After all," he said to me, "with the available reports of your *political unreliability* I have found in your files from party officials in your school town," etc. and bla, bla, bla.

It seemed to me the son of a bitch *Ortsgruppenführer* wouldn't let go of me.

Helmut, Hans and I said good-bye and wished each other good luck for the rest of the war. My mother and I went back to Berlin, where I discovered that my father was seriously ill.

Years later I heard that *my* JU 52 had been shot down shortly after transporting me to safety, this time leaving directly from Stalingrad. At the beginning of the winter of 1942 the Russians closed the circle around Stalingrad. The encircled army was doomed, and very little could be done to extract anybody. Because of Hitler's refusal to let Stalingrad go, 284,000 men of the 6th army were either killed or taken prisoner. 34,000 wounded soldiers had been evacuated earlier either by the heroic pilots of the JU 52, or by other means. None of the 284,000 men ever returned. They died either fighting in subzero temperatures in the ruins of the city, or later during the march into captivity.

Our contingent of *RAD* men had played a small part in a big battle. They had been extracted in time.

I had been lucky. The Good Lord was watching over me!

2

THE WAR, THE INJURIES, AND THE SUFFERING

From *Eberswalde* I went home to Berlin; Berlin at war. One could see this clearly when riding through the city on public transportation. Damaged buildings were everywhere. The bombardments by the U.S. planes and the Royal Air Force were showing their marks.

My mother went to her apartment and told me to spend some time with my father. He was ill, as I've already mentioned, very ill. The doctors diagnosed him with cirrhosis of the liver prompted by some bad oysters he'd eaten in a restaurant. Considering wartime logistics, reduced importance of civilian freight and everything else, one can only assume that the oysters had spent too much time out of the water.

At first the doctors diagnosed his complaints as the results of an upset stomach or a bad case of food poisoning. Then his liver stopped functioning. His abdominal cavity filled with a cloudy, watery fluid, which had to be drained once a week. Over three gallons of the murky liquid filled the receptacle every time the doctors performed the procedure. The liquid was running slowly through a glass tube sticking out of his belly. Fortunately he didn't seem to be in pain during the procedure and insisted that the quantity of the fluid each time was measured accurately. He also measured every drop of liquid he drank during the week to compare it with what was extracted.

He had never been a skinny man, to say the least, but now he looked emaciated and had lost a lot of weight. Otherwise he was in good spirits, most likely because the doctors had convinced him that the liver was the only organ in the human body that could restructure itself and would do so repeatedly. He believed them.

He also was happy to see me, because I had come home from the war relatively unharmed. With the exception of school vacation I had not been home in a long time. Surprise, surprise it was one of his rare

71

shows of affection towards me. I felt bad looking at him in his misery, lying in bed, skinny as a rail, suffering each time they drained him. There was nothing I could do to help him.

During the relatively short time in the RAD we didn't have many opportunities to write home. Now I sat down on his bedside, and told him about my experiences in the camp in Poland—not the story with the Polish girls—and of the fighting we were involved in near the Don. He listened proudly to my adventures, and asked zillions of questions about the weaponry we employed and the weapons the Russians used to get back at us. He wanted to know about the availability of ammunition, the morale of the guys I had been with and the leadership of our officers. These discussions gave him plenty of opportunity to make comparisons with his own experiences as an officer during the last war and to theorize about the differences in tactics and strategy.

At first, when he started to dig into the details of my experiences I didn't want to talk much, but in the end I gave in to his persistent questioning and told him about all, or most, of my 'adventures.' I showed him the decorations they had given to me in *Eberswalde.* He considered them to be a great honor, especially the EK II (Iron Cross Second Class), which he had been awarded during the First World War, fighting the Russian invasion of East Prussia. He proudly told me that he now considered us brothers-in-arms.

I should've known that he wouldn't keep all this to himself. I was right. He talked to his friends about my experiences. They came to visit him because of his illness and wanted to see my medals. Much to my embarrassment he showed them to everybody who entered the apartment.

Right then and there, when I saw how my father's visitors behaved, drooling over a piece of metal, I decided never to wear any of the Nazi decorations if I didn't have to. I hated all this adulation, because I hated the Nazis who had started this war, had drafted me and had put my mother and me into this predicament. No, in my opinion they had forced me into their army, and now I was supposed to wear their decorations? No, not me! The only feelings I had about the fighting were feelings of gratitude towards My Maker who had protected me at a time of great peril.

Prematurely, I thought myself to be very clever and strong enough to resist the system.

And then I saw Marianne again. We certainly had lots to talk about. She was the youngest of four sisters. Two of them were married to submarine *Kapitäne* (Captains). I was eager to meet them. I finally managed to do that at Janne's home when I picked her up for our date. Now, *they* certainly looked like heroes to *me*. I couldn't possibly imagine myself going under the surface of the ocean in one of these floating sardine cans—what a horrible thought!

Janne and I had a good time together, went to the movies and the circus, held hands rather innocently. In spite of my time in the military, my experiences in shooting at people and with the Polish girls, I just couldn't muster the courage to do anything with her, I mean, not even kissing her. Janne did not give me any indication that she would let me, at least not to my inexperienced way of thinking. Usually, after coming back from one of our excursions like going to the movies, we would spend the evenings in my mothers little apartment, listening to records and talking about *Gott und die Welt* (God and the world). My mother loved these visits, because that was her chance to see me and to spoil me before I would go back to the inferno. Janne always had the latest English and American recordings of the British Brunswick label with the newest and most popular music. She borrowed them from her sister's husbands, the submarine commanders.

During the beginning of the war the German U-Boots still dared to stop merchant vessels in the North Sea and the Baltic searching for contraband. Contraband was everything on board designated for England. If they found contraband the ship would be redirected toward a German harbor with a detachment of German sailors aboard. While checking on the cargo aboard ship, going through the bills of lading, they convinced some of the captains to 'lend' them recordings from the ship's officers' quarters for the U-boots officers' mess. This happened before the submarine warfare became ugly. The Germans had not yet occupied Denmark and Norway. These countries were still neutral trying to ship merchandise to England. England paid with real money, not worthless *Reichsmark.*

To us, the English recordings on the Brunswick label were a musical treat I will never forget. Janne and I both favored Louis Armstrong's, *"Jeepers creepers where'd you got those peepers,"* and many others as well.

My father was angry when I came home as late as I did many times, mostly because I didn't tell him beforehand. But one day he really made me mad when he slapped my face when I came home after 12 o'clock, because I didn't tell him the truth right away where I'd been that night. I stepped back from him and almost shouted, "Have you forgotten where I just came from and of my recent experiences? It was okay, I guess, to get shot up by the Russians, destroy their tank and get all kinds of decorations. Beyond that I'm sure you are aware of my forthcoming draft into the German army with more of the same to come? You know, Papi, really, if you want to slap me now for coming home late from visits with my girlfriend, do I have to remind you that nobody watched my late hours while huddling in a Russian foxhole? I was so fearful for my life that I shit in my pants. It's not exactly my doing that I'm in this mess; I didn't volunteer for any of it!"

I felt sad our relationship had developed so disappointingly. It was too late now to retrace the many wrong steps we had taken along the way, both of us. My mother was upset and cried. I handed her my handkerchief to dry her face, which didn't help much to calm her down. Ten days after my release from the RAD my draft notice arrived via registered mail. It specified that I was to report to the 122nd Infantry Communication Company in *Kottbus,* south of Berlin on December 1, 1942.

"Peter, I am so worried about you. Don't stick your neck out again. You don't have any business in this war anyway. You don't need to be a hero for the Nazis. Be careful and don't climb onto any tanks anymore, please, promise." My mother pleaded with me.

She reminded me, over and over again, to be careful and not to force my luck. Mothers all over the world have such a strange conception of war, of the things that happen when opposing armies are out to kill each other. About what soldiers are forced to do if they don't want to get killed by their own people and what they will do when their life is at stake.

But, let's face it, without mothers and their love, soldiers could not endure any of it. We hugged and my mother called upon the Almighty God to protect me—I sincerely hoped that her intervention on my behalf would help. Marianne woke up to the realities when I said good-bye to her and kissed me passionately. Did I miss anything? My experiences with girls in those days left a lot to be desired. My father and Marcella insisted on accompanying me on my way to the railroad station in *Charlottenburg,* a suburb in West Berlin.

Whenever I stayed at my father's house, during the last few weeks in Berlin, Marcella had become very, very friendly. She came into my room to say good night when I was already in bed. She would sit down on my bed, giving me a goodnight kiss on the forehead, her soft blond hair, let down all the way to her shoulders, gently brushed past my cheeks. If it was meant to excite me, she did all right. But I couldn't quite understand why she did it to begin with, and in my youthful innocence and inexperience I didn't understand that she was totally aware of what she was doing. Like in my relationship with Marianne, I wasn't experienced enough with women, or let's say too naïve to draw the right conclusions about her behavior.

On the final day in *Berlin-Charlottenburg,* as the train left the platform, we waved our handkerchiefs endlessly. I soon had forgotten most of Marcella's behavior, but I can still remember to this day my father's frail body standing there on the platform with his loosely fitting overcoat hanging around his shoulders. His hat was held up from sliding over his face only by his ears. He waved his handkerchief after the disappearing train. He'd lost over sixty pounds. It was the last time I saw him alive.

Years later it amazed me in my own mind, to be confronted with unimportant little details I remembered under those circumstances. For instance on my last evening at my father's house, before leaving for the army, he opened one of his remaining two bottles of French champagne, which he had hidden in the cellar for special occasions. The bottle he opened was a *Dom Perignon 1936 Millesime.* Marcella

In the German army. Winter 1942, Kottbus

baked a strawberry short cake. Where did she get the strawberries? She knew it was my favorite. The cake was excellent, but the bottle of champagne tasted of cork. I drank it anyway, who wants to waste a *Dom Perignon Millesime?* I was sick all night. I woke up the next day with a splitting headache. It taught me a lesson about drinking wine tasting of cork. My departure from Berlin took place in a haze and with terrible foreboding of things to come.

The 122nd Infantry in *Kottbus* was a communications company. The first official act of the administration was to test everybody's IQ. Thorough as the German military is, they also conducted aptitude tests. The more intelligent men—guess where I fit in—were commandeered to learn the Morse alphabet and to train as short wave operators. The others were relegated to be telephone operators. The difference in the training was vast. Short wave operators had to learn the Morse alphabet and a coding and decoding system. For six hours of every day our lessons took place in a comfortable classroom, while the telephone operators had to practice to lay cables in the fields and woods surrounding the barracks. The drums weighed almost 120 pounds, each carrying 300 feet of insulated cable. Unwinding of the cable, while carrying the drums on your back running and jumping up and down, was extremely taxing physical work. It was even worse rewinding the cable, because during rewinding the drum was attached to the chest. Jumping up and down under simulated enemy fire was the worst. Only much later did the young recruits learn about the telephone equipment, switchboards and portable field phones and the actual rules and procedures of conducting a telephone conversation under combat condition. In retrospect I was glad I did not decide to play dumb, as some smart alecks in our group had suggested. We went through all the routines for fresh recruits, the drill and the training of becoming an infantry soldier, suffered through exercise-ground chicanery devised by vindictive training personnel, went to the range for shooting practice and, naturally, did lots of work with the Morse alphabet. The standard drill was tiresome. If it hadn't been for our sergeant, an experienced veteran of the winter of '41 in Russia, it would've been worse. Sergeant Trepper knew what was necessary, and that's what he demanded of us, not more and not less.

The rooms in the barracks housed ten recruits each. Rooms had to be spotless at all times according to military discipline. This was a rude awakening for many recruits away from home for the first time. It was necessary as an integral part of training and regimentation of young soldiers. Sergeant Trepper made sure we accepted the drill and inspected the cleanliness and the orderliness of our lockers meticulously every night. One sweeping motion of his arm emptied the locker and turned the entire room upside down if anything didn't meet his expectations. We learned quickly to watch each other, help each other and depend on each other.

We were permitted to write home and discovered to our great surprise and astonishment that three of the ten guys in our room couldn't read or write. They were analphabets. Can you believe that? In Germany! We couldn't believe it. They had juggled their way through school just as they had managed to slip through the military aptitude tests. We had to write the postcards to their families and sweethearts and enrolled them in special classes to learn belatedly what they had missed in school.

Most of all we liked the practice sessions on the shooting range, because during shooting practice we didn't have to sweat on the exercise grounds. In the beginning the distance to the target was 300 feet and they were large, 3 by 3 feet, almost like a barn door. You wouldn't believe how many guys missed the targets.

I didn't tell anybody of my experiences in the *RAD;* what for, to show off? The sergeant was surprised when I hit the center of the target three times in a row. Two or three of the others had learned shooting at the pre-military training of the HJ and were also doing well. Shooting expertise was awarded with a pass for a one-day leave into town. We picked up our passes from the office of the First Sergeant. He congratulated us on our excellent shooting. With our permit in hand we left and went through the gate past the guardhouse.

The barracks of the 122nd infantry were way out of town. We took the bus for a ride into *Kottbus.* Obviously, I didn't know anybody in *Kottbus.* I strolled around aimlessly getting to know the place. The war had left its telltale signs even in this little town, away from the main stream and without any industry. *Kottbus* was a sleepy little town far away from any wartime activity. The stores looked drab and the windows void of any saleable merchandise.

I entered a café to order a cup of light brown wartime coffee, to eat a piece of cake and to read the newest magazines on display. The waitress asked for my ration card for the cake. As a soldier I didn't have any ration cards, and I asked her to bring me only coffee. As I sat down to read my magazine an elderly woman entered the restaurant, took the empty chair next to mine and immediately started to talk to me. She was about 50 years old, very plainly dressed with a kind face and was friendly right from the start. She looked at me inquisitively and asked whether soldiers in the barracks got enough to eat and other details about life as soldiers. Her son was in Russia, she told me, and she had not heard from him in a long time. She was a worried mother wanting to chat a little and wanted to know from me about life while facing the enemy and what the soldiers were doing with their spare time. I told her stories from the *RAD* and what we had done to pass our time. I didn't get into too much detail about the fighting, the fear that struck everybody, the wounded and the dying. It seemed to help her to talk to a soldier like her son and before I knew it, she invited me to come to her apartment for a home-cooked meal. After weeks of military food, it turned out to be a fabulous treat. In the end, my visit to Kottbus had been a success.

The following day, while exercising with our carbine, learning the special handling and saluting with this weapon, a runner from the office of the first sergeant came. He told our drill sergeant that soldier Schwarzlose should report to the lieutenant and the first sergeant immediately. I searched my mind what the reason could be for this urgency but felt totally innocent.

As I entered the office, I came to attention and said, "Soldier Schwarzlose reporting," looking straight ahead at the wall in front of me. After all, I had been in the Army for a few weeks and remembered the RAD; I knew what was expected of me.

"Tell me, soldier," the first sergeant started sanctimoniously, deliberately walking, no, strutting back and forth in front of me with his arms crossed on his back. "Aren't you keeping things from us? I mean standing here in front of us with a bare uniform? Is that really the way—according to military code—you should be dressed? Are you, for some reason or the other keeping things hidden from us?"

I could see that this was leading up to something. He was talking himself into a rage. I knew instantly what he was talking about. The first sergeant was one of these typical army men. If he were in civilian clothes, he would've looked like a first sergeant. His face was getting redder by the minute and his eyes were bulging from their sockets. He looked intimidating, and he was.

According to prevailing military code every soldier was obligated to visible wear on his uniform, at all times all decorations awarded to him by the *Führer*. The *Führer* was awarding all decorations, though he didn't award them personally. Not to wear them was considered an insult to the *Führer*, as I was to find out immediately. Of course I knew that I was in violation of the code of conduct, but I had thought that I could get away with it.

"In your records I am reading all kind of interesting things, soldier," he continued, holding my file in his hands and leafing through it.

Uh oh, I knew what was coming now. Fuck him, I thought, I had made up my mind, and I was going to stick to it.

"You went to a swanky boarding school to the north of Berlin. I am reading here reports by the *Ortsgruppenleiter*"—him again—"Of irrational behavior during that time. You insisted that you were not a German National but an American instead; you opposed party discipline, etc. You want to comment?"

"No sir, I cannot add anything, I'm sure that you have it all in front of you," I said, continuing to stand at attention.

"You were enlisted to the *RAD* on the 15th of August and sent to Russia, south of Kursk. The report goes on to say that during a battle, and an attack by superior Russian forces with tank support, you single-handedly destroyed a Russian T 34 with an anti-tank charge. It goes on further, saying you turned back an assault of Russian troops with the help of two other *RAD* men. You were severely wounded and received a purple heart. You were awarded the Iron Cross 2nd class for bravery. Is this correct?" (Lieutenant Max had filed his report as promised and, in my opinion, had grossly exaggerated my part.)

"Yes sir, that's correct, sir," I replied

"If that's correct, soldier, why aren't you wearing the decorations the Führer graciously and proudly awarded to you? You know that this is part of the honor code of the German army, don't you?"

"Yes, sir, I do, sir," I answered without hesitation.

"Well, if you do know, why don't you oblige, soldier? But never mind, aside from committing you to three days of solitary confinement for this infraction of the code, the army has ordered me, and it's my pleasure to do so on account of your deeds of heroism, to promote you at this time from soldier to corporal. I'm complying. Starting tomorrow I also order you to wear the signs of your new rank together with all your decorations on your uniform. Let me say that, personally, I am almost positive that you are one of these troublemakers the army has to face from time to time. I assure you, that the army knows how to deal with this problem. I only hope for your own sake you are aware of the consequences of your behavior. Don't try to fight the army; it's bigger than both of us. Go to your room and do as I ordered. Apply all decorations and the signs of your new rank to your uniform and report to the brig. Dismissed!"

The lieutenant didn't say a word during the entire proceedings. He was kind of dense anyway.

I saluted, turned on my heels and left the office. When I arrived in the room of our platoon, Sergeant Trepper was waiting for me. He had a kind smile on his face. The men were still outside, exercising.

"Corporal, congratulations." He stretched out his hand to shake mine. "I only wished that I had guys like you with me when I was stuck in the mud, near Moscow, during the winter of 1941 with the Ivan coming at us in never ending waves, but," he injected softly, "that was another time. For the rest of your time in the army let me give you a piece of advice: Run with it, don't buck it. You'll lose. It isn't worth it. Now, report to the brig; they are waiting for you."

He left the room, and I sat down on my bed all alone to contemplate what to do. Should I be pigheaded? The war was certainly going to last for a long time. I had experienced the power of the army, and in the end I decided that Sergeant Trepper was right. I sat down, pulled out my sewing kit and sewed everything onto my uniform, the ensign of my new rank, the ribbon of the EK II and two loops for the black medal for being wounded once (the equivalent to the purple heart). After I was finished I wondered what my comrades would say when they saw me again. I was disgusted and angry with myself to have broken my principles, but at the same time I was rather helpless. To hell with the army!

Three days of solitary confinement were peaceful, only the food was sparse, just dry bread and water. It was frugal and too little, on the other hand I had plenty of time to contemplate my conduct in the future. I decided of the two available roads, I should better choose the one of compliance. To resist would mean continuous harassment maybe even severe punishment, most likely further incarceration or worse, that would be *"Bautzen"* (the most notorious military prison complex of the German army in Saxony), or, God forbid, a penal battalion near the front lines to clear away mine fields. If I complied, on the other hand, I would live the life of an ordinary infantryman, going to Russia, Italy or Africa, wherever the army would send me. I decided to choose the latter.

My comrades were surprised when I returned to my quarters with my uniform prepared according to regulations, congratulated me, slapped my back and asked many questions about my new rank, and how I'd earned the decorations. They were good guys, and in general treated me as they'd treated me before, only with a little more respect.

As far as the army was concerned I was a recruit, albeit with a rank. Only my pay increased.

Basic training continued, in our case with the emphasis on the Morse alphabet. Sending and receiving messages and learning to convert clear language messages into coded ones were practiced exhaustively. The sergeant told us we would be called "Operators," by the time everybody was able to send 90 symbols a minute and receive 80.

I wrote a long letter to my mother. I didn't know whether she would agree with my decision of compliance but tried to explain my reasoning to her. The main thing for me, as I explained to her, was to get out of this war alive. Nothing else mattered. I mailed the letter via the civilian mail system. I didn't trust the bastards. They sure as hell were going to check on my mail.

Ten days later the answer from Olga arrived. In my thoughts I always called my mother by her first name; to me she was "Olga." She agreed with my decision whole-heartedly, told me that she loved me and I should stay out of trouble with my superiors. She also wrote that my father's health was deteriorating. The doctors talked a lot of gibberish. They were of the opinion, and told him so, that his liver could and would recover. It was more a question of whether his heart would be able to put up with the strain long enough for the damaged liver to recuperate. His only hope was to wait for his body to do the healing. I wrote a letter wishing him the very best, from all my heart and also made some general observation of life as a soldier. I left out any description of my experiences with the first sergeant. It was no use to upset him with my troubles. He had enough of his own.

*   *   *   *

In the meantime Olga was in Berlin, and she was rather alone and unhappy. She wrote letters to me, and I wrote to her, but she noticed that I was growing up fast. I had written to her about all this soldiering and very little about things she wanted to hear from me most. She wanted to hear about my plans for the future, after the war, what I'd do after the fighting was over, of my memories of our time together in New York, how lonely I was without her. For some reason she didn't understand my priorities had changed, my life was drifting away from her in another direction.

She'd been able to live in Berlin almost unnoticed and unmolested by the Nazi authorities. Once a month, as a matter of routine, she reported to a local police station. The authorities had grown considerably unfriendly since the declaration of war between the USA and Germany. Her friends were guarding her so far, and protected her from internment or worse. Every once in a while Bill, being on a business trip, arrived from Switzerland using his Swiss passport. He urged her repeatedly to leave Germany. He would help her across the Swiss border if things would get tight. Olga, however, wanted to stay were her son was or at least in the vicinity. Since I was soon going to be transferred to some occupied country she began to have doubts about the wisdom of her decisions. In the end she decided to rejoin her friends in Switzerland to find out what she could do for me from there.

On December 30, 1942, one day before the beginning of the New Year, four weeks after I had been drafted into the army, an order was issued to the 122nd infantry communications company to assemble immediately. We were transferred to France. It was rumored our destination was near the English Channel. Of course, it was a secret, but the location would be somewhere in France for sure.

I departed with my comrades of the 122nd. To my great disappointment the first sergeant stayed with us, and Sergeant Trepper stayed behind.

"You are doing fine, Peter," he had assured me when we parted. "Be smart and not a smart-alecky. I prefer to stay behind to train another group of recruits. It's safer that way."

He knew the army and was doing the right thing in order to survive.

By now the ten guys from our room at the barracks had known each other long enough and a few friendships were developing. Ever since I had been promoted and after seeing my decorations my comrades treated me differently. To them I now was an authority about the war and also of things to come. It was awkward for me at first. They constantly referred to me with any subject of concern, but after a while I got used to it.

Our transport consisted of normal third class passenger carriages. Those old wagons of the *'Deutsche Reichsbahn'* had a separate door for each compartment on both sides of the wagon. They looked strange, almost like a continuous row of doors on wheels. Inside each compartment had two rows of wooden benches facing each other, large enough for three passengers to sit on with strong baggage nets, supported by iron crossbars, hanging overhead. Six guys were ordered into each compartment and the jostling began immediately. Who would sleep where? We decided two of us would sleep in the nets, two on the benches and two on the floor. The floor was the worst location it was tight and dirty. For the first time my rank and my authority saved the day. I told them that I would sleep in one of the nets and the others could have their pick. At night six backpacks hung underneath the net. That didn't leave much room for anything else in the compartment. On the third night, while the train was rumbling slowly through the French countryside one of the backpacks broke loose, they were heavy and the steel helmets were tied on top. It fell down and broke the nose of a guy sleeping below. His luck was he was taken off the train to a hospital, and his misfortune that he came back to rejoin us four weeks later. By that time we were stationed on the French coast. After that accident we were only five left. The man on the floor had more room to sleep and to move around. Sometimes in life, especially in the army, one man's misfortune is another ones luck.

As the train continued it's way through France, always in westerly direction, the weather became warmer. Soon snow disappeared all together. The proximity of the Atlantic Ocean's Gulf Stream had changed the climate.

Three days later we arrived in *Fécamp* a small fishing port located at the English Channel south of Dieppe and north of Le Havre. *Fécamp* had only a small harbor mostly for fishing boats. During summer people were trying to make an extra franc from the visiting big city folk who come on vacation to enjoy the soft white beaches. *Fécamp* is near an ancient *Bénédictine* order of monks. It is known for their famous *Bénédictine* liquor. It also had a small whorehouse.

As soon as we left the train everybody was assigned quarters. Our group was sent to a medium sized house on top of the northern cliffs of the harbor and away from town. The house had a good location way above the harbor, high over the city. We had a beautiful view over the town to the south and the ocean to the west. The owners of the house had been forcefully evacuated for security reasons, to make room for the German army and because it was too close to the cliffs. The area was a defensive parameter.

One day, shortly after our arrival, the quartermaster sent two of us to the *Bénédictine* cloister to exchange a 200-pound bag of sugar for two-dozen bottles of *Bénédictine* liquor. We went to the cloister with a team of horses and a heavy supply wagon. The cloister was six miles inland from *Fécamp*. We negotiated successfully with the monks for one extra bottle of the sweet stuff before concluding our deal, just for the two of us. On our return trip to *Fécamp* we finished it off, one sweet sip after another. Has anyone ever tried to finish off a quart bottle of sweet liquor in a short time with only two people? The sweet stuff made me rip-roaring drunk and after first falling asleep, I fell off the wagon onto the shoulder of the road, much to the distress of the other guy who was not too sober either. After we finally made it back to *Fécamp,* I was a mess. First sergeant almost sent me to the brig again.

At this stage of the war, in early 1943, the Germans were feverishly developing *Fécamp* and the areas up and down the coast into massive fortifications, the so called *Westwall,* to guard the European main land against a possible invasion by British and Americans forces. Areas close to the English Channel were one solid construction site. Hundreds of crews pored concrete for artillery bunkers and other buttresses. Trucks were rushing back and forth day and night as if there was no tomorrow. Most of the workers were French, former prisoners of the early days of war. Even though they made good money and liked the work as they told us, I was wondering about the quality of the work they were doing.

We never really got a chance to get a closer look at the town of *Fécamp.* Before we departed for France our officers had briefed us about some isolated activities by partisans *résistance* as the French called them among themselves. After we arrived in *Fécamp* we never saw any or heard of any *résistance.* As a matter of fact, on the few occasions that we made contact with the civilians they were friendly and helpful. May be the *résistance* was someplace else. *Fécamp* was small, three thousand people at the most, and they were used to tourism. Maybe they looked at us as passing tourists, though that sounded a little farfetched.

Our officers involved us in military drills to keep us busy and to continue our basic training and make believe missions. Soldiers of all armies have to be kept busy lest they start spreading scuttlebutt and get into trouble. After all we were recruits in training; we had only been soldiers for five weeks and had to learn more about soldiering.

For the short-wave operators it meant practicing Morse code and learning how to judge distances. UKW (ultra short waves do not follow the curvature of the earth) can only cover a short distance and any obstruction from buildings or hills would severely limit transmissions.

Our house had sleeping facilities for twenty men. Ten had already been there when we arrived. These guys were 'old hands' and had one priority and one priority only, to stay in France!

They proclaimed to us to know everything about town and were letting us know graciously where the bars were, and *'der Puff'* (The brothel). These guys seemed to spend all their free time in the brothel. They knew all the girls by name and used the place not only to get their rocks off, but also as a center of social activities. They immediately recognized some of us younger ones had never seen the pleasure-sights they were talking about, much less had enjoyed our first penetration. They made fun of our inexperience and kidded us unmercifully.

"Can you imagine," said Erich, a natural loud mouth and a member of the older group, "the expression on Peter's face, when he looks straight into the mouth of hell and heaven for the first time? I bet he'll scream for his mama, and run as fast as he can."

Everybody had a laugh at my expense as if this were the best joke they had heard in a long a time. Those dumb asses! I could only imagine what Erich had meant with his metaphors and didn't dare to inquire any further about details of what he insinuated, for fear of being ridiculed even further.

The bantering about whores and screwing and pussy went on day and night, whenever we sat down to have a meal, or to rest, or before lying down on our bunks, always. It was subject number one. Young soldiers seemed to have only one subject on their minds, how to get laid!

"Ahhh, nothing more beautiful as when they spread their legs and let you look into the gate of heaven," Erich sighed. "I have to go soon to see *Chou-Chou,* my little sweetheart. I haven't fucked in two weeks and feel horny as hell."

Chou-Chou apparently was the name of a very young, good-looking whore in the brothel that everybody knew and preferred to be with.

"What do you say, comrades, shall we go there on Saturday and initiate Peter at the same time?"

I knew my face was crimson red, but I couldn't possibly admit that I was scared. What if I would go there and catch a case of the clap, or even worse, syphilis? And anyway, I just didn't know how to react. What business did I have to be in a French whorehouse provided and controlled by the German army? Outwardly I acted and bantered with them as if I wanted nothing more than to join them during their upcoming excursion.

There was also a guy in our group who was about 32 years old, much older than the rest of us and very, very short. He was only five foot one. His name was Kurt. Back in Berlin he was a tailor and had been doing his job unmolested all through the war. I must say again he was really short, very short. He was the smallest man outside of the circus, of course, I had seen during my entire life.

During the first three years of the war the German army had followed its old tradition. Nobody who wasn't at least five foot two inches, the size of a 'rifle 98' would be drafted. Well, as the war progressed it turned out that losers couldn't be choosers and when the casualties mounted, the army finally drafted him. Kurt had left a wife and four children in Berlin and told us when we asked about his four children that he would only have to hang his pants on his wife's bedside and "bingo" she would be pregnant. But, small as he was, he had one other problem.

One day when we were all taking our shower he was the last to come into the bathroom. We were all standing there soaping up and enjoying the hot water. There he came, the little guy, ridiculously frail with a short white body. But, can you believe it his penis was hanging down all the way to his knees, *to his knees*! There was dead silence. Aside from the noise of the running water, silence, as everybody stared at him. The guys slowly turned to look him, up and down. The THING, his penis, was enormously long. We continued to stare. I had never seen a penis that long before and apparently neither had the others. It was actually hanging down all the way to his knees! Unimaginable if I hadn't seen it with my own eyes. Suddenly the silence was broken and the howling started. Erich was the first, naturally.

"My God, Kurt, you must have been in a circus. Is your name in the Guinness Book of Records? How do you stow that prick in your pants, I mean, does it fit?"

Poor Kurt wanted to turn and run away but some of us stopped and consoled him telling Erich to shut his filthy mouth. The situation was funny to say the least; actually it was hilarious for everybody except Kurt.

None of the whores at the brothel had seen an organ of that size either and that was a problem for Kurt. He told us that he had made several attempts to persuade one of the girls to have a go with him but they flatly refused as soon as they saw the size of his member. They wouldn't let him enter the portals of heaven, not a chance.

"Can you imagine the size of that prick when it's alive and ex-ited?" they had said. *"Non, jamais!"* (No never!) That was their final decision.

Later during that day when we were sitting together, talking about the possibility of a Saturday filled with fun at the local estab-lishment, everybody kidding me about my innocence, I desperately wanted to divert the attention away from me. Then, suddenly, like a stroke of lightening, I had an idea how to do it.

"Listen fellows," I said loudly, "I think it's high time that we help Kurt to have some fun too. I mean it must be terribly frustrat-ing for him to be refused by the girls at a time when everything seems to be the matter of only a few francs. In my mind it can only be a question of mechanics."

Everybody started talking at once.

"Listen to him, hasn't fucked an ant in his entire life, much less a decent French whore, and he talks about mechanics."

"Baby talk, still wet behind the ears, doesn't even know whether to fuck them from the front or from behind, and wants to give us seasoned fornicator's advice."

They all laughed and the banter was ferocious, one guy trying to outdo the other with their comments. After awhile they calmed down, and I was able to make myself heard again.

"Okay, have you finally exhausted your limited imagination and your brain power? I'll tell you what we'll do and how we explain our plan to the girls. What we'll have to do is this: Kurt has to lie down on his back, one of the girls will give him a nice blowjob so his member gets really excited, I mean until it reaches its full size."

Here the howling and laughter started again. I managed to stop them and continued with my words of theoretical wisdom.

"One of us grabs the bottom of his prick with two hands, one hand on top of the other intending to get that huge prick of his to look normally sized. Then we promise the girl who is willing to ride on top of him that we won't let go of it until he has blown his nuts."

I looked at them waiting for a response; there was an eerie silence. Erich sat there with his mouth open, spit drooling out of its corners, staring at me. Then it was bedlam.

"Peter, you have been lying to us, you must be the most talented cocks-man of them all. You must have been hiding your experiences behind that innocent baby face of yours, you S.O.B."

The ribbing got worse but now with a totally different slant. I fathomed what would be coming next from this rough, reckless and inconsiderate group of soldiers.

During the shouting, back and forth, Erich became once more the leader of the gang. He was a lousy soldier, and I wouldn't have entrusted my life to him, like I did with Helmut and Hans, my old *RAD* buddies, but here he was king when it came to ribaldry.

He climbed onto the table and proclaimed over the din, "My dear comrades, this Saturday we'll all go into town, to the *bordello*. I'll see and talk to *Chou-Chou*, and I'll organize a good time for Kurt. I don't want anybody to chicken out, especially Peter, our experienced man of the world. Ha, ha!" Everybody yelled and shouted and agreed with Erich's plan. The only two embarrassed faces were Kurt's and mine.

It may sound as if the German army had nothing else to do during this war but to think about whoring and drinking, that was not always the case and not more than in any other army in this world. Attached to each infantry battalion was a trench mortar company. The trench mortar, in the eyes of military experts is an accurate and effective weapon to repulse an attempt of an invasion by allied forces from the sea. The mortar shells were deadly. Especially when they hit the hard, compacted sand, they would spill thousands of small, murderous shrapnel to all sides. To keep us busy as additional extension of our military know-how we had to practice with the mortars to learn something more besides communication work. I'm telling you, moving the 4-inch mortar with its heavy bottom plate around in the trenches above the harbor of *Fécamp* was heavy work. Each battery of three 4-inch mortars was assigned its position and fired enough practice rounds to find its range for possible landing sites of enemy infantry. The coordinates were written down, and stayed in the logbook of the noncom officer in charge of the site.

I preferred my challenges as a short wave operator and was happy when we returned to work with our DORA. My superiors picked me, because of my rank and previous experience—there we go again—to be the lead man in a DORA unit, a two-man team assigned to an infantry company of a regiment whenever the need for wireless communication arose. Mostly this would happen during an assault or retreat situation with no wires on the ground to communicate by telephone. Each one of two men in a DORA unit had to carry a heavy metal box on his back. The boxes were 24 × 17 × 12 inches in size. The unit with the "brain" was the lighter one containing only electronic transmitting components. It was the master unit. The second box, the utility unit, was fitted with two large, heavy, dry batteries and one wet battery. It was much heavier. To carry this second box, in more sense than one, was an absolute pain in the ass. The second man assigned to my DORA unit was Oskar. Oskar was about ten years older than I. He was from *Kolberg* located in Pomeranian on the Baltic Sea, the northeastern part of Germany. *Kolberg* was not far from where I had spent my summer vacations with the Laurenz family. Oskar and I talked a lot about his home in *Pomerania*. He was quiet but reliable, not a loud mouth like Erich. We collaborated well in our work and daily routine. The only bad thing about him was that he was a rabid, 100% communist. How he had survived in the army up to this point with political spies hanging around was an absolute miracle. The best part was he didn't make any bones about his political beliefs, and, to top it all off, tried incessantly to draw us into debates about Nazism and Hitler, "the murderer," as he called him, and *Himmler,* "the cruel butcher." He had degrading adjectives for the other leaders as well. He used descriptive names for every one of them and had a good reason for each one of the names. That made his talk extremely dangerous for those who listened to him without reporting him. I didn't want to be shipped to *Bautzen,* the most notorious military prison operated by the army, and I didn't want to have any more trouble with the first sergeant than I already had.

"Oskar," I said, "You are a great guy, but keep your political beliefs to yourself, I don't want to know anything about them; I have
my own problems. Talk to anybody you want to, but not to me."

"But you are an intelligent man, Peter; you know what I am
talking about. The others are anencephalic turds. What little gray
mass there was has been washed away by the indoctrination of the
Nazis. They are nothing but cannon fodder, and we will need people
like you when the war is over."

"No dice, buddy," I protested vehemently. "If you think they are
brainwashed, that much the better. Clean their brains one more time
if you want to. Wash them with your ideologies. I don't care, but I
do not want to be any part of it."

He kept quiet for a while, but not for long. When the plans to
visit the whorehouse on Saturday surfaced, he flatly refused to join
us, and murmured something about imbeciles, and infantile juve-
niles who could never improve the lot of the masses.

Erich supervised our attire. He was eager to show off at the
brothel with his new buddies. He thought the whores would consider
him to be a big shot. When everything was just right and we had
passed his critical inspection we marched down the steep hill past
the harbor filled with French fishing boats. We only had to go to the
edge of the little town, right next to the harbor, where the brothel
was located. I was so nervous. My hands were shaking, twitching
and sweating and I was hiding them in my trouser pockets for fear
of attracting even more ridicule from my seasoned comrades.

A member of the military police was stationed at the entrance
of the brothel. He was an older guy, about fifty years old, who would
probably do nothing else until the end of the war than to check on
soldiers at the entrance to a French brothel. He scrutinized our permits and also ascertained that everybody was equipped with con-
doms. In the anteroom a medic took us aside and led us into a cubicle,
where I had to pull my pants down when my turn came. The medic
took a very large syringe, filled with a yellowish liquid, to inject into
the top of my penis to wash out my urinary tract. What a procedure!
It burned slightly and felt awful. He explained that this procedure
was for sanitary reasons—to avoid the transmittal of sexual diseases

and that, on my way out, I would have to come back for another dose of the same.

The dreaded moment had arrived. There was no backing away anymore. I had to go inside. An elderly lady, heavily made up, reeking of a cheap perfume, sold each one of us a metal chit for RM 5— "Good for one screw," (which it read on one side). We took it and went inside.

The first impression was disappointing. The interior was frugal. No, it was ugly and primitive. I'd imagined that it would look as I remembered it from the movies, gaudy, colorful and sinful, with a piano player in the background, just as any a decent brothel should look. Instead, it was drab and plebeian and definitely not sexy nor glamorous. The whole room smelled of cheap perfume. It displayed a dozen worn and cheaply upholstered chairs a dilapidated sofa and a bar were in the background backed by a few mirrors illuminated with several naked, pink bulbs. The girls, though, were young and pretty, clean looking and full of laughter. We were the first customers of the day and received lots of attention. A good-looking, blond girl came over to greet Erich.

"Bonjour, Erik, comment ça vas?" She smiled and kissed him on the cheek. Erich pranced around like a peacock and made a feeble attempt to speak French with her. It sounded awful and nothing like any French I knew. Gesturing with his hands and feet, he tried to explain Kurt's problem to the girl, and our plan to convince one of the girls to take him on. The girl shrugged her shoulders; neither she nor any of the other girls understood what he was talking about.

This was my chance for the second surprise of the day. It was the first time to prove my years of studying French at school had not been wasted. Inwardly I was laughing at myself. I was sure that this was what my father had always visualized when he had sent me to the Gymnasium: His son an interpreter in a French whorehouse!

"Allo, Chou-Chou, tu es très jolie," I said. *"Je vois que tu es la plus belle de la maison."*

She turned to look at me, at first critical and astonished one of the Germans had spoken to her in French, but then a big smile crossed her face.

"Oh lala, mon jeune ami, tu parles Français, pas d'accent non plus, incroyable! Tu viens d'Allemagne?"

"D'accord, mademoiselle, mais j'ai vu dáutre pays aussi; l'Amerique, l'Espagne et l'Italie, et maintenant je suis arrivé a votre établissement."

I was really showing off with my French and my comrades by their looks thought so, too. I used the interval to translate a description of Kurt's problem.

"What is all this," Erich blurted out, "are you going to let us know what you two are talking about?" He was angry that I made out with 'his' "whore.

"Of course," I said and translated everything. *Chou-Chou* was laughing her head off, as were the other girls.

Right then I saw a great chance to cover my tracks without further embarrassment. I approached her with my chip in hand and asked her for her time. She laughed and giggled and told me how delighted she was I was the first one of the day, and not this "oaf." She meant Erich. Obviously she wanted to keep this conversation only between the two of us, as she blinked her left eye furiously at me. Erich was foaming at the mouth, but by the rules of the house he had missed his turn and couldn't do a thing about it.

I went 'upstairs' with *Chou-Chou* to a small room and asked her to order a bottle of Champagne for us.

"Certainement, mon ami, chaque bouteille de Champagne vaut une autre demie heure avec moi." (Of course my friend, each bottle of champagne means another half an hour with me.)

I knew that the moment of truth was approaching fast. I would have to confess soon the worldly traveler was a virgin. First, however, I tried to stall.

"Tell me, Chou-Chou," I said to her, as I was trying for time, "I've always been wondering why goodlooking girls like you choose to do what you are doing now, I mean, is that what you want to do, or does anybody force you to work here?"

"Peter," she said with an exasperated sigh, "you're a little idiot, like so many of the other soldiers. You know nothing about France.

Before you pass any judgment you should first familiarize yourself with our customs."

It was obvious that she hadn't gone through these explanations for the first time. She continued getting serious and sounding very grown up.

"In every village in France you'll find a house, which belongs to the lady who gives pleasure, upon request, to the men of the village, married or otherwise. She's an accepted member of the community, the women greet her when they meet on the street and the men treat her with respect. Whenever a man has the need for entertainment he goes to her house, meets other friends, drinks a glass of wine and satisfies the desires he may not be able to satisfy at home. A father may also approach her with his son so that the young lad can be properly introduced to the pleasures of the world for the first time."

When she came to this point I must've looked embarrassed, because she interjected, "What's the matter, don't you believe me? You can ask the madam, she'll bear me out."

I calmed her down and told her that my embarrassment was of another nature, which I would confide to her shortly. She continued, apparently content with my explanations.

"Most of the girls here are from little villages in the southern part of France, Vichy France as it is called at the moment, presently not occupied by the Germans. We all have plans what to do with the money we earn. I, for instance, want to get married. But neither my fiancée nor I have the money to do so. He went to occupied France to work for the Germans, building fortifications, and I, I must confess without his knowledge, have come up here far away from home where nobody knows me, to make money too. I believe that in another 3 to 4 months I can return with enough money to get married."

I was stunned, even after this lengthy explanation, by her reasons for being in this establishment, doing what she did.

We opened a bottle of Champagne, which had arrived in the meantime, and I wished her the best of luck for her plans. Now my stalling had come to an end. *Chou-Chou* looked at me and said, *"Alors, Pierre, qu'est-ce que c'est que tu préfèrs?"* (Now, Peter, what do you prefer?)

This was it, now I had to confess.

"Chou-Chou, you may not believe it, but I've never been with a girl before, you're going to be my first experience, I ask you not to laugh and not to divulge my secret to the others outside, because that would be terrible for me."

She opened her eyes real wide and said, "Oh, Peter, how wonderful, I am honored and proud, don't you worry one bit. You'll have a wonderful time, I'll have a wonderful time, and the others will know nothing, promise."

She came over to me, kissed me on the cheek, and proceeded to help me with myself, very tenderly and expertly. As she'd promised, I had a wonderful time, and as far as I could tell, she did too. We must have exceeded the permissible time limit, because there was a knock on the door, to remind us that our time was up.

I followed *Chou-Chou* on the way out trying to act nonchalantly. She immediately mingled with the others, chattering away at a hundred miles a minute. She was a good actress.

After a few minutes she came towards me, smiled conspiratorially and said, "Now, since we have settled down, we've got to take care of Kurt. Tell me again the cock and bull story about the longest prick we have ever seen. You know my friend, amongst us girls we are a very seasoned group of professionals. I can't believe that we might see anything that any of us has not seen before."

Kurt was called to the forefront. He had been waiting impatiently, drinking one glass of wine after another, jumping up and down, getting progressively drunk, incoherent and yelling repeatedly:

"Get me a girl, I finally want to fuck, I want to stick it in, I want to feel pussy, soft and silky, no more excuses and false pretenses, I'm the guy with the longest prick in the world, and I'm going to prove it to all of you. Peter, you can lay two hands on it, and I'll still beat every one of you by two inches!"

The girls were screaming loudly as he went totally out of control. Nobody had ever seen him behaving that way, ranting and rav-

ing like a lunatic. He usually was a very quiet man. He wanted to
have a girl he wanted her now. There was no doubt about it, and to
make matters worse Erich started to tease him.

"Kurt, the girls in this establishment are seasoned and sophisticated whores. They can't possibly believe that you have the biggest
prick in the world," he said teasingly, dragging out every word he
said while Kurt sat there with blood shot eyes.

One girl sauntered over to where Kurt was, sitting, half lying on
the old sofa with his legs slightly parted. She stroked with one hand
down his thigh, while her eyes were widening steadily. *"Mon Dieu,
c'est incroyable!"* she exclaimed. (My God, that's unbelievable.)
The others came over also, for a *'feel.'* Soon all the girls had handled
his member with their groping hands up and down his thigh and, naturally, it was not tame any more; it had swollen considerably from
all this handling. They were oohing and aahing and I started to explain our plan, before they had a chance to beg off because of the size
of his member. One of the older girls finally agreed to handle the situation, for a double charge. We all crowded into one of the little 'private' rooms to watch the action. The room, jam-packed as it was with
a bed, two chairs and a small table, couldn't handle the onslaught.
We moved everything outside, except the bed, just to be able to fit
everybody in. Kurt was lying down on the bed two girls were pulling
his pants off; revealing his member, which by now had achieved its
full size. The girl, who had committed herself, talked to me anxiously and made me promise we would hold on to Kurt while she was
on top of him. She rolled on the condom, which covered only a little more than half of the actual length, and one of the guys settled
next to the bed to hold on with both hands to its lower part. The
whore climbed on top of him and the action began. Everybody in the
little room started yelling and shouting, and encouraging the two
participants. It was gross, terribly grotesque but hilarious at the same
time. The girl's movements became faster and faster and Kurt kept
yelling:

"Let go of it, let go of it, I want to feel it all the way, I'm coming!"

Fortunately, the guy who held on to him didn't comply, Kurt afterwards complained bitterly with his friends.

"Inconsiderate bastards, I wouldn't have hurt her, do you know how it feels to be halfway out and halfway in when it counts?"

He was upset; we could tell; and the whore was still shaking her head about the experience.

After the others had their turn with the girls, we started to leave. Everybody had to visit the medic at the entrance who gave us the same treatment as before. I didn't mind the syringe, I promised myself to be back as often as my time and my money permitted to see *Chou-Chou.*

Back at our little house on the hill there was a message for me. I was to see the first sergeant. I was immediately apprehensive. What could be the reason this time? The first sergeant informed me stiffly—we continued to nurture our mutual dislike—the company had received a communication from headquarters that my father was seriously ill. I had been granted a five days leave to go to Berlin. I obtained my papers the next morning took a train for *Reims* and another one from there to Berlin.

The town of *Reims* was where most of the soldiers from the northeastern part of France had to change trains to go to Germany. I discovered that my train connection afforded me three hours intermission. I went to the NCO club near the station, available to corporals like me, and learned from the other soldiers that all kinds of goodies were for sale provided you could display valid papers for home-leave. None of the items had been seen in stores in Berlin for a long time, nor had we seen them in *Fécamp:* Chocolate pralines, alcohol of any kind, silk stockings, Italian salamis, cigarettes, French cognac and many other delicacies. At the entrance to the *magazine,* I received three coupons to buy three items of my choice. I observed almost nobody was buying anything. When I asked, one man explained that after all the partying and whoring that was going on in occupied France nobody had any money left.

I was in a better position. I still had plenty of money and approached the lingering soldiers and offered to exchange their useless coupons for packs of cigarettes. They were delighted to make the trade and in the end I had twelve or fifteen coupons to go shopping. I picked six bottles of cognac, three pair of silk stockings, several salamis and one box of pralines, to satisfy my own sweet tooth. I even managed to store everything in my duffel bag and my coat though some bottles were sticking out of my coat pockets.

The train slowly pulled into the *'Bahnhof Zoo'* (Zoo station in the center of Berlin) at 5 o'clock of the following morning; it was till dark outside. The black marketers who were waiting for the new arrivals from France could see what I was carrying and harassed me aggressively as I was getting off the train. They wanted me to surrender some of my prized possessions and offered me the incredible sum of RM 1000—for only one bottle of Cognac (A soldier's pay was RM 10—for every ten days). I told them, "No dice." I bought my treasures legally and carried them all the way from France and they were intended for my family and money didn't mean a thing to me.

I climbed down the stairs to the subway, took the train in the direction of *Ruhleben* and left it seven stops later in *Neu-Westend*. On my way to the apartment building I was beginning to get nervous.

Marcella opened the door, tears flowing down her cheeks. Two days ago, she told me, my father had been taken to the hospital. He was not well at all. She explained to me convincingly that she alone would visit him later on and emphasized repeatedly that everybody, but everybody, had advised her not to take me along. She would tell him that I had arrived in Berlin. I was supposed to be on a special leave, so her story went, to be transferred to some other place of the war in the east. Everybody had been of the opinion that my father, as an old soldier, would know immediately how grave his situation had to be in order for me to be granted a special leave.

In later years I always blamed myself for not insisting on going with her to the hospital. In spite of everybody's opinion I should have gone. That very morning, with the help of my father's lawyers Marcella drastically changed his will to my disadvantage. This was done after she had welcomed me at home and kept me from visiting my father at his bedside.

I'll explain the changes without going into the details.

In business matters concerning my father's company Marcella would be my guardian until I reached the age of twenty-eight. Until that time she had the authorization to run the company in conjunction with an appointed administrator. I would only assume my place after I had proven the necessary expertise to her and to another guardian, also appointed by my father. In a peculiar twist, my father left me his shares of the company, thirty-five percent, but stipulated that the income derived from these shares would go to Marcella during her lifetime.

I never had a chance to discuss the details with him because my father died at 1:30 P.M. of the same day.

In later years my mother blamed me for not calling her to seek her counsel. She would have warned me, she said, of Marcella's obvious self-interest in keeping me out of the company as long as she could. It was 20/20 hindsight. I could not anticipate the consequences. To an eighteen-year-old, money and power meant very little.

The employees at the company were upset because Marcella was now the boss. They didn't know what she would do with the company. They didn't even know her. After the probate of the will, the remaining family members, who also owned shares in the company, wanted to contest the will. It was a terrible situation. By this time I was back in France and there was very little I could do about it.

While I was still in Berlin the family went to the crematorium, listened to eulogies and contrived accolades, accepted condolences, cried crocodile's tears and buried my father in the grave of his ancestors.

Marcella was desperately trying to convince me that she had done everything for my own good. The lawyer had told me about the rewriting of the will and I asked her about it. She only wanted to handle the affairs of the company in my favor, she said, while I was away during the war, she protested. She wanted everything to be all right for me after I returned at the end of the war. In my mind the doubts remained; why did she change the testament at the last minute? Even though I read and reread the document several times I must admit that my thoughts were on other matters; like my present situation, the continuation of the war, where I would be going and what other horrors were waiting for me.

Dumb, that's what I was, extremely dumb and too young, naive and inexperienced.

I spend a day or two to visit Marianne, my mother and a few others, mainly to distribute the presents I had brought from France, which made everybody happy. Especially the silk stockings were a big hit. They were not available in stores, but even if there had been any, they would have cost points from the textile ration card.

Because of legal details connected with the probation of my fathers will, I was able to convince the military authorities to extend my leave by three more days.

In the days since I had been home, something had developed between Marcella and me, which was becoming a problem, at least in my eyes. She became extremely attached to me, constantly asking my advice, and she was "close." In previous years our relationships hadn't been that bad but let's call it unexceptional, or even better, normal between stepmother and stepson. Now it was "chummy"; it was so close it was almost bizarre. When I left the house to go on one of my errands she kissed me goodbye, you know, tenderly (lovingly?). In any case it wasn't a normal behavior for a stepmother. She was twenty years my senior, and she was my stepmother. I didn't think that it was up to me to stop her.

In the evening we would sit together in her living room until all hours of the night, or morning, talking about life, the things we were missing or, in great detail, of the intimate things *she* had been missing during the last year of my father's illness.

Brother, her story and what she was confiding in me was really something. It was a lot to handle at my age.

On the last day of my leave, virtually during the last hour of my stay in Berlin as I was leaving the apartment, I said goodbye to her. I wanted to go alone to the train station, only with my mother and not with her. She put her arms around my neck, pushed herself real close and kissed me, I mean kissed me warm and tenderly and with a little bit of tongue probing gently:

"Oh, Peter, this is insane! We can't do that! No, stop it!" she exclaimed breathing heavily. What was she talking about? I wasn't doing anything! I was just holding still. It might have been that I re-acted with a little bit too much enthusiasm, feeling no pain so to speak, you know. Finally, as I was beginning to feel some excitement stirring in my loins, we drew apart and she promised to write to me every day, "at the front" as she put it.

I must say that she kept her promise. With mail in light blue en-velopes, smelling of French perfume I received during mail call, I was an easy target for my comrades' facetious remarks.

My mother went with me to the station and was surprised I made comments about Marcella at all. In the past I had never mentioned her; she smelled a rat but was too smart to question me on any details.

In *Fécamp* there were plenty of surprises. In my absence the whole outfit had been inoculated with several different vaccines, two or three a day. The 223d infantry division was going to Africa. At least that was the rumor. Our gear and clothes were exchanged for tropical attire, which included a tropical helmet as a replacement for our customary steel helmet. Our officers received new instructions about water, the climate, people and about tropical diseases. We were not exactly delirious about going to Africa. General Field Marshal Rommel wasn't doing so well at the beginning of 1943. However, it would be far better than going to Russia, especially since we were now in the midst of winter. I knew all about Russia, and I didn't want to see it again. The battle of *Stalingrad* was over. The 6th army had been lost. Who wanted to go to Russia? If that was at all possible we were more demoralized than ever.

Before we were loaded into one of those "lovely" boxcars, I had time to visit *Chou-Chou* for one more time. I had a soft spot in my heart for her, since she had been the girl who initiated me to the phys-ical pleasures of love. By her reaction she made me believe she en-joyed seeing me and would miss me. (What comfort for my soul, I was missed by a French whore.)

"Peter, *mon amour,* how nice of you to visit me. The fellows told me about your father's death, I'm sorry. But remember in these times of war it is most important for everybody to survive; take care of you at all cost. I hope that you'll watch out for all the wild animals in Africa."

I was flabbergasted, how did she know where we were going? That certainly was privileged knowledge. It was supposed to be a big secret! Then again, I thought, with all the tropical stuff hanging around in the depots and with French civilians doing all the loading and unloading it wasn't difficult to put two and two together. On second thought, maybe her customers had talked?

It wasn't my business to worry about the Government's secrets. What I was interested in, as I stood in front of her, was her warmth and her softness. Chou-Chou and I made love passionately with all the abandon of youth and—as far as I was concerned—with desperation in my heart about things to come.

"Good bye, Chou-Chou," I said, "don't forget your plans for the future and have many children, each one of them as cute as you are." She cried a little, and I left the establishment to acquiesce to the unavoidable treatment with the syringe.

When I reported my conversation with Chou-Chou to my comrades, and commented that I thought she really missed me, there was roaring laughter all around, particular from Erich. I was upset that nobody understood my feelings.

Our transport went according to plan. We climbed into the boxcars with all our equipment ready to be dropped as a fighting force wherever we were needed. Oskar and I spent a lot of time together. Not because I really wanted to, but because he continuously tried to convince me about the superiority of the communist ideology. Aside from the fact that his theories sounded ridiculous to me, it was dangerous stuff. I brushed him off time and time again. First of all, because I was not interested and secondly, while he was trying to indoctrinate me, he was not shy about who was listening. You could never know whether somebody would rat to the political officer. Didn't he know that spies were everywhere?

After two days our transport arrived in *Leipzig* and stopped on a rail siding of a huge freight yard. *Leipzig* is a city in Saxony, well known before the war for its annual International Fair. It was the last possible opportunity for the train to turn south, towards Italy and Africa. Instead the transport was positioned far away from the regular track. At night there was hectic activity. Trucks with barrels of white paint and tons of clothing, white winter clothing arrived alongside. Every piece of clothing reminding us of Africa was exchanged for white, camouflage overalls and warm clothes. We also received white windbreakers to blend in properly with the snow.

We applied the paint to our infantry carts and other rolling equipment. Russia! This was Russia, for sure, damned to hell, now we were in a real pickle. It was good-bye Africa!

By two o'clock in the morning—with typical Prussian efficiency—everybody had new winter clothing; all vehicles had been painted white and we were exhausted.

I was restless, very restless, not that I'd been crazy about going to Africa, but my experiences at the Don were vividly in my mind. I couldn't sleep for the life of me. I stepped outside walking alongside the train, lost in my thoughts and memories of Helmut and Hans. I was thinking where they might be at this moment until I heard people talking at a distance. I went closer, carefully not to be observed by anybody and made out two men in uniform, together with a woman in civilian clothes, loading cartons out of a supply boxcar into a VW command car. One of the men in uniform seemed to be an officer. The other one was a common soldier; he did all the lugging. Both were trying to be very quiet carefully checking around constantly. The unloaded boxes were stored into the back of the VW. From there they drove carefully to the far side of the tracks and reloaded the loot into a small truck. I was following carefully wondering; what was going on? Then, as I was hiding behind the next boxcar in line, I heard the soldier, "Yes, colonel, sir, I'll take your wife home now, put all the things into your cellar and return the truck to the barracks. I'll be back here before the train leaves."

The truck left with the merchandise, with the wife and the soldier as the chauffeur. I had just witnessed a huge theft of a large quantity of alcohol, chocolate, cookies and other precious supplies by the regimental commander, his wife and his aide. This merchandise was intended as rewards for the soldiers of the regiment on special occasions. I was in shock. What should I do? For once I recovered my senses in time. I acted smart and decided to keep things to myself and to use this knowledge to my advantage if, and when I needed it and when it would count the most. I couldn't forget the first sergeant and his vendetta.

To this day I don't understand how I arrived at that decision. It was gut felling, pure gut feeling, and it probably saved my life. More changes were planned for our transport. The African adventure had been an interlude soon to be forgotten. The train was speeding towards the Russian front to fill a gaping hole left by the disappearance of the Sixth Army near Stalingrad.

My experiences in Russia became a subject of interest and discussion by the others who had never been exposed to any fighting anywhere much less on the Russian front. Erich became conciliatory, his big mouth subdued for once. Oskar was the only one happy to get closer to the real communist world. What an idiot. It wouldn't help him with the Ivan or save his life when bullets were flying.

"Are they as dumb and ruthless and willing to die as the propaganda tells us?" Erich wanted to know, "I mean, coming at you without arms, ready to die by the thousands?"

"I don't know where you get all this nonsense," I replied. "The ones that were coming at me during the one battle I participated in were excellently equipped, well trained and supported by artillery, Stalin organ and T 34s." I continued, idiot that I was, "Look what they did to the sixth army. They obliterated it, all 300,000 of them." Oskar, the commy, couldn't keep his mouth shut. He insinuated that the superior morale of Russian soldiers was a result of their Marxist training and more of the same hogwash. He was a well-trained dialectician and knew his Marxist theories by heart, but nobody wanted to hear it.

Just about that time, I was cleaning my mess kit rinsing it with water after eating a horrible pea soup and did something very careless. I tossed the water out of the open door of the moving train. But my spoon went with it, my only spoon. What was I supposed to do now? I had to wait at chow time until somebody else finished eating, to borrow his spoon, or until the soup was cold enough so that I could slurp it out of the mess kit. This incident provided my initial impulse to learn how to speak a few words of Russian.

West of *Charkov* the train started to slow down. *Charkov* is a large industrial city halfway between Kiev to the west and *Stalingrad* to the east. We saw less snow on the ground than we had anticipated. After going through all this camouflage stuff and the repainting in Leipzig we certainly had expected tons of snow. It was white all right, but the snow was at most two to three inches deep.

After the train stopped it we received fire from light Russian artillery. Jumping through the open doors, the soldiers scrambled, seeking protection on the ground near and under the train. The engine still seemed to be working because the train backed away slowly as soon as we were out of it. Gradually we got things under control, dug in with our spades and waited for our officers to decide the next move.

Oskar and I were ordered to set up our Dora unit to find out where the fire had come from so unexpectedly. The Colonel, our larcenous regimental commander, didn't have the faintest idea. We'd have been better prepared for this had he been more experienced and alert as our train approached the lines of battle. He hadn't even checked how far the train could go before making contact with the enemy; at least that's what the coded message we received from the Division headquarter spelled out unmistakably. I carried this information to the Colonel personally; no needs to embarrass him by letting others see it. Everybody else around us, that are all the other regiments assembling in the area, had been well aware of the proximity of the enemy units. We were the *malenki,* the greenhorns, as the Russians would call us in the future. No sooner had we settled down when a Russian loud speaker blared across the field at us from several hundred yards away, *"Dasdrastuitje malenki divisia"* (Welcome, baby division.) It was a play on the average age of our newly formed replacement division. On average the soldiers of the division were twenty years old, all youngsters, with a lot of Polish speaking recruits from Upper Silesia. The enemy was well informed about the composition of our division. Most of our soldiers knew more Polish than German.

The unit of the Russian army, which had penetrated our lines deeply didn't stay long enough to be routed by superior German forces. This gave us time for a breather, to get organized, to proceed to wherever we were going.

The Ukraine has a pleasant countryside. While the terrain is mostly very flat, ideal for farming, it is laced with many small villages, which are hidden away in small valleys, crowded with farm animals and lots of chickens. We wondered how they had kept alive with all the fighting going on.

After a few days, at the end of a day covering about 30 miles we entered one of these villages and were dispatched six, or seven, or even ten soldiers to one house, to share it with the civilians. My first order of business after I entered the house was to try to talk to a woman—the lady of the house—to ask her for a spoon. I held a spoon, one of our army issue spoons, up to her and used the only Russian words I knew, *"Stotakoi pa Russki?"* (What is this called in Russian?) Now that was real coarse, but one has to start somewhere and these were the only Russian words I knew. She looked at me suspiciously, looked at the spoon and spat out, *"Loschik, takoi loschik, ponjumaitje?"* (Spoon, that's a spoon, do you understand?)

Now came the difficult part. How was I to ask her if she had a spare spoon for me? It was awkward, and I used two hands and all ten fingers to make myself understood. Finally a smile of comprehension and recognition what I wanted crossed her face. She'd finally understood and disappeared to the back of the house returning with a spoon. It was carved of wood, a beautiful spoon, highly polished, with delicate paintings on the handle. I kept it throughout the whole war as my favorite eating utensil.

Of course, she wanted something in return, which was fine with me, but what? The gesticulating started all over this time with the old lady taking the lead. She desperately tried to explain what she wanted. In the end I understood that it was a needle and white thread. I was happy, because I had what she wanted in my backpack and gave it to her. She gave me a big toothy smile, we both were happy and she said, *"Spassibo, spassibo bolschoi"* (thank you, thank you very much). I had learned two more words.

We stayed for two days in the house. After these two days I had lice. Her house had been infested with the vermin. We had to rush to a delousing establishment to get cleaned up. Every village in Russia had a delousing installation. The surprising part to us was that the family had not availed itself of its services. There is nothing more disagreeable than lice. They must be millions of years old, and when you catch lice they seem to come from nowhere. Lice multiply extremely fast and seem to be indestructible. You cannot simply pick them off your clothes to get rid of them, because every day they lay thousands of eggs. Instead your clothes have to be put into the heated chamber of a delousing establishment; it's heated to over 200° F and kills all lice and their nits efficiently. It was our first exposure to lice and regrettably enough it was not our last.

Our regiment moved on. Without much fighting we slowly gravitated toward Charkov. The Russian army seemed to withdraw voluntarily.

Then one day, we had covered another thirty miles, we came into a pretty, green village with a pond in the middle surrounded by trees. Most of the houses—as a matter of fact the whole village—looked as if it was in great shape. They were white washed on the outside (the customary color to paint houses). We saw no people anywhere. For a while we were mystified.

"Where have they all gone," the lieutenant asked, "Let's be super careful and watch that this is not a clever trap. You know, the Russian partisans are liable to have booby-trapped the houses. Maybe they have hidden somewhere around here."

He was probably right to be careful. In the end it turned out to be something totally different, and I must say, eerie.

Never in my life before and never again have I seen a village taken over by flies, billions of flies—the common type every one-day-fly you'll find in the summer in every house.

As the soldiers entered a house in the village a loud buzz greeted them. The walls inside were black with a thick layer of flies, unbelievable. Since flies will always move towards light we came up with a clever idea. We covered all windows with blankets to darken the room completely. After that we opened the door a small crack, letting a bright ray of light enter the room, and waved blankets to chase the flies. The flies responded instantly, departing the house in black, loudly buzzing clouds, rushing towards the light that came through the crack in the door.

So far so good, now we could remain inside for the night, but the air was sticky and moist and too many flies were everywhere. Our horses on the outside couldn't be contained much longer, because they were covered with flies. To chase away the pestering flies they were slapping their tails and its long hair back and forth constantly without any relief. The soldiers in charge of the teams led them away from the village; there was no other way. Just 500 yards from the perimeter of the village the nightmare ended, no more flies. The colonel decided to stay for only one night and then move on. He called me to his command post and told me to prepare a message explaining the situation to the Division Head Quarters.

I came to attention and asked, "Yes sir, what would you like me to write, sir, everything that comes to mind sounds either awful or silly?"

"Oh, never mind, corporal," he responded. "Just explain the situation clearly, you should be able to do that. I'm very busy right now. Why do we have you people anyhow? Dismissed, and show me a copy of what you have written before you send it, okay?"

I turned on my heels, left the command post, puzzled. A regimental commander a colonel in the German army had asked a lowly corporal to contrive a message to his divisional commander, in our case a general, because he didn't know how to explain the situation? What did he his adjutant do?

I made several attempts to write a brief description of the situation, and why we had to leave our designated quarters and finally settled on the following one:

"The village of Belickojewski is inundated by billions of flies.
The village is void of any living creature, except flies.
There is no civilian to be seen anywhere. Soldiers and especially the horses
cannot endure the situation and we have no means
to get rid of the pest. We are asking permission
to leave for alternate quarters in the early morning hours."

The Regiment always had orders for alternate quarters, just in case. I delivered the message to the colonel for approval and he was visibly pleased with my composition. I asked him to sign it, transcribed it into code and sent it to the Division.

Well, all hell broke loose and the airwaves really got busy that night. We sat in our little house, not daring to go outside because of the flies, and our officers sent messages back and forth doubting each other's sanity. I let Oskar deliver them to the command post. After each one of his trips he came back waving his arms frantically to fend off the flies until he reached the safety of the house. We fled the next morning as fast as we could.

Soon thereafter our infantry met stiffer resistance; we had to dig in and waited until the strategic assembly of all resources of the Division, including artillery, had been completed.

One of these charming, small Ukrainian villages, which I described before, but without flies, was our next objective. This time the civilians had not fled before our arrival. The layout of the village was expansive. The houses were standing wide apart with little gardens in front. Every one of them was painted snow white and looked very clean from the outside. In the middle of the village was a huge 300 × 300ft square featuring the community hall. At least we gathered that's what it was, because of all the banners with propaganda slogans stuck to the outside walls. It was the only ugly building in the village and did not improve any after we tore the banners down. One of the major crops of the Ukraine is the sunflower. During harvesting time fields upon fields of sunflowers are everywhere. At the time we arrived they were only a foot high and one could still look over them. Soon that would be different and we wondered how we could attack an enemy, or conversely defend ourselves, if we couldn't see across the field to know who was out there or coming at us.

Sunflowers and the seeds from those flowers was the main staple. After harvesting the seeds they are pressed to extract oil, and the residue is compressed into cakes for animal feed. The Ukrainians also roasted seeds on their stoves to supplement their dull diet. They'd developed a fantastic talent to throw the seeds, one by one, into their mouths, cracking the shell with their teeth and separating the kernel from the shell with the tongue, spitting the shell out instantly while eating the kernel. They could do this everywhere, walking, standing in the streets, or sitting in front of their houses. The girls claimed that the seeds were good for their breasts. Looking at their figures one could easily believe that it was true. Ukrainian women have big, well-proportioned breasts, which they display proudly and, as it appeared to us in the beginning, without being supported by a bra, free swinging so to speak. It was unbelievable. Hadn't they heard about bras? And how did they keep them up? The girls wore loosely fitting white blouses, tightly closed around the neck and we could see that the breasts moved freely underneath, but nothing was ever 'hanging' or looking droopy. Of course, we were curious until one of our guys from Upper Silesia, a Polish-speaking guy did more "serious" research in the matter. He explained to us that the girls, upon developing a bosom, had a hand carved balcony made.

"What kind of balcony?" we shouted at him. "What kind of balcony, explain?"

"Well, it's like this," he said. "They go to a local artisan and have a piece of wood carved to fit around their ribcage below the chest; kind of tight, you know. This piece of wood is about one inch high and fits snugly half way around the body. It has two protrusions, balconies as I call them, one under each breast. When they get dressed they help each other, winding ten feet of linen bandage around the body over this piece of wood so that it can retain its position supporting the breasts. When they put the blouse over it you don't see a thing and the breasts appear to be totally without support and free swinging, and there you have it, a Russian bra."

We wanted to find out ourselves, because his story sounded unbelievable, but the girls were indignant about our curiosity and turned us down.

Sunflower seeds contain large amount of vitamin A, which is good for a girl's chest. I don't know what else is in these seeds but they are good for you and taste good. Fortunately it didn't work on us and we all ate piles of sunflower seeds, without, I might add, acquiring the talent to throw them into our mouths, cracking them with our teeth and picking out the kernel with our tongue. For us it was a slow process involving our fingers.

The main battle line was two miles east of the village. We could always hear the rumbling of the artillery. Most of the time our officers kept us busy digging trenches, fortifying our defenses or exercising. Off duty we were slowly getting to know members of the families where we stayed. For the first time we met some younger people. Usually the Russian military took great pains not to leave any young men or women behind, but in this little village they had stayed put. Especially our men from Upper Silesia, who could understand the language, Polish and Russian are very similar, were happy and quickly became friendly with the girls much to the annoyance of our officers who continuously issued stern orders, forbidding any kind of fraternization with the 'enemy.'

Several weeks later on a lazy Sunday afternoon, a messenger from the regimental command post arrived at our quarters with orders for Oskar and me to report to the colonel, on the double. We were wondering what the reason was but didn't imagine it would be anything serious.

When we got there I was told to wait outside with a guard standing nearby watching me suspiciously. Oskar was ordered inside to see the colonel and the first sergeant. After a few minutes I heard loud shouting from inside, first the voice of the first sergeant and then the colonel's too. At one time a loud and angry voice seemed to be Oskar's.

After ten minutes of back and forth shouting inside the house, two corporals of the military police arrived. They entered the office and came out with Oskar in the middle; he was handcuffed. He looked at me kind of triumphantly but couldn't, or didn't care to give me any clue as to what had transpired inside.

Now it was my turn. I was called into the office and found myself confronted with the colonel and my beloved first sergeant. The latter immediately started to accuse me in a loud voice of seditious behavior, demoralizing speeches and presentations of a political nature to other members of the German armed forces and other similarly idiotic innuendos. I tried to think as quickly as I could what to do to gain time for myself. When my turn came I replied deliberately and firmly, "First Sergeant, sir, you are making serious and preposterous accusations. I hope for your own good that you can back them up. Otherwise I'll be forced to call upon a hearing to clear my good name, which has been recognized by the military's high command and the *Führer* himself when he awarded me the decorations I am wearing."

I turned to the colonel, thinking intuitively that it was high time to play my ace in the hole and continued.

"Furthermore, Colonel, sir, before we continue with this charade, I request to have a word with the colonel in private."

The colonel looked at me, not unkindly, turned to the first sergeant and said, "Okay, First Sergeant, leave us alone for a minute. We have to get to the bottom of this before it's blown up unnecessarily."

The first sergeant, mumbling something to himself about the old communist bastard and his little helper, left the office.

By now I recognized precisely what this was all about and why we had been called to see the colonel. A cold shiver ran down my spine. I could be in deep trouble, indeed, if other soldiers had reported the content of discussions Oskar had originated in our boxcar during the long train ride from Leipzig. Oskar had used these talks as a platform, to expound his idiotic theories about Marx and the World Revolution. The Nazis where unforgiving in that regard, sedition or the claim of it was deadly.

I looked the colonel straight in the eyes and decided that this was a fight I couldn't afford to lose, or I would be lost. Silently I said to myself, *"Mom, I hope you are with me right now, because I need every help I can get."*

"Colonel, Sir," I started out, taking my heart in my hands, "at this time I would like to report an incident I observed while our transport was standing at night on a rail siding near *Leipzig."*

I related what I had observed in *Leipzig* of the removal of prime merchandise from the supply wagon and worded my report in such a way as not to mention the names of persons I observed, or to implicate the colonel in any way. I thought it might be better to leave an element

of doubt with the colonel as to what I had seen, to be careful not to co-
erce him, or to paint him unequivocally into a corner.

When I was finished the colonel looked at me with piercing
eyes. This was dangerous stuff. The best thing I had done in a blink
of time, without thinking, had been to ask the colonel to send the first
sergeant out of the office. There was no witness to what was being
said between us.

The colonel, pacing back and forth through the small room,
crossed his arms behind his back without looking at me once. After a
minute or two of pacing without a word from either side, he stopped
at the window and looking outside, said slowly and quietly, "Who else
knows about this?"

"Nobody, sir," I answered.

He turned and looked at me with hate in his eyes and said,

"Okay, Corporal. See that it stays that way. I don't believe the
accusations about you, and I'll order the first sergeant to stop all further inquiries into this case. You, Corporal, you better watch out for
yourself. We're in enemy territory, and a lot of bullets are flying in
all directions. One never knows where they're coming from. That's
all for the moment, dismissed."

I saluted, turned on my heels and left in a daze. What the colonel
had said or implied was dynamite. Was he really trying to threaten
me, or had he wanted to warn me? Every soldier knew that extremely
disliked officers or noncoms had met a mysterious death while near
the front lines.

"With lots of bullets flying in all directions," that's what he
had said. I was a nobody; I didn't have an enemy among my comrades; except now, the colonel and possibly the first sergeant. With
my guarded statement and my apparent knowledge of the theft of
valuable merchandise, I realized, I must've become a real danger
to him. What would happen to him if I talked, or he talked? We both
would land in *Bautzen* for the rest of the war and beyond. I decided
to follow his advice, to watch myself very carefully, and to keep my
mouth shut.

Most of the spring off 1943 went by with lots of digging and construction of underground shelters. Some of the older officers, forty-

five years and older, remembered the First World War, 1914–18, with cholera, horrendous stench in the trenches and endless artillery bombardments. Nobody really knew how this war was going to proceed, now that the Germans' quick advances were a thing of the past. The officers wanted to make sure that they're well protected if the 'war of the trenches' should commence again. The construction of the fortifications kept the soldiers busy. And it's always a major concern for officers of any army in the world to keep that way.

Shortly after my explosive discussion with the colonel a new man arrived as replacement for Oskar to render the Dora team operational again. Oskar had disappeared. We never heard from him again and didn't dare to inquire. The new man was from Dresden. In our eyes he was old. He was all of 32 years. We considered him to be a "really, really old man." We had our discussions and made our observations and concluded if the army drafted old people like him, the Germans were losing the war, for sure.

His name was Karl Schmitz and he was, will you believe it, an opera singer, a tenor in the permanent ensemble of the Dresden State Opera. Nobody, not even he himself could understand why he had been drafted into the army, at least that's what he told everybody. Normally the propaganda machine would rather employ people like him to entertain the soldiers at the front. Almost every month some entertainment outfit was visiting the area immediately to our rear. Visits to these performances were considered a special treat and were awarded to deserving soldiers.

Whatever Karl had done in Dresden, he had fallen out of favor with the Nazi party big wigs and was drafted to join the real war. I was immediately confronted with the unpleasant discovery that his training as a short wave operator was inadequate. This was happening more and more often with replacements from home. As the war wore on, training of new recruits was sketchy, to say the least. Karl and I had to spend a lot of time together to improve the speed of his work, receiving, transmitting and decoding. He was an intelligent, gregarious man and we laughed a lot and worked together well.

After another month, we were approaching the summer at the end of May 1943 the two of us were ordered to join an infantry company at the *Hkl*. Our assignment was to assist with communications to and from the regimental headquarters. Was it significant that we were the only ones sent to the front lines? *Nachtigall ick hör Dir trapsen"* ("Nightingale I hear your heavy footsteps"). This is a badly translated version of a German, or even better, Berliner saying. It means you are becoming aware of something very obvious. I was reminded of the colonel's last words before I departed his office. As we made our way to the *Hkl,* I decided to share my little secret with Karl. Since we were close to each other at all times and depended on each other and were, so to speak "in the same boat" I felt he deserved to know what could possibly happen if he was around me. He was a sensible man and I felt he would understand. He gave a short snort after I was finished with my story and said,

"I trust these bastards as far as I can throw an elephant. They'll dream up anything if it serves their purpose. When the time is right I'll tell you why I'm in this bloody army."

"Okay. Whenever you're ready, in the meantime we'll watch our behinds," I concluded.

Up to now there had been no serious entrenchments, I mean like in World War I. The battlefront was made up of loosely connected trenches and foxholes, much like the ones we dug up when I was at the Don, with the *RAD.* Maybe now, in contrast to my Don experiences, we were protected a little better with several barbed wired studded stakes in front of the foxholes. But still, the defensive positions I saw were not deep enough to allow for a fall back into a second line of defense, if attacking infantry should overrun us. I explained this to Karl after I reported to the officer in charge. To my understanding, even with my limited experience from the *RAD,* I didn't think it was very well engineered.

"Corporal Schwarzlose and Soldier Schmitz reporting for communications duty."

The lieutenant and his staff sergeant wore no decorations or service medals whatsoever on their uniform. They were green and untried. Like the majority of the 223d Division, they were in combat for the first time.

Why did this always have to happen to me?

I saw the disaster coming. The lieutenant was okay. He asked me where I had been before and where I had earned my decorations and some other things to get to know me and where I was coming from. I told him that I came from Berlin, no use mentioning New York, and we exchanged some lapidary stories about Berlin before the war.

After that we set up our DORA unit, established contact with regimental head quarters and got our coordinates. Then we settled down in one of the foxholes.

At first nothing happened. During the afternoon, several artillery rounds were traded between the Ivan and us. Other soldiers told us this was a routine bombardment, which occurred every day at about the same time, nothing to worry about.

Early in the morning of the next day mortar fire hit our positions. I was slightly wounded by a small splinter in the right index finger. It was nothing serious and the medic, after examining my pay-book for the last tetanus injection, put a bandage around it and entered the date as my second injury in battle. My hand hurt, though, and I became clumsy with my work at the DORA. Fortunately, Karl by now was able to take over from me for a few days. After dark we were sitting in our foxhole, reminiscing about home and our loved ones. I started to tell him about Marcella, and how awkward I felt about her and our last embrace. I felt at ease talking to Karl. For me he was an older man with lots of experiences, besides, when I compared him with the crowd I had met in *Fécamp* and considering his education and intelligence, he was my man. He listened to my story, looked at me and laughed.

"Boy oh boy, you really have a thing going there, Peter. Tell me, do you know why your father changed his will shortly before his death and who made him do it? How much money is involved, in your father's will?"

At the time of my father's death I had other worries, I never thought very thoroughly about the money involved. But now, since Karl mentioned it, I started to think about it and tried to explain the situation to him.

"My father left the shares in his company to me. The income from the shares will go to Marcella as long as she lives. She'll be my custodian until I become 29. After that I'll take over the company. Money wise? I can't answer that. It'll depend on the profitability of the company."

"My friend," he interrupted me, "there you go. Without her you won't have any money, and without your cooperation and benevolent consent there might not be any profits for her. When she convinced your father to change his will she most likely saw that very clearly? She wanted to make sure that she would have a steady income. She wanted to know what you were going to do, and she wanted to be able to control where the money was going. I mean, do you understand, or do I have to draw a picture?"

I was very quiet for a while, letting his precise and cynical evaluation settle in. What a coldhearted point of view. Surely, I knew Marcella, and I knew she wouldn't do anything like that; or would she? She had been writing to me, as she had promised, faithfully, almost every day. During mail call my name was always called up several times. Every time I received a stack of letters in those wonderful, sexy smelling, blue envelopes. She didn't write anything about money but lots about the war in Berlin, the bombing raids, lack of food items, her fox terrier Curry, our friends and how much she missed me. You know, not real love letters, but pretty close to it. I pulled one of the last ones out of my breast pocket, where I always kept them, and let Karl read it.

"What do you think, Karl, does that sound very calculating?"

"No, it doesn't, Peter, but then, that would be stupid. From what I'm reading here, and from what she did a minute before your father's death; that women is anything but stupid. Never mind, don't trouble your mind more than you have to. We're in enough of a mess as it is, and our first thoughts have to be how to survive. We can tackle the rest later, should we still be alive after the war is over. To change your train of thought and to explain why I've become rather cynical about people let me explain to you why and how I lost my cushy job in the ensemble of the opera in Dresden. You must know I was a well-liked tenor at the opera, had lots of admirers and fans, male and female and made enough money to lead a good life. I received enough special privileges to always have plenty of food and alcohol. Yes, and women too. To be precise; I was interested in one woman in particular. And she was interested in me too, very much so. To be honest, she was mad about me, and I was mad about her. There was only one thing wrong with our relationship; She was married. Now, this happens often in life and wouldn't have been really that bad, BUT. . . . she was married to the local head honcho of the Nazi party and that was bad. As a matter of fact, it was fatal. He was an older man; she was twenty years younger than he and terribly in love with me. She thought she could treat life as it pleased her. One day she came to visit me in my apartment and told me happily, to my utmost horror, after a fight with her husband, she had thrown the truth right into his face, accusing him of his age and his impotence and told him she was in love and wanted a divorce. Can you imagine what happened? To say the shit hit the fan would be an understatement. The guy found out easily enough who the object of his wife's affection was, and that's how I became a soldier in our *Führer's* army."

Karl was silent, lost in his thoughts, and I felt for him.

"Tell me Karl, did the guy threaten you, did you have a fight, or how did he react?"

"Peter," he chuckled, "you have to learn the ways of the world. These men never expose themselves unnecessarily. What for? In my case, as a case in point, it happened much simpler, by the book, so to speak. One day his wife was suddenly gone on a previously unannounced holiday to the Bavarian Alps. Two days later I found my draft notice in the mail. That was it, and here I am."

Nights in our foxhole were quiet, especially after we had transmitted our daily messages about usage of ammunition, status of food supply and a report about the health of men in the company. The only thing bothering both of us was the inability to perform any personal hygiene. We started to smell and to itch, and we suspected lice as the cause of the itching.

At times when it was real dark at night, I climbed out of our hole to stretch my legs and walked back and forth thinking of the possible consequences if Karl's evaluation of my father's will and of Marcella and me were correct. One night walking about, I heard the typical sound: pluck, pluck, pluck three rounds of mortar had been fired by the other side. Instead of diving for the hole, as I should have, I looked around to see where they might hit. Just in time I managed to flatten myself to the ground as all three of them fell rather close by and, while exploding in a bright flash, spread their deadly compliments of thousands of sharp little steel shrapnel. I felt a piercing pain in my right knee, but after a minute or two I could get up again and jumped into our hole.

"What happened to you?" Karl said with a grin. "First you are starry-eyed and walk with your head high and then you went down rather fast."

"Come on, Karl, shut your mouth and light a match. Take a look at my knee, it hurts, and I feel as if something has hit me."

I pulled my pants down and we searched the area where I felt the pain. The only thing we discovered was a small, bloody scratch in the middle of my right kneecap. It hurt a little, but I could bend the knee and I could walk so we didn't make too much of it.

Fifty years later, after having an x-ray in preparation for knee replacement surgery, the doctor said to me, "That's strange; you have a small splinter embedded in your knee cap, about one half of an inch long, where'd you got that from?"

That had been number three.

We spent a few more days in the foxhole with the Infantry, before being called back. I went to the lieutenant to report to him that we had been ordered to return, and that we would be leaving him and his men the next day. He would have preferred us to stay, because from now on his only connection to and from the Regiment, in case telephone lines were cut by enemy fire was by messenger.

"Stay well, Sir. Watch out, and if I may say so, build another trench for yourself and your men, just in case you have to fall back or are overrun. Your available perimeter is very shallow."

He smiled and thanked me for my well meant but unsolicited advice.

"You too watch out for yourself, Corporal," he replied. "You do not only have friends at headquarters, you know." I looked at him and wondered.

When we arrived in the village, the whole place was in an uproar. Young Russian girls were running back and forth, loading bundles with their belongings onto army trucks, crying and saying good-bye to their families. A commando of the German SS Division *"Dirlewanger"* carried out an enforced evacuation of all young women. They were to be transported to Germany.

The SS Division *"Dirlewanger"* was the most notorious unit of the SS, especially trained to do the Nazi regimes dirty work. It was composed up to 80% of pardoned convicts straight out of jail.

All SS Divisions had names of big shot Nazis, or were named after the areas, which had supplied the young recruits, like *"Sepp Dietrich"* for a famous General, or *"Flandern"* for the Dutch Division. On top of the list: *"Adolf Hitler,"* the most elite and best equipped of them all.

Our soldiers were standing on the streets saying tearful goodbyes to their Russian girl friends. With their Polish backgrounds they easily had made friends and felt for the girls. Most of them hated the German army anyway. The scuttle but had it the women were transported to Germany to work in the factories for the mutual war effort.

The young women suspected what was going to happen to them, even though the *"Dirlewanger"* men didn't know or revealed any details. Some of the girls tried to run away into the nearby woods only to be pursued by the SS men, were caught, brutally handled and dragged back to the waiting trucks. We could see they came from penal institutions of the worst order and enjoyed the assignment.

Nobody knew what to do. The family in our house was affected as well, having their only daughter taken away. They begged us to do something about it, but what? We were as helpless as they were.

The families in these small villages in the Ukraine were really close. They endured a lot of hardships in their lifetime, had survived the creation of the soviet *kolchos* system, Stalin's persecution and eradication of the kulaks (farmers) in the early thirties and had prevailed. Most of the people we met lived in total harmony with three or even four generations in one house. Upon entering a typical house you came into a big room. All of them were built flat on the ground, no cellars and no attics. Every house was on one level only and covered by a thick thatched roof. The floors were of compressed clay. In one corner of the room was usually a gigantic stove. It was built on three levels all the way to the ceiling. The stove and the oven were for cooking and for baking and the oven were large enough to bake several loafs of bread at the same time. The draft was provided by a one and one half foot square funnel, which stretched like a bench all around the room, exiting at the door. Hot air from the stove circulated through the bench keeping the room pleasantly warm. This was important during winter with nighttime temperatures below zero. Family members slept on the bench with exception of the old people. We only discovered the great grand mother after living with the family in the same house for two weeks. The old woman was too weak to come down off the stove. The family cared for her up on the stove, providing her with everything she needed, feeding her and cleaning her. Even at such close quarters we never experienced any fighting or bickering among the family members. The young people did most of the work.

Now the German SS took the young ones away, kidnapping them without any regard to the families' needs, without any regard for international law or human decency. It would be extremely hard for the older members of the family to provide for their livelihood without help. And what would happen to the young women? Heavy work was waiting for them in Germany, with nothing to sustain them but the German ration card system?

It was one of the most despicable and insidious episodes of the entire war, the deportation of hundreds of thousands of Ukrainian women to Germany as slave laborers. And that's what it was, pure and simply: slavery.

When the invading German army first entered the Ukraine in 1941, the population had welcomed the Germans as liberators. Ever since Stalin had deported and cruelly starved millions of *kulaks,* there was no love lost between them and the Bolsheviks. They had hated the communists and the Russians. Now the Germans were hated even more intensely than the old communist enemies had been hated before. No wonder our relationship with the local populace was never the same again. We left the village shortly after all this happened. Karl and I talked a lot about our feelings in this matter. Our opinion about the atrocious behavior of the Germans was identical. I knew his feelings couldn't be any different. He had his own experiences with Nazis. Mine didn't have to change. They were just confirmed one more time.

"It's difficult to trust anybody, you know, there are always people around and nobody knows who is a member of the party or one of their spies." Karl said to me one evening as we walked through the middle of the village discussing the latest happenings in the most critical of terms. We couldn't be overheard; we were at least 100 yards away from any building or any people.

"And we don't know who is listening to us when we talk." He continued," I would suggest we continue to be extremely careful with our discussions, keep our own council, tighten our lips and try to survive, lest the big bad *Dirlewanger* and his SS executioners comes to get us too."

He was right, of course. I had been warned often enough about my big mouth. If anybody would report me again to the colonel or the first sergeant, I would be a goner for sure.

A new officer was introduced to us. Lieutenant Seuffert, 35 years old, a teacher by profession, about five foot five tall with narrow beady eyes. He was someone who had managed to stay at home until this late in the game. I didn't like him from the word go. In many ways military life near the front lines was relaxed and in-formal, not so for Lieutenant Seuffert. Just coming from the military academy, he wanted everything to be done by the book. Rise and shine early in the morning, a little exercise, uniform inspection etc., etc. We could easily see where that would lead us.

By the end of May 1943 the 223d division was transferred fur-ther north. We were now 60 miles closer to Bjelgorod, to take part in a summer offensive and to regain the initiative. After the disaster of the previous winter it was hoped that the German army would chase the Ivan eastward once and for all. The colonel, in a speech delivered on the occasion of Hitler's birthday on April twentieth, had pompously announced these plans. I couldn't help but remember a similar speech delivered by a major during my time in the *RAD,* at the Don not too long ago. It was the same bullshit and we saw what had happened.

How these plans were supposed to be achieved was a mystery to anybody with two eyes in his head. We had seen few heavy weapons and very few German planes in the air; ammunition was al-ways scarce; and the replacements were constantly getting younger or older for that matter. New arrivals were less prepared for the job than ever before. Maybe we, at the 223d were just an isolated infantry division, but it didn't look like we were in a position to chase anybody anywhere. However, during the first days of June the SS elite division *"Gross Deutschland,"* (Greater Germany), equipped with plenty of tanks, armored vehicles and motorized artillery, pulled up alongside of us. We had an opportunity to talk to a few of them. They were so full of themselves and so indoctrinated with political propaganda that it was absolutely sickening. They, the SS, that's what they told us, were the greatest fighting force in the world and they were going to rip the Russian defenses to shreds. Those were their very own words. They would accomplish this for us, and then they'd let us handle the pursuit of the fleeing enemy and the mopping up operation. These loud mouths almost made us ill.

"Why do they think that they're any better than the rest of the army?" I said to Karl.

"Because of the armor," was his reply. "Look at the tanks and the attack-carriers, equipped with four inch howitzers, rocket throwers and automatic weapons in everybody's hands. Look at us, what do you have? You have a carbine with five bullets in the chamber and another sixty as reserve on your belt, period. How can you compare yourself with them? But let me tell you another thing. Twenty percent of them will have stopped breathing by the time they are through with this attack; and that's for sure. After that they'll be transported to the rear to polish their battered egos." He was right. The casualties would be horrendous.

At about 5 A.M., on a bright and sunny morning, the bombardment started. One hour later the SS started to attack the Russian lines, which, as we found out later, were staggered thirteen trenches deep. Several barbed wire barriers fortified every trench. The Russians had not slept during the winter they had worked tirelessly. Losses of the SS Division were phenomenal. Twenty percent casualties surmised by Karl were exceeded by far and the Russian defenses were not broken. The SS withdrew with more than a bloody nose, and it was left to us to withstand the counterattacks of heavily armed and very capable Russian elite divisions.

Karl and I once more were sent to an infantry company and were sitting in our foxhole trying to maintain communications with our reliable DORA unit when the Russians began their counter attack. It started with an uninterrupted barrage of artillery. We could see a runner from head quarters coming towards us, jumping up and down. But he never made it. An artillery shell exploded nearby, lifting him into the air and slamming him down to the ground hard. He was dead on arrival with a few pieces of his anatomy missing.

"Which idiot is trying to send a messenger to us?" Karl exclaimed. "Can't they contact us on the DORA? There you have it again; the total disregard for human lives."

Of course, he was right. We had seen it often. Soon enough the regimental commander, in his unfathomable wisdom, must have had the same idea though it was one useless casualty too late. Our DORA started to peep, and we recorded an incoming message from the regiment.

Our instructions were to request fire support from the artillery. Why us? They were the regiment and the colonel certainly outranked a lieutenant? We complied. The answer was brutal and to the point, "We have six shells per gun. We are only allowed to employ our resources on the direct order of the division commander and only in case of an enemy attack."

There we were. After weeks and weeks of "All quiet on the Eastern Front," the German army had started a major attack, and after a few days of serious hostilities they were out of ammunition? We passed the message on to the regiment, and made ourselves real small in our foxhole.

It was difficult to understand the intention of the high command. They didn't make any sense. What did they plan to do to extricate the Division from the position it was in? We had no ammunition, no tanks, and had suffered heavy casualties. An attack, or the attempt to dislodge the Russians from their positions under these circumstances, and after the bloody experiences by the SS Division, was out of the question.

By now the fighting had gone on uninterrupted for a couple of weeks, and we hadn't been able to take a breather. Life was getting rough without washing, shaving or cleaning. Lice were beginning to eat us alive. One of the famous *Rollbahns* (A German word coined to describe a wide road etched into the land by lots of traffic, but without any foundation or embankment) passed immediately behind our holes and our main trench. This former *Rollbahn* was about seventy yards wide. If we wanted to go to the other side we were forced to leave the protection of our trench and to run across the *Rollbahn* unprotected and in full view of the enemy. The trench continued on the other side of the *Rollbahn*. A ten-day-old, grossly bloated carcass of a dead horse, was lying right in the middle of the *Rollbahn*.

It was now June and already very hot. On top of it, it was a sunny day. Lieutenant Seuffert had come from the other side of the *Rollbahn* on one of his dumb inspections. Standing in the foxhole across from ours he yelled at us, "Why haven't you tried to do something about your cleanliness? You look unshaven and unbecoming a German soldier."

He must have just arrived from the village nearby, had his shower and looked nice and clean. Why was he picking on us at a time like this? He simply was out of his mind.

While he was carrying on his tirade, the Russians continued their bombardment with mortar and artillery. The lieutenant was about sixty yards away, in a fox-hole and almost foaming at the mouth.

"He has lost his marbles," Karl murmured under his breath.

"Corporal Schwarzlose, why don't you wear your steel helmet as its standard regulation under combat conditions? I'll report you to the first sergeant, do you understand?"

"Lieutenant Seuffert, Sir," I yelled back rather sarcastically. "If you would look into army regulations you'll also find an exemption for wireless operators while they're working and while they're wearing headsets. The headset won't fit over the helmet, Sir, and you can't hear anything as delicate as an incoming Morse signal, Sir, if you wear the headset over the helmet, Sir. Do you understand what I'm trying to explain, Sir?"

By now he was almost ballistic, ready to blow up. An incoming message prohibited me from continuing this fruitless exchange.

We did our recording and decoding and I took the message, which was for the company commander, waved it at Lieutenant Seuffert and yelled, "Message to deliver," and jumped out of my hole intending to cross over the *Rollbahn* to the other side and into the trench. Wouldn't you know, the Ivan must have observed all this traffic back and forth across the little stretch of real estate and started to shoot at me with everything they got. I barely reached the carcass of the dead horse and threw myself down behind it. Dozens of bullets were hitting the carcass, each one with a dull thud. Karl yelled at me not to lift my head. The lieutenant had suddenly become quiet, disappeared in his hole and didn't dare to move either.

The stench of the decaying horse was unmerciful. I repeatedly vomited compulsively. Now I was lying flat on the ground in my own vomit. Every time I tried to raise my head, to find out whether it was safe to move, the shooting started all over again. After several hours, when darkness finally descended, I made a successful attempt to get away from the dead horse and delivered my message.

The company commander's cleanliness was not all that great either having been with his men during the entire time. He asked me, "What is this with Lieutenant Seuffert, he certainly acts strange doesn't he? Almost as if he is scared out of his wits."

I didn't answer. I didn't have to. His was a candid observation and didn't require any answer. When Lieutenant Seuffert had started to act up, I hadn't thought about fear. But that's what it probably was, *Angst*, pure unadulterated fear. Time and time again men would act absolutely strange when exposed to enemy fire for the first time; it was the first time for Lieutenant Seuffert, and it had happened to him too.

I found Karl in good shape with several more messages to deliver. Fortunately Lieutenant Seuffert had disappeared.

"He left after darkness set in," Karl said. "I believe he needed to clean his pants."

Shortly before daybreak we were called back to the regimental headquarters. The scene was bedlam. The Russians were on the verge of breaking through. Our orders were to leave the DORA equipment behind to join with a platoon of infantry advancing toward the enemy lines to retake our trench.

We were badly prepared for the fighting; solely equipped with our five shot rifles 98k. Our infantry had suffered heavy casualties during the last few days and needed reinforcements. The Russians had overrun them. There was a gap in our defenses. They needed help urgently

"Try to do your duty, Corporal," the first sergeant called after me, smiling rather happily while we went on our way. My God, idiots surrounded us on all sides.

The infantry attacked the trenches near the *Rollbahn* where their previous positions had been. The trenches had been taken over by the Ivan who had chased our infantry like rabbits.

Before we started our attack we were laying in the open field, in shallow holes dug with our spades, under heavy fire. Bodies from both sides were everywhere. Nobody had a chance or desire to bury dead corpses.

A master sergeant, jumping up and down, came towards us and yelled, "Our lieutenant has been wounded and is on his way to the field hospital. In the absence of an officer I am the new company commander. Get ready. We're going to attack the enemy lines and will retake our old trench. Shortly after our artillery has softened them up we'll jump."

Sure enough, fifteen minutes later ten rounds from our artillery came flying overhead hitting somewhere in front of us.

"Is that all?" Karl asked. "They haven't even found their range yet."

No sooner had he said that than the master sergeant gave the command to attack. We got up, held our carbines in the crook of our arms running towards the trenches ahead of us. We zigzagged and were bobbing up and down to project a more elusive target to the enemy. During one of these jumps I felt a violent slap to my left hip, like a jolt, almost as if a horse had kicked me. I was thrown to the ground like a bag of potatoes and was lying there for a few seconds. I felt up and down my left side with both hands, but couldn't feel any blood or any torn clothing. I got up rejoining the others ahead of me, jumping and weaving and shooting with my carbine at anything that moved. We continued to run forward forty to fifty yards and saw Russian Infantry climbing out of the trenches disappearing in the background into a field of fully-grown, seven feet high, sunflowers.

The trenches, originally dug by the enemy, were seven feet deep. We had to stand on ammunition boxes if we wanted to look over the edge. Like all trenches they weren't dug in a straight line, but rather zigzag. Every leg of a zig or zag was six yards long and then turned at a forty-degree angle.

The intention was to prevent an attacking enemy to run through the trench looking down a straight line and shooting at everything that moved ahead of him. The intruder had to search and fight around every corner of the zig and the zag, to find out the hard way if a deadly surprise might be waiting for him.

Several dead Russian soldiers from the previous attacks were still lying in the trench. One of them looked particularly gruesome. A burst from a machine gun had taken off half of his skull. He was lying there his brain totally exposed, oozing out of its cavity, with green flies crawling all over it.

We didn't pursue the attack any further, because the enemy fire was still heavy and where were we going to go anyway? To leave the trench at this time would have been suicide. An hour had passed since I felt the kick to my left hip. The action had slowed and the adrenaline was flowing slower. I started to feel a persistent and growing pain in my hip. Looking down my side Karl couldn't find anything either, but it was beginning to hurt badly.

"Look over there," somebody yelled, "They're starting to attack again. I can hear tanks."

He was right. We could see Russian soldiers at the distance running towards our position. The unmistaken noise of moving tanks was drifting across the field. I still remembered the sound from my days with the *RAD*. Some soldiers became real panicky about the noise and wanted to jump out of the trench to run away. The master sergeant had a hard time to contain them.

And then you could see them coming, bobbing up and down hidden partly by the field of sunflowers. Six T 34's were rolling slowly but steadily toward our position, firing away from their turrets with automatic weapons and cannons in sweeping motions from right to left and back again. Our soldiers were jumping out of the trench. The master sergeant couldn't stop them even though he shouted threateningly to shoot them.

Karl looked at me his face twisted, fear in his eyes. It was his first exposure to a tank attack and I knew how he felt in his gut.

"Peter, I'm not going to stay and let them kill me. There're so many more of them than of us and they have tanks, and we don't have a chance, let's go."

"No," I said, "if we run they'll get us for sure, don't waste your ammunition at this distance, wait, 'till they come closer."

I could see that he was scared and ready to abandon our position at any minute.

The Russian Infantry kept coming closer and closer. As I said before we had almost no automatic weapons only the carbines 98k. The carbines fired too slowly to make an impression on the attacking Russians. We had no MG 34 or 42, or any other automatic weapon to deter them. It wasn't an equal contest. The master sergeant couldn't stop his men any longer. Soon they were jumping out of the trench. Karl turned to look at me one more time with terrified eyes and, climbing over the edge of the trench, disappeared with the others. It became a full flight.

By this time I would have jumped out of the trench too, but I couldn't. My left leg had become totally numb at the hip, almost paralyzed. I stood there trying, frantically, to climb over the ridge of the trench, but I couldn't do it with one leg alone and my left leg wasn't obeying my orders. From the near distance on my left and on the right, only a few zigs and zags away, I could hear the Russians yelling and jumping into the trench. I was panic-stricken. They're going to slaughter me, pump me full of bullets, or gorge me with their bayonets; what could I do?

I turned and saw the dead Russian soldier nearby with his skull half cut off and his brains oozing out, exposed to the flies. I threw myself down next to him, half over his lifeless body and buried my face into the ground, dug my hand into the slimy substance of his brain and slapped as much as could get hold of on the back of my head. No sooner was I finished than I heard movements behind me. Some Russians must have come around the bend of the nearest corner and stopped. I heard them talking furiously to each other until one of them stepped onto my back with both feet. I felt two sharp, piercing stabs penetrating my back.

It's the God honest truth that to this day I don't know how I managed to lie motionless while the Russian stabbed me in the back twice with his bayonet. How I could've remained still while the pain raked through my body is a mystery to me. Most likely a tremendous rush of adrenaline exited my brain and raced through my body as a result of mortal fear and made me oblivious to any pain.

My luck was Ivan had other worries than to stay with me and check my condition more closely, whether I was alive or not. Apparently they didn't want to waste more bullets or time on a seemingly dead enemy. They moved down the trench with others who followed them, trampling over the dead Russian's body, and mine. The dead man had saved my life with his life and, "literally" with his brains.

It was an interminable time. I must have become unconscious from pain. German infantry started a successful counter attack and chased the Russians out of the trenches one more time.

I was bleeding like a pig from the stab wounds in my back. Karl arrived with others to reclaim the trench. They would have left me there for dead, had I not managed to let out one single piercing scream. They rushed over, picked me up and carried me out of the trench down a small hill to the nearest first aid station. The Red Cross tent was filled with wounded soldiers lying around moaning and groaning. I thought nobody would ever pay any attention to me. The medic, whom I'd met briefly while being with the infantry, stopped to take a look at my wounds. He ordered some soldiers to pour water over my head to wash off the stinking mess that was still stuck to it and told them to put me on a passing truck, which went to the nearest field hospital. I lost sight of Karl.

The field hospital was an assembly of large tents with hundreds of wounded soldiers lying on the ground. Medics unloaded the wounded, put me on a stretcher at the entrance of a tent, and I waited. Every once in awhile an orderly with a basket-full of limbs, arms and legs mixed together came out of the tent. If I hadn't been in such a terrible shape I would've thrown up, but in my condition I hardly noticed my surroundings.

After an endless time of waiting they carried me into the operating tent and addressed the stab wound on my back. Luckily, the penetration hadn't been deep, and to my relief the doctor murmured,

"No punctured lung. The stabs didn't penetrate deep enough, must've been caught by the rib cage."

Then he turned me over to investigate my leg. He took a thin metal probe, without even bothering to apply any painkiller, and pushed it deep into the small hole in my thigh. The pain of the examination woke me up with a jolt. These were injuries four and five.

"Keep still, soldier, I don't have enough pain killers for little things like this. You might need some later, when I've got to amputate your leg. That's probably what I've got to do anyway, because you have a bullet in your hip joint, and if I can't remove it you'll get gangrene, or worse, and you'll die." (These were the days before the invention of penicillin or antibiotics.)

He called out to the operating nurse: "Nurse, tie him down so that he can't move before I cut into him and bring me the saw. We need to take his leg off."

When I heard that I panicked. The guy wanted to cut my leg off!? I would be a cripple for life! No way! I wasn't going to allow that, I rather die of anything, gangrene or whatever he said, but I wasn't going to be a cripple!

Pictures flashed in front of my eyes sitting on a street corner, hat in hand, begging for support from disinterested passers-by like I had seen many times as a young boy in the late twenties on the streets of Berlin with soldiers from the other war.

I took all my strength, lunged out with my right arm and backhanded the doctor across his face. He tumbled, and almost fell to the ground.

"Get the dumb ass out of here right away," he yelled. "There are many others who understand I want to help them, I don't have time for idiots like him."

They carried me out of the operating room. I was strangely happy, almost serene. I still have my leg! I still have my leg! That message raced through my mind repeatedly until I passed out.

When I woke up I was in a moving vehicle with several other wounded soldiers. The truck was on its way to a hospital train, which would be taking us to Vienna. The minute I was carried onto the hospital train I felt like 'déjà vu.' I'd been on one of these trains before and felt safe immediately. It wouldn't have surprised me at all if my nurse, from the other train, eight and one half months ago—was it only that short time ago—would have stepped up to my bedside to clean me up and to take care of me.

Red Cross nurses inspected us before the train finally started to move and put bottles of liquor, compliments of the Red Cross, next to every bed. They had all kinds of different liquors, *Holunder Schnaps,* cognac, coffee liquor, cointreau, gin and more. Our nurses decided to pour all bottles into one large army issue, coffee jug. Wow! The mixture tasted strong and sweet, but it was very effective. The tranquilizers we swallowed together with alcohol did a thorough job. We were fast asleep when the train started to move.

I woke up the following morning with a splitting headache. It was daylight outside and the train was moving at a fast pace. A doctor came for an examination and after seeing my injuries and reading the tag attached to my leg he decided to put my left leg and lower torso into a cast. He told me that since he didn't have an x-ray on the train, he couldn't determine whether any bones had been chipped or broken. In all probability my hip joint was fractured, he said. It would be safer to have the leg in a cast before the bullet, which he estimated to be located near my hip socket, could be removed. Those were his very words. With no x-ray facilities available on the train the doctors had to do a lot of guesswork. Whatever was the matter with my leg, the cast certainly couldn't do any damage. The nurses came, undressed me, and wrapped my lower body in soft white cotton and covered everything with gypsum bandages. I wondered out loud how I would be going about doing my business, but the nurses laughed and said that was no problem at all; they would help and assist me.

The lice, nobody had thought about lice, lice loved cotton, naturally. It was like a giant bed for them to make love in and to multiply ferociously, which they started to do day and night. The only tool I had, to alleviate the excruciating itch was a six inch long copy pencil; my upstairs bed-neighbor had given it to me. The pencil was intended before the invention of the ballpoint pen to write with pressure on normal paper lying upon copying paper to make copies. For some reason it had a purple lead.

During the remainder of the transport I kept pushing that pencil downwards under the cast on my belly, up and down, up and down to get relief from the terrible itching caused by the lice. I did this often during the day and the night and the results gave me some relief.

It took the train four days until it arrived in Vienna. After unloading the wounded that were eventually distributed throughout every institution in the city, the medical staff got us cleaned up and deloused.

During the month of July of 1943, 230,000 wounded soldiers arrived in Vienna. The city was inundated with them. Every available hospital bed was occupied and the military requisitioned every building suitable as make shift hospital. The casualties from our hospital-train were directed to the edge of town to a very old and grandiose looking institution. It was a government-run senior citizen home in the suburb of *Wien-Hütteldorf*, which had been converted into a hospital.

When the nurses cut off my cast, my belly was one infected, bluish-red mess. It looked frightening to everybody, even to me. I had discarded the pencil before leaving the train and wasn't going to help the nurses or the doctors with the diagnosis of the infection, or the cause for the purple streaks on my belly.

I had plenty of time to think during the four days on the train. I was determined to milk every last day out of this misfortune to avoid another stretch of duty in a location where shooting and killing was going on and where, sooner or later, I would be killed too.

A *Stabsarzt* (Doctor with the rank of a Major) came into the hall where we were bedded down to conduct a preliminary examination of everybody's wounds. When he arrived at my bed, he looked at my leg, which had no visible sign anymore of any wound or penetration of a projectile and barked to an orderly, "This soldier is a malingerer. He pretends to be wounded most likely to get away from the shooting and from performing his duty as a German soldier. See to it that he's turned over to the provost marshal at once."

I couldn't believe my ears, and the nurses around the doctor looked embarrassed. What kind of a clown was that? I turned slightly on my bed to pull my uniform jacket from under my head where it had been placed as a temporary pillow and opened it up to display my decorations and said:

"Sir, you may also want to look at my back, because I have two stab wounds from Russian bayonets. I also request respectfully that an x-ray of my leg and my lungs should be taken before you arrive at your rather insulting conclusion. However, *Stabsarzt,* Sir, one more thing strikes me as odd with the men of the medical profession; the first doctor wanted to cut my leg off, right at the joint. The second one in the train wraps me in a cast because of a possible ruptured joint-capsule and you the third one call me a malingerer? I expect an apology from you after the x-rays are taken and have been evaluated, and I expect an apology in front of the same people who were present when you insulted me."

The man turned crimson red and called for an orderly to take me to the x-ray room. The x-rays revealed that the second doctor had been right. I had better remain in a cast. A few days later I received his apology. He also presented the *Verwundetenabzeichen* (Purple Heart) to me, in silver, a medal for three injuries received in battle. The case was closed.

I called Berlin to inform the people of the Schwarzlose Company of my whereabouts, without telling them I'd been wounded, or any other details of why I was in Vienna. After four days a long letter from Marcella arrived asking me how I was, why I was in Vienna and telling me how much she missed me. She went on to say if I would have a chance to come to Berlin, she would show me in person what she meant by that. I wondered!

Two days later a nurse came into our room, or should I better say hall, because the room where we were bedded down was large enough for fifty beds, and told me with a big smile on her face that my mother was waiting at the entrance and wanted to see me.

My mother, I thought totally flabbergasted? The last time I had heard from her was that she had returned to Switzerland an eternity ago? With the help of a nurse I got out of bed as quickly as I could and made my way downstairs using a pair of under arm crutches.

As I was slowly descending the stairs with my crutches I could see my mother standing in the huge entrance hall, looking to me the same as I had left her the last time I had seen her. She had tears in her eyes when she saw me hobbling up to her on my crutches and took me carefully into her arms.

"Hallo *Mutti,* how have you been?" I said in English trying to sound nonchalant. "You can see I did as I promised and followed your instructions. I didn't climb on top of any tank and I got out of the last skirmish alive and that is the main thing. Don't cry, Mom, please, otherwise I'll do the same, and that would look awful for a soldier."

We hugged carefully so that I wouldn't be thrown off balance and sat down to talk.

"Oh, Peter, I am sooo happy to see that you are alive and in good spirits. Tell me what has happened to your leg. How and where were you wounded this time? I'm very curious to hear how you'll explain your latest adventures. You always seem to get in the way of flying bullets. I reminded you more than once to be careful."

I had to laugh. What could I say? I didn't let her know all the gruesome details of the war in the trenches. I told her briefly, very briefly, what had happened and emphasized over and over again how happy I was to see her, "Mom, who told you where I was and how did you get here so quickly? From what I gather it's not easy to get travel permits these days to leave Switzerland and come across the border to *Gross-Deutschland,* or Austria as it used to be called."

"Well, my son, I was in Switzerland with Monica and Bill, as I had written to you in my letters before I left Berlin. Somebody from the Schwarzlose Company sent me a wire with the details of where you were. Bill got me a ticket and," she bent over and whispered into my ear, "I'm traveling on a temporary Swiss passport, which I'll have to surrender again the minute I'm back. I have permission to stay in Vienna for two days. During these two days I want to see you as often as possible. I'm staying with business friends of Bill, very nice people with a lovely apartment. I hope you can come to visit me."

She gave me her address and phone number, and I promised to find out if I could get out of the hospital or not and also how I would arrange transportation with my awkward cast.

Wow, what a surprise that was, a temporary Swiss passport? I couldn't believe it and waited for the rest of the story.

I talked to the same *Stabsarzt* who wanted to turn me over to the provost marshal the day after I had arrived. I approached him during his next visitation. He must have still had a bad conscience because he promised to help me, which he did. He even arranged for his personal car, with chauffeur, to pick me up, and to take me to the address my mother had given to me. The orderly picked me up two hours later.

My mother and I were sitting in the "salon" of Bill's friend's home. It was in one of these old rooms with high ceilings and lots of gilded ornamental stuccowork on ceilings and walls. It was an old beautiful Viennese apartment filled with gorgeous antique furniture and paintings, a virtual art gallery. A maid, a Russian girl from the Ukraine, served coffee and delicious pastry. I met the owners of the apartment briefly. They were gracious enough not to intrude letting my mother and I talk to our hearts content. Especially with the experiences of only a few days ago firmly engraved in mind, I felt transported back into the distant past almost as if I'd be in a movie or in a museum. This scene of splendor, old world charm and unreal tranquility was unreal. A sensation swept over me as if the time had stood still, and as if I was transported to another planet, the war had suddenly disappeared.

Olga told me that she'd left Berlin two months ago because of increased harassment by local authorities. With Bill's help she had managed to cross the border into Switzerland without incident.

"Mutti," I said, reverting to the German version of Mom, "your life is much more dangerous than mine was in Russia where the shooting was going on. What do you think is going to happen to you if the Nazis arrest you and put you into one of their infamous concentration camps? They're awful everybody says, and more people die than get out again alive. You remember my father's uncle who was sent to the concentration camp in *Oranienburg* for black market activities? When he got out he told terrible stories. Do me a favor this time; get back to Switzerland and stay there. Wait until the war is over and then, so God will, we'll both return in good health to the USA. The way I judge the condition of the German army, the availability of supplies and weapons, it can't last much longer." (It was July 1943 and I had underestimated the tenacity of the Nazis and the durability of their war machine.)

"You're probably right, Peter, I'll see whether I can manage to do that. I can't promise what I'll do, because a great deal will depend upon what happens to you."

"Mutti, let me tell you one thing, which I firmly believe; let the Good Lord keep an eye on me and you watch out for yourself. You should keep in mind, I'll need the Lord for sure if they manage to fix me up again and send me to the front again. Only He will be there to protect me. His guardianship has been well established otherwise I wouldn't be sitting here. I don't want to imply that He doesn't lose sight of me every once in awhile, like this last time, but when it counts He is on my side, you bet."

"I pray to the Lord every night, Peter, and ask him to watch out for you," she replied with fervor. "Let's hope He listens to either one or to both of us."

We parted a few hours later under tears. I told her again to be careful crossing the borders and asked her to give a hug to Bill and Monica. She implored me, for the millionth time, to be watchful. That's what we always seemed to be doing when we met, telling each other to watch out for danger. The world certainly had become crazy.

The battles in Russia raged on through the remainder of the summer of 1943. The Germans didn't get anywhere. On the contrary they were retreating. The best divisions had been annihilated, the resources were depleting at a rapid pace and Hitler's moves became crazier with each passing day. More casualties kept streaming into Vienna and hospital beds became scarcer. The *Stabsarzt* visited one morning and asked me.

"Do you want to go home to Berlin, Corporal? Just for six weeks, until the time when your cast has to be changed, or we take it off completely, depending of what the x-rays reveal. We need hospital beds and room for the more urgent cases."

When the *Stabsarzt* asked me that question I had to make a decision. I hesitated with my answer. I contemplated the consequences for one long moment. Was I scared of something, or what? Then I made up my mind and said, "Yes, sir."

The following day I picked up my papers from the administration together with a new set of more comfortable under-elbow crutches. I left the hospital in *Hütteldorf* hobbling badly and caught a *tram* just around the corner, a streetcar, to go to the nearest train station. It was one of these old electric conveyances with a passenger compartment in the middle high above ground. As a matter of fact it was so high older passengers had a hard time climbing up several steps to reach the platform. This one had three rickety metal grated steps to negotiate, what a construction; I finally made it into the compartment, but only with the help of two passengers who grabbed my arms as I was stumbling forward.

The train ride to Berlin was interrupted several times by air raid alarms. Each time the train stopped. To protect the train from damage the engineer tried to stop outside of stations or, if at all possible, in tunnels. By the time we finally arrived in Berlin it had taken us more than twenty-four hours, a trip, which normally lasted twelve hours.

And now came the good part. At least that's what I was hoping for.

3

RECUPERATING WITH MARCELLA IN BERLIN

The train rolled slowly into *Bahnhof Zoo*. It was 6 P.M. I looked out the window, before getting off the train. I noticed people darting nervously back and forth on the platform. First, I assumed they were trying to get home from work as quickly as possible. I carefully climbed with my crutches down three steps, one step at the time. Then I stopped a passing woman inquiring why everybody was in such a hurry. She looked at me as if I were coming from another star and answered curtly.

"It's already late and those bloody bombers are going to come as early as 8 or 9 o'clock. We're anticipating an air raid almost every night. Everybody wants to be home before these bastards drop their bombs. If you're not home and get caught by howling sirens in a strange neighborhood, you may not find room in a shelter. Most cellars are small. They're just big enough to accommodate the tenants of the house without any room for unwanted strangers trying to get in. Who wants to be in the open without protection from bombs and from millions of pieces of shrapnel raining down in a steady downpour? You know, and I'm talking about shrapnel shells fired by our own anti-aircraft guns after they explode high in the sky. I've got to hurry now and you better get going too. With your crutches you can't run."

She chuckled at her own sick humor and disappeared. Off she went. I put my crutches under my armpits and climbed slowly down the stairs to the adjacent subway. I was used to crutches by now and managed to hobble down the steps in time to catch the next train without waiting. It was my train to *Ruhleben,* towards the old Olympic Stadium. It was the last stop in the western most part of the city. The passengers in the subway looked drab and smoked the cheapest smelling cigarettes you can imagine. I'd entered the smoker's car without bothering to look first. Aside from the stench

141

of smoke it stank offensively of sweat and unwashed bodies. No wonder with rationing for everything; including soap. It was difficult to stay clean or to wash clothes with one piece of soap per person per month and warm water was scarce in most houses. Nobody talked much less smiled. What bothered me even more being on crutches, swaying back and forth in a moving subway car was, that nobody made an attempt to get up to make room for the wounded soldier! I concluded that morale must be very low and that I was probably right.

My stop called *"Neu-Westend"* was seven stops away and two stops before *Ruhleben*. Each stop took about three minutes; time enough to let passengers in and out and to go to the next station. Twenty-one minutes is not a long time. It was my last opportunity to sort out my course of action with Marcella, and whether or not I was comfortable with it. Should I consider the good advice from people like my friend Karl? Should I play it like the "son," or should I let her take the lead? Let her decide where our relationship was going?

To make a decision like that in eighteen minutes is a short time, indeed. But to be honest about it, I had to admit, I wasn't thinking about it for the first time. These weren't new deliberations or new thoughts. It was just getting tight right now. I had twenty-one minutes to finally make up my mind. The problem, as a matter of fact, had been churning in my head for a long time.

"All right," I finally said to myself with two stations to go, *"Your father explained that you shouldn't hesitate to get involved with older women. He said they are more experienced and more gratifying. Just for once, my friend, take his advice and don't think about money and inheritance and all the other shit. It will be cleared up when the time comes and after you have survived this mess of a war—hopefully."*

The dice had been rolled and had come to a complete stop. Snake eyes?

Marcella's apartment, my father's apartment, was pretty close to the subway station. I had my difficulties climbing up the stairs getting out of the *U-Bahn*. The escalators had been shut down a long time ago, because of wartime restrictions, for lack of electricity, or for lack of spare parts.

Once I reached the top I took a deep breath of fresh air, leaned on my crutches, placed them deliberately in front of me swinging my feet forward between them again and again. I hobbled a few hundred feet down the sidewalk and across the street until I arrived at the house I knew so well. I stood in the dark entrance for a minute or two, nervously contemplating my plan of action one more time or, to put it more succinctly, my pattern of behavior. All the lights had been turned off on account of the air raids. The city was pitch dark.

Horseshit! No more procrastination! I had made my decision. Marcella was the older, experienced one: that was an understatement. The way I remembered her I was absolutely certain she always had her plans and made her own decisions. She would leave no doubt now where the ride was going.

I rang the bell where the label said 'Schwarzlose' and waited. The loud speaker sprung to live and a voice said guardedly: "Who is it?" I responded:

"This is a tired soldier coming home from the war, looking for a warm and friendly bed to sleep in." For three seconds there was dead silence. Then she cried out, "Oh, Peter, it's you; I'll be right down with the elevator to pick you up."

The apartment was three flights up, and I had hoped she would come to get me with the elevator. It wouldn't have been easy to walk the three flights using my crutches. She didn't have any idea that I was injured or about the nature of my injuries or that I was using crutches. I was wondering what kind of a face she would make when she saw me. As I said before, when I phoned the Schwarzlose Company from Vienna I hadn't divulged anything about my condition, about being wounded, or given any other explanation why I was back on home territory. Women can easily get upset for the strangest reasons, and I just wanted to show up to face her in person, to tell her myself.

As the light in the stairwell came on, I couldn't see anything through the slits in the protection covers at the doors. Protective covers on all windows and openings of houses were obligatory. It was a total blackout intended to 'hide' the city from enemy planes.

The door flew open, and there she was with her eyes wide open in anticipation of seeing me. She took it all in with one quick sweep of her eyes, the crutches, the cast and my bent figure, "My God, what's the matter? Have you been hurt, Peter? Are you in pain? Talk to me, please?" Before answering I gently nudged her off the street into the hallway of the house and hobbled up three stairs to the elevator. I entered the small cage. She let me go in before she squeezed herself into the tight compartment. As we rode up to the third floor she looked up at me silently, her huge blue eyes opened wide. Now is the time I thought to myself; she threw her arms around my neck and kissed me warmly and passionately. Her soft lips and her moving tongue gave me the feeling of a kiss with an intensity I had never experienced before. We lost all track of time until some persistent knocks on the door of the elevator on one of the upper floors reminded us that other people were living in this house. We got out and entered the apartment. I had only brought a small bag with me with an extra set of army issue underwear and a toothbrush. With the crutches in my hands, I couldn't have carried a suitcase anyway.

"Peter, what happened? Tell me. What's the matter with your leg? Did you break it or what?"

"No, Celli," I said, using the nickname my father had given her. "Where could I have possibly broken my leg?" Women! "Erroneously and carelessly I got in the way of a bullet from a Russian Kalashnikov," I explained, trying to sound nonchalant. "X-rays show the bullet is embedded in my hip, and the doctors have confirmed it. There is a fracture. That's why I have to wear a cast all the way up to my hip, and that's the reason I walk on crutches." I went on to explain further., "The cast has to stay in place for the time being, for six weeks to be exact. Then I have to return to Vienna for further examinations and evaluations by my doctors. Right now hospitals in Vienna are overcrowded with wounded men. The administration wants as many soldiers as possible to recuperate at home, especially those soldiers who don't need continuous medical care and attention as I do. The trick for me, or for us, will be to find a way to prolong the hardships from this injury until the war is over, if at all possible. Now, Celli, we can talk about this some more. But please, let me take off my uniform and the rest of these army rags, and let me take a bath. That is, if I'm able to manage a bath with this cast on and then put on some of my own things. I presume that this house has hot water? I desperately would like to feel like a civilian, even if it's only for the short time I am permitted to stay in your home. Maybe you are also having a bite for me to eat and a glass of wine to refresh my spirits."

All the time I was talking, she stood there in front of me looking up at me with her eyes wide open, her lips slightly parted, just being gorgeous. I felt a stirring in my loins, thinking what it would be like to climb into bed with her right now. I don't know what her thoughts were, but she came real close to me and stroked my head. Holy smokes! She looked lovely with her blond hair and those deep blue eyes. I didn't know what to say. I just looked back at her, pulled her closer toward me with my free arm and kissed her. It was difficult to separate again, but we finally did, each of us at a loss for words.

Only a few minutes ago, standing in front of the door downstairs, I'd wondered about my 'pattern of behavior.' This wonderful woman had blown all my doubts and uncertainties away. They'd vanished the way the early fog on a summer morning disappears when the sun is rising over the horizon. My heart was beating like a sledgehammer, and I had trouble containing myself.

I attempted to take a sponge bath, which was easier said then done with the cast reaching all the way up to my hip on my left side. Afterwards I put on some of my own clothes and sat down to eat a few pieces of bread and drank a glass of red wine. Celli wanted to know everything about my injury, whether or not it bothered me, hurt me, what the doctors had said and so on and so forth.

Then she started to tell me about her difficulties in war torn Berlin.

When I said I "sat down," I must explain that it is extremely difficult to sit down with a cast and an immobilized hip joint. I practically had to sit on the corner of the chair on my right bottom cheek and then lie back a little to accommodate my stiff left side under the table. It not only looked strange. After practicing the last few weeks I was used to it by now, but Celli, when she saw my contortions, was upset and thought it must be painful, which it really wasn't, just uncomfortable.

Then she got up to get a piece of paper and a pencil. Putting a finger across her lips to keep me from talking, she started to write, "The Nazis have connected many homes to a device called *Drahtfunk* (broadcasting by wire). It supposedly guarantees radio reception during air raids when all normal radio signals are discontinued. Since *Drahtfunk* is transmitted by telephone wire it doesn't require aerial signals and doesn't betray the city's location, or give navigational assistance to incoming enemy planes. At the time of the conversion of our radio, a small microphone was placed inside, to allow the *Gestapo* (*Geheime Staatspolizei*) to listen to our conversations. Please watch what you are saying, okay?"

I read the note carefully, nodded to her and took a match to burn the paper in an ashtray. The world was getting crazier by the minute. Those Nazi fuckers! What could they think of next?

"The sirens are sending us to the air raid shelter almost every night," she continued. "Not that our part of the city gets hit every night or has been hit seriously so far, but everybody has to go into the shelter anyway. Down to the dirty cellar we go where everybody in the house waits in tight quarters until the raid is over. You can't get any sleep under those conditions. Of course, everybody has found his personal routine which items to take to the cellar. For instance I take a small suitcase with me. You must have seen it standing at the entrance. I packed my important papers, my jewelry, one change of clothes and a blanket. Peter, I am so glad you're here. My nerves are raw after weeks and months of this perpetual hassle. If it were up to me, I would stay up here. But the air raid warden checks on every apartment and issues summonses to anybody who doesn't obey his instructions. In the past some raids have been pretty bad for Berlin, especially when the American bombers drop those big bombs. They call them 'block busters.' When they fall close to our house the whole house shakes. Hearing the terrible and frightening howling sound of one of those falling bombs, I always wonder how close it's going to be this time and whether or not the whole house is going to collapse on top of me. We will take the subway into the city while you're here, and you can see the damage from the air raids. Literally thousands of houses have either burned to the ground or have been totally destroyed by blockbusters. The people are afraid to open their mouths for fear of being sent to one of the *Konzentrationslager* (Concentration camps). They are only talking about the camps behind closed doors. Nobody even dares to mention the word in public."

I remembered that our soldiers in Russia, coming back from home leave, had mentioned that they much preferred the artillery fire to the bombs of the Americans. The noise of falling bombs, they said, and the claustrophobia in the cellars had been worse than anything they'd experienced in the trenches. I also remembered the word *Konzentrationslager* being mentioned.

Celli started to cry uncontrollably, and, when I took her into my arms, I could feel that she was shaking and trembling. She calmed down after a while, and I tried to console her, kissing her on her mouth, her eyes, her nose and her ears.

Things were definitely developing in a promising way.

We'd only eaten a few pieces of bread and drank a sip of wine when sirens started to blare for yet another air raid alarm, my first one in Berlin. I didn't want to go to the cellar, and, without Celli's insistence, I wouldn't have gone. My luck was that the electricity was still working, and I was able to use the elevator.

As we stepped through the reinforced door of the cellar I recognized several familiar faces of people whom I knew from past visits. They had lived in the building for a number of years. We exchanged our "hellos," they asked a few questions about my injury, and we sat down on a wooden bench and kept to ourselves. From the disinterest they displayed I gathered that they must've seen many injured soldiers before. The war was lasting too long and had affected everybody's life.

Sitting on the hard bench for a long time was more than uncomfortable and still, I couldn't keep my eyes off Celli. The hell with my buddy Karl and his Cassandra warnings I thought. The more I looked at her, the more beautiful she became to me. With all these people around I had to watch to keep my hands off her while we were in the cellar. It wouldn't have looked too good to flirt openly with her. Our neighbors would have wondered what stepmother and stepson were up to.

A half an hour into the raid the anti-aircraft guns started to throw their deadly load up into the sky. Everybody in the cellar was getting nervous and fidgety. The raid was on in earnest. I could see that many in the fearful crowd around me spoke silent prayers. I must admit that I felt pretty shitty myself.

The British bombers, mostly smaller than their American counter parts, didn't carry large bombs. Instead they dropped thousands upon thousands of small incendiary devices. They couldn't demolish a house instantaneously by sheer impact alone like the big bastards could, but they were dropped in a close pattern, by the thousands, from each plane. Those incendiary bombs were 24 inches long with a heavy cast-iron head. The heavy head facilitated a relatively straight fall. The incendiary part, which harbored the phosphorus that burned at several thousand degrees Fahrenheit, was in the rear behind the iron head. After dropping 20,000 feet from the plane, the bomb gained enough velocity to penetrate any existing roof construction; I can attest to it that they did so most effectively.

The night I'm talking about was a night for the British bombers. We soon heard the staccato noise of hundreds of small bombs falling onto the neighboring streets where they started to burn without causing any harm.

"What's that noise, Celli?" I asked her.

"Those are these terrible incendiary bombs that the British are dropping. If you hear so many of them falling nearby, it is quite possible that our house has already been hit. No matter what anybody says about staying in the cellar, let's go upstairs to inspect our roof top to see what's going on."

Our apartment house had a flat roof construction, not very solid, and most likely constructed of wooden beams covered only by boards and tarpaper. That construction was an easy target for the bombs to penetrate. If they did, they landed immediately inside the apartments on the top floor.

We rode the elevator to the top floor, because fortunately, and, at the same time, unexplainably, the electricity had not been cut off. Then we climbed the few remaining stairs to the door of the roof entrance, opened it, carefully peeked outside and were confronted with an eerie sight.

Beams of hundreds of high-powered anti-aircraft floodlights were sweeping back and forth across the dark, cloud-covered sky. The floodlights looked like huge, searching, dancing fingers, moving slowly across the low hanging clouds as they tried to find their targets. Most of the time the clouds rendered them unsuccessfully, and they couldn't lock the beam onto the planes flying overhead to get a bearing for the anti- aircraft batteries. Thousands of shells were exploding all over the sky like gigantic fireworks, and the shrapnel was raining on to the streets clattering in a deadly staccato. Some houses nearby, and others as far the eye could see into the distance, were already burning.

"I can't see any fire or smoke rising from our roof, Celli," I yelled at her through the earsplitting noise. "But look at the building next to ours, there is some smoke rising from the roof. Do you see it?"

"Let's go down quickly in the elevator and up the next building, but get the janitor first. I know that he has the keys to every apartment in both buildings," she yelled back.

Down we went back to the cellar where our heroic janitor was trying to stay away from trouble.

"Come on; let's go, Mr. Sedlmaier," I barked at him. "Take all your keys for the building next door and some manual operated water pumps. There is fire on the top floor."

He followed us quickly but reluctantly dragging two pumps with him. We went up with the elevator next-door. Sure enough, as soon as we stepped out of the cage, we saw smoke oozing out from under the door of the apartment on the left. He opened the door with one of his many keys. The flames suddenly released from captivity, fed with fresh oxygen caused by the suction of the open door and the hallway behind it, exploded in our faces like from a flamethrower. We backed away quickly, which was difficult for me on my crutches, and slammed the door shut.

"Get a blanket! Drench it in water! Wrap it around your head! That way you can go inside and connect a hose to a faucet. Hurry, or the whole house is going up in flames. Don't forget, Sedlmaier, your apartment is in here too," I shouted at the panic stricken man.

Finally, when I mentioned his apartment and his own possessions, he saw the urgency and understood that time was of the essence.

"And get me the key to the apartment below this one as well. I'll need to open it, to make a phone call to the fire department. I don't know whether I'll succeed, but we have to try to get whatever help we can on a night like this. I think that this fire is too big for our little pumps."

That's what I did. Marcella stayed with the *Hausmeister* to make sure he would do as he was told. He was working with the little hose, spraying a thin jet of water at the roaring flames. Our pump was a joke and only helpful for a short time, as Celli told me later on. The fire grew bigger, feeding hungrily off the dry furniture and the carpets on the floor. The flames quickly got the upper hand. With the little pump alone, we would've lost the battle against the fire for sure, and the building would've burned to the ground and with it, our building too.

By comparison, the disaster hadn't been too bad for a night like this with relatively few fires burning around us. A fireman at the fire station answered after the tenth ring. I gave him the address of our house and a little sob story about a soldier on crutches, just home from the war. He said that he would see if he could spare a few men. Wouldn't you know six minutes later three guys came rushing up to the fourth floor? They took one look at the situation, ran downstairs again and came racing back up the stairs hoisting and dragging a professional hose behind them. They'd hooked the hose up to the hydrant on the street. Water with plenty of pressure and in vast quantities poured out of the hose. To my great relief I saw that they would be able to handle the situation and extinguish the fire.

To be frank, it was high time that help arrived. If I hadn't gotten off my feet, I would've fainted. Hopping around with the crutches and spending weeks in bed at the hospital hadn't improved my over-all physical condition or stamina. I was exhausted. The women in the house were also worn out from fighting the fire and from running about. Most of them weren't the youngest any more and wouldn't have been able to handle the situation by themselves. I told Celli to stick around for a while and left whispering to her, "I'll hobble to our apartment. I have to lie down."

I made it back with a concentrated effort, crutches and all, went into her bedroom and fell on her bed fully clothed, filthy from the fire and the soot. Within seconds I was sound asleep.

I must've been dead to the world, because I didn't hear her come home. She had undressed me as difficult as that must've been with my cast, and she had cleaned me up. I didn't feel a thing.

I finally woke up to a wonderfully excruciating feeling. At first it appeared to me to be one of those pleasant dreams young men have when their juices become too abundant and are overflowing all by themselves. Then I opened my eyes and saw Celli kneeling at the side of the bed, and I realized totally startled that something else was happening. Actually, she had all of me in her mouth, between her lips, and her tongue was dancing a tango around the tip of my meat man. She didn't pay any at-tention as I lifted my head, and she hadn't noticed my opened eyes. She kept her eyes closed while continuing her activities with great passion and deliberation. I thought I would explode any minute and opened my mouth to cry out, but all I could produce was a slow agonizing moan. She raised her head looking at me with a big smile crossing her face.

"Ah, my tired old warrior has recovered. I'm glad I found the right medicine for you, my darling Peter. What do you say? Want some more?"

"Oh, Celli," I moaned, "I feel as if I've woken up in heaven. No, don't do that again, or we'll have a serious eruption. You'd better find a way to get us together quickly and more comfortably for you with this darned cast in the way, or we'll both die of frustration."

"Don't worry one sec, Peter. While waking you up, I've made exact plans for the two of us. Lie back comfortably and I'll put a pil-low under your head. You know, your head has to come up a bit so that you can better observe what we're doing. Otherwise it's only half the fun for both of us. And don't forget the most important thing when making love is that you have to give a running commentary on how you feel, how things are developing with you what you want to do and want me to do. And all the time you have to tell me that you love me."

She busily arranged the pillows behind me and moved my head on the pillow the way she had planned. Only now did I notice that all she was wearing was a beautifully transparent, flimsy something or the other, which permitted my hungry eyes an almost unobstructed view of her beautiful, trim body.

Celli had just the right size breasts, not too boyish, but sexy, up-right and firm, and her equally firm behind was to die for. She hud-dled over me permitting me to cuddle those two wonderful breasts of hers, which I'd only just discovered while kissing and squeezing them lightly. She threw her head back and moaned from the depth of her throat. I pulled her down a bit to kiss her on the mouth and to sink deeply into those luscious, enticing, hungry lips.

I'd seen these lips in front of my eyes during countless dreams in lonely cold foxholes, on smelly straw bedding and in hospital wards, tempting me teasingly to kiss them and to taste them, only to elude me and to fade away as dreams do when you wake up.

Now it was for real, and I was savoring the feeling in total ec-stasy. At this moment the world owed me nothing, and I didn't worry about anything, "I was in heaven."

Celli was excited, very excited, but she wasn't in heaven yet. She was going to show me what it would take to transport her to the same level that I was on. She was going to teach me, in detail, all those things, which a good lover—in her eyes—should do and say. I finally understood what my father had tried to convey to me with his advice about older women.

"Peter, Darling, if you love them that much, you have to give both of them a name, you know. That way we can talk about them in the presence of other people who are not supposed to know about what and whom we're talking. Come on, one name for each of them, never to forget! Think of a nice name."

She kept coaxing me while I had totally different ideas and de-sires. I was as anxious to start with the real thing, as any young man in my situation would've been. I looked at them, kissed them and thought that they looked rather audacious with their pink nipples standing straight in the air tempting me to do more caressing and kissing.

"I tell you, Celli, these two beauties look as brazen as anything I've ever seen, so, I'll call them after two brazen characters from stories by Wilhelm Busch, Max and Moritz. That's it."

For a moment she turned white as a sheet, and I thought she was going to faint. Then she bent down, kissed me on my eyes and said, "That's what your father called them, and, if that is not a coincidence, I don't know what is. But," she continued laughingly; "this way they don't have to get used to a new name."

In my own mind I thought that my old man must've had a laugh at that, wherever he was.

"Darling," she continued, 'we've to name two more members of the group before we really can get acquainted."

Straddling me she lifted herself up onto her knees straightened her upper body and held her love nest in front of my face. She had light blond hair everywhere like she had on her head. A little pink was peeking out through the middle.

"Come on, Peter. If you want to love her, we have to be able to talk about her, and I'll have to be able to tell you how she feels at all times. I have to be able to write to you about her when you are gone again and do so without the censor's interference. Same as with Max and Moritz, I want to be able to talk to you about how she feels regardless where we are and with whom we are at any moment."

This was a great idea, and I couldn't think of anything that I would've liked more to talk about than her pussy.

"Susie," I blurted out. 'That's what I'm going to call her from now on. She laughed happily and accepted my name without further ado.

"Now we have to give you a name, my huge upright love." She took my penis into her hands and said: "I christen you Leu, the name for all fairy tale lions. He looks strong like a lion, and I'm sure he'll be firm and strong like a lion."

I thought that with all this name giving we would never come to the interesting part.

I took her down over my face and was kissing "Susie" with my lips and tongue passionately and with abandon. Of course, with her directions on how to go about it, what to touch, where to lick and where to suck until, with an exuberantly lustful and shattering cry of pleasure, she'd her first roaring orgasm.

"Man, oh, man, Peter, baby. If you're new at this, you're learning fast, this was exquisite, better than I have ever experienced before. But now comes the real action."

Slowly she lowered herself onto "Leu" and me. "Little Susie" finally swallowed up "Big Leu." I'd almost thought it was never going to happen.

Of course, I hadn't told Celli about my adventure in France with Chou-Chou. Something told me that it wouldn't have been such a good idea. To Celli I was a virgin, and it was better that we left it that way. It probably added to the thrill she was experiencing. These two women and my feelings for them couldn't possibly be compared. Right now I was in love, terribly in love, which made all the difference.

"Tell me how you're feeling, Peter," she purred, as she was moving up and down slowly. "Remember when we're together you always have to tell me everything you feel."

She exhaled, arching her back, breathing heavily and moving ever so slowly.

"I can't describe what I feel, Celli," I moaned. "The feeling is too wonderful to put into words. Susie is the softest and at the same times most muscular creation on earth. Stop massaging me like that or I'll blow my load right into Susie's face."

She didn't listen to me but kept on going, moving slowly up and down, moaning with her eyes closed and her head thrown backwards. We both stopped making intelligent noises now as she was beginning to move more aggressively. We were nearing the end of the road, which we both reached at the same time. The sensation was that of excruciatingly bright fireworks exploding in my brain, taking me away into a heretofore undiscovered realm.

She was on top of me now, Susie still twitching temptingly and at the same time very softly and totally drenched.

"Darling, you made love exquisitely. I don't think I have ever been as satisfied as I'm now. . . . even though right now it feels more and more like I could go another round."

I couldn't have agreed more, and together we were traveling again on the road to heaven, talking, groaning and moaning and giving each other the feeling of never ending love until another mind boggling orgasm left us lying in each other's arms, totally spent.

She stopped twitching. She kissed me softly on the lips, just on the lips and without her tongue intruding into my mouth in search of mine.

"Did I hurt your leg by moving up and down?"

"Of course you hurt my leg," was my reply. "But it was my third leg, the one in the middle. Look how soft and weak Leu has become."

We laughed and cuddled and were happy in each other's arms repeating our tryst passionately in the early hours of the morning as first night lovers often do.

In between, during a waking moment all by myself, I determined that I didn't regret for one minute my decision to let her lead me to wherever we were going to go.

Everybody can guess what we did for the next few weeks morning noon and night. Celli lived, breathed and thought about nothing but sex. That's what her life was all about. She was not a nymphomaniac, hating men. No, she sincerely enjoyed sex. The ideas and techniques she could develop to change the routine and to give everything a new twist were unbelievable. In a way she was insatiable, which for me, at nineteen, was just what the doctor ordered.

We would go out, for instance, visiting people or watching an early movie at the cinema, and she'd turn around looking at me seriously and intently and say, "We have to go home, because we can't leave Susie alone that long. I can feel that she is terribly lonely."

We would rush home as fast as we could and screw our brains out.

My cast, of course, was a limiting factor, and I wished that I could've moved more freely. I also began to be sick and tired of the crutches.

The day arrived, after six weeks had passed, when I had to return to Vienna to see the doctor and hopefully to remove the cast. Celli accompanied me to the station, of course. When I leaned through the open window of the passenger compartment she said within earshot of about a dozen people, "I don't know about Leu, but Susie will be so lonely I can't even begin to tell you."

I must have blushed because she laughed mischievously and blinked her left eye at me.

"Don't worry, Darling, there are things between heaven and earth only you and I are able to understand."

She threw me a kiss, while the train started to move out of the station. To tell the truth, I was grateful for a little rest.

My old friend, the *Stabsarzt* in Vienna, was satisfied with the condition of my leg. After looking at my x-ray, which displayed the position of the bullet and the mended bones, he decided to leave it where it was. He explained to me that it would encapsulate fully and wouldn't hurt or do any further harm. He ordered physical therapy for me to regain the mobility of the hip joint and also asked me whether I could and would exercise by myself. If I could, he would send me home to workout by myself, or he could get me supervision and help. I accepted the offer to learn my exercises in the hospital's rehab center. I realized as soon as I was peeled out of the cast that my limbs wouldn't obey me. All my upper thigh muscles and tendons on the left side had been immobilized by the cast and hadn't been used for six weeks. They needed to be trained and exercised.

Six weeks later I was transferred to a hospital in Berlin to spend the rest of my rehab closer to home. Actually the hospital was only a half-mile from where Celli lived.

Wow!!! Wouldn't you know? The *Stabsarzt* in the end had come through as a compassionate man? He had come a long way since our first encounter, and I couldn't thank him enough. He also wrote a grave "expert opinion" of my injury and the consequences for the mobility of my leg if the bullet were not given enough time to encapsulate in the muscle or in the tissue structure near the joint. He wrote further that the bullet could also move sideways and lodge itself in the muscles of the thigh away from the joint. Either way, he stated that in his expertise, I needed rest and continuous physical therapy.

So far, so good. What I needed now was for the war to be over in a hurry. Christmas passed and spring of 1944 arrived. The war wore on with no sign of abating. The Germans were hanging in there with next to nothing. The doctors in the hospital in Berlin were sympathetic to my desire to prolong my recuperation time as long as possible, but they also had to live by the rules of the powers in force.

Four weeks later a commission of SS doctors arrived in the hospital to check on the performance of the staff and to insure the strict observance of regulations. They examined several other soldiers as well as me. After examining my leg they said abruptly: "KV" those famous two letters that decided so many lives during the war (KV or *Kriegsverwendungsfähig* = okay for war).

When I came home from the hospital that night and told Celli about it she started to cry. No, she was screaming hysterically, but there was no way out. We had spent three fabulous months together loving each other with the abandon of lemmings ready for the plunge into the ocean. We'd exploited the possibilities of love making to their ultimate depth, Celli, with her never-ending inventiveness and I, submitting to her as an eager pupil. I'd take this experience with me and never forget any part of it. My education had been detailed full of pleasure and only needed a little polishing every once in a while.

The 'goodbye' was tearful. She told me the same nonsense that my mother had told me: "Be careful!"

If it had been up to me, I would've hidden in the Black Forest just to be careful, but it wasn't up to me. I would have to think of something else. The Americans were in Italy. Maybe I could get a transfer to Italy and a chance to defect?

My conscience was bothering me, because I hadn't called and had written only a few times to my mother since her visit to the hospital in Vienna. I went to the office of the Schwarzlose Company and tried to place a call to Switzerland. It was a difficult undertaking, because the censors wanted to know what my call was all about and whether or not it was urgent. I finally convinced them that it was a business matter, vital to the war effort of the German Reich and more of the same bullshit.

After a four-hour wait I finally heard her voice.

"Peter, where are you? I haven't heard from you in ages, I didn't seem to be able to get a connection to talk to you from here."

"*Mutti*, I am sorry. I should've tried myself before, but time was flying by and rehab in the hospital didn't give me a chance," I lied shamelessly. "My leg is much better now, but no sooner did it improve than they're sending me back to the shooting war. If the scuttlebutt I've been hearing is correct, my outfit will be sent to Italy. I'll call you from there, okay?"

It was time to end our conversation, because the operator cut in and reminded us that many other people were waiting to make calls, and our conversation didn't sound very important to the German Reich. Bastards!

We said good-bye quickly and were cut off.

I felt awful. I'd acted like a real skunk shacking up with the woman my mother hated most of all in this world and forgetting her in the process. I promised myself that would never happen again.

4

THE WAR IN ITALY

When I arrived in *Kottbus* it was early March of 1944. The hospital administration in Berlin had ordered us to return to the barracks of our reserve units. For me that was the 122nd Communication Company in *Kottbus*. To my reckoning, and my ever so wishful thinking, the war should've been over by now or should be soon.

At this stage of the game the Germans were certainly running the war on a shoestring. While in Russia I had seen that ammunition wasn't only scarce for the artillery, but also in many cases for the Infantry as well. We didn't have any air support for the ground troops and let's not talk about the paucity of tanks. Where were the famous *Panzer?* Germany's resources were spread extremely thin. With the war conducted on four fronts, in Russia, Africa, Italy and on the Atlantic coastline, the Biscayne in France all the way to the northern most point in Scandinavia, without mentioning Yugoslavia and Albania—there was hardly enough hardware to go around.

The lack of equipment was especially frustrating for the units involved in day-to-day combat. An enormous amount of equipment was tied up in anticipation of an Allied invasion on the coast of France. This material was badly needed, to hold off the rapidly advancing Russian armies in the east.

The so-called Allies were no allies but rather a burden. German paratroopers had to free *"El Duce,"* Benito Mussolini, after an uprising of some of his own generals who had incarcerated him, the nincompoop.

The African theater of war was on the verge of collapsing, and in Italy the Germans had a hard time holding off advancing Americans and their allies who had plenty of ammunition, artillery and airplanes. Once they'd gotten a hold of the continent, landing in Sicily and wading ashore near Anzio, 60 miles south of Rome, the Germans were on the run. The Nazis were only able to hold onto to power by applying all the brutality they could muster.

So far there was no visible sign of any move by the Allies on the Channel coast. I clandestinely listened to the BBC news broadcasts, but they didn't come forward with any predictions for the end of the war either. The Allies would certainly succeed if they attempted an invasion of France. At least I felt they would succeed, and the war would be over in no time at all. But . . . could I and would I survive that long?

I had nursed and prolonged my leg injury as long as possible. Now, in the spring of 1944, I had to admit that I failed. I was on my way to another theater of the war.

The 122nd Communications Company in *Kottbus,* from what I could detect, was replenishing its reserves either with children, old men, or cripples. For me it was one more sign that it looked bad for the Nazis if they were now depending on men like me to continue the war.

On the very first day after my arrival in *Kottbus,* I ran into my old buddy Karl. We fell into each other's arms happy to see to see each other. Happy that we'd both weathered our misfortunes on the Russian front and had come out alive. As we sat down in the canteen for a cup of watery coffee, he told me he had suffered a slight injury to his left arm during the debacle near *Bjelgorod.* He'd been able to delay his recovery—same as I had—but was now pronounced KV. He was no more keen to return to the shooting gallery, where we were *"the set ups,"* than I was. We hugged again and exchanged tales of our adventures of the last several months.

"What happened to all of the others after I was carried off?" I inquired. "How did you ever get out of that shitty mess?"

"Looking back on the horror of the moment now and with the benefit of time, it was rather comical," he replied chuckling quietly to himself. "All of a sudden Lieutenant Seuffert appeared out of nowhere. You know he had the tendency to disappear when too much lead was flying through the air. He jumped on a passing personnel carrier and yelled to us: *'Rette sich wer kann'* ('Save yourselves if you can').

"With those very words as his parting message, he was gone—the idiot, the coward. I don't know what happened to him afterwards. He was totally out of his wits and couldn't be contained. He simply didn't know what was going on. And what was even worse he didn't care anymore! Of course, you know as well as anybody that when the enemy is in hot pursuit, you have to take a stand someplace or you're dead. Once you turn your back and run they can annihilate you with the greatest of ease. Consequently, the rest of us consolidated under the leadership of an astute captain and turned, dug in, and defended ourselves. To our great surprise we were supported by a few of our Panzer from an SS Division, which had finally reappeared. The whole area slowly stabilized. I guess Ivan was out of breath too. Soon thereafter our regiment, which had suffered heavy casualties, was withdrawn from the battle lines. Yes, and one more thing. The colonel and the first sergeant, your two favorite people, were killed by artillery fire; at least that's what I heard, by a direct hit on their command post. Now, that should give you piece of mind, Peter. Doesn't it?"

It did for more reasons than one. And now I was curious to find out what Karl had discovered about the plans by the "Brass" for our future.

"Do you know where they are planning to send us this time? I still have great difficulties walking and would like to be anything but an infantry soldier, that is, if I have a choice. I hear rumors that the 122nd, or what's left of it, is going to Italy."

"Yes, that's what I heard also; the scuttlebutt is about Italy. Some other units of the 223d Infantry Division are assembling near *Rimini* on the Adriatic coast. It's only scuttlebutt for now, but Italy is pleasant at this time of the year, don't you think? Much better than Russia, I'd hate to be in that mess again. Tell me, my friend," he asked, as he glanced at me sideways, "before we get any deeper into speculations about our next assignment, whatever developed in the relationship with your beautiful stepmother? Did you follow my advice? Or did you succumb to temptation?"

"Without telling you a long story, Karl, I succumbed. Considering what may lie in store for us if this war continues much longer, it was worth every minute of it. She was very sweet, very sexy, and, frankly, I don't give a damn what happens afterwards. Let the war be over first, and let us return safely with all our limbs in place. Then and only then will I worry whether it was right or wrong to fuck my stepmother, okay? And now let's close the subject; I don't want to talk about it anymore."

Karl shrugged his shoulders, and the subject was never mentioned again between us.

In *Kottbus* we were training with new wireless equipment and were introduced to new codes. I didn't go into town. I knew it from my last visit, and it wasn't worth the trip.

Our orders to transfer to the divisional staging area came at the end of March. Karl had been right with his prediction, it was Italy.

A German soldier, a corporal like me, not involved in actual fighting, received only RM 10 every ten days, and RM 20, if he was in actual combat. That's nothing now and it was nothing then. It was enough to buy cigarettes from the commissary and an occasional beer, but that was all. Other soldiers who had been in Italy told us that wine, food and girls were good, and all three were available everywhere. It sounded great, but in order to enjoy all or some of it, you needed Italian Lira. Naturally, we were debating what we could do to exchange money. Or, even better, get something of value to the Italians we were going to deal with. They explained to us that we had two choices of payment, since no Italian in his right mind would take paper Reich Marks in payment or in exchange for anything. We needed either RM 5 coins, or we needed flint-stones for cigarette lighters.

Let me explain. The RM 5 coins contained about 50 percent silver, and Italians accepted them gladly in exchange for paper lira, which to them were worth nothing, but it was the legal tender. The silver in the coins would retain its value even after the war.

Flint-stones were another matter entirely. In those days Italy had a "State Match Monopoly." Some clever financial adviser of *El Duce* had convinced his government that taxes collected from selling matches would create far more revenue for the state than if they permitted the use of lighters, which earned nothing for the government. Consequently, possession or the sale of lighters was strictly forbidden by the fascist regime of Benito Mussolini. There was a substantial penalty if one disobeyed. Even if you wanted to disobey you needed three things—a lighter, lighter fluid and flint-stones. You couldn't buy replacement flint-stones in Italy, though there were lighters, and that was the opening for us to beat the system. Karl found out that flint-stones were sold for 100 Lira each on the black market. A hundred Lira was enough to buy plenty of delicious Italian wine and many other wonderful things to eat or to drink. Flint-stones served well as trading items for everything. That was valuable information. We had to get flint-stones.

Luck is an extremely necessary commodity not only in normal life, but especially if you are a soldier and are involved in a war. Karl and I had already proved that we were lucky. After all, we were still alive.

Our good fortune was confirmed once again when we heard of a small workshop in a village near *Kottbus* whose owner made a living by manufacturing and selling "Flint-stones" and other parts for lighters. We went to see him immediately. It was not easy to convince the proprietor that we needed flint-stones desperately. With our irrepressible charm we promised him we would be making it worth his while if he would be willing to circumvent the ubiquitous German rationing system and its watchdogs and sell us some flint-stones. He explained to us in great detail how he was obligated by rules of a wartime economy to deliver his entire production to the Government. We listened to his arguments with great though strained patience. He started to listen to our overtures and pleas only after we promised to send him a few cases of delicious Italian Chianti as soon as we had arrived in Italy in lieu of payment in Reich Marks. He considered our offer for only a short moment and gave us a bag with 500 *(FIVE HUNDRED!)* flint-stones. In Germany a flint-stone was worth pennies. In Italy they would be worth a fortune. Within weeks we filled our part of the bargain and sent him fifty bottles of a special *Chianti Classico;* by courier from Bologna. The courier was paid in (guess what?) flint-stones.

Now we were ready to face Italy, its beauty and its challenges, if only we could stay away from its shooting gallery.

Our first destination was Milan where we received new uniforms and a new advanced DORA communications unit. While we were in Milan we also had to face inspections by some military big shot every second day.

One of the inspectors was the notorious Colonel General Heinrici, a particularly objectionable "warmonger" who had key responsibilities on the Italian front at that time.

We assembled and stood at attention as he examined our attire and military bearing. Of course, he had to make a speech. They all have to make speeches about heroism, the *Führer,* the war (which would be won, of course) party discipline and a lengthy enumeration full of ineffectual, pathetic encouragements to go out and fight one more time and to die for the *Fatherland,* willingly.

During his speech he emphasized that he favored and especially respected those soldiers who had bullets or shrapnel embedded in their bodies as a irrefutable proof of their selfless service to the Fatherland. Soldiers who were here in Italy to fight for the final victory of Germany and its glorious *Führer,* Adolf Hitler, *der grösste Feldherr aller Zeiten* (the greatest General of all times, his very own words). To us soldiers that abbreviated into *Gröfaz.*

Listening to this horseshit almost made me sick to my stomach, but I managed to keep my face under control. I had learned it the hard way. When he was finished, he looked around with a smug, self-satisfied face and strutted down the line of assembled men asking them, one after the other, a few personal questions about their past military history. He stopped in front of me and barked in a loud grating voice and in staccato sentences.

"Nice decoration you have, Corporal; Iron Cross second-class, Silver Medal for three injuries, soldier, why are you still a corporal?"

"Generaloberst, Sir, I don't know, Sir. It might be I have spent too much time in hospitals, Sir. I also still have a bullet in my hip joint. I cannot move around well. I know of no other reason, Generaloberst, Sir."

"I'll check you out, Corporal; I need people like you even if they are limping."

He moved on down the line to continue his inspection, and I never heard from him again. He probably discovered my "questionable" background, so much the better for me. I wasn't eager to be near this guy or to be pushed by him most likely from one suicidal mission to another.

Karl had excellent sources to get information, because after a few days we received our marching orders for *Rimini*.

Nobody who knows the bustling resort town of *Rimini* today, located on the beautiful, blue Adriatic Sea, 35 miles south of *Ravenna,* would imagine that once upon a time, in 1944, it was a small, sleepy little town. For Italians it was a resort with the benefit of the sea, a very pretty one. Back then, foreigners, especially German civilians had not discovered it.

We were directed to battalion headquarters located a few miles out of town in a beautiful villa with a huge park. Our officers surely knew how to requisition the best of the best. They had been spoiled by wonderful *chateaux* in France, which they had occupied before they came to Italy via Russia. Our designated quarters turned out to be in a small house at the edge of town. The house was kind of square and ugly, built of solid red brick, two stories high with ceramic tile floors throughout to keep it cool during the hot summer. Other soldiers, telephone guys from the 122nd, were already there. We actually met quite a few men who had been with us in Russia. Most of them had also been wounded near *Bjelgorod* and spent time in hospitals and at home. The central switchboard for the Battalion was located on the ground floor of our house. Even we, the short wave operators, had to take turns working on the switchboard to keep the telephone lines open day and night. What an insult to our status as the cream of the communication group. I am kidding, of course. Our telephone buddies were all nice guys and would help us with our work of decoding, or with messenger duties when the going got rough, so we helped them with their tedious switchboard duty.

The man in charge of the entire communications group for the battalion was Staff Sergeant Losanski. The Iron Cross II and I class, the Black Medal for one injury and, very exceptionally, the Silver Infantry Close Combat Wings for twenty-five close combat engagements, were attached to his uniform. The exact definition for the latter was: *Twenty-five attacks on an enemy position where you see the white in the enemy's eyes.* He was seasoned, calm and exuded confidence. I was happy to have him as a superior rather than a cowardly, inexperienced idiot like Lieutenant Seuffert. Losanski was a

straight shooter and a man one could get along with. We would find
out more about him as soon as we got closer to actual fighting. In the
meantime our life was routine and easy going and as far as we're
concerned could've gone on forever.

The house had been "intervened" by German armed forces. We
never saw the owner. It was completely empty, and we had to go to
the quartermaster to obtain some bunk beds with straw mattresses.
In the back of the building was a small garden with a narrow brook
passing by. The brook was also the border to the adjacent property.
We pushed a board, about a foot and a half wide across the six feet
wide brook. In the morning that was our "bathroom," always with
running fresh water. Kneeling on the board we dipped our hands in
the cool water, washing our faces to wake up, brushing our teeth to
get ready for the day.

One morning, as I was kneeling on the board scooping cold
water onto my face to overcome my hangover from the previous
night's drinking too much Italian red wine, I felt something wiggling
and squirming in my hands. As difficult as it was to open my eyes in
my condition I looked at it and discovered a small puppy, just a wet
ball of fur. It must have been born only minutes earlier. Its eyes were
still closed. The owner of the mother-dog had thrown the entire lit-
ter into the brook to get rid of it once and for all.

I carefully carried the puppy inside to show it to my comrades.
I wanted to ask them whether anybody knew what to do with a newborn dog. We had a few farmers' sons amongst us who told me immediately to put the puppy back where I had found it. It was too
young to make it without the bitch's milk, they explained to me. That
wasn't good enough for me. I always loved dogs and wanted one
badly when I was a child. Now I had one, and I wasn't going to give
it up without making a determined effort to save it.

"Peter, listen to us experts and throw the pup back into the water
where you've found it. It's too young. You'll not be able to feed it.
You don't have the right size tits."

My old friend Erich from the brothel in *Fécamp* had made one
of his "intelligent" remarks. The Russians had shot his pinky off, but
it hadn't changed him one bit. He was still as stupid, ignorant and

foulmouthed as I remembered him. The guys who overheard him all laughed cruelly, those assholes. I didn't think he or his cruel remarks were funny at all. Erich's negative interference, if anything, stiffened my resolve about the puppy. He wasn't going to change my mind. This dog was going to live even if I had to inject milk directly into his stomach.

"Maybe I don't have the right size tits," I replied, "but in contrast to you I have the right size brain. I'll make some right size tits. I already have an idea how to do it. As soon as the dog gets big enough, I'll train her to take a piece out of your fucking ass."

I put the pup on my bed, wrapped it in a blanket and asked Karl to watch it carefully, while I went to a candy shop nearby. I bought a small toy-baby-bottle filled with candy-coated sugar pearls, like young girls use when they're pretending to feed their dolls. The bottle was small, just big enough for one ounce of liquid. Even so, for lack of anything else, it had to do. I carried it back to our house where Karl and I warmed up some regular milk on our stove, just enough to be lukewarm. Then I heated a sewing needle to puncture three holes into the thin, tiny rubber nipple. If this thing was good enough, according to my thinking, for the little girls to play their games of mother and child feeding the dolls, it certainly was good enough for my little dog. Karl was a real buddy and watched the little pup in the meantime. I thought I had done as good job as I could, when we turned the bottle upside down and saw that some milk penetrated through the punctured nipple. Now came the test—would the puppy be fooled?

"Karl, take the puppy and we'll see if we can make her drink from this 'thing.' Just put her down on her side as if she was feeding from her mother's tits."

Karl did what I suggested, and I pushed the tiny rubber nipple into the mouth of the puppy. Nothing happened during the first two or three attempts. The puppy turned its head slightly displaying a total lack of interest, quacked a little and let go of the nipple.

"Maybe you've got to wet the nipple with warm milk on the outside to give the puppy a taste of milk. The taste of dry rubber must be awful," Karl suggested.

"Man," I shouted. "What a great idea! We'll make you the official wet nurse."

I dipped the nipple into the warm milk and we tried again. This time the puppy kept the nipple in its mouth to lick off the milk and low and behold continued sucking. It worked! It worked! The milk in the bottle gradually disappeared into the tummy of our ward. When the bottle was empty the puppy quacked a little and we hurried up to prepare a refill, which disappeared into her stomach just as quickly.

"I hope she keeps it down and doesn't throw up," I worried.

We were lucky. Asta, that was the name Karl and I had given our puppy, prospered and drank, kept us up all night, peed into the blanket and opened her eyes after a few days to take a look at the world around her and at her foster parents.

We both were as happy as we could be. We had adopted a little puppy.

"I hope we don't have to go on some stupid maneuver, because I don't think the others would be going through all the troubles that we've been going through to feed her. Let's get Staff Sergeant Losanski involved. He seems to be a reasonable individual and could keep us covered until the pup grows a little bigger and more independent." I proposed.

And that's what we did the very same day. When we approached him and told him the story of the puppy, he was very sympathetic to our plight.

"I had three dogs at home," he told us. "One of them was a German shepherd and from the looks of it, that's what this dog is going to be. I miss my dog terribly. They are great company. I've no objection to this one. Just watch out that he does not chew on wires or electric cords, it might kill him."

Of course, we agreed with him enthusiastically. We were also very relieved and promised to keep him abreast of the progress Asta was making.

He'd taken a liking to our puppy that had acquired a powerful guardian.

Our life in *Rimini* proceeded as life in a communication group usually does; this one located one hundred miles behind the front lines. We practiced incessantly, kept our weapons clean, and tested our equipment. It also kept us busy.

Every so often American Super Fortress bombers on missions to targets further north flew high overhead trailing white vapor. One day one of them, a huge bomber with four engines, passed low over *Rimini* with black smoke trailing from its engines. A lonely ME 109 chased it. The bomber was limping badly with only three of its four engines running and sputtering. To become lighter and more agile, trying to get away from the deadly fighter plane, the bomber dropped all of its remaining bombs right over *Rimini*. On their way down the bombs made the same terrible howling noise that I remembered from the air raids in Berlin, sitting in the cellar with Celli. We took cover until the last bomb hit the ground. We didn't see what happened to the bomber, but its deadly load of bombs caused destruction to civilian buildings in town. A farmhouse near our quarters was hit and severely damaged. We knew the farmhouse and the people because we bought fresh milk for Asta from the farmer. Staff Sergeant Losanski ordered a rescue party to go to the farmhouse. We grabbed some picks and shovels and ran over, on the double, to see how we could help. The farmhouse had collapsed, and people seemed to be buried underneath the rubble. We started digging furiously and soon we had found the farmer. He was still alive but had suffered a badly crushed leg.

Just at that moment an older woman came running over to where we were digging. It was his wife. She was cursing violently, swinging at us wildly with a piece of wood in her hands as if she were out of her mind. "Those cursed Germans," she was yelling, "had already killed her son and others in his family as well. These sons of a cursed Madonna were to blame for all the evil, which had conquered her blessed homeland. We should all die and rot in hell, and our women at home should die of the plague instantly."

She didn't complain about Mussolini, though. The precious *"Il Duce"* had joined the Nazis in their war in 1940. He was eager to participate in the spoils, to get some pieces of real estate from France and maybe all of Albania. No, she cursed us as we were trying to extricate her husband. To add insult to injury, everybody knew that the rural population had been the biggest supporters of *"Il Duce"* during gigantic rallies, when he was dressed to the nines in an ornate uniform of a General Field Marshal of the Fascist movement wearing a ridiculous, polished steel helmet on his bald head.

We made a feeble attempt to calm her down, unsuccessfully I might add, and continued to dig through the rubble until we were certain that no more casualties could be found.

The episode with the old farmer's woman who had been vociferously venting her hatred of Germans bothered us a lot. Karl and I were sitting together discussing it until all hours of the night, wondering.

"If even our Allies hate us," he observed philosophically, "how can we manage to win this war? I know that opposing nations hate us intensely, that's normal, but our Allies? I'm starting to believe the stories about atrocities and slavery and other things I've been hearing. I mean, at home, you hear those stories in cellars while bombs are falling and people get angry about the war. But I never believed it. I'd thought that these stories were only inspired by fear and disgust about the war."

I didn't know how to reply. Karl was my friend. I trusted him, but I wasn't going to reveal that I'd heard these and similar stories before while listening to the news from the BBC. With my earphones on my head, the volume turned real low, I'd listened to reports about concentration camps and the conduct of the SS murderers and all that. It was better to keep my mouth shut. All I said as a comment was, "I guess there must be something to it. Why would people be talking? Let's just you and I make a strenuous effort to get out of this war alive, not get shot by our opponents, not get killed by our own assholes; otherwise these bastards will be the lonely survivors and God help us if that happens."

"If the hatred of the Germans is as deeply imbedded as we have witnessed today, even among the population of our allies, tell me, what'll happen after the war?" Karl looked at me expectantly with a troubled face, thinking I could alleviate his worries.

"You know where I am going my friend after all this is over? I've told you. But I'm sure that coming out of this mess, everybody who participated in it in any way will be tainted, no matter what his excuses," I theorized.

Karl was silent for a long time and then addressed me again.

"You know, Peter, I wished that I could escape the consequences of this war as quickly and as painlessly as you probably will
but there's not a chance. It'll take generations until enough grass has
grown over all the miseries created by the Nazis and millions of people who have been killed during this war. Fortunately for me I have
no family left. My father died during the last days of World War I.
My older brother died in France, early, during the first days of this
war. My poor mother died a year ago of a broken heart. For her it is
better that way. It will take strong people to survive the aftermath of
this carnage, and to tell you the truth, the way I am feeling right now,
I don't know how I could return to my previous life, singing at the
Opera."

We became silent, each of us lost in his own thoughts and worries, and I might add, our hopes. We had an extremely naïve conception of how it would all end. Not even in our wildest dreams did
we imagine how terrible the end would really be. We had no idea at
all. We were just speculating. But, our final conclusion was that Germany would lose the war.

Weeks passed, and the summer of 1944 approached. It was getting warm as it should in Italy at that time of the year, and Asta grew
like a weed. Did she ever grow! We could only guess what kind of a
dog she would turn out to be. The Staff Sergeant was probably right
with his guess of a German shepherd. Asta ate lots of food by now,
and we had our hands full acquiring the necessary quantities, especially meat. Karl ventured a guess one day and said,

"I'll bet she will grow up to be a big dog. Look at the ears, the
tail and the big paws; she'll be a beauty. My God, she's going to eat
enough to send us to the poorhouse." We both laughed.

I went to the local butcher and asked him for scraps. He understood what I was talking about. My Italian was good enough for that.

Talking to girls we met at the local pub and conversing with
other civilians when the need arose, I'd made strenuous efforts to
pick up enough of the language to get around. I even went to the
movies, convinced that the combinations of words and pictures
would hasten my learning process, and it did. Aside from learning
Italian—little by little—it also turned out to be an education about

the differences in cultures. When entering a movie theatre I could hardly see the screen, because the patrons seemed to smoke without interruption. The noise from the film and patrons talking and yelling at each other was unbelievable. Different countries—different customs!

The staff sergeant made use of my talents, particularly my newly acquired language skills and asked me often to interpret for him. To learn Italian was not his cup of tea. I guess my studies of French and Latin in school finally paid off. It definitely helped me to speak and understand another difficult language even if it was only marginally.

The butcher was surprisingly cooperative. Normally the army's relationships with the local merchants weren't very good because the merchants didn't like to get paid in worthless paper money. It may have helped that I immediately slipped him two flint stones and indicated that there were more where they came from. Asta loved the scraps from the butcher. She ate like a horse and grew like a German shepherd. She also appeared to be a great diplomat, smiling at everybody and dancing around the guys, wagging her tail happily when they came home from their assignments. Her efforts were rewarded by the other who started to love her almost as much as we did. Even Erich joined the Asta fan club. Begging like an old pro, she got many little tidbits from all of them.

Occasional duty at the switchboard gave me the opportunity to make private phone calls, just what I'd been looking for. I did this with the help of female military operators working across Italy in major exchanges of the military telephone network. For them it was easy to invade the public telephone system. Once you were there, you'd connect to other countries as well. I talked to Marcella repeatedly who told me how lonely Susie was. For heaven's sake! What was I going to do? I was not any happier either, and, as the saying goes: "There is nothing you'll fall behind on so quickly . . ." and I had no opportunity to catch up anyway, and wasn't interested in taking advantage of the opportunities that were available. Her letters kept coming two or three times a week with pages upon pages of detailed descriptions of her life without me and of the war in Berlin. They were filled with declarations of how much she missed me, all of me, together with detailed descriptions how Susie felt, and what both of them would do to me, when they saw "us" again. I didn't have as much writing paper as she did, but I tried to respond as often as I could without telling her where we were and without revealing any other "war essential" military secrets.

The Italian girls I met in the local pub, which we frequented, called me *El Alemano biondo,* because of my blond hair. The women were friendly and flirtatious, but I just couldn't convince myself to crawl into bed with any one of them. Staff Sergeant Losanski who was involved with several of the girls laughed about my compunctions and advised me to carry a condom with me at all times.

"Forget your unwarranted scruples and whatever or whomever you have left behind," was his advice. "Give them some pleasure and enjoy yourself. They don't take it seriously, and you shouldn't take it seriously either. Have fun while you can, Corporal; you know as well as I do that under our present circumstances, life can be terminated rather quickly. I don't know how long we'll remain in peaceful, beautiful *Rimini,* but since the war continues unabated, a need for fresh troops (pardon the pun) increases daily."

Of course, he was right. But, considering my youthful and still idealistic opinion of love, the mating process was rather personal and had something to do with being at least a little bit in love with the person I made love to. The girls in the pub were too coarse for my taste, and, to tell the truth, I was spoiled. At this juncture I couldn't envision myself tumbling in the hay with any of them.

On rare occasions I also managed to get a telephone connection to Switzerland and was able to talk to Olga. Like mothers are all over the world, she was always happy to hear from me. She was full of worries and practical advice.

"Oh, Peter, Sonny Boy, am I happy to hear your voice! It means that you're alive and well. Be careful and don't volunteer to participate in any dangerous assignments, promise me, will you? Never forget; it's the German's war, not ours."

Ihr Wort in Gottes Ohr (Her words to God's ear), but what was I going to do about it? And when did I ever volunteer?

I promised, though, seeing no sense in arguing with her, or to open old wounds, to heed her advice and explained to her for the thousandth time that my feelings about the war were no different than hers. She was having a good time in Switzerland, though the country was experiencing some shortages of supplies and had introduced ration cards to its population like all the other European countries. Switzerland was not at war with anybody and, most importantly, had managed to keep the Nazis away from its territory.

"Mom, what are your plans? Do you want to remain where you are until the end of the war?"

"I don't know, Peter. But promise me to get in touch as soon as you know that you're coming home. I'll be in Berlin in a jiffy, okay?"

I told her that I'd keep in touch and promised the switchboard operator in Milan a case of wine for her help and cooperation.

Every day we were in Italy our flint-stones became more useful. We had never anticipated what a brilliant idea it would be to buy those little stones. They were worth their weight in gold. As far as food and drink went, Karl and I lived a good life. Almost everything was paid for in flint-stones. From our point of view the war could've gone on like this.

Spring had ended and summer was here. My dog was growing up to be a healthy German shepherd. Asta and I went on long walks together through the countryside, which she enjoyed like all dogs do. She ran into the fields, dug holes to find mice, or other creatures and barked excitedly when she returned, proudly showing me her prey. Italians, however, she detested like the plague. She must've known instinctively, or detected from their scent that one of them had tried to kill her at birth. At least I didn't have to be afraid of partisans during my walks. Asta could smell or sense a human being a mile away. She would perk up her ears and dart into a cornfield, barking, growling and making scary noises. I could often see figures disappearing on the far side of the field that she was exploring. Nobody wanted to tangle with a hostile, aggressive dog of her size, and she was growing up fast.

Asta was always lots of fun and good for a story. While she was still a puppy she was full of mischief and had to be watched constantly. One time, our cook had "requisitioned" a pig from a local farmer to get some fresh meat for us. He'd slaughtered the pig and had removed all the intestines, but hadn't cut the carcass into two halves. Sometime that afternoon we discovered Asta had disappeared, seemingly without a trace. Virtually everybody in our outfit was searching for her. We accused every Italian around us of having abducted, killed, or drowned her, because they had not succeeded the first time. She had perished from the face of the earth.

It was already getting dark, and we were still searching for her feverishly. Then as I passed the kitchen area—we were fed from one of these camp kitchens, a big kettle on wheels with a funnel on top—I heard loud snoring. There was nobody there; no person to be seen anywhere, except the carcass of the pig, carved out and lying there, on a low table, next to the camp kitchen. Then I saw it, a tiny piece of a dog's tail peeking out of the pig's rear side. Asta! The dog must've crawled inside the pig, feasted until she was ready to burst and then had fallen asleep.

I called everybody involved in the search to look at this picture of tranquility and total contentment—a dog's tail hanging out of the corpse of a slaughtered pig. We laughed and laughed until the cook came. He wasn't amused; he was ready to slaughter Asta but he calmed down quickly, and we added this story to the many other adventures of "Asta, Peter's dog."

It must've been at the end of May when "Alarm" sounded in the middle of night. The entire battalion scrambled and assembled in a hurry. We had orders to gather all our gear, to disassemble the equipment and to march south on the road alongside the Adriatic Sea, past *Pesaro,* towards *Cap Ancona,* a distance of about sixty miles. After months of idleness, in the hope that we could endure the rest of the war in *Rimini,* we were totally unprepared for this physical exertion, especially me.

I had been out that night with my usual gang and with a few Italian girls having a ball in the local pub, drinking, joking and laughing about nothing and everything. I had drunk much too much wine, not knowing that we were going to embark on a forced march with all equipment. I was still lying incoherently on my bed when the alarm surprised us. I didn't fathom what was going on.

A few weeks earlier we had received brand new uniforms with pants cut very similar to ski pants, tapered towards the bottom and fastened by a ribbon under each foot. The narrow cut of these pants saved precious cloth for the army's supply department. They were nice and tight and looked good on us when we were prancing around town. But the tightly fitting band under the foot was impractical as hell, especially for marching.

In the hectic minutes after the alarm and in my foggy state of mind, I'd tied the ribbon under each foot much too tightly. That drunken stupidity had disastrous consequences.

We packed our things in a hurry, disassembled the equipment, the switchboard, the DORA unit, everything. Asta was still too young for a long march. Besides, who could have marched in the dark amidst a column of soldiers with a young dog running back and forth? I put her into a carrying bag, hung the heavy beast around my neck and went to the assembly point for the battalion at the edge of town.

Our march began in a southerly direction—destination unknown. Everybody was unaware of what the night might reveal to us, but we knew we were going to join the *mêlée* again.

If anybody had asked me beforehand, I'd have given him a most convincing argument why my hip with the embedded bullet could never endure a march of sixty miles. However, while marching, and before the bullet in my hip joint had a chance to act up, or bother me in any way—whatever good it would have done me anyway—the tightly bound ribbons under my feet were demonstrating how small omissions can produce excruciatingly painful consequences. After fifteen miles of aggressive marching the ribbons caused the most painful pair of blisters I had ever experienced. They had formed all the way around the bottom of each foot, each blister three inches long.

After the first fifteen miles of our march we were granted a brief respite. I called the medic to check on my feet only to find out that he could do nothing to help me or to stop the pain. He took one look and said, "Wow, these are the biggest blisters, in the worst place, at the worst time I've ever seen. The only thing I can do is to open them up, disinfect the wounds and bandage your feet. After that I wish you good luck and endurance. From now on every mile will feel like twenty to you."

The reason for our march was a military emergency. There were no subterfuges or excuses I could have used as a plea not to march, when I might have made if the march had only been a maneuver. Worse, there was no transportation of any kind available. Even if we had transportation on wheels, we couldn't have employed it anyway. During the first night we crossed three riverbeds with totally demolished bridges. The American planes had bombed all of them meticulously. The riverbeds we crossed were at least a half-mile wide and filled with the remnants of the crumbled bridges. Though they were without water, that could change suddenly even after the smallest rainfall. We had seen how they would swell to torrential, devastating streams after only a short downpour and how they'd pull everything within reach downstream.

Since Italy had no natural resources, like coal, steel or oil, generation after generation of Italians had depleted the forests for the purpose of turning the wood into building materials, or, in the old days, wooden sailing ships or for charcoal to be used as fuel for cooking. Bare and without trees, slopes and mountainsides had no way to absorb the water. The remaining thin layer of soil couldn't retain any serious precipitation.

No motorized column had a chance to cross the rivers without bridges. The American bombers had done a thorough job of destroying the German supply lines.

I will not attempt to tell you in detail about my agonies, marching for the next forty-five miles on blisters. It was an almost unbearable experience. The key word is 'almost,' because I made it. Even Asta made it with the help of many of her friends. Karl carried her most of the way without complaining. He was a great friend, not only to me, but also to *our* dog. Asta demonstrated with her behavior later during the campaign, whenever Karl was around her, that she remembered his TLC and loved him dearly.

After arriving at our destination south of *Cesano,* a small town on the Adriatic coast, we were granted a day's rest for recuperation. The men had lived a soft life for too long. Nobody was in shape physically for an ordeal like this march. The soldiers fell to the ground and slept wherever they had stopped walking.

I was tired too, but my mind was elsewhere. We were getting closer to the front lines, and it was high time for me to give serious considerations to my options. This wasn't the Russian front any more where a desertion would have been deadly. Now our opponents were members of civilized western nations, maybe even American soldiers? How could I jump ship at the first possible opportunity? I knew I couldn't talk about this to anybody, not even to Karl. To make him an accomplice or an accessory to my traitorous plans would have been unfair to him. A German soldier caught in the act of deserting, or knowing of another soldier, who was intending to commit such an act, was shot without further ado. My first priority was to find out who the opposing troops were. The Allies had British and US troops but also polish units in Italy, and I didn't want to fall into the wrong hands.

The Poles, we had heard, killed all German prisoners without asking any questions. They had an ax to grind for the cruel conduct of the German army in Poland in 1939 and thereafter.

I couldn't even talk to my mother on the phone about my deliberations because the SD (*Sicherheitsdienst* = Secret Service) most certainly was eavesdropping on all telephone conversations with neutral Switzerland. The best part was that I was still able to establish a telephone connection to Switzerland and was able to talk to Olga. These were great moments of rejoicing and commiserating. I explained to her only briefly how I was. Any further detail of my whereabouts, etc. would have caused the connection to be interrupted promptly. She, in turn, could be more explicit about her plans, and what she was doing. She begged me for the hundreds time to let her know as soon as I could, when and if I would be in Berlin. She promised that she would come to see me immediately. For my part I promised to do so hoping I would still be all in one piece, without saying so much.

We continued marching down the coast for several days. We passed *Senegallia, Ancona, Civitanova,* and *Guillanova* until we reached *Pescara*. This small town on the Adriatic Sea is about 100 miles south of Cap *Ancona* and almost straight across the peninsula from Rome. The enemy was still south of *Pescara*. So far there was no contact, and nobody knew where and exactly how far away from us they were. The exact position of enemy lines across the Italian peninsula was kind of muddled. From now on the infantry probed carefully to find out how far the enemy had come north, in order not to get caught with their pants down.

The Germans had retreated along the coastline after the Americans landed on the beaches of *Anzio*. They did this on both sides of the mountain range, which stretched from the north to the most southern point of the peninsula. The war took place mostly in the coastal plains of the Mediterranean Sea in the west and the Adriatic Sea in the east. Very little serious fighting, if any, was going on in the rugged *Abruzzo* Mountains, the *Gran Sasso* or further north in the Apennine. It made no sense for the Germans to take a stand in the almost impenetrable hills, and the Allies didn't do the Germans the favor of picking a fight they couldn't win. If the Germans had made a stand in the mountains, the Allies simply would have passed them on the right or on the left. After a costly battle at Monte Casino, where they had suffered heavy casualties, the Allies were pursuing the German retreat carefully, and the Germans didn't have the resources any more to start a major battle.

Pescara was well known from prewar days. In peacetime it had been the sight of an annual professional car race. The race was a mountain event with cars racing up the mountain against the clock. Each car started two to three minutes apart and raced one way only. Whoever clocked the fastest time of two runs was the winner. The track had forty-three sharp, serpentine curves with a total change in elevation of 3600 feet. It was difficult to negotiate.

As soon as we arrived in the area and had properly settled in some deserted farmhouses, left behind in anticipation of heavy fighting, we had our little thrill negotiating the racetrack with whatever vehicle we could muster. We found an old Fiat Topolino, an extremely small car, requisitioned the regimental VW and an army Opel-blitz truck and tried our luck. The road up the mountain was a bitch to negotiate—winding narrowly along the side of a mountain sloping steeply towards a deep valley. The valley was about one and one half miles wide at the bottom. I am explaining this in detail, because our knowledge and experience in negotiating the track became a major factor later on when the Allies were in hot pursuit.

Whenever we had time and gasoline we practiced racing up the mountain until some envious officer complained about the waste of precious gasoline.

Asta liked the neighborhood, because the farmhouses smelled yummy and there were always chicken to be chased, and all those other wonderful things young dogs love to explore when they're running freely in the open.

"She is growing like a weed and eating like a horse," Karl remarked for the tenth time. "And I'm glad she wasn't that big a couple of weeks ago, I don't think I would've managed to carry her." He was right. We put her on a scale found in the barn, and its scale tipped at 35 kg (77 pounds). Incredible how much the dog ate and how fast it grew. Asta loved to sit next to us her ears perking up, her wet tongue hanging out. She was totally absorbed watching people coming and going, what they were doing and the strange peeping sounds that they were listening to. Everybody coming by had a little bite for her, a huge attraction for a growing and perpetually hungry dog.

It was too good to last. The infantry made contact with the advancing enemy five miles south from our position and called for artillery and mortar support and for communication units as well. Once more our group bundled up to join the fight.

Having experienced the fighting style of the Russian army, we wondered how much differently the Allies troops would be in conducting the war.

I was contemplating day and night when my chance might come to take a powder.

The behavior of the Allies was certainly different. While the Russians had often been visible to us in the flat terrain of the Ukraine, we never saw a single enemy soldier attacking us in Italy. They employed more artillery and also a super 20-mm caliber automatic weapon, but we saw nobody in the open. The latter weapon was especially annoying, to say the least. They fired over the nearest hill on indirect trajectories, apparently guided by forward observers. We not only had to seek protection from the artillery, which could be heard long before the grenades arrived and detonated, we also had to guard against these large caliber 20-mm shells, which we would hear only after they hit the ground when they splattered into deadly pieces.

In contrast to our own supply situation the Allies had ammunition to burn. They used this weapon to spray the countryside without aiming at anything in particular, purely for the purpose of intimidation. I must admit that they were successful. We never showed our faces in the open if we didn't have to and almost never during the day. In contrast to the Russians, who avoided night-time fighting and hated the dark, they loved to attack at night, sneaking up on our positions, throwing hand grenades into every hole and cavity in the mountains where they thought we might have taken refuge. And, of course, if they could find our foxholes, they dropped the grenades into them only to disappear quickly and as quietly as they had come. We heard the noise of the explosions at night and found the bodies of our comrades in the morning. Yes, the fighting style was different, but we got used to it fast.

One day our infantry got smart and caught a guy at night as he was sneaking up the mountain. Guess what? As I had feared and had suspected all along, he was from a unit of the Polish army and spoke a little German. He was terrified that we would shoot him immediately. That's what they'd been told and that was, as he told us, what they would do with any prisoner from our side. We passed him on to our rear with a guard.

Now I knew. Our opponents were Poles fighting with the Allies for a free Poland. It was scary and for me nothing to look forward to. If I defected and fell into their hands, they'd shoot me before I was able to explain my situation to them, and I couldn't speak a word of Polish. What a mess! I decided to delay my plans for defection and wait until other nationalities, preferably Americans, were opposing us.

Our "Brass" on the east coast chose to fall back just as slowly and at the same pace as our army on the other side, near the Mediterranean

Sea. The majority of the fighting took place on the western shores anyway. The Adriatic side was more mountainous all the way to the sea and difficult to oversee and to traverse. Any serious fighting, as I said, would have caused heavy casualties for the Allies. The Russians in contrast never seemed to care about casualties.

Every night we relinquished our positions from the day before to the advancing enemy. We walked up to ten miles through the night and took up our new position as soon as daylight broke. Not realizing, sometimes, that we had sneaked away during the night, the Allies fired artillery upon the previously occupied positions or bombarded them with planes.

We, the wireless operators, moved with the infantry every step of the way. But in contrast to us, the soldiers could sleep during the day—while we had been marching together during the night—keeping only a few guards to watch for possible action. They recuperated from the rigors of the night as well as they could under the circumstances without losing any sleep.

For the wireless operators there was no rest. We had work to do during the day, coding, sending, receiving and decoding messages about casualties, spent ammunition and necessary supplies. The retreat didn't allow the telephone operators to put down wire for the telephone. What for? The DORA was the only solution. Karl and I were as tired from marching as the others but there was no letting up. You would be amazed all the stuff the officers could think of transmitting.

Asta was lying next to me snoring away most of the time, doing what the infantry did, and Karl and I were "dog" tired. One day when I was particularly exhausted, I looked at Asta in her sleep, gave her a little push to wake up and said, "It's about time you earn your keep, you mutt you—here," and I pushed the earphones over her head, saying, "Listen to the noise, and if you hear anything at all, wake me up."

Naturally, I never expected her to understand or to show any reaction, and I seemed to be right. At first she shook the earphones off vehemently. I tried again and again and talked to her soothingly. After a while she kept them over her ears and went to sleep again. I slept too, only to be woken up by some pinching ever so slightly in my left leg. I raised my head sleepily and saw Asta, gently pinching me with her front teeth, her lips curled back. The earphones on her head emitted a peeping noise: "ditdaditdit, ditdaditdit." I pulled them quickly off her head and over my ears, acknowledged the call and wrote down hastily what the other side was telling me.

My dog had woken me up because she had heard the same noises in the earphones she knew were important to me!

"Karl did you see what Asta just did?"

The poor guy was still asleep and didn't know what I was talking about.

"What? Who did what?" was his sleepy reply.

"You can help me with the decoding," I said, as I got busy with our work.

We finished what we had to do, and then I told him what Asta had done. We were both totally flabbergasted. An animal is supposed to have no reasoning power, and here, this dog, our dog Asta, had heard the same noise coming from the earphones she'd always heard when we were working. She'd decided to wake me up. Incredible! We both determined that Asta was a genius. We talked to her and praised her. She was pulling her ears back, her eyes smiling the way only a happy dog can smile and tried to lick my ears.

"You're a great dog," Karl petted her, and gave her a piece of sausage. "But I hope you're aware that you have opened a Pandora's Box. From now on you will be the third partner of this DORA team. But don't nibble on my leg when the unit is making noises, just your Daddy's leg will do, okay?"

Asta pointed her ears and looked at him with big, brown questioning eyes. To understand such a long sentence was expecting too much of her. She seemed to say, "Make it brief. I'll listen."

What a dog she'd turned out to be! I hugged her again, which she disliked intensely, but I continued to praise her lavishly.

We continued withdrawing every night a few miles deeper and deeper into the rugged Gran Sasso D'Italia, about twenty miles inland from the Adriatic coastline, climbing continuously. The territory was wild and was the poorest in the entire country. The farmers here, high up in the mountains, were sharecroppers with a 50/50 contract with the owner of the land. What they were able to retain from the crop after a season of backbreaking work was not enough to live on and too much to give up and die. They raised a few chickens around their little houses, pressed a little oil from the olives on the trees around the area and grew wheat for flour but otherwise ate mostly millet. Some flax grew sparingly on the steep hillsides. They spun the flax and wove it on very primitive, ancient looms. This provided them with twenty-inch wide, endless rolls of rough, pale linen cloth. Otherwise they had no real clothes to wear and couldn't afford to buy any clothes. All they wore, sort of like a long shirt, was a piece of this linen material, doubled up and sewn together on the sides. A hole was cut with a knife for the head where the fold was. They simply pulled it over their heads and used a piece of rope as a belt. It looked like a crude nightgown without sleeves. I swear that this was all they were wearing summer and winter. It reminded us of pictures of Vikings or Roman slaves, which we'd seen in the movies. The owners of the property, *"Latifundi"* as the Italians called them, lived off the proceeds in splendid surroundings. (A land reform at the end of the war put an end to this exploitation by feudal landowners.)

The house of a sharecropper, if that's what you'd call their huts, was one room. Upon entering the house through a narrow, low hung door a single dark room, with pitch-black, greasy feeling, walls, confronted us. We wondered why the walls were black and discovered that the only material available to these people to make a fire in the stove was charcoal. Charcoal, however, was used sparingly, only to cook, never to heat the room. After many years the fatty smoke covered the walls with black soot. These dreadfully poor people had no other material to make a fire. To keep warm during the winter they slept with the animals, mostly dogs, a sheep, a donkey or a mule. A mule already meant wealth, because it could do many jobs a smaller donkey could not do.

We wondered how they cooked with charcoal since charcoal by itself doesn't burn it just glows slowly. With our limited Italian it was difficult to strike up a conversation and to ask questions. On top of it they spoke an atrocious dialect. I think we spoke more Italian then they did. Finally, after much gesturing we comprehended what they'd explained to us.

The stove on the side of the room was built very simply. The farmers put blocks of square fieldstones together creating a flat top. A hole, more like a tunnel, was left open in the middle of this construction. The tunnel was about thirty inches deep and ten inches wide. Crude iron rods covered it lengthwise like those on a normal grill. The front was left open without a door.

To start a fire they placed some finely shaved dry wood and dried moss inside the tunnel and heaped charcoal on top of that. To this day I don't know how they lit the wood and the moss before we came. They certainly had no paper, and they'd never even heard of matches. At first they didn't even know what to make of a lighter and certainly not of the importance of our flint-stones! But let me continue.

Once the charcoal was lit and started to glow slowly they fanned it vigorously with a fan made of chicken feathers. The feathers were aligned in parallel and held together between two pieces of wood with a handle on the bottom. It was primitive, but it worked. To get enough glow and heat from the charcoal for cooking required strong and continuous fanning. In short, they were as poor as church mice.

We traded with them, gave them some of our flour in exchange for eggs and a chicken, and before we left we presented them with a spare lighter together with a brand new flint-stone. They'd never seen anything like a lighter before and talked excitedly about this marvelous invention and gave us a big hug when we left. The lighter would be an invaluable treasure for them.

We didn't see many farmers though. Most of them, rich or poor, had fled the fighting and the majority of the houses were deserted. Before they fled, they'd stashed their biggest treasure away, the olive oil. They had hidden it somewhere in the walls of the house. After the harvest and the pressing they filled wine bottles with the oil and placed them into gaps in the wall, closing the hole with stone and mortar until the wall was smooth again. Nothing of the cache could be detected from the outside. Talking about being poor, this was the limit!

It was not that we had plenty to eat. With the exception of flour we had nothing. Our supplies kept coming sparingly over the destroyed bridges. The lack of trucks and constant bombardment by Allied bombers made a regular chain of supply for the troops precarious if not impossible. Only ammunition was supplied on a regular basis. The flour was transported on the back of mules. Our high command probably figured that if we could defend ourselves we could certainly manage to get food from the farmers. That was true, and the farmers, sometimes voluntarily, sometimes as the result of requisitioning, supplied us with flour, abundance of eggs, and with oil. We found the oil in the walls of abandoned houses by systematically tapping the walls with a hammer or other hard object. Whenever the knock on the wall produced a hollow sound, we opened the wall, and, voila, there it was, the precious bottle of oil.

Every one of us carried a large frying pan to make omelets, large omelets. We ate omelets in the morning, at noon and at night. At times a chicken graced our meals. We also discovered that drinking a cool, raw egg, directly out of the shell, was a terrific thirst quencher.

The Poles were following us, and I was too afraid of them to trust them with my life.

June 6, 1944 arrived. It was a long anticipated day. The radio was full of news and reports of the Allied forces landing on the coast of the Normandy. The German propaganda machine treated this as a simple, routine event in an ongoing war. We believed that the landing was the beginning of the end for the German army and the war. Karl and I drank a bottle of local red wine to celebrate the newest developments. The battalion propaganda officer—every battalion had one—distributed a heroic statement, issued directly from the *Führerhauptquartier* (headquarters of the *Führer*). It grandiosely proclaimed that he would personally take charge of the situation and would—in his unfaltering wisdom and as the greatest military tactician of all times—drive the invaders back into the ocean within a short time.

For me it meant that I wouldn't have to put myself in jeopardy with the Poles anymore. I only had to wait until the Allies would force the Germans to surrender. The war would be over soon.

Once again I had underestimated the longevity of Hitler's brutish regime. By June 15, 1944 we'd retreated over ninety miles back to *Pescara,* the town where we had started. This time we arrived further inland from the city, high in the mountains and at the end of the race-track, which we knew so well. Our supplies came from the port of *Pescara* where they'd been transported by small fishing boats and then by trucks to our position, using the former racetrack. Exactly a mile and a half away on the other side of the valley was the enemy. Even at night it was impossible to negotiate the road unmolested by artillery unless . . . unless the driver was very good and was coming up the road at breakneck speed and put on a good show of skillfully negotiating the track. Only then did the enemy leave him alone some-times probably to watch and enjoy his driving performance rather than to kill him. Can you imagine it was war and we were playing games? Our experience with the track came in handy, and now our officers ap-preciated that the guys driving the supply trucks had taken the time to practice and waste precious gasoline when we were here the first time.

But, as I said, we were on the move, and even this interlude did not last long. The enemy was pushing forward on the other side of Italy along the Mediterranean plains and we had to follow suit if we didn't want to fall behind and be cut off.

The only appreciable fighting force the Germans had left at this time of the war was the infantry. There was almost no artillery left, few tanks and no heavy weapons of any kind, and definitely no air support. If we were lucky, we saw a lonely Me 109 patrolling the coastline only to disappear in a hurry as soon as Allied planes ap-peared on the horizon. Time and again we had to relinquish our po-sitions to the enemy without much of a fight. After a month of backtracking through the hills and mountains of the *Monte Grosso,* we arrived at a little town called *Iesi.* It was twenty to thirty miles in-land from *Cap Ancona* and straddled a prominent ridge. A little church was positioned dominantly on the eastern edge of town. The top of the church tower afforded a terrific view over the entire valley toward the south where the enemy was. Master Sergeant Losanski or-dered our DORA team to proceed toward the church together with a platoon of infantry to report the moves of the enemy to the battalion.

"Idiots," was his comment to the order he had received and passed on to us. "If these assholes can see a chance to pin a medal to their chests then lives mean nothing to them. What do they want to hear? We know where the enemy is, and we certainly are not going to put up any more resistance than we have so far." But he couldn't change it and we went.

The platoon, Karl and I climbed up the hill until we arrived at the church. As we struggled up the barren hill, we noticed that the farmers had not even bothered to plant a crop. We made our way under the helpful protection of darkness, but could clearly see that the hill and the bare field didn't provide any cover anywhere in case we had to retreat in a hurry. The platoon leader examined the defensive position around the church before we entered the building. It must've been a poor parish because inside were only crude wooden benches and a frugal wooden altar with a crucifix hanging on the wall. There were no other ornaments inside, which you usually find in Catholic churches—even the poorest ones. The windows were very high above the main floor. No chance to use them to look out to see who was approaching.

"Karl, I don't like it," I said to my friend. "I'll climb the ladder to the top of the steeple to investigate our surroundings from up there. You'll keep in touch with the sergeant in case he has any messages to relay. The way I've understood him, he wants to get all of us out of here at the first opportunity."

I was right. Before I could even climb the first stairs, the sergeant arrived, puffing and blurting out angrily, "What a trap this is. Don't go too far, we aren't staying long, I promise. I'll compose a report of the situation for the benefit of the battalion, and you'll pass it on pronto, okay?"

It was dark by now and of no further use to climb up to the top of the steeple anyway. I couldn't have seen anything anyway. A few guys had been stationed outside as lookouts to warn us of approaching enemy troops. Karl and I set up the DORA to be ready when the Sergeant was ready with his report.

His message, which he finally concocted and handed to us, was a convoluted assortment of lies about approaching enemy infantry with artillery support and armored vehicles. He combined it with a request for permission to withdraw immediately. We passed it on to headquarters in clear text. Ten minutes later we had the reply.

"Those bastards!" the Sergeant grumbled. It read, "The platoon will remain were it is and, if necessary, defend its position. If enforcement is needed, we'll send it."

The officer who sent the message must have been stark raving mad. The sergeant called a corporal from his platoon, and debated what could be done. We were interrupted by a soldier coming from the outside telling us that there was a lot of commotion on the street to the south of the church, about a hundred yards away. The way he described it, it looked like a large number of enemy soldiers were approaching. The sergeant ordered everybody outside, positioned us around the church and told us to fire at anything that moved. It was dark but one could almost feel the presence of the enemy all around. We could also hear distant noises of moving vehicles and subdued voices.

At about four o'clock the dark void in front of us started to explode. We took an avalanche of infantry fire from all directions, rifles, automatic weapons and machine guns. Mortar shells dropped through the roof of the church and exploded inside. It was an ear-splitting noise. Hand grenades flew through the windows and exploded spreading shrapnel everywhere. It was a blessing that we'd vacated the church when we did.

Being on the outside, and relatively safe in a ditch alongside the roadway, we tried to defend ourselves in the semi-darkness of the predawn with everything we had, which wasn't much. One could clearly see the enemies gun muzzles flashing in the dawn of an arriving day, and we threw our hand grenades in that direction. The sergeant crawled over to me and screamed into my ear, "Tell headquarters that we need support immediately, now, and that we're running low on ammunition. It's getting light. If we have to run, the only protection we'll have is the darkness. With the small amount of ammunition available we either have to run down the hill in a minute, or raise our hands, which I'd hate to do considering that we are facing the Polacks."

We got busy on the DORA with voice communication, which was only permitted in extremely precarious situations and with no other option available. A lieutenant from headquarters responded, telling me to get into code and not to dramatize our situation unnecessarily. Listening to the response the sergeant grabbed the mike and let out a stream of profanities. He told the lieutenant that without any artillery support we'd withdraw, and then he severed the connection.

The explosions around us got worse by the minute. The Poles were pushing us. One after the other we were running out of ammunition, and the casualties were mounting. Finally the sergeant gave the order to retreat. Karl and I started running down the hill with our cumbersome DORA boxes on our back; the same way we'd come up a few hours ago. This was easier said than done. By now it was early daylight and the Poles, positioned on the ridges and hills around us, could see clearly what we were trying to do. They weren't letting us get away as easily as we'd hoped. They wanted us dead, all of us, and they covered the hill with whatever they could throw at us. They fired mortar shells, automatic weapons and light artillery.

The hill we were descending had a few shallow trenches going straight down and away from the church. They were from a plow a farmer had made with his horse, and we were using one to hide as best as we could and to wriggle downhill on our bellies. We were inundated by enemy fire and frantic to get out of danger. Karl and I kept the heavy DORA units on our backs as we slid down the hill. Suddenly, close by, with a foot or two to spare, there were three enormous explosions. I felt a sharp pain jerking my head around, an instant pain on my left jaw and a hard impact in my back where the DORA unit was. My left arm went limp. As I touched the side of my face I felt warm blood running down my neck. I turned around to look where Karl had followed me only five yards behind. All I could see was a mangled, bloody mess where he'd been seconds ago. He must've taken a direct hit by a mortar or artillery shell. Not a sound came from where his body was lying and I saw no movement. I saw one of his arms lying a few yards away from his body and called out to him but there was no answer. On top of my own injuries I was shocked senseless by the sudden loss of my friend. He'd died; he'd been slaughtered; and I was seriously wounded. All because of a stupid, very stupid order by an officer who didn't know fuck all about infantry combat and was trying out idiotic tactical moves as a way of gaining recognition and glory.

I was lying in my trench not moving. Strangely enough, I was feeling no pain from my injuries. The sudden burst of adrenaline suppressed the pain. But I felt infuriated and terribly distraught by what had happened to my friend, Karl. I don't remember how long I lay where I was. It may have been ten seconds or ten minutes. The appreciation of time had left me until I recognized the situation I was in. I returned to the present with a jolt as I felt blood from my neck and jaw running down my body inside my uniform. Coming back to my senses I knew that with the loss of blood I'd soon be too weak to move. For the first time in my life since I could remember I cried violently. Tears were running down my cheeks as I was crying for my friend Karl who didn't have to die.

My injuries didn't give me much time to consider my options. With my remaining strength I jumped up without any regard for enemy fire and flying bullets and ran all the way down towards a prominent gully at the foot of the hill. Luckily, the Poles must've been surprised by my sudden move and my audacity and that I was still alive after lying there motionless in front of them. I drew relatively little fire and fell down in the safety of the gully and cried desperately.

When I pulled the DORA off my back I discovered that a huge splinter, almost a foot long, from the grenade, which had exploded nearby was embedded in the unit and had totally destroyed it. The DORA was busted, but it had saved my life. A piece of metal of that size would've crushed my spine and killed me instantly. I kept looking up the hill where Karl's remains were lying motionless. The enemy kept firing at his position to make sure they got him, those bastards.

A medic came by and took one look at my wounds.

"You've a gaping hole in your jaw, and your left arm doesn't look too good either," he observed factually. He called another soldier to carry the ruined DORA, put a bandage on my face and arm and sent me on in the direction of the battalion headquarters a few hundred yards away.

When I dragged myself into headquarters, the lieutenant, this murdering fool started to open his mouth to say something, but he kept it shut when he saw that my face was full of blood and the DORA was hanging in shreds on the back of the other guy. With great difficulty, because my tongue was swollen and filled my mouth, I reported the death of Karl and asked for a medic.

This second medic was more experienced than the first one. He also had no enemy fire to contend with. He carefully took his time looking at my injuries. He discovered that I had a piece of metal in my upper arm, no broken bones but that I had lost lots of blood and had a damaged muscle. My face was the worst. Shrapnel had penetrated my neck, just to the side of the aorta and shattered my jaw also cutting my tongue; he couldn't be sure where the shrapnel had settled. My inner mouth, my tongue, everything was bleeding, and I'd a hard time speaking and swallowing, and my aorta was pulsing in full view. He was afraid it might rupture. With the blood still running from the wound, the poor guy couldn't make a proper diagnosis and feared that he would make matters worse, whatever he did.

Asta, my faithful dog, which Karl and I had left behind with Staff Sergeant Losanski came creeping towards me on her belly her ears hanging down; she was whining loudly trying to lick my hand. The poor animal didn't even know that her best friend, Karl, would never come back. The staff sergeant commandeered a Red Cross truck, and they put me inside. He got in after me together with Asta and off we went towards the harbor of *Cap Ancona* where a hospital ship was loading the wounded. The guards at the ship wouldn't let Asta come aboard with me; I had to leave her at the pier with Losanski. He promised me to treat her like his own. As I was lying there on the stretcher the dog sat next to me, licked my face, and I stroked her head with my good right hand. We both knew that this was a final good bye; one look into the dog's eyes spoke volumes.

I was so terrified, shocked and worn out by the day's events that I must've passed out shortly thereafter. When I woke up I felt the slight rocking movements of a ship at sea.

The wounded were lying in a huge room, probably the converted ballroom of a passenger vessel. Nurses were hurrying from bed to bed to check the new arrivals and the severity of their wounds.

From what I could hear and understand, the "Venetia," our ship, had traveled along the coastline loading wounded soldiers at every port that was large enough for her to dock.

When the nurses finally came to my bed they attended to my arm first. It was a simple flesh wound looking worse than it really was. Only later did they pay any attention to the wound on my neck, which was bad, very bad. It didn't only look frightening, when I sneaked a look into a handheld mirror, but it continued bleeding profusely. The doctors didn't want to operate especially after they had made certain that the aorta was not in immediate danger of rupturing. The extraction of the shrapnel from my jaw would be a major undertaking, and the ship's operating room was not equipped for a delicate facial operation. I gathered all of this from their conversation at my bedside.

"Let's keep him stable until we get to Venice and put a rush on him for an operation in the mountains," one of them said. They injected me with a sedative and I fell asleep instantly.

It must have been something potent, because when I came to, I was in *Cortina d'Ampezzo,* high in the Dolomite Mountain Range. A ride from Venice to *Cortina* in an ambulance, or a train, is at least an eight-hour trip.

Today everybody knows that *Cortina d'Ampezzo* is a fashionable winter resort, which it was even then. *Cortina,* for short, as people call it, is located deep in the Tyrol tucked in among the monumental Dolomite Mountains. It's beautiful and the scenery is breathtaking, though in 1944 the town was much smaller than it is today. Only the Winter Olympics, after the war, made it big, but it was already full of hotels and resort buildings. Every roof of every hotel and hospital had a large Red Cross painted on it to protect the town from Allied bombers. It worked, and the US bombers that flew across almost daily honored the internationally recognized safety zone.

The morning after I arrived a nurse told me that in *Cortina* was a special hospital for soldiers with facial injuries. The doctor who looked at my wounds gave me a long explanation why he didn't want to put me under during the extraction of the shrapnel. I didn't understand all the medical stuff, but from my experiences with doctors in field hospitals in Russia and Vienna, I'd developed a deep distrust for the members of his profession in general. He made sure that I understood that for my own safety I'd to lie absolutely motionless during the entire procedure. He didn't want to injure my aorta any further during the extraction of the metal, and he wanted me to be conscious. Well, he managed the extraction all right. After the operating came the part why, truthfully, he wanted me to be conscious. The orthodontist put wires around my teeth, to keep my jaw from moving and to let the jawbone heal unimpedded. To hold my jaws together tightly they connected the wires around the upper and lower teeth with little rubber bands. The jaw had to remain motionless for two months, he explained, to allow for heeling of the jawbone, which had been shattered. The entire operation took three hours. I don't know who was more exhausted in the end, the doctor or I. Afterwards . . . afterwards the doctor, the sadist, gave me a sedative.

The nurse was the only honest one. She explained that they preferred to keep me conscious during the procedure to prevent my tongue from sliding back into my throat, choking me.

During his next visit the doctor told me that I couldn't chew any solid food. He promised that I'd get wonderful chocolate and vanilla soup to supply me with nourishment.

Virtually every house in *Cortina* had been turned into an annex to the main hospital. Our house stood on a hill overlooking the town. My bed was near the window with the sun shining through the curtains in the afternoon. If it had not been for the discomfort of my wired jaw, it would have been perfect.

As I was lying in my bed with only one other postoperative casualty in my room, I reflected upon my fate. The Good Lord certainly protected me otherwise the grenade that struck Karl would have struck me, or the one that showered its shrapnel upon me would have struck closer. My poor friend Karl; I was thinking about him constantly. Where was the justice in this world if a man like him had to die? There were so many bastards in the army who had never been wounded only once. I missed Karl terribly, and more than once I talked to him in my dreams.

One thing was certain; I was exhausted. I needed rest, physically and mentally, but more than anything I was glad to be alive. All

I wanted to do now was to sleep for 48 hours, 96 hours, not thinking about the nightmares that lay behind me. Karl and my dog Asta were constant companions in my thoughts regardless or whether I was awake or asleep.

One night as I was lying in bed dreaming I started to bleed profusely. With the loss of blood, life was seeping out of me slowly. The other soldier in the room noticed the red spot spreading gradually around the area of my head and rang for the nurse. They rushed me to the operating room and applied another set of stitches while I kept on dreaming terrible and frightening dreams, too weak to wake up from the loss of blood or to notice anything around me. From that night on, the nurses checked on me more often, and I was fed intravenously for several days.

Cortina D'ampezzo. I have to hide one
side of my face

Your resilience is excellent when you are twenty, and my powers of recuperation were fabulous. Only one week later I was eating my vanilla soup regularly and was gaining strength by the hour.

My thoughts were turning toward my mother. How could I inform her of my where-abouts. The nurse helped me to compose a cryptic wire and promised that she would try her best to send it where it was supposed to go. We included my present address in violation of all prevailing regulations.

My health was improving, and my jaw didn't feel as sore any more. My left arm was healing slowly.

A few days later, at three o'clock in the afternoon, the door of our room opened, and there stood my mother, a big smile on her face and worry in the corners of her eyes. I must have looked frightening. With bandages around my head and neck, speaking was still difficult and my left arm was in a sling, but I managed a "hello" and gave her a hug with my right arm as she sat down at my bedside.

"Peter, what did they do to you? The doctor told me that you cannot talk much, and, as a civilian, I'm not supposed to be here in this hospital, but you know me, I just had to see you. And, after all, I'm your mother. I think that convinced the doctor to make an exception."

She kept rambling on for a while, trying to suppress the urge to cry on account of how I looked, the sight of the bandages and her happiness at seeing me alive and safe. I'd never been so happy to see her before in my entire life. I felt like a little boy who'd never been separated from her. I wanted to preserve that moment and wanted the blasted war to go away. She stroked the healthy side of my face carefully with her hand and sat there looking at me until the nurse came to interrupt our reunion.

"Mrs. Pütz"—I thought I was not hearing right—"you have to leave now. Although it is difficult right now with over 3000 wounded soldiers and all the medical staff, I found a room for you, if you come back here tomorrow, I'll let you come in to see your son for a short while."

We parted and I was left wondering what this "Mrs. Pütz" was all about. I would talk to her in private to clarify that mystery.

My mother's visit had given me the incentive to get up, move around and make a determined effort to get my strength back. The nurse laughed at me struggling and helped me to walk up and down the short hallway.

The next few days passed with the same routine. My mother visited me in my room where we weren't alone, and we had lengthy, innocuous talks. I was waiting for the day when the doctor would permit me to go outside on my own to talk to her in private and to question her about "Mrs. Pütz."

The doctor finally removed the stitches and appeared to be satisfied with the results of his work. An x-ray revealed that the bone was healing nicely and that I would be almost like new with the exception of a large, ugly scar on my left cheek. My arm healed well too. My most pressing concern was how soon and whether or not I'd be KV again. The doctor explained very patiently and understandingly that it was much too early to consider anything like that and I shouldn't worry too much about it. In general, he informed me, a KV ruling occurred when all the wounds had closed, had healed properly and the mouth could be opened wide enough to insert an upright thumb between the front teeth, in his opinion that was a long time off. The hospital started the mouth exercising as soon as the wires were removed. They inserting a reverse clamp into my mouth, which would help me to pry my mouth open slowly further and further. I decided right then and there that my mouth would never open wide enough to insert an upright thumb; at least not before the war had ended.

When I was strong enough to take a short walk I took my mother to a quiet park with a bench, and we sat down to have a little chat.

"Mother," I started pompously, "what is this Mrs. Pütz business? What possessed you to travel under the name of your first husband who deserted you?"

She laughed and then grew serious. "Peter, I would've preferred to keep that issue my little secret. It would be better for all of us if I were the only person who knew. If you ever talk to anybody about it, you'd not only endanger your life but mine as well. You know how the Nazis are with their secret police. They'll find out almost everything. I'm so afraid of what they would do to me. I've read and heard so much about the torturing that goes on in the cellars of the Bendlerstrasse [Headquarter of the *Gestapo* = Geheime Staatspolizei in

Berlin], and I know that I'd break down before they started putting
the screws on me. You must promise not to talk to anybody about it,
will you do that?"

"Of course, Mom, don't be ridiculous. How can you even think
that I'd talk to anybody about our secrets? We have enough of them
already, I'd never put you in jeopardy, you know that."

We'd progressed too far in our discussion for her not to tell me
the whole story, so she continued.

"You know that I'm a stickler for keeping things, documents,
certifications and records of all kind. You always laughed at me, but
sooner or later it pays off. In 1919, after the first war, when I went
to the American consulate to reclaim my US citizenship, they did-
n't ask me to turn in my Spanish passport so I kept it after they had
helped me to annul my marriage to Egon. That passport was in my
possession all these years, and I thought it might come in handy.
When I went to Switzerland to visit Bill and Monica I took it along
with me, just in case. Later on, in Zurich, I went to the Spanish Consulate and simply told them that I wanted to renew my passport. Of
course, they asked me a million questions—where I'd been for the
last twenty-five years, why the passport had no exit and entry
stamps into Switzerland, and why the last entry stamp was from
1913 when I'd entered Germany with Egon, which was true. I'd discussed all that with Bill beforehand, and together we cooked up a
story, which was believable if you stretched it a bit. As a matter of
fact Monica was more inventive than Bill and I were. The story was
that I had been their companion in Switzerland for all these years
and that I'd lived with them content with the quiet life in a Zurich
suburb. Now, I told them truthfully, I wanted to travel to visit some
old friends in Germany. The deal went through, you won't believe
it, but they renewed, stamped and updated my passport (they told
me to be careful with the Germans)—and I was a Spanish *Senora*
again. There's my story. Now, how do you think I was able to visit
you in Vienna? How'd you think I went back to Germany and returned to Switzerland? Certainly not with my American passport, or
with an outdated German *'Kennkarte'* (ID paper given to all Germans for identification), and certainly not with a Swiss passport,

which is impossible to get anyway. I hope that nobody finds out about this until this war is over, or they'll throw me into a concentration camp and throw the key away."

I was stunned, my mother as an international impostor, a woman with three nationalities. She was bolder and more daring than I'd ever have imagined in my wildest dreams.

I started laughing, squeezed her and replied, "Now, we only have to manage the trick of getting my picture into your Spanish passport, like when I was a baby and became an American with the help of your passport."

"Peter, don't think that Monica and I haven't discussed how to exploit that possibility. We believe, however, that at your age it wouldn't work. The Spaniards wouldn't go along with it. And, let's not forget the inquisitiveness and resourcefulness of the German border guards. I don't know how they'd react if you'd try to cross the border with me with your baby picture in my passport."

She took me into her arms and cried a little, and we talked about the good old times we had on Long Island before this crazy war started, and we talked about Bert Larson and his parents and where they might be in this ugly war. We rehashed for the hundredth time and criticized our stupidity by traveling to Germany in 1939 to fulfill the stipulations of her divorce agreement.

Yes, if one could turn the clock back we'd all know what to do right, and we'd all be rich and in the right place at the right time—20/20 hindsight.

I turned around automatically to see whether anybody was eavesdropping before I asked my next question. My mother laughed and said, "You have, what we call in Switzerland, 'the German look.' You are always looking over your shoulder to see whether somebody is listening or watching. I guess people get used to the circumstances in which they live."

"Mother," I interrupted her train of thought. "Tell me the latest news of the Allied invasion in Normandy. I mean the truth, the unadulterated truth. Are the Allies successful? Or are the German papers correct in their evaluation of the situation? You probably know that the German papers tell us that the Allied casualties are enormous and that they'll be thrown back into the English Channel where they came from, any day now."

"No, Peter, the German papers aren't correct. They're lying as usual. The invasion is a great success, and the Americans, with the assistance of mainly the British and some of the French, are advancing rapidly. The Germans cannot contain the onslaught, and we must hope that by the end of the year at the latest, the nightmare will be over. Monica, Bill and I always listen to the BBC and the AFN, the newly established daily newscast of the American Forces. Between these two stations the news coverage and news analysis is straightforward and exhaustive. All you have to do now to pay attention that your jaw doesn't heal too quickly. If you manage that you have it made. I pray every day for you that this is your last injury. I don't want to visit you in another hospital any more. I want to take you back to America where we can live in peace."

"How do you think I feel, Mom?" I blurted out. "I have a bullet in my hip, a torn muscle in my left arm, a broken jaw, a couple of holes in my lungs, courtesy of some Russian bayonets, and a few other minor injuries, which I don't want to detail at the moment. I'll soon go out to join the carnage one more time, if the doctor is right in his evaluation. That'll happen the minute I can put my thumb upright between my teeth. The next time, Mother, that you'll visit me in a hospital it'll be either in a psychiatric ward or in the morgue."

I shouldn't have said that because it was rather theatrical and not the way I truly felt. In the state of mind I was in, everything ran off me like water from a duck's back. I felt numb, and the number of positive expectations for the future was zero.

She cried a little; I consoled her, as we sat on a bench in the park in beautiful *Cortina d'Ampezzo,* thinking of a safe future in New York. It would take a little while for that to come to fruition.

As I said, *Cortina* was then, and is today, a very picturesque resort town. Small cafés and restaurants were operating even during the war. My mother and I visited many of them and the last of my remaining flint-stones helped us to get the best coffee and the best cake available. I was glad that they were the last, because they reminded me of Karl and that was very painful for me to bear.

On the southern side of the town, going up the Mountain by a cogs wheel railway was a huge shrine dedicated to the "Unknown Soldier" decorated, no, I should have said desecrated by a statue of Mussolini, *Il Duce,* overlooking the valley. This egomaniac really must have had delusions of grandeur, I mean, building something like that, during his lifetime!

It was a quiet place with a gorgeous panoramic view of the town and valley beyond. We sat there talking about us, about the future, and what we'd do once peace had become a reality.

Everything must come to an end sometime. My mother left for Switzerland after a tearful "Good bye." During the third week of July 1944 the hospital transferred me to Berlin as an outpatient, to make room for the next group of casualties.

Strangely enough I never made any contact with the other soldier in my room. Half of his lower face was gone, he couldn't talk now and probably would never be able to again, but the worst was that he'd given up on life. He rejected all my attempts to develop even a fleeting relationship in order to cheer him up. Poor guy, I didn't give him much longer.

They had chosen a recuperation place in Berlin for me specializing in facial injuries. Hospitals all over Germany where crowded with wounded soldiers and needed rehab centers. The doctor in *Cortina* assured me that the healing process of my jaw no longer required a precious hospital bed. My home was in Berlin and that was where I was transferred.

Of course, I had a terribly guilty conscience. I had not called Celli as soon as I had been able to. Worse, I hadn't called her at all. Somehow I felt that the time I'd spent with my mother in *Cortina* was between my mother and me and didn't call for any interference by anybody. Nobody should've disturbed our privacy—not even in thought, especially not my father's second wife, my present girlfriend. Boy, oh, boy, life can become complicated especially when you're involved in an affair with your stepmother.

Guilty conscience or not, I would have to live with the consequences of what I'd started and in this case I did so without losing much sleep over it.

The day before I was released from the hospital, I managed a telephone connection to Celli's home in Berlin. She was surprised to hear my voice, and that I was calling her from a ski resort.

"Where have you been? I haven't heard from you in such a long time. I was terribly worried. Has something happened? Don't tell me that you are injured again?"

When I told her what had happened she seemed relieved. "Oh, Peter, I am so happy that you are still alive."

So was I! It sure as hell almost didn't work out this time.

I explained the circumstances as well as I could, without resorting to outright lies and described my injuries, which were the reason for my mumbling. If you talk with your mouth closed—the wires—you sound as if you are standing in a closet with the door closed. In the end she believed me and was happy that she was going to see me soon.

Once I arrived in Berlin I reported to the designated hospital where they gave me a bed to sleep in for the night. They also gave me the time for the examination of my jaw on the following morning.

The doctor who performed the examination was of the cheerful kind, acting as if he did not have to deal every day with a lot of misery.

The facial-surgical ward in any hospital was a gruesome sight. Soldiers in this ward had ugly wounds, had half their faces missing, or were otherwise seriously mutilated. Some were without noses or chins, had their ears torn off, or disfiguring facial burns. The worst case in this respect that I had ever seen was a poor young fellow in *Cortina* who had the entire front of his face blown away. After I had seen him, I had nightmares for days imagining that the same thing had almost happened to me.

Maybe the doctor was happy because he was healthy and safe and far away from all the shooting with the exception of the falling bombs. He complimented me on the excellent work done to my jaw by the doctors in *Cortina.*

"That ugly scar can be removed by plastic surgery when the war is over. After all these injuries and the mangling and disfiguring, the plastic surgeons will have a field day for the next few years. Just be sure that you pick the right guy because some of them have a heavy hand. It always helps to ask for recommendations first and to take a look at the work that the doctor of your choice has done on others. For now I will leave the wires where they are. You have to come back every two weeks. After four weeks we'll take another x-ray to check on the jaw bone, but I'm sure that by then we'll take the wires out and you can start with your rehab."

"Yes sir, the doctor in *Cortina* gave me a device, a clamp, to stretch my jaw after the wires are gone, to chew better, he said, and to speak properly. My present speech pattern drives me nuts," I answered.

"Very good advice," he replied. "We will practice the stretching together. I don't want you to overdo it in the beginning and do any damage, prolonging the healing process. Experienced and decorated soldiers like you are needed at the front lines to defend the Fatherland. See you in two weeks."

The idea of visiting a plastic surgeon was good advice. Under the circumstances it took me twenty-nine years to follow up on it, but then I did exactly as he had recommended and was surprised what one could do to improve an old face with few cuts and stitches.

His other comments sounded absolutely crazy! Did he really think the front lines would see me again? I surely didn't want to hurry things, just stay at home as long as I could in a warm bed with pleasant company; that was my intention.

The rehab center was located in a vacated lyceum (a gymnasium for girls) right across from the *S-Bahnhof Heerstrasse,* in the West End of Berlin, within walking distance of Celli's apartment. I called her to tell her that I had arrived. And I started walking slowly down *Preussenallee,* which connects *Heerstrasse* with the suburb of *Neu-Westend,* a pretty street lined with gorgeous old plane trees.

In a way I was looking forward to our reunion. I had to think of Karl's words of caution and my brazen reply at the time. I concluded, as I was ringing her doorbell, that my comments to Karl were still right; what the hell did I care as long as this carnage was going on.

The door flew open and there she was gorgeous as always. She hugged me and kissed me and only stopped after her tongue got entangled with the wires in my mouth.

"Peter, that's awful! How will we kiss each other? How long will these terrible wires stay? Does it hurt? And how about your arm, you seemed to flinch when I embraced you?"

I had to laugh; the first thing on her mind was the tumble in the hay.

"They have to stay for a few weeks longer, Celli, and it doesn't hurt. It is only uncomfortable for the girls when they get their tongues into it, and, yes, my arm still hurts a lot. But don't worry. I remember that the full cast I wore the last time we were in bed didn't represent any insurmountable obstacles to your endeavors or to our lovemaking. And, don't forget the most important consideration; the longer the wires stay, the longer I'll be home."

I tried to be loose and not let her know that my nervous system wasn't unaffected by all the things that had happened to me. My experiences had taken their toll. I wasn't exactly virgin material any more. The years at war, the things we had seen, the injuries, had left a mark. But having been in Berlin for two days, I'd come to realize that somehow it was a different story to fight a war in the open, as we'd done in Russia and in Italy, or going into the cellar every night to listen to the howling bombs falling towards you and wondering whether or not they would hit your house, bury you, or spare you one more time until the next night.

Nevertheless I was hell bent not to go back to the front lines, if I could help it. I preferred to stay in Berlin as long as I could. I would find out soon enough how that would work.

We talked and talked like two people in love who have not seen each other in a long time and are happy to be together again. We went to bed and made love as if drowning, only to come up for air every once in awhile to start all over again and managed to forget the misery that surrounded us. Celli was incredible. The dedication, energy and passion she put into making love and the obvious enjoyment she derived from it was 'phantabulous.' She still had a boyish figure with small breasts and blond hair. She was tight all over but soft and nimble at the same time. It's said that the young women of the North African Tuaregg nomads are trained to do just about anything while making love. Well, I was convinced that Celli must have taught them.

We were into one of the most enduring sessions ever, and I enjoyed the marvelous warmth of a perfect penetration, when the sirens screamed their warning blasts.

"Stay here," I said. "If the house falls on top of us, I may really get into you."

"No, Peter, darling, first of all, I'm afraid of the howling bombs, and, secondly, I don't want to be reprimanded by the air raid warden and dressed down in front of the others. He is a real Nazi and takes his duties seriously. The people in the cellar are his watchdogs. They'll report to him if I'm not down there within five minutes after the alarm goes off. Let's get untangled, grab our things and run. If we're lucky the raid won't last too long, and when we come back up, we can continue with these wonderful exercises where we've left off."

We were lucky that night with the destinations of the bombers, and, later on, we did exactly what Celli had suggested. At this rate I wasn't sure that I would survive the war at home.

After a few weeks the air raids and the visits to the cellar at night got to me too. To spend the nights anticipating falling bombs, the house crashing down, being buried alive was nerve wrenching. I visited the hospital for the removal of the wires and was introduced by the doctor to a set of stretching exercises to do morning, noon and evening. Following his instructions I made sure that I didn't stretch my jaw too much. I didn't want my thumb to fit upright between my teeth for a long time to come.

In the afternoon Celli and I often went to the movies, at night to the cellar and, in plain English, fucked day and night whenever the thought entered our minds and the air raids didn't interrupt us.

Christmas 1944 had came and passed, and the news from the front lines was good, good to my thinking and bad for the Germans.

The progress of the Allies was slow, however. In the west they were taking their time, and in the east the Russians had come to a complete stop near Warsaw on the far side of the Vistula River. They had stopped to watch the fighting in the city. The Polish freedom fighters had started an uprising and were giving the Germans a hard time. The SS was slaughtering them. The way the Russian army reacted almost gave the impression that they were permitting the Germans to kill off the Polish nationalists because they didn't belong to the communist faction of the resistance and didn't fit their ideology. The fighting went on for weeks, and the Soviet army stood idly by, watching the killing.

The Nazi war machinery pulled out the last stops at the home front, true to minister of propaganda Dr. *Goebbels* famous speech in the Kroll Opera, when he had asked the assembly of deputies, "Do you want total war?" Well, they got it.

The Nazis recruited old men up to sixty years old and boys as young as fifteen. They called these last reserves, the *Volkssturm*, the "People's Force". The young boys were sent to help the anti aircraft units that tried unsuccessfully to keep the bombers at bay and the old men took over the nonessential military duties, guarding thousands of bridges and other noteworthy military installations against sabotage. If worse came to worse, they were employed as infantry. The regular soldiers they relieved were organized into new companies, battalions, regiments and divisions and sent to the front lines. Field Marshall Hermann Göring *"donated"* an entire *Luftwaffe* division to the SS to fight as infantry. Of course, the propaganda machine promulgated the enthusiasm of these young and old people day and night, not mentioning that they had only one thing in mind: TO SURVIVE AT ANY COST. Maybe a few idiots still believed in the invincibility of the *Deutsche* W*ehrmacht* and its glorious *Führer,* but they were few, very, very few.

As I checked in one day at the outpatient ward of the hospital to have my weekly examination, I noticed a group of very active looking SS officers darting in and out. If anybody had asked me I would've bet that even those faithful followers of the regime were trying their best to stay away from the shooting in an effort to survive. I should've turned around immediately because it didn't take me long to find out the reason for their presence. They were searching for new cannon fodder.

They cornered everybody who was in the hospital. The exits were locked. Nobody could get out. When it was my turn to be examined, my doctor told me that the conditions for KV had been lowered by orders of the *SS Reichsführer Heinrich Himmler,* the highest in command of the SS and favorite among Hitler's cronies. My jaw was good enough as it was, he said; I was pronounced KV and was told to report the following day to my reserve unit, which was located in *Guben* near the Oder River in the east.

I was terribly disappointed. I didn't make it! I had underestimated the Nazis again. They wouldn't fold, and I had to go to join the killing one more time.

I can't remember exactly how painful my departure was for Celli, but I know that I was terrified to go back to face the killing. I even contemplated sneaking away to cross the border to Switzerland. Getting my senses together, I realized that there were better ways to commit suicide. I was a tearful goodbye and a hurried departure, which didn't leave much time to tell anybody where I was going. Even a phone call to my mother had to wait until I was near a military phone.

My old unit, the 122nd, wasn't located in *Kottbus* anymore but had been moved to *Guben*/Oder for logistical reasons. The city of *Guben* was further to the east, straddling both sides of the Oder. It had several large complexes of military barracks on the hills to the eastern side of the river. I reported to the office of the first sergeant of the 122nd. He turned out to be a straight guy for a change and took a liking to me at first glance. First Sergeant Kaiser didn't search my files before talking to me and had a surprise waiting for me.

"I've been expecting you, Corporal, ever since I received a little package from headquarters with your name on it," he said with a smile on his face. "You now have a total of five injuries officially registered in your pay-book. I know that in reality you have seven or eight, but regulations are that more than one injury received on the same day counts only as one. According to its rules the army has awarded you the Purple Heart in Gold for five injuries. Now, don't get any more injuries, otherwise they'll have to invent a new medal for you."

We shook hands, and he helped me to take off the silver emblem from my jacket to replace it with the new, shiny medal in gold. We exchanged a few words about the futility of the war, and he sent me back to my quarters, a room occupied by six other guys and told me to report back in one hour.

In my quarters I met a soldier whom I knew from my old outfit in *Fécamp* and Russia, though he'd never been one of my favorites. Scuttlebutt was circulating through the barracks like wild fire. Official news was scarce, often contradictory and warped in favor of the Germans. One rumor was that the Russians had broken through the German defensive positions to the north and south of *Warsaw* and were now on the west side of the *Vistula*. Of course the official government announcement only spoke of valiant efforts by the German forces to defend the Fatherland and about "shortening" the exposed flanks in order to regroup for future attacks. The same excuses had been used ever since the debacle at the gates of Moscow in 1941. Who was going to believe it?

The Americans and the British troops were still biding their time west of the Rhine River while advancing with extreme caution. There was talk of a decisive battle in the Ardennes and of the Germans beating the Allies, but official reports remained evasive.

"That's nice," I said to Walter, my old acquaintance from the 122nd, after we had listened to the news. "In a few days we'll see the Russkis again either because they'll send us there or because Ivan will come looking for us."

"Are you kidding?" he replied with his eyebrows raised in disapproval and his narrow forehead wrinkled in consternation. He looked as dumb as they come. "We are deep inside Germany? The *Führer* will never permit Ivan inside German territory. He has vowed that in all his speeches to the German people, and he would never go back on his word. I have heard we will unleash some of our secret *Wunderwaffen* [miracle weapons] and send them running back to Moscow as fast as they came. The whole maneuver near Warsaw was just a trap set by the *Führer* to enable us to catch as many Russkis as possible."

I couldn't believe what I was hearing. Was this guy really that dumb? Now I knew why I didn't care for him and never had. He had been one of the guys around when Max—the old commie from my DORA unit in *Fécamp*—had held his propaganda sessions, praising the communist party. I wouldn't have been at all surprised if he was the one who denounced Max and me to the first sergeant. The guy was typical in his political nearsightedness, an incurable idiot. There were still too many of them.

I went back to First Sergeant Kaiser to hear of my new assignment, hoping it would keep me away from any monotonous exercising or boring guard duty.

He sent me to a neighboring barracks. "They're about a mile away. Report to the lieutenant in charge. It's about training a group of newly arrived recruits to become field telephone operators," he said. This meant that they had to learn how to put a wire down and to handle telephone equipment. Putting wire on the ground was heavy and dangerous work, but somebody in the army had to do it. I remembered the work well from my early days as a recruit in *Kottbus*. Every one of us had gone through the exercise in basic training. Before I grabbed a bicycle to peddle to the designated barracks, I asked the first sergeant if I could make a phone call to my mother.

"Sure," he said, "by all means."

I didn't tell him where my mother was. I had the right numbers to dial to get my connection to Switzerland, and I knew the right girls at the switchboards in Munich and Stuttgart. I hoped that my mother would be at home and not gallivanting in downtown Zurich. Monica, her friend, picked up on the first ring and put me through to her immediately.

"Hi, Mutti. How is everything?" I started the conversation on an easy tone not wanting to scare her.

"My God, Peter, I haven't heard from you in ages. Where are you? And are you in good health? What's your jaw doing? Will you be out of the army soon? By now you have been shot so many times that they hardly can keep you much longer. Bill always says they must let you go now."

"Well, Mom, you have lots of questions as always, but I'm so glad to hear your voice and to be able to talk to you, so I don't object being put through the third degree. My health is okay. At least that's what the SS officer determined when he pronounced me KV, which answers the other questions you were asking. At present I'm in *Guben* with my old reserve outfit, about ninety miles from the Russian front, or at least I think so. I don't know what's going to happen from here on. I just wanted to tell you that I'm alive and well. I'm glad that the same applies to you."

"My Son, we're thinking and talking about you constantly, stay well!" It was a closing sentence from her, as the operator was cutting us off.

Olga had been greatly upset by her son's call. He was back in the midst of the fighting, and she was in Switzerland enjoying life with her friends. She had a sleepless night, and on the following morning at breakfast she turned to her friend Monica to announce, "I'll go back to Berlin. The war must be over shortly, and when Peter returns, he'll need my help. I know it sounds foolish, but I'm confident that nothing is going to happen to me. The only treacherous part will be crossing the German border. I plan to walk across the narrow Rhine-bridge near *Dornbirn,* north of where the river flows into Lake Constance, as I've done before, just as if I were a local resident visiting a neighbor on the other side. I hope that the customs people are sleepy, careless or both."

She said good-bye to Bill and Monica in the early morning the following day and rode by bus and train to her destination. The customs people were as careless as Olga had hoped. She was on her way to Berlin to wait for her son to return from the war.

The lieutenant to whom I reported for my assignment was young, barely out of officers' school, and had his hands full with the unfamiliar duties of leading a consignment of raw recruits and bringing them up to snuff. The recruits, he confided to me, were more mature, around 45 and older. He gave me the room number of the platoon I was supposed to introduce to the secrets of communication and told me to report back to him at the end of the day or if anything extraordinary happened.

I walked up two flights of stairs in a bare and ugly stone building, which had not seen a new coat of paint since 1938. When I stood in front of the designated room I glanced over the list of names posted on the outside of the room, right next to the door. I wanted to familiarize myself with the names of the men I would meet. I looked and read and didn't realize at first why something struck me as odd. Then I saw it. The handwriting— I knew the handwriting! It was the handwriting of the boss from my boarding school. I checked the names and true enough there it was—"Soldier

Weimann," the "boss," the man who had turned me over to the *Arbeitsdienst* with the help of the *Ortsgruppenleiter,* the party official who had earlier forced me to participate in the drills of the HJ organization. I stood there, digested the information for a minute and entered the room.

I was confronted with a typical barracks arrangement, fifteen recruits in one room, crowded with bunk beds, positioned narrowly on a hard wood floor with sheet-metal wardrobes lining the walls. A naked bulb hung from the ceiling. The smell of thousands of sweaty soldiers who had paraded through the room hung in the air. Everybody in the room jumped up and stood at attention. One recruit started to report when a voice from the back of the room interrupted, "My God, Peter, It's nice to see you. How'd you get here?"

I turned to face him and barked at him like a true corporal should:

"Recruit Weimann, I am corporal and 'Sir' to you. Do you understand that soldier? I am here to make soldiers out of you. We are going to start right now, and if I may say so, with your kind permission, Soldier Weimann, without any further dumb remarks from you, do you understand?"

"Yes, Sir, Corporal," he replied instantly.

He was speechless, and the others were snickering slightly.

The men were all forty-five to fifty years old and would never have been drafted under normal circumstances. But these were not normal circumstances—rather the final twitches of a dying dictatorship and of the country it had ruled with an iron fist for the last twelve years. Recruit Weimann, apparently, had made himself popular with the group. Otherwise they would've reacted differently.

I ordered them downstairs to the exercise grounds on the double to receive some basic telephone equipment from the quartermaster. The first thing the guys had to learn was how to deal with a fully loaded drum of telephone wire, to splice two wires together and to hook up the end of the line to a working field telephone.

The fully loaded drums were heavy. To deal with them they were hung into a special carrying device, which one could either strap on the back—for the disposal of the cable to the ground—or to the chest, to retrieve the cable from the ground later on. On the right side of the cable drum was a winch for turning the drum during the rewinding process. The capacity of the drum was one hundred meters (110 yards) of insulated two-ply cable. As I said, it was heavy, and these guys were no youngsters any more and had probably not exercised or done any physical work since their youth. Putting the cable down, while being under enemy fire required running and jumping up and down, to avoid being hit. I explained that this was our exercise and ordered them to break up into five groups of three. One recruit in each group had to carry the drum, while the other two were laying and securing the cable on the ground, fastening it on trees where necessary. I explained that the carrier would have to hold the drum down with one hand on his lower back, especially when he had to go down on his belly, otherwise the drum would jerk forward and hit his head from behind. I'd done it many times in basic training and knew that it could hurt you or even knock you out. Soldier Weimann, I will call him the Boss now, because to me he still was the objectionable character from my school time. I could never forgive him for forcing me to be with the Hitler Youth. The Boss seemed to be happy that he wasn't carrying the drum. I had reserved the best part for him, for later. After we'd placed the cable, I explained and we practiced splicing the wire to attach it to the succeeding cable on the new drum. The men were actually pretty good and adapted quickly to the new job and the strange environment. After a brief rest I ordered the retrieval of the cables and picked the Boss as one of the cable retrievers with the drum on his chest. To move, run and jump up and down with a drum tied to your chest—while it becomes progressively heavier as you turn the winch and pick up more and more cable—is a bitch, and that is putting it mildly. The Boss was having a hard time, and I didn't have any mercy for him, or his age, or his physical condition. I really was a bastard, but I felt he had it coming.

Guben is a small provincial town, not far from Berlin, about one and a half hours by train. As soon as Celli found out where I was, she decided to visit me. She was having withdrawal symptoms, and I was getting restless too. She checked in at the one and only hotel in *Guben,* the *Gasthaus Zum Schwarzen Bock,* not far from the bridge over the river to the western side. The hotel had been kept open to the public in spite of wartime restrictions and lack of food in order to accommodate visiting wives and sweethearts of soldiers in the barracks. After my work with the recruits was finished, I went into town to visit with her. I checked with the man at the desk. He was the owner, barman, waiter and cook all in one person and went up to her room. She kissed me passionately and immediately sat me down on the only available chair in the frugal room. It was furnished with a bed, two chairs and a small round table. She opened my fly and started to go down on me. I mean I still had my coat on, but she couldn't wait, straddled me, and, after a furious workout, had an orgasm with all the accompanying exclamations of pleasure.

"Peter, I needed that; now let's move to the bed and do it once more but this time nice and slowly."

She was, as always, insatiable in bed and not interested in anything else. There wasn't much else in *Guben* anyway, and the room was at least warm in contrast to the wintry January weather outside.

Later we went downstairs to the *Gästezimmer,* the dining room, to see whether we'd be able to get anything to eat with the help of some ration cards, which I'd obtained from the administration at the barracks. Lo and behold, Soldier Weimann's wife, whom I knew from my days at the school, was also at the hotel, hoping to visit with her husband. She approached me for help in this regard, but I couldn't help her. I wasn't the commanding officer. But I told her that I'd seen him and had been assigned as his Drill Sergeant. I listened to her pleas to treat her husband with understanding because of his age, because we had known each other so well and for such a long time and because he wasn't the youngest any more. Her pleas fell on deaf ears. I couldn't forget what he'd done to me.

Recruit Weimann and most of his fellow recruits disappeared one month later without a trace in the ensuing battle for the bridgehead of Guben on the Oder River.

The following morning it started to snow heavily and exercising in the severe cold with telephone equipment became slippery and unpleasant for the recruits; I didn't like it too much either.

Returning to my own barracks in the evening first sergeant Kaiser advised me to send Celli home immediately because we were going to go on an extended maneuver. Before she departed, with tears flowing, she dragged me upstairs one more time to make love on the tiny table of that ugly room.

There was plenty of nervousness and haste among the officers and men. The first sergeant called for everybody to assemble the next morning on the barracks assembly area. He meant everybody, wounded and crippled returnees from the hospitals and all the stragglers who had not been sent back to their units so far.

"Listen everybody and listen good. It looks as if we will be involved in the fighting near the Vistula sooner than we thought. The regimental command wants us ready to go. We will go east for a few miles and set up a fictitious battalion head quarters and establish communication links to two fictitious regiments of infantry to the north and to the south of us. Do a good job. Don't mess around, and we'll be back in no time, dismissed."

We were issued weapons, same old carbines again, with 60 rounds of ammunition for each of us. Two others and I received an old, beaten up DORA unit. It was snowing heavily without letting up. By now we had two feet of snow on the ground and our only hope was that we would not have to bivouac in the open.

Nothing had changed this was still the infantry. For the next five hours we trudged through the deepening snow. After arriving at our destination in the evening, we, the DORA team, luckily found an old, very small empty barn to stay in away from the falling snow. The barn also protected the equipment. We set everything up and sent an acknowledgment of our arrival to Headquarters.

So far so good, but now . . . comes the rest of the story!

The infantry went through all kinds of exercises and deployment drills, and we did our spiel as the communicators, sending fake messages back and forth, practicing the coding and decoding. Our position was deep in the woods, and there were no wires on the ground anywhere. Everything had to be transmitted via Morse code, enciphered and deciphered, which was cumbersome and slow, especially with ice-cold fingers. Three days into the exercise, sitting at the DORA, listening to the occasional traffic on our frequency I caught a signal I had never heard before. It was repeated several times, it read:

"-.- .. -.-" Did I hear right? "KIK"? That was the accepted signal for: *Kamerad im Kessel* or in plain English: "Comrade, you are surrounded."

I answered immediately with the standard reply I had learned in basic training: "-.- .- -.-" KAK: *Kamerad ausserhalb Kessel.* (Comrade on the outside).

"What are you talking about?" I encoded and transcribed as fast as I could, "What *Kessel?* We are on an exercise, hundreds of kilometers behind enemy lines. We have not even heard a single shot, and you tell us we are surrounded?"

The immediate answer was plain and a rude awakening for my friend Walter, the believer.

"In a surprise move the Russian army has reached the Oder north and south of *Guben.* The military complex of barracks remains the bridgehead on the east side of the river and will be defended to the last man by order of the *Führer, Adolf Hitler.* Get back to the Oder and to *Guben* as quickly as you can, and make yourself available to the commander in charge of the barracks. We cannot provide any more support or further information to you. The consolidation process for the regiment will take place around *Guben.* You are seasoned soldiers; get going or Ivan will get you going, over and out."

We were in deep shit. The Soviet army must have crossed the Vistula, raced west chasing the German army all the way to the Oder. We had to get back to *Guben,* otherwise we would be captured, or left hanging out in the woods without any assistance, food, ammunition or supplies.

We still didn't hear anything, no noise of any fighting, no small arms fire, no artillery, no tanks or engine noise, nothing. The surrounding woods were as peaceful and silent as the snow that fell upon it. The first sergeant assembled everybody after reading the transmitted message. He divided the contingent into six groups of twenty men each, gave everybody directions how to get back to the river on whatever maps he had available, told them to make it back to the barracks, to avoid enemy contact and to follow the orders from the battalion. He joined our group to return to *Guben* and to join the fighting near *Guben.* The snow continued to fall and our progress through the wooded area was slow, wet and cumbersome. When we left the barracks a few days earlier we didn't know what this exercise had been all about. Now we knew it even less. Most of us were veterans of the war. At first we had thought it was a little late to practice tactics. Now we knew better.

After marching only a few miles we settled down in the snow for the night. It would've been impossible to proceed in the darkness. We were on the west side of a large clearing in the woods. The other side of the clearing, hidden in the growing darkness and the falling snow, was about 300 to 400 yards to the east. The low hanging clouds and the falling snow didn't permit the moon to throw too much light on our position. We hoped, and I prayed silently, that the enemy wouldn't find us, or catch up too fast.

"Shit, crap and corruption. How did I get into this mess? How did I manage to attract all the bad luck?" I was thinking to myself.

I went over to where the first sergeant had settled in the snow under a low hanging tree and started to discuss the situation with him.

As I said, he was as blind as a bat in the dark and relied upon me to guide him through the woods. He couldn't see where he was walking most of the time, and I was wondering how he'd made it through the war so far.

"First Sergeant, Sir, may I may make a suggestion. Even though we don't know how close the enemy is, shouldn't we better set up a defensive perimeter, just slightly inside the woods and have our weapons ready? I would place the heavy machine gun in the middle. I'm detecting movements on the other side of the clearing, between the trees to the east, and while this may be a figment of my imagination or deer or wild boar, one can't be sure what one sees in this driving snow. It's really dark. I think it's better to be prepared, you know. We should be ready for them if they mount an attack. The way I know the Russkis, they'll do it in the early morning hours as they always liked to do."

"You must've good eyes, Corporal, because I don't see a thing. But you're right. I'll set up everything; it's good to have an eagle eyed soldier on the team."

The other eighteen men weren't happy with the situation. Who was? But after years of fighting they knew pretty much what they had to do. The comments from the soldiers weren't compliments for our officers.

"How can the 'BRASS' always fuck up so expertly?"

"Can anybody tell me how to get out of this fucking army in a hurry?"

Those and some even more caustic remarks laced with the usual expletives were thrown around and fell onto the virgin snow like duds with no replies expected.

I prepared myself in my own mind for anything, and though I didn't hear any engine noise, the thought of tanks rolling slowly across the clearing was crossing my suspicious mind. We didn't sleep much during the night, just dozed off now and then and kept a couple of men on guard duty.

It stopped snowing during the night. A half moon illuminated the winter scenery, which looked beautiful with the trees covered with fresh snow, the branches hanging low from the weight and hiding everything from sight, friend and foe alike. Even so, nobody was in the mood to appreciate the scenic beauty properly.

I was freezing while being reminded of a beautiful hot summer day, way back when, deep inside Russia, with birds in the air and rabbits hobbling around, when Ivan had attacked early in the morning. It had been a deceptively peaceful scene just as it was now and Helmut, Hans and I had been waiting.

As soon as the early light of morning was coming up from the east over the rim of the forest, we could detect commotion on the other side of the clearing below the edges of the trees. At first we couldn't make out clearly what was going on, but then we saw horses, so many horses we hardly believed our eyes. It was really a cavalry unit, getting ready to cross the clearing. *CAVALRY?*

During my time in Russia, in the Ukraine in 1942 and '43, I had never seen Cossacks on horses or any other cavalry units for that matter. Where were they coming from now after four years of war?

After all, it was the end of the war, and horses had been replaced by tanks or personnel carriers, or had they?

An idiot on our side—there is always one—instead of keeping it nice and quiet to see whether we'd been discovered or not, let off a few rounds, and the cat was out of the bag. A hundred or so horses, I didn't count them, broke into a trot and then into a gallop throwing up mountains of pulverized snow as they thundered across the clearing. They stretched into a line and galloped towards our position. What a sight!

I think it is superfluous to ask anybody alive today whether they've ever seen or experienced a formation of cavalry coming at them in anger, as fast as the snow on the ground permitted the horses to run. If you haven't seen it by now, I guarantee that you'll never see it. But let me say this, it's a frightening sight and just as scary, if not worse, as any attack by the dreaded, bullet-spitting, unrelenting, modern steel tanks.

I took one look at the first sergeant and new that he was, as the rest of us, on the verge of bolting from our secure position. My stomach did a few convulsions before I yelled, "Everybody get ready to fire! Aim low and we'll create the biggest pile of horse meat you've ever seen."

Even though it was muffled by the snow, the drumming noise of the galloping hooves of hundred or more horses increased by the second. The first sergeant, suddenly realizing the responsibilities of his rank and position, barked an order. Sixteen rifles and one '42 heavy machine gun, firing at one thousand rounds per minute, started to burp their deadly load toward the enemy. The results were not pretty but effective and life saving for us. The horses went down in clusters and the riders with them. We used the confusion on the enemy's side, the screaming of the horses and the cursing of the Cossacks as a welcome diversion to disappear into the woods and head in a westerly direction towards the Oder River as fast as our feet could carry us.

We hadn't eaten anything substantial for two days and trotting through the snow in the woods was exhausting. My leg gave me a lot of pain, but I kept going for fear of being left behind with obvious consequences. A few others felt their handicaps too, and the moaning and complaining became louder. The first sergeant ordered a brief rest, calmed everybody down and tried to figure out our approximate location.

"We must be about two kilometers (one and a quarter mile) away from the river, south of *Guben*. Come on everybody. Get your ass in gear and get up. We'll need all the time we have when we arrive at the river to figure a way to cross it."

5

THE LAST CONVULSIONS

When we finally reached the Oder, totally exhausted and worn out, two men were missing. In our anxious and somehow weakened condition we hadn't even noticed when that had happened. The first sergeant dispatched a group of four men, who seemed to be in the best shape of all of us to go back and search for them. The others rested outside of the adjacent woods on the snow-covered banks of the river. After two long hours the group returned with nothing to report. They told us that they had retraced our steps in the snow as best as they could. The freshly falling snow steadily covered everything within a short period. They hadn't seen anything of the missing men or of the enemy either. The latter was good news, but it was unfortunate that they didn't find any sign of the two missing soldiers.

Now came the hard part for us.

In February of 1945, it had been very cold for weeks; way below freezing, and the Oder had masses of rapidly drifting ice floes coming down stream in large chunks. The only *"vehicles of conveyance"* that we could make out in the rising fog were three old, rickety looking rowboats tied to a landing nearby. The good news was that the boats were afloat and usable. The bad news was that they had no oars. We scurried around and found a few lose boards, which we intended to use as paddles, to get to the other side of the river. Where we stood the river was about 200 to 300 yards wide.

It was one of those wet, ice-cold days when a thick fog hangs over the water and the air smells of moisture from the riverbank and its terrain. Visibility was barely good enough to make out the other side of the river. Wet snow kept falling, even though—when I think back to that moment—we were much too apprehensive to feel anything except fear.

While we were waiting for the missing men, we also anticipated the pursuing Russians to break out of the woods any minute. Our anxiety grew by the second. We desperately wanted to get away from the Russians. Continuous muffled explosions from the fighting further to the north, which drifted upstream, increasingly magnified by the cold and wintry air, indicated to us that the Russians had already reached the river near *Guben*. It would've been downright foolish and hazardous for us to try to stay on the eastern banks and to go north to reach our barracks.

The first sergeant made the decision to attempt the crossing with the boats. Eighteen guys with three rowboats to share is not much. He didn't want to leave any valuable equipment behind, but the equipment was heavy and needed space. Six guys plus equipment in a rowboat was a heavy load. The boats were beginning to take water the minute we left the safety of the banks. It was difficult to paddle through the rushing ice chunks with the cumbersome wooden boards. At our location the Oder flowed north in a long sweeping curve and the natural drift of the water helped carrying us slowly to the other side; at least that's what we could detect from the movement of the ice. The ice floe was pushing and scraping at the side of the boats as we slowly traversed the river in a hurry for more reasons than one. More water was slowly seeping into the boats. Our fear grew that the enemy would appear on the banks to kill and obliterate us with their bullets. It gave us wings. We didn't dare waste any time contemplating our chances of safely crossing the river before we got in the boats. Frightened and scared out of our wits we would drown and be swallowed by the angry river, or crushed by the grinding ice, we paddled for our lives.

Everything was okay until we reached the middle of the river. The water was churning and gurgling wildly with terrific turbulence. The drifting blocks of ice were pushing and squeezing the boats ferociously. Rowing and at the same time pushing the ice away with the wooden boards was only possible if we leaned out of the boat always in danger of capsizing. Suddenly we heard a scream from the left and saw one boat turning over with everybody falling into the water. The occupants were trying to hold on to the floating blocks of ice and the capsized boat with bare hands. Heavy winter clothes were soaking up the water and dragging the men down. We heard cries of *'Hilfe'* (help) and saw several men disappear beneath the icy surface. One guy made it onto a floating chunk of ice, approximately eighteen square feet in size, which slowly drifted to the other side. The other five drowned in the angry river. We jumped into the water as soon as reached the other bank and his float drifted close enough, to pull the prostrate figure off the ice. We had to hold on to each other for fear of being pulled away by the sucking current.

It was indescribably cold now and we were soaking wet from the water. We gathered the equipment that was left, including the DORA, and started running as fast as our feet would carry us to reach the first houses of *Guben* aching for a warm spot anywhere before we solidified into blocks of ice. The first sergeant was really with it. He could've made the experience even more terrible by acting like a stupid jerk, but he didn't. During this crossing we became friends and began trusting each other.

Somehow we made it, actually entering the hotel where, just a few days ago, Celli and I had made love passionately. We hung our clothes near the hot ceramic tile oven in the main guest room and drank tankards of hot, red wine; courtesy of the proprietor. He was glad to see that German soldiers were still around to protect him and his property. As soon as the Russians would come he feared for his life and that of his elderly wife.

Late at night of the same day we had recovered sufficiently to report back to the barracks, which so far had not come under enemy fire. The commandant of the bridgehead, a colonel, had thrown up a defensive perimeter to be prepared for the assault.

The first sergeant couldn't see and I became his seeing-eye dog.

"How did you make it through the war?" I asked unbelievingly. "Half the time that I can remember we moved during the night just to be safe from getting killed."

"It was bad," he replied, "but I always found a guy like you who could help me. Right now I'd give anything to be able to see in the dark like you. This war is winding down, and I'm nervous. Let's go and inspect the forward positions to find out where we're standing, where the Russians are and what supplies we'll need. We won't get any smarter if we stay here in the barracks. We only get more nervous than we already are close to a large complex of barracks with no communications. I'm not only blind but deaf too."

"Let's go," I replied, "but don't expect me to do any shooting or standing in foxholes; I won't. I don't want to wind up in a hospital again, and I mean it." He laughed.

We made the rounds and were told the Russian infantry was out there. They were slowly inching up to our positions, getting closer and closer, probing here and there to see how much and what kind of opposition they were facing.

Whenever the enemy fired toward the barracks, and the volleys struck the brick walls behind us, there were secondary explosions. We deduced that they were using the newest type of rifle ammunition, explosive bullets. That was a nasty surprise. If one of these bullets got you it would explode as soon as it hit a hard surface, like a bone inside the body. We had heard about this ammunition, and I had seen some ugly casualties in the hospital, but I had never been exposed to it in combat. The stakes were getting higher.

We could also hear engines rumbling, big ones and many of them.

The enemy kept probing and stabbing as time wore on. We could only guess that after racing from the Vistula River to the Oder they waited with the next assault only long enough to catch their breath and to refurbish their supply lines. The barracks to the north of the military complex where the "Boss" and the recruits had been were already in Russian hands. Nobody knew what had happened to the hapless recruits.

A few days after we made it over the Oder, the first sergeant excitedly called me to his command stand and told me with a big smile on his face, "The Army Corps has put in a request for an experienced wireless operator. I put in your name, and they accepted immediately. Pack your things. You're out of here. When you get there, don't tell them right away that you only have infantry experience, or they'll send you straight back where you came from. We don't want that to happen, do we?"

I couldn't believe my luck and stuck my hand out to shake his. I was sincerely grateful for what he had done for me. We hugged, and he whispered into my ear, "It's over soon, Peter. Keep your nose out of trouble. You'll be riding in a motor vehicle from now on. No more walking for you, my friend. And, Peter, I live near *Königsstein,* west of *Frankfurt.* Everybody knows the Kaisers there. Look me up when this is over, okay?"

A few years later when the time came I did, but he never made it.

I crossed the bridge over the Oder in westerly direction breathing deeply with a sigh of relief and bummed a ride to the Army Headquarter on a passing truck.

The soldiers at headquarters were actually happy to see me. I found out that first sergeant Kaiser had been correct. I would ride in a *Kübel* (truck-like vehicle similar to nowadays SUVs) The entire rear of the *Kübel* was filled with short wave equipment but was otherwise comfortably arranged with a fold down table top to write on in front of an upholstered bench. What a change in comfort from an infantry wireless operator's life!

I met the crew of four corporals, Kalle, the driver of the *Kübel,* who was from *Oberhausen* in the Ruhr River Valley with a real name of Kalweit. He was the only one who had seen action during the war and had a bad arm injury to prove it. Toni who was from East Prussia, the cipher man, and Erich and Paul two short wave operators like me. Toni was a small, blond man with a dashing mustache on his upper lip and the oldest of the group.

"The ladies like it," he confided to me. "That's why I keep it."

He'd spent the entire war in his present position and turned out to be a great comrade, dependable and helpful.

In essence, they all knew the KW short wave equipment and worked with it expertly. I had some catching up to do. My working experience was limited to the slow and primitive Dora unit used only by the Infantry in forward positions. This was the real stuff, big time!

While the infantry, at least under combat conditions, never received—that is, took messages—at speeds of more than 80–90 letters per minute, these guys easily took 120 to 140 lpm. Not only that, the speed of the incoming signals at times reached 180 lpm, depending on how good the guy on the other end was with his hand. I was totally out of my class, to me the incoming messages sounded like an undecipherable blur. Whenever we had a free minute, Toni tutored me patiently to bring my speed up to snuff.

It wasn't only the speed of the transmissions, which was new to me, but also the coding and decoding. In the infantry we had used printed diagrams—new ones were issued daily—to code the messages after a prearranged pattern. Here we used a coding machine, which needed typing skills and was kind of tricky to operate and to reprogram every day with the newest code.

The DORA units of the Infantry employed UKW (FM) frequencies with the advantage that you never had to listen to more than one signal at a time. The incoming signal was meant for you and nobody else. The first time I put my earphones on to listen to the KW traffic it was like listening to a cacophony of an orchestra playing dissonant music by Bruckner or Shostakovich. There must've been twenty or thirty stations on the same frequency sending Morse signals at the same time.

"What is this?" I exclaimed. "Which one in this noise is my party? This sounds like a howling herd of cats! I can't understand a thing!"

"Try it like this," Toni remarked laughingly, wanting to help me. "You know your station symbol, in our case WW1X. Get attuned to the rhythm of that signal, and whenever you hear it, you have to absorb the music and the handwriting of the man at the sending station and then immediately stick to it. Block out the rest of the noise in your mind as if it isn't even there. At the moment it may sound impossible to you, but you'll see it works, and you'll do fine," he said encouragingly, until somebody called WW1X.

"See, here it is. By the way he is slurring his W's; that's probably Hans over at the 256th. He never learned how to move his hand rhythmically."

With the old Morse code—hitting the keypad rhythmically during transmission—everybody developed a recognizable "handwriting," clearly distinguishable from anybody else.

"You and I, Peter," Toni said confidently, "we'll practice a little more and then you'll be perfect."

During the following days he did so with great patience and determination until my speed improved to the point, which permitted me to sit alone at night to listen to the traffic on the KW band as if it were music I could understand. Without him and his patient help I would've been a goner in no time. I would've returned to my old outfit with first sergeant Kaiser and to the useless annihilation process that was continuing unabated.

At the *Armeekorps* we never had any contact with the enemy and were at least three to six miles away from any fighting. While this was okay and a welcome relief for me it exposed me at the same time to the political badgering and manipulation by a type of soldier who had spent the entire war in safety and near the "BRASS." Few of these soldiers had any front line experience or decorations to prove it. Maybe I saw a "frozen meat" ribbon tucked to a uniform here and there, because the guy had been in the army long enough to experience the winter of '41 in Russia. But they certainly wore no mementos of any fighting. Now they tried everything to hide until it was over. "Stay away from the fighting at all cost; use all your influence to let somebody else go where the bullets were flying."

The questions that were on everybody's mind were rather obvious:

"How long can this war possibly last, and how will I survive until the end?"

"When the time comes, how will we manage to surrender to the Americans and not to the Russians, who most likely would ship everybody off to Siberia?"

"How can we possibly be where the American forces are, and what will be the armistice arrangements between the parties when everything collapses?"

Only the dear Lord knew the answers, and he was not talking to us.

Our unit, which was attached to the 5th Army Corps, was sent all over the place to do emergency communications work and to keep the "BRASS"—which in our case was the infamous *Generalfeldmarschall Schörner*—informed how everything was going or, even better, was going to pot. The sudden and rather hasty retreat of the German divisions from the Vistula all the way to the Oder—with heavy losses of men and material—didn't give the front line battalions, regiments or divisions enough time to reorganize or put telephone wires on the ground. Many times whole regiments were left hanging in the air, literally.

Once a demoralized army starts to run there is nothing to stop it and everything goes to hell. The German army was plainly demoralized beyond repair; there was no doubt about it. In spite of draconian measures by the military police, in German jargon called *"Kettenhunde"* ("chain dogs"), because a silver-plated metal shield attached to a chain hung around their necks depicting them as military police—desertions were plentiful. The morale of the German soldier had gone south, all the way. For the officers it was difficult if not impossible to get anybody to risk his live for a lost cause.

With troops in deplorable psychological condition the high command decided in early April of 1945 to shift us further south towards central Silesia to the neighborhood of *Breslau* (It is now Polish and is renamed Wroczlaw). For what we had in mind, when the end came—question 1, 2, and 3, above—Silesia was the worst of all possible places to be. One look at the map to locate Silesia will prove my point. It is like a long appendix, split in two on a north-south axis by the Oder River tucked between Czechoslovakia in the west and Poland in the east. If we wanted to go to the west to reach the American troops we would be totally blocked by Czech territory. It would be difficult in any case to cross Czechoslovakia without harassment and possible belligerent engagements with Czech partisans. The one thing we didn't want to do was to fight anymore, to fight anybody, or to kill anybody.

During March and April of 1945 we were ordered back and forth, riding in our *Kübel,* to help the struggling front line units communicate with each other. Often we observed openly displayed panic in the eyes of the civilians, especially the women fearful of the raping that would most likely take place by the advancing Russians. The civilians didn't have any place to go and were painfully aware that they couldn't cross Czechoslovakia. They were waiting fearfully for the Russian army to arrive.

On one of these assignments we were put up in a farmhouse at the edge of a small village, it was occupied by four women all of them refugees with their children.

As usual we were working through the night transmitting supply and casualty figures. It was boring work with lots of figures and statistics. Two of the women kept Toni and me company. More to the point they were trying to find out from us what method of survival would be the best for them, in our expert opinions.

"Tell us where to go before it is too late, and the Russians are here. We're in deadly fear of being gang raped," One of them, called Ilse said to the two of us. "We're not from here, you know. The local Government of *Düsseldorf* transferred us to Silesia, to protect us from the continuous air raids by American bombers. At first it was okay. We worked for the farmers, had enough to eat and didn't have to go into the cellars any more. Our children could sleep again and gradually stopped crying all the time. But now it appears as if we have jumped from the frying pan into the fire. We're stuck in this village with the Russians approaching fast. We have no means of transportation, and the railroads have stopped running. None of the locals really like us, the *Rhineländer,* and we don't know what to do. Could you possibly take us with you? I mean, we don't even have bicycles to move faster and my child is only two years old, Maria's is three, we are kind of limited in our options."

Both of the women, Ilse and Maria, were about 22 or 23 years old and had been married for only a short time.

Toni asked them where their husbands were, but neither had any idea nor had heard from their men in over a year.

"I'll give you some advice, but you won't like it," he said. "Stay here. You have a roof over your head; it's a farming community with enough food for all of you. You don't want to be out on the road with young children to worry about. Yes, yes," he continued as Ilse tried to reply, "I know what you'll say. The Russians will rape us. Well, that may be true. We have seen lots of women being raped, but they were still alive when it was over."

"That's a rather callous observation. Would you give that advice to your wife too?" Ilse replied angrily.

"I don't have a wife," Tone replied quietly, "but I have a very dear friend at home, whom I intend to marry when all this is over, and I don't even want to think about her being in a situation like you are in now. I'm from East Prussia. I don't know whether my family escaped, is on a trek through Poland, or is dead. But, Ilse, the scenes we have seen on the roads coming down here were pretty grim. Often they were clogged by thousands upon thousands of refugees without food or shelter, and the end result will be the same or worse when the Russians catch up with these *treks.* "

We didn't get a reply from either one of them, but they became quiet after Toni had bluntly outlined the grim alternative for them.

We continued our work on the KW unit, and the women were talking agitatedly amongst themselves debating one solution against the other. When our shift ended Erich and Paul took over, and we took the women outside for a smoke. They were grateful for the company and didn't object when we invited them to come with us to our beds of hay in the attic of the building. Ilse was nice and cuddly and Toni must have felt the same about Maria. They were two lonesome women fearful of the future, and we were not too sure of what lay in store for us either. Lying in each other's arms gave comfort to all four of us. Most likely everybody had their own thoughts and anxieties, but for the rest of the night we stayed together, comforted each other, made love to each other and finally fell asleep holding each other.

The next morning was the day we were going to depart. Ilse asked me to take a walk with her into the nearby forest. It was a warm and sunny day and the first signs of budding spring could be seen on the bushes. Ilse told me of their decision. They were going to stay, no matter what, because of the children she said. We sat down on the ground; she quickly slipped out of one side of her underpants and invited me to be with her one more time.

"Before the bad guys come," as she put it.

On the 6th of May 1945, we were positioned in a small *Strassendorf* (a village built alongside a road instead of in a cluster), which was common in this part of Silesia. Since leaving the women behind in late April we had retreated sixty miles further towards the *Riesengebirge* and the city of *Hirschberg.* The *Dorf* stretched for two miles on both sides of the road. Headquarters was on one end of the village while we were on the other. A call came in from HQ on the short wave requesting a messenger come pick up a *Führerbefehl*—an order by Hitler—to be rebroadcast to all units. I was told to go and fetch it, but

I didn't dare leaving our quarters without appropriate protection. We arranged for three guys to follow me at a distance of 100 feet with automatic weapons in the crooks of their arms, as a precaution, of course. The MPs were running wild because of rampant desertions and had already strung up four guys—whom they had suspected of desertion—on trees and telegraph poles alongside the street. They were left hanging for everybody to see as intimidation, their feet swaying slowly in the breeze. The soldiers had been caught on the road without proper marching orders. The MPs had hanged them without asking any questions. Those bastards! I didn't want this to happen to me.

A good thing we did what we did, because the MP's were lurking behind one of the houses as we were walking down the street through the village. They withdrew quickly when they saw that my protection meant business.

At headquarters I received a written proclamation, to be broadcast to all units. The *Führer* and Chancellor of the *Reich,* Adolf Hitler, had died on May 4th in the cellar of the Chancellery in Berlin in defense of the Fatherland, and *Admiral von Doenitz* had been named his successor. All hostilities would stop on the 9th of May at 12 o'clock noontime, and every unit of the Army would have to remain exactly at the location where it was at that time. And now came the interesting part; the demarcation line between the advancing Russian army on one side and the Americans on the other side was the Moldavia River in western Czechoslovakia, about 120 miles from our present position.

We ran back, did our transmission to all units in clear text and contacted our buddies from the infantry to decide what route to take across enemy territory to save our collective asses and to be in the right place on the 9th of May, the magic day. Now was the time not to hesitate and to do the right thing.

"I don't think it's a smart idea to remain where we are," I volunteered. "Let's take the two cars we have. We have enough gas for both of them, cross the *Riesengebirge* near *Oberschreiberau* and drive through Czechoslovakia until we get to the Moldavia where the American army is waiting. We have until the 9th at noon; that should be time enough."

"And what happens if the Partisans have established road blocks and won't let us pass?" somebody objected.

"Yeah, I agree, do you want to defeat the Czechs or start another war?" was a remark from another wise guy who had never seen any combat during the entire war.

"No," I replied brusquely, "but I most certainly don't want to become a Russian prisoner either, and, if I look around this room, it seems to me we have enough able men to hold our own against a few Czech civilians. We'll put one man with a machine gun on the roof of the *Kübel* lying between the antenna rods facing forward and another man facing backward to guard our rear. If anything unfriendly develops or only appears to develop, they'll fire a burst of lead in the air. I don't believe that any of the partisans are eager to die now that everything is over."

"He's right," was Toni's opinion. "And a second vehicle will follow us with the same setup, okay?"

A few more ideas were thrown back and forth with nothing intelligent being said. The two factions, the "go" faction and the "no go" faction couldn't agree. Kalle broke it up by announcing, "I'm going outside to start the car and load all the gasoline we have. You better get your things together and get into the car too—otherwise Peter and I'll take off without you."

That seemed to be the proper wake up call. Everybody scrambled for their belongings. We set up the two guys on top of the car. One could never know; there were also our own MPs to guard against too. Our two cars left ten minutes later in a westerly direction driving past *Hirschberg* and continuing toward the *Riesengebirge*. In essence, we were deserting, but we didn't care any more.

For the first few miles the roads were crowded with soldiers. Most of them had thrown their weapons away. Ten miles further towards the mountains and Czech territory the traffic became lighter and lighter. On one corner of the road we saw a sign:

> 5th Army Central
> Medical Supply Depot

"Let's make a quick detour, Kalle," I said. "Maybe we can find something useful in the depot. We are running low on food too."

Kalle agreed, turned off the main road and continued for about three more miles until we saw a group of administrative officers, *Schmalspurindianer* (small-gauge-Indians, so-called because of narrow epaulettes on their uniforms, hardly translatable), as the soldiers called them derogatorily, were waiting for us at the entrance to the depot with their side weapons drawn.

"Halt! Nobody enters the premises. This is property of the *Deutsche Reich* and nobody enters without proper authorization." One of the administration officers announced loudly and rather pompously.

"Show this asshole in uniform our authorization."

Toni called to the guy on the roof of the *Kübel* who was lying there with the MG 42, ready for action.

The corporal on top of the car obliged by hammering a salvo into the upper windows of the building, and the supply officers succumbed quickly. It was the beginning of the end. The common soldier, even a good-natured guy like Toni, was feeling his oats. Anyway, these officers were bureaucrats in uniform and had never used their pistols during their entire lives. We took the pistols away from them to avoid any unnecessary damage, to be on the safe side, and entered the building. It was huge, about 100,000 square feet under one roof and loaded up to the ceiling with pallets upon pallets of medical supplies, but, as we discovered, also with food items. Where had all this stuff been when we needed it? The shortage of medicine, bandages and especially anesthetics had been critical for a long time. Those bureaucrats had been sitting on them while the wounded were suffering. We loaded what we needed in the food department. I found a securely locked room containing narcotics. Just in case, I took a box with 100 vials of morphine. I didn't really know what to do with it at the time, but I took it anyway. I thought it might help our finances later on. The little convoy stopped again after we made it back to the main road to wait for nightfall, and we slept somewhere near the roadside. It was no use driving in the dark and being surprised by something we couldn't see or evaluate properly. We had been soldiers too long to be that stupid.

At dawn, as we entered Czechoslovakia, we proceeded cautiously down the road. At first all was clear. But slowly more and more

Czech civilians lined the side of the highway, shaking their fists and yelling something in their language that we couldn't understand. They carried weapons all right but were not eager to use them after wisely observing that we were prepared and ready to defend ourselves.

The first serious roadblock appeared 50 miles into "enemy" territory. We stopped the Kübel a couple of hundred yards short of the roadblock and held a war counsel.

"I don't think it would be wise to drive up to them and start negotiating," Kalle said. "Once we get near them we are trapped. We shouldn't stop too close so we can be rushed. There are more of them than us, and I wouldn't want to be within shooting range. If we do that our goose is cooked."

"Okay," Toni said. "Good thought! What would you do or anybody else for that matter?"

I opened my mouth and suggested that we put a few shots into the air with the MG over their heads to see what would happen. A salvo of an automatic weapon always had a sobering effect.

That's what we did, one sustained salvo from the 42 over their heads, and the little convoy started to roll. It worked. Cursing and shooting in the air the group of civilians removed the roadblock, and we passed by at high speed, continuously threatening with our rifles sticking out of every window and with the two 42's. We had to repeat this procedure several times on our way west, and we also listened to newscasts from all sides during the day to gather new information which could be useful for us on the 9th at 12 o'clock, when the historic moment of the end of the war would finally arrive.

We spent one more night in a fortified position in an open field, together with other soldiers who had taken the same route. A broadcast by the BBC informed us the next morning the Moldavia River had definitely been designated as demarcation line between advancing Russians from the East and the Allies coming from the West.

I got a real warm feeling in the pit of my stomach; I would finally meet American soldiers. What would they say to my story? How would they react? How should I present my case? I decided that if I could get anybody to listen, I would tell them the truth and nothing but the truth.

But, no matter what happened or what they might do, the main thing was the war was over, and I was still alive. There was no question in my mind after checking us out and removing all of our weapons that the Allies would set us free, and we would be sent home. What else could they do with us? The war was over?

I planned to go straight to the next civilian telephone to call my mother, who, I was hoping fervently had remained in the safety of Switzerland.

On the morning of May 9, 1945, after 129 miles of driving through belligerent territory, we arrived at the banks of the Moldavia. The river was not very wide, maybe 150 yards at the most, and the water was moving very leisurely. Some anxious *pioneer* officer with wrong ideas of strategy had blown up the only existing bridge upstream. Two ferrymen occupied a small ferry, hanging on a rope in the middle of the river in front of us. One of the two men spoke some halting German and shouted at us, "What can you present in form of payment if we ferry you across?"

The guys pulled bundles of money, German money, from their pockets, but the ferrymen only laughed at the sight of the paper *Reich Mark.*

"Nicht gut, nicht gut" (Not good), they shouted repeatedly.

Next to me stood an officer clad in one of these fancy peacetime uniform jackets that had disappeared from sight a long time ago.

The buttons of his jacket were neatly covered with gray cloth evidently made by a real tailor. I watched him curiously as he started twisting and turning one of the buttons until it came off. He peeled the cloth from the button and, lo and behold, what appeared under the cloth was a gold coin, a real RM 20—gold coin, from Kaiser Wilhelm II. He put it between his thumb and index finger and held it up for the ferrymen to see, and shouting at them, "Do you take gold?"

You should've seen how quickly the guys moved the ferry to our side. The officer—I forgot his name—asked us if we would give him a ride in our *Kübel* to Winterberg; we answered in the affirmative. He then ordered our two cars and some of his men onto the ferry.

I'd learned a valuable lesson about the value of paper money.

Everybody let out a sigh of relief as we crossed the river. We'd reached the American side. We were safe! The war was over, and we'd escaped the imminent danger of becoming captives of the Soviet army.

Somebody produced a bottle of cognac, and we drank to our survival and to what we thought would be the beginning of a new life.

I am sure all of you know the saying, "Don't count your chickens until they are hatched."

Silesia, 1945. Totally worn out.

6

THE GERMANS LOST AND NOBODY BELIEVES MY STORY

Now here we were almost precisely where we wanted to be. We had driven completely across Czechoslovakia, speeding like maniacs, and were in the midst of the Bohemian Forest very close to German territory. A few more miles and we would be safely in *Winterberg* where the old border between Germany and Czechoslovakia had been.

This war of wars was over. I had waited through hell and damnation for it to end. I'd fought and suffered, walked thousands of miles. My constant thoughts were of survival, staying alive, not becoming a total cripple, not getting caught by the wrong people. I was always painfully aware I was in the wrong uniform, fighting on the side of a criminal organization, which had been heading towards disaster from the outset.

But I had fought my way through. I *had* survived, somewhat bruised, but still one of the few who had come through. I learned later that of the twenty-three healthy young men from my high school class, I was one of the last remaining five; most of the others had perished—killed in action or dead of malaria, typhoid fever, or hepatitis. The Nazis had imprisoned one in one of their infamous *Konzentrationslager.* Only God knew where he was now. Another had gone insane.

Most of the guys with me now had endured the fighting for three or more bloody years, though only one had lasted through the entire war. Some, like me, were barely twenty-one years old. Some had been wounded three or four times. We were damaged goods, to say the least. I myself had been hit seven times. I could hardly chew properly or open my mouth and was barely able to walk. We'd been in and out of hospitals so many times they'd become a second home to us. Many of the guys were virgins; most had neither wives nor children.

And now, as we raced our *Kübel* the last few kilometers toward German territory, we were certain we were the chosen ones. We would not be caught by anybody! We would not be shot or hanged by one of the hated *Kettenhunde*. We had made it!

The convoy raced over a small hill, steep enough so we couldn't see the other side. Our group consisted of four vehicles driving at sixty miles an hour, singing old songs until our throats ached because *Winterberg* lay only ten miles away. And *Winterberg* meant freedom. There would definitely be no Russians or murderous Czechs no matter what new disasters awaited us.

I hit Kalle on the back and shouted over the din of the engine, "We're almost there! Step on it and don't look back. I never in my whole life want to see another bloody Czech again!"

As we raced over the crest of the hill, there they were—the whole bloody American Army, or so it seemed. Kalle, driving the lead vehicle, stomped on the brakes and brought the car to a screeching stop.

"Look at it! Have you ever seen so many Sherman tanks before?" I shouted in total awe.

Spread across the plain, which opened before us were at least twenty Sherman tanks flanked by trucks, jeeps, and personnel carriers with the Star Spangled Banner flying from the lead vehicle.

"Where are we?" Kalle shouted. *"Ich glaube mein Bett brennt!"* (I think my bed is on fire!) This can't be for real! We can't even turn around on this narrow road, or they'll pulverize us."

No sooner had he spoken than a round exploded to the left of our column. The Americans closed in fast and stopped a hundred yards in front of us. An officer jumped off the lead tank, which pointed its canon threateningly at our *Kübel*.

Oh my God, I thought, *this is what I've been waiting to see for six years. But what do I tell them now? I am an American in German uniform? I have been forced by the Nazis to serve in the German Army? They'll die laughing,* I told myself. I could almost hear their response. *You're wearing the wrong uniform, Kraut. Just because you speak some English doesn't make you an American."*

That's exactly what they would say. Speaking English could even make it worse.

"We met a lot of you guys at the Bulge, all properly fitted up in American uniforms speaking excellent English, making us believe you were one of us. A lot of our guys bit the dust because they believed you. We're not falling for that crap again."

That's what they'd say.

No, better keep my mouth shut. Now as we were finally American prisoners—something we had planned for over the last several months—I would have an opportunity to tell my story. This moment, with tensions running high was not the best time. I was safe. Let that be enough for now.

Everybody was kind of excited, but apprehensive, too. The Americans looked a little uptight. Anything could set them off.

What a frigging mess we were in.

The GIs jumped off their vehicles and ran toward us, their M1s leveled and ready to shoot at the slightest provocation, shouting constantly.

"Hands up, hands up."

We watched fearfully in anticipation of what they'd do next.

"Hands up! Hands up! Get the fuck out of your cars and put your fucking hands up! *Snell, snell!"*

Nobody in our group was even mildly inclined to disobey. All fifteen or twenty of us clambered quickly out of our vehicles. Our hands over our heads, we attempted to do nothing that might look the least suspicious, no move that might give the impression we were going to put up any resistance. All our side arms were thrown into the road, and the GIs moved quickly to remove our watches and other valuables. Fortunately I carried my watch in a bag in the car, which they did not search thoroughly.

What is this thing victorious soldiers have with watches? Most of them must have their own. Maybe it's the souvenir value or some other secret impulse of the winner when meeting the loser, but they all seem to love watches.

The GIs searched the four *Kübel* looking for weapons. What they found right away were the 200 vials of morphine, which I had swiped from the depot near *Oberschreiberau.* I had intended to make a fortune with that stuff but no dice. It was already gone.

"Hey, look at this! This'll keep us happy for a while," the lucky discoverer shouted to his buddies.

The excitement between the GIs was great. They immediately sensed the value of these vials. Their commanding officer, a captain, wasn't fast enough to secure the loot before it had mysteriously disappeared.

Another thing the Americans seemed to be interested in were our medals. My *Verwundetenabzeichen in Gold* was gone in no time.

Kalle and I looked at each other, each seeing in the others eyes the incredible disgrace, humiliation, and disappointment engulfing us.

Arms above our heads and surrounded by GIs, we felt most deeply the frustration of not having made it to freedom, to *Winterberg,* where we would've been safe. We knew *this* would be our final stop.

"Get back in your cars and follow our jeep," the captain ordered after the GIs had satisfied their curiosity about the contents of our vehicles.

The car started to roll, and Kalle grumbled about our stupidity rushing over that last hill without first investigating what lay ahead, while he shifted noisily through the gears.

"How dumb could we be? Peter, you spent the whole war in the infantry. You of all people should know how to survive. No wonder they got you seven times. Damned shit, fuck, fuck! How did we get into this mess?"

Nobody in the *Kübel* said a word. Even though I didn't exactly agree with Kalle's negative assessment of my wartime skills, I had to admit our negligence and stupidity had been extraordinary. It could only be excused by our eagerness to get as far as possible away from the Russians and our euphoria to see the war was finally over and we'd survived.

The American officer made us turn our cars around and head back in the opposite direction towards the hell we'd been trying to escape: Czechoslovakia. After about ten miles, just past *Strakonice,* we saw a sign that read "Pisek 4 km". Over the next hill and in sight of the town of *Pisek,* we saw a camp nestled against a small forest. Already occupied by many vehicles and by more than 400 people, the field seemed to be full of vehicles and overrun with German soldiers, but we also recognized a number of women and children as well. Driving off the road and into the field, the GIs directed us to an empty spot then left us to our own devices.

Our sergeant, the ranking member of our group, had been generally useless throughout the entire race across Czechoslovakia. He had joined up with us in the last Silesian village after the armistice had been declared, as we were leaving German territory east of *Oberschreiberau.* He'd displayed no initiative, no original thought, nothing and disappeared whenever we encountered difficulties or when decisions had to be made. He'd survived the war as a bureaucrat, never closer to the actual fighting than wherever the divisional headquarter was located. But he was always very important looking, always with a big mouth and a clean uniform, a good gofer for the officers.

Only after I'd been wounded several times and been disabled for front line duty had I become acquainted with this type of soldier. Most of them were absolutely healthy, aside from some so-called illnesses like ulcers or asthma. But our sergeant wasn't the only one. There were men like him in every unit of the army.

"Come on, Wilhelm," Kalle prompted him, "you're in command here. Go find out what's going on. We'll check around and talk to the others in the camp."

Wilhelm ambled off toward the entrance to the encampment where German officers stood around looking important.

Kalle called out to Toni and me to join him. At thirty-four, Toni was the oldest of our group. We headed toward a nearby personnel carrier occupied by soldiers, noncoms, and a few women as well.

"Hallo, comrade," Toni addressed one of them. "Do you know what's going on here or what the *Amis* are planning to do with us?"

"No idea," the guy answered. "They stopped our convoy just after we crossed the Moldova, shortly before we reached *Pisek.* We were happy to be on the western side of the demarcation line. Our main goal was to get as far away from the Russians as we could. The radio has been full of news of the conditions of the armistice agreement, you know. We heard the Moldova River was the dividing line between the Russians and the Americans, and anybody who could make it to the western side of the river by the ninth at noon would be an American prisoner. Everybody on the eastern side would be in the hands of the Russians."

The guy busied himself lighting a cigarette, then continued.

"You see, that was the reason we picked up our wives in Silesia to come with us. We wanted our families safe with one of the Western Allies and not expose them to being raped by the Russians. The party big shots back home had evacuated them to Silesia a few months ago to protect them from the continuous bombing raids around *Düsseldorf.* Many of us lost our families to the bombs, you know? It was about time the party bosses did something about it. Life in Silesia was good until about two weeks ago. In general those little villages had more to eat for the civilians than the big cities in the west. It was a stroke of luck our unit came by, and we were able to pick up our families. At least we're together now, which makes everything easier to bear."

It seemed to me they'd jumped—like Ilse and Maria whom we had left behind—*"vom Regen in die Traufe,"* from the frying pan into the fire.

"If the Czechs ever get a chance to lay their hands on us, God only knows what they'll do," the guy continued. "Especially to our wives. But then, I don't think this will happen, because the *Amis* will need us when they try to finish off the Russians once and for all."

The three of us looked at each other thunderstruck! This was the first time we had heard anything about a possible confrontation between America and Russia.

"What are you talking about?" Toni shouted at the guy angrily. "The *Amis* want to start something with the Ivan? And what have we got to do with it? You must be crazy." He calmed down a bit and continued, "Oh, by the way, I'm Toni, and this is Kalle and Peter. What's your name and outfit?"

The guy lit another cigarette while displaying an air of importance, because he seemed to know more about the situation than we did, and finally answered Toni's question.

"My name is Horst, and this is my wife, Helga. Before we started slogging our way across *Czechoslovakia* and everything began falling apart, I was with the 5th *Panzer division.* I don't even know what happened to the rest of my outfit. It kind of dissolved the minute the armistice was officially declared. From the way you're looking at me I guess you don't believe what I'm telling you, but everybody around here talks about nothing but the *Amis* using us to finish the war against Stalin. We haven't heard anything definite, but believe me we're listening to every newscast we can catch on our wireless. Up to now there's been nothing to hang your hat on, but the story makes sense, doesn't it? We have all the experience fighting against the Ivan. Our arms must be around here somewhere, and you'll never convince me the Americans are friends of the Bolsheviks. And besides, why else would they assemble us so close to where the Russians are?"

I couldn't believe my ears. These guys must be stark raving mad! Where had they been during the last two months? How could they possibly believe the Americans would want anything to do with the German Army? I knew they considered the Germans a bunch of murdering criminals. Besides, by now they had to be so sick and tired of the war; they'd do anything to keep from prolonging it. But then I had to remind myself these guys probably hadn't listened to the English language broadcasts as often as I did.

I heard them regularly from the BBC or from the U.S. Armed Forces Network during the last months before the war ended. Of course, this was done always in secret with Kalle standing guard outside the *Kübel*. We didn't want to get caught by any of the political officers, the *Kettenhunde,* or any other fanatic party member. Even though it was late in the war and most people seemed to be sick of it, there were still quite a few diehards around.

Horst probably had no idea how appalled and shocked the world had been when the advancing American forces first encountered the German *Konzentrationslager,* the concentration camps, filled with starving Jews and corpses.

But Horst was proud of his own theories and continued to expound upon them and the stories he had heard from "reliable sources" while Kalle threw impatient glances at me.

"Well, okay," said Toni, "let us know if you hear any more about this. After all, we wouldn't want to miss out on the next war."

He laughed disgustedly as he turned and waved at us to come along.

"What about you?" he asked us, with cynicism dripping in his voice. "Are you eager to jump into the next fracas? Not me. Before I pick up another gun again they'll have to tar and feather me."

We all nodded in agreement. Horst's story might have sounded to some like a possible solution to the mess we were in at the moment, but not to my friends and me.

As we returned to our *Kübel,* we could see the sergeant coming back from his scouting expedition. Everybody scurried around him, questioning him eagerly.

"What did the brass say?"

"What's going to happen now?"

"What about food?"

"When are they going to release us?"

"Are we going to be transported to some other place, or are they going to release us to go home from here?"

"Did you hear anything about the rumor that we'll join the Americans to fight the Russians?"

The sergeant quieted everybody down. "They don't know a thing. The Amis either don't know themselves what to do with us, or they aren't telling. You can believe it or not, but the only thing they seem interested in is having a race between one of their Jeeps and one of our amphibian *Volkswagen.* Kalle, how about you? You're a good driver, and you know how to handle that little thing. Even though we've lost the war, we don't want to lose a race against that funny looking Jeep, do we?"

Kalle laughed. He was all for it, but first he wanted answers to all the other questions we had asked.

The sergeant obliged. "So far I can't really find out anything. The Amis don't have any food except the rations for their own men. The only thing they promised was water, which we need badly. Right? They also told us to start digging latrines to keep the place from becoming totally unsanitary. Our officers—those who arrived here before us—have promised to provide a work detail. And the

Amis also promised one role of toilet paper for everyone, which is a joke. Without food how are we going to shit? I know it's not much, but I think by tonight we'll know more. No one said a word about us joining them to fight the Ivan."

"Where do I go for the race?" Kalle asked the sergeant. "And who's coming to watch it?"

"Come with me," the sergeant replied.

The two took off to organize whatever there was to be organized.

I didn't like the news one bit. How could this bleeding idiot be concerned about a car race when we were in the middle of Czechoslovakian territory, surrounded by revenge-seeking Czechs? The situation was as dangerous as it could possibly get, and we were talking about a car race?

We had to get away from this camp fast. Nothing else was of any importance. Nevertheless, I followed my friend to help with interpreting to the American driver. Somebody had to tell them what was going on.

Kalle was checking on the mechanical condition of the one and only available VW *Schwimmwagen* (amphibian car), indicating to me from a distance that everything looked okay.

Nine or ten GIs stood near the starting point, laughing and joking, thoroughly convinced this race between their Jeep and the German *Volkswagen* would be as easy to win as the war.

I found out which of them was going to drive the Jeep and went over to talk to him.

"Hi, I'm Peter," I introduced myself. "I hope you'll understand my English. I'm a little rusty. Tell me how this race is going to work."

"I'm Joe, and I've never heard a fucking German speak English as well as you do. A little Brooklyn accent there, but otherwise okay."

"Actually, that's something I wanted to talk to you about," I began, deciding to explain my special situation. But then I thought better of it. I should probably wait for an officer, so I changed course. "Lots of English in school. I'll explain later. But it comes in handy now, don't you think, Joe? Tell me, what does my friend Kalle have to do?"

Joe laughed. "Tell your friend we'll drive up that hill over there, turn the cars around at the top and begin the race. I'll use my fingers to count to three then we'll start. When I lift the third finger, down the hill we go, right past the camp to the intersection just before the beginning of the town. We turn around and head back to the entrance of the camp. First one there wins. And tell your buddy, just for the heck of it, the winner gets a carton of Lucky Strikes, okay?"

I translated all this to Kalle and told him about the carton of precious American cigarettes if he won. For a smoker it was a fantastic incentive. To be able to experience the taste of real American tobacco was all Kalle had to hear. But he had to joke.

"Damn the cigarettes! Why don't you negotiate for our release, Peter, instead of a carton of cigarettes?"

The two contestants got into their cars, and Kalle followed the Jeep up the hill.

The Volkswagen and the Jeep looked very small up there. We could hardly see them, and everybody—friend and foe alike—was yelling and backslapping.

Bets were made, marks against dollars, food items or cigarettes. All of a sudden we were not Germans against Americans, but a bunch of young men having a great time and rooting for their man.

"Here they come," somebody yelled. "The Jeep is ahead," and right he was. The Jeep roared by, closely followed by the VW. Down the hill they went to make the turn at the intersection. The Germans knew that the VW with its wide tires and very low mid-section was great at cornering.

"There they are at the intersection, and the Ami has to slow down otherwise his Jeep will topple over," a German shouted while the VW made the turn smoothly and passed the Jeep.

"Joe, step on it! Let's go! Don't give the fucking Kraut an inch," came the shouts from the Americans.

By this time half the people in the encampment, soldiers and civilians, were near the road. The *happening* of the race had made the rounds quickly, and nobody wanted to miss it. The hoopla and the yelling from both sides were deafening. Everybody wanted his man to win.

Then they raced up the hill on a small, narrow road. Kalle was not about to give the Jeep an opportunity to pass if he didn't have to. Besides, it appeared as if the VW had a little more speed on the incline. The VW came roaring by five yards in front of the Jeep with Kalle waving happily.

Now, wasn't that something! The ratty little Volkswagen had won against the Jeep. The American soldiers were speechless.

"My God, what do you have under the hood? This must be a V8 with compressor," one of the U.S. soldiers shouted.

"Come look for yourself. The engine really is a marvel." Kalle laughed, prepared to use the oldest trick in the book when it came to the engine of a VW. The soldier came over, and Kalle obligingly pulled the wire for the hood opener.

As it popped open, the soldier stared at the spare tire and otherwise empty cavity. His eyes flew open.

"Where's the engine?" he shouted. "There's no engine? This guy must have made it on foot."

All of us laughed, and the German prisoners loved it.

Kalle magnanimously waved his arm. "Come over here to the back, and I'll show you a piece of German engineering designed by Professor Porsche. Air-cooled, needs no water, runs like the devil as you've seen. And more importantly it uses very little gasoline."

Joe studied the small engine with the big belt for the cooling fan and shook his head. "It's a wonder you lost the war with such great equipment. But then you fought for the wrong side, and that's what made the difference."

Kalle kept his mouth shut. He gently reminded Joe of his carton of cigarettes.

Joe was a good sport. He congratulated Kalle and handed him the carton of Lucky Strikes. "Good driving. I have to admit it's not only the car. You really did a good job. You earned your cigarettes."

"You're not so bad yourself." Kalle grinned and accepted the carton.

The Germans had their happy moment at a time of worry, and the GIs were good losers, marveling at that little amphibious VW, which really looked like a bathtub on wheels.

Soon the excitement was all over. Our group went back to the *Kübel*. We decided it would be wise to take an inventory of the eating stuff we had left until our captors could come up with more supplies. Everybody was willing to contribute to the supply of food and to share with the others.

Many times in later years I remembered this moment when people still appeared to be human and sane.

Several loaves of bread turned up, along with a few cans of soup, some candy and chocolate, butter, and tea. That was all. We decided to determine the size of individual rations frugally to have enough food for everybody over the next two or three days. Hopefully the Americans would soon come up with something edible for their prisoners of war.

The days were already getting longer. It was the eleventh of May; and, fortunately for us, it was getting warmer, too. In the falling dusk of the early evening, Kalle and I walked to the edge of the camping field not more than one hundred yards away to check out the situation and see what guards, if any, our captors had put in place. At the edge of the encampment we found a thinly wooded area, mostly pine trees, and no American guards to be seen anywhere.

We probed deeper into the woods until, after about 150 yards, we heard voices. We stopped dead in our tracks and remained silent and motionless. We could faintly hear some Czechs talking to each other in the distance.

"Those bastards," I whispered to Kalle. "Not American guards, but Czechs. Guess what they're going to do if anyone in this camp tries to escape? They're going to slit our throats."

Slowly and quietly we retreated. As we came out of the forest, we encountered a few soldiers and their wives, their faces troubled.

"Did you hear them, too?" one of them asked. "The whole camp is surrounded. Thank goodness for the Americans. I don't think they're here to guard us. They're here to protect us."

We discussed this back and forth but came to no conclusion. On one side was the town of *Pisek* and the road, on the other side, dense woods. There was no fence, but we were trapped, nevertheless.

The ensuing night was not very peaceful. We heard women sobbing, children crying, and the men debating the situation endlessly from all sides. Our little group was fortunate enough not to have any children or women around to burden us. We had that much less to worry about, but it didn't make the situation any better.

7

AND NOW WE'LL GO
AND PICK GRAPES

Ir was late; we had an eventful day behind us and camped down underneath the *Kübel* seeking protection from the cool night temperatures.

But no matter how late it was, or how tired we were, we couldn't go to sleep and were laying awake most of the night, talking and discussing our options backward and forward. Not knowing what our captors planned to do with us. It was an uncertain situation. People were talking all around us. Some of the more light-hearted ones were snoring loudly.

Nudging me gently, after resting for a few hours, Kalle asked, "Are you sleeping?"

"What do you mean sleeping?" I replied indignantly. "How can anybody sleep under these circumstances? I must admit this is a new one. I had thought that nothing in this war could surprise or frighten me anymore. But now my brain is numb, and my thoughts are running in circles. I don't know what to do next or even what to think next. Here we are in the middle of Czechoslovakia; we are American prisoners of war, and the war is over. Kalle, I am suspicious as to why the Americans are holding us here? Something doesn't smell right, I'll tell you. I'll only be able to sleep in peace again when this uniform is off my back, when I wear my civilian clothes, and when I know that I can do as I choose. Do you understand what I am talking about?"

Kalle understood very well; he was not one of these stupid army blokes who could only think of women and alcohol.

Though we knew each other for only a short time, we had become friends quickly not only because we were of the same age, but also because we had been working together, decoding messages, and doing our thing during long nights of a seemingly endless war. We had had

251

many opportunities to exchange our views about the war, politics, how the war would end and what we would do as civilians. We had agreed on most subjects.

Now he didn't know what to reply.

"If the Amis wouldn't only look so confused, I mean. Have you ever seen a group of soldiers so totally at ease? I believe they would behave differently if it were true what some are saying that they are planning to start a new war with the Russians, don't you think? They would look more concerned and not as happy and relaxed as they do now."

Kalle was silent, unable to help me abandon my doubts, my fears or add anything to alleviate them. Nobody had the faintest idea what was going on, and that truly was the most frightening part. The victors seemed to be no wiser than the losers.

Though the end of the war had been coming for a long time, nobody, not even the leaders and planners on the other side, whoever they were, had been doing anything to prepare for the logistical consequences that would follow the collapse of Nazi Germany. It seemed as if they probably didn't give a damn. Over night the Allies had more than 70 million Germans, prisoners, refugees and the entire civilian population on their hands. The German's own logistical system, stretched to its limits as it was, had come to an abrupt halt for sure. Now with the breakdown of authority no supplies of any kind were moving in any direction. Nobody was in charge any more. Everybody was out for himself, and had to be, in order to survive. There was no semblance of order, and, lets face it, who would have been there to give directions?

One side had been too busy losing, and the other side too busy winning. The idea that there would be an onslaught of millions of prisoners to feed and many more millions of civilians had not been part of the winners' planning process. The fighting had been too intense and had been too filled with hatred and vengeance to permit such thoughts.

"How about getting up tomorrow morning and walk off? Disappearing? *Ne Fliege machen* [getting lost] so to speak. Not staying here any longer?" I offered after a while, while the night was dragging on, seemingly without an end. The darkness made everything even gloomier.

"Look at this road which passes the entrance to our camp. You never see any guards at the entrance. Nobody would notice if we would get up to leave. Besides the Amis appear to be terribly disinterested in what is going to happen to us. If we'd just walk through the exit of the camp and simply leave, they wouldn't realize or care what happened. The exit of this camp is just a drive-in anyway with so many people coming and going all day long; we can just get up and go."

There was a long silence in the dark night as we lay there thinking, listening to the constant chatter and the lamentations that came from the direction of other vehicles and pitched tents.

Kalle mumbled and groaned, did not listen to what I had said, or seemed to be undecided.

"Okay," he finally replied. "So we walk out of here and somebody stops us. What do we say? We can't say that we're going for a walk. I mean they're not that naïve. They'll want to know were we're going and why and will stop us immediately."

"Of course, maybe you're right" I replied. "But maybe we should take a chance in this general tohawubohu and walk away. Maybe nothing is going to happen and maybe something will. But *'maybe'* is just the thing. I believe we have a chance. And if we walk down the road and none of the Americans stop us even the Czechs are less likely to go after us than if we attempted a getaway through the woods. They are waiting for us behind every tree and bush to see whether we'll make a run for it. Come on, Kalle, let's think up a good story."

"How about if we play up our disabilities," my friend volunteered after a long pause. "After all, that's what got us into this outfit in the first place. I mean, until we were too much *'damaged goods,'* they wouldn't have let us ride in a car, and heaven knows, where we would have been by now." Neither one of us has been far behind the front lines at any time during the war. "Basically, in our present condition we aren't even fit to serve! If *Schörner,* the bastard, [General Field Marshall *Schörner* in command of the 6th Army corps] had not been in dire need of good communications people, we would be in a hospital somewhere in *der Heimat* (at home) licking our wounds. But, he needed us, and his henchmen pulled us out of rehab, the S.O.B.'s. Here we are in this bleeding mess, cripples in uniform and prisoners too. Maybe we can turn the table after all and make some positive use of our disabilities and misfortune. For instance, Peter, you could act up by emphasizing the pain in your leg, use your walking cane, which you often use anyway, and I could put my bum arm in a sling, and off we'd go. I have noticed a few other guys around here who are unfit under normal circumstances for soldiering with their injuries. I'd be a monkey's uncle if they don't count now. We could convince some of those guys to come along on this little adventure, or we can get at least ten guys together. It would make up a nice, pathetic looking group. If any American soldier stops us, we'll be in need of a good story and you're the guy to give it to them, Peter. I am sure you'll do a good job of it."

Kalle was out of breath after his "little" speech. This guy was not a talker. My friend usually talked in monosyllables at best. The plan he had presented had been a long, elaborate and a detailed delineation of his thoughts.

I was absolutely elated. "My God, Kalle, where in hell did you hide your strategic talents? You're an absolute genius! Now we can go to sleep and look forward to tomorrow with peace of mind." After a few moments of silence, I added, "Don't think any more about it now. The more you add the worse it's going to get. We are a bunch of idiots, sinking steadily deeper into this cesspool of catastrophic events without anything to hold onto. Our minds are going to go soft, if we don't do something soon. Nobody will do it for us, and we'll lose our last little bit of initiative. Let's get some sleep and rehash your plan tomorrow. We are assuming there is a tomorrow."

The next day was bright and sunny, very promising looking with not a cloud in sight. It was almost as if nothing in this world had gone wrong—as if there had not been a war and no trepidation about an unknown future or prison camp with a thousand people and nothing to eat.

The encampment woke up gradually. People were trying to clean up without using too much water. Some were cooking water over open fires to prepare tea or coffee to fix some kind of a break-fast. They were using whatever resources they had, and they worked together.

Some American soldiers could be seen hanging around the pe-riphery of the camp. At least this was a good sign and helped us to alleviate some of our fears. Without any weapons we felt naked with the Czechs lurking in the woods. And we were not foolish enough to speculate about our status. We were POWs now and nothing else. It was a terrible, hapless feeling for sure. We had a hard time adjusting to it. The world had collapsed.

I decided to approach an officer the minute I saw one. I deter-mined to get my story across or at least find someone to report to. Idiot that I was, I didn't do it and for all the wrong reasons. I didn't want to leave my friends behind and that's what it would have meant, if anybody believed my story. I was naïve about what would happen next to us and how our friendships would weather this new upheaval in our lives.

The best would be Kalle's plan, if it worked. Then we would be out of here, I thought.

Soon enough some American soldiers arrived on a Studebaker truck with a huge barrel on top. Water! They had kept their word. Our officers and noncoms got busy with the distribution, and after a few hassles, everybody had some water again. True to their word, another truck arrived loaded with enough toilet paper to serve a reg-iment for a month.

"What the hell are we going to do with that?" asked Toni. "I haven't seen that much toilet paper since we left the supply depot near our chateau in France in 1942. Trust me, that's a lot of 'shits' ago. Take a look at the quality of the paper. Did you ever see soft toi-let paper like that in all your life? It's incredible."

"Oh, forget it," grumbled the sergeant. "If you didn't get any at all, it wouldn't be right either. And if the quality is too good for your own ass, take it home to your wife. But you better look at this: one tablespoon of raisins for everybody!" he exclaimed, as the Ameri-cans pulled a big bag of raisins from the truck. "Don't chew too quickly, otherwise you might choke."

We were flabbergasted, a tablespoon of raisins per person as rations? How long would that last? This must be a joke or an error of some kind. So far we still had some food left, it would last for two or three days. Then there would be nothing, and it seemed we would starve for sure.

The officers decided to send a delegation to the American officer in charge to voice a formal protest and to recite a paragraph from the Geneva Convention. Idiots! Did our officers really think that anybody would listen? The world, as we knew it, had come to an end, and they were concerned about arguing their *'rights,'* according to the Geneva Convention? Where had these guys been with their arguments about the Geneva Convention? Where were they when the Nazis killed all those innocent people in their concentration camps? And who had treated the Russian prisoners like animals? The hypocrisy and stupidity of our officers was unbelievable.

They would find out soon enough that from now on and for a long time to come the victorious parties would not be interested in the *'rights'* of German prisoners of war.

After trying to get in touch with just about anybody, our officers found out that there was nobody among the Americans present who was in charge or responsible for organizing supplies for the prisoners. The delivery of raisins was an act of unexplainable kindness by a lower ranking American noncom who had found several sacks among the supplies available. No more distribution of food had been planned at this time for the German prisoners.

The situation became more confusing as time went by.

I reminded my friend Kalle of our discussion and his plans of the previous night. "There is no time to lose, Kalle. We have to make a break before it's too late and everything gets out of control. No guessing what's going to happen if we let this go on any further. In two or three days everybody around here is going to go nuts if there isn't any food."

Kalle agreed and we talked to seven more "cripples," encouraging them to join us in our attempt to escape. After a lot of talking they were ready to come along. We were ready.

We took along some essentials: our canteens, our mess kits, blankets, some bread and tea. Kalle, for emphasis, put his arm dramatically into a sling, and I grabbed my walking cane. All in all nine guys were walking or limping towards the exit. As we reached the road, walking slowly, we turned left towards Winterberg and kept on marching. Nobody was at the entrance of the camp. Nobody paid any attention, and nobody gave a damn where we were going.

At first we continued limping, walking and stumbling forward, anxiously looking around from time to time to see, whether an American soldier would possibly shout from behind, call us back, or come after us, or if a jeep might follow us. Nothing, absolutely nothing happened. Nobody cared.

Our group limped along, putting on a great display of our various disabilities. One of the guys still had a gory looking bloody bandage around his head. It was a reminder that the Czechs had tried to stop the German soldiers who crossed the country to reach the Bavarian border. One of those Czech bullets had grazed his head. It really wasn't a bad injury, but the bandage hadn't been changed and was soaked with dried and caked blood. To suit our purposes, it looked just right.

After a while we relaxed, believing that we had succeeded in making a clean getaway. Jokes were flying around, and the tension subsided. Suddenly two Jeeps appeared from over a hill, from the direction of Winterberg. The Jeeps stopped abruptly when they reached our little group, and a lieutenant, sitting next to the driver, waved at us to halt. The lieutenant leaned out of his vehicle and yelled:

"Stop! Stop immediately! Where do you think you're going, you mother-fucking *Krauts?*"

Our small contingent came to a stop. We looked rather bedraggled and downtrodden. Everybody realized immediately that this was serious. The guys looked at me expectantly, as the only one who could speak and understand what the American was saying.

"Where do you think you're going?" The lieutenant yelled again. "Who told you to leave the camp? Does anybody speak any English?"

I raised my arm and volunteered, "I do, Lieutenant."

"Okay. Tell everybody to turn around and head back toward the camp."

By this time we had covered about two and a half miles, and the camp had disappeared out of sight, but somebody must have informed this guy about our departure.

"Lieutenant, Sir," I replied, "we are all wounded soldiers and we should be in a hospital rather than in that dusty, unsanitary camp or on this road. We were only in this camp by accident, because shortly before reaching Pisek the ambulance that was taking us to the hospital in Winterberg broke down."

Of course, this was a lie, but it was the story Kalle and I had dreamed up the night before. We had figured that the Americans with their relaxed behavior would swallow it and, maybe, even drive us to the nearest hospital, which we thought to be in Winterberg.

"I don't give a shit what you have and whether or not you are wounded," shouted the lieutenant. "As far as I'm concerned, you can all drop dead, you fucking Krauts. Now, turn back immediately, and don't give me any more smart answers."

The situation became tense, and the others in the group who didn't understand what was being said, became extremely agitated, shouting at me, at each other and the American soldiers.

"Explain to him what's the matter with us, you asshole."

"If you don't open your mouth he'll send us back, Big Mouth." And some other similar remarks were thrown in my face.

One of the GIs pulled up his M 1 and fired a few shots into the air. This idiotic reaction caused a panic among the German soldiers who believed that the next salvo would be directed at them.

To avoid being shot, everyone, with the exception of Kalle and me, jumped off the road into the ditch and disappeared in the adjacent cornfield. It was a difficult escape, because at this time of the year the corn had not grown high enough to give adequate cover while standing up or while running away.

The two Americans in the Jeep lowered the M 1s and fired a volley after the escaping Germans. Most of them ducked below the height of the corn, to get away unseen and kept on hurrying away.

The GIs became excited, shouting after the men and shooting their guns at the escaping prisoners.

Holy cow, I thought somewhat abstractly, the way they are shooting and aiming, they don't look as if they have used their guns often.

One guy in the group of quickly disappearing prisoners, who had been grazed by one of the bullets, put his hands up and came back. The others were nowhere to be seen. You only noticed some corn stalks swaying in the distance. The Americans were debating among themselves whether or not they should pursue them, but the lieutenant ordered, "Don't follow them; one of them might have a gun. It's not worth getting anyone hurt at this stage of the game."

Even several more volleys from the M 1s did not bring the fugitives back. Now there was real confusion. The Americans were cursing the fucking Germans, and I shouted at the lieutenant to stop shooting. He yelled back that he would shoot me, if I did not bring the others back.

"How the hell do you want me to do that?" I shouted back. "Why did you start shooting? The war is over, or didn't you hear about it?"

But the guy had lost it. He was furious and made moves which looked as if he wanted to shoot Kalle and me.

He yelled that we all should be shot right away, and that the whole group was a bunch of mother-fucking lying bastards.

Finally he started to quiet down, and I decided to make one more try with my story. I had decided, while the turmoil had developed, that everything had gone too far anyway, and that it was now or never to pull my final trump card. I had promised Kalle that if push came to shove, I would no longer hold my "American card." I would tell my story to the first American who would listen to me, that I was an American citizen, or, anyway, that I thought I was, and how all this had happened to my mother and to me.

But how do you tell a complicated, long story like that in one short sentence and in a tense moment like this? Well, I tried, "Lieutenant, Sir, please listen to me for a moment. Through some strange circumstances my mother and I were detained in Germany at the beginning of the war, in September of 1939, when I was 15 years old.

My father is a German, divorced from my American mother. I spent the summer with him vacationing that year. The minute the war started the German authorities kept me in Germany and drafted me into their army when I was 18, and here I am. I know it's hard to believe, but given the circumstance that's the best explanation I can give you. My mother and all our relatives would be devastated, if you don't let me go to the hospital in Winterberg. You could just as well turn us over to the Czechs or Russians, and we'll all be sent to Siberia. You don't want to do that to an American, do you?"

The lieutenant took a deep breath and rolled his eyes unappreciatively, "Listen, Buddy," was his answer, "I couldn't care less what happens to you and your bloody friends. I don't believe your hair-brained story for one second. You're in the wrong uniform, O.K.? You should have thought up a better explanation than this cock and bull story. It's unbelievable! Now turn around, or we shoot the lot of you."

I summoned all the nerve I had and asked, "Lieutenant, Sir, where are you from, and what's your name?"

"My name is Lieutenant Snyder," he answered self-importantly, "and I'm from upstate New York, Batavia, to be exact, if you have ever heard about it, you phony American. I'm not going to stand here and strike up a conversation with you. Now, turn back or else."

I replied, trying to stay calm, "Batavia, oh yes, I remember it well, that's near Buffalo. My mother took me there in 1937 to see Niagara Falls. We spent a great vacation there. If you have never seen the falls before it's a breathtaking sight. But, Lieutenant, since you seem to have made up your mind, I will promise you this, "I will certainly remember your name and I will not forget our encounter here on a country road in Czechoslovakia. I don't know how long it will take me until I'm able to return home to the USA, but some day I'll return, you can bet your life on it. And then, a few days after my return, I'll be standing in front of your home in Batavia, and I'll remind you of the decision you made right now."

The lieutenant was not impressed. He had made up his mind and was not going to change it, no matter what my arguments were.

"I couldn't care less about your story and whether or not you'll show up in Batavia. Yeah, come and see me, if you'll ever make it to the United States, and, if they let you in, I am looking forward to it."

He repeated his order to his men to shoot us at the slightest provocation. That did it. I could do no more without endangering the lives of the three of us. I translated to Kalle and the other guy what the lieutenant had said to me. Then we turned around and hobbled back to the camp.

During the next two days the continuous worry about food grew more and more desperate. The men with wives, children or girlfriends were seriously upset. They were running from one car, or tent, to the other, to solicit support for their plan to approach the Americans one more time. But nobody could see any sense in doing that.

We stayed near our *Kübel,* played cards and talked incessantly about the opportunities we had missed to be elsewhere, and not here of all places, and also exchanged the latest scuttlebutt.

When one gets into a situation, like we were in, one starts to wonder where things had gone wrong. What one could have done to *"changez la fortune,"* we thought. We all speculated but to no avail. 'What if' was the subject of the hour, not that it could have been changed anything, but it seemed to give the men something to hold onto. Yeah, that's what you think. Bullshit!

Sometimes later Kalle started to philosophize about things he should have done but did not do. He talked about his last stay at a hospital in *Hagen,* an industrial town south of *Dortmund,* while recuperating. He felt that he had not made enough of an effort to drag his stay out, to demonstrate convincingly enough to the examining *KV Kommission* that his arm was ruined beyond repair, that it hurt like hell and that it was too mangled to return to the front lines in any useful capacity.

"No," he said, "I pretended that everything was fine and that I wanted to get back to my outfit, away from the nightly bombing raids and the sticky, stinking air raid shelters. You know, Peter, not the worst enemy bombardment, *Stalin organ* and artillery could've been as bad as the howling of a 500 kilogram (1000 pound) bomb falling towards you. Listening to that sound, when you are sitting in an air raid shelter under four stories of loosely constructed apartment masonry is unbearable. You can visualize how the building will collapse on impact, right on top of you. During these months at home I'd seen too many houses in the morning after the raid, reduced to heaps of rubble, with all the people in the cellars buried alive. I also saw the pitiful few that made it out of the cellars. To me that experience was worse than the worst enemy fire I experienced at the Russian front, in Italy, or in Africa." Kalle fell silent and then he continued, "On top of it, I must admit, I wanted to get away from my nagging girlfriend. All she ever wanted to know was whether or not I'd been faithful to her while I was in France, in Italy, or someplace else. She couldn't understand my frustrations. She insisted on remaining a virgin until we got married, after the war. How could I have explained to her, that it really didn't matter to me whether she was a virgin or not. In the end it really was more important for me to survive from day to day and to be able to enjoy life and 'love' now. What should I have done, rape her? Of course not!"

He was lying there, lost in thought for a while until he continued talking to himself rather than to me.

"I tried to reason with her that a young man doesn't appreciate the ideals of an 18-year-old girl about being chaste, faithful and celibate, especially if he faces mortal dangers everyday that no human being should ever face, much less one who has barely become a man. Maybe it was unjust of me to feel that way, but I couldn't help it. And now, I'm here, and like many times before in life, I'm much smarter than I was then, but it doesn't help me one bloody bit."

He paused, and I did not want to interrupt his thoughts, as I was having some of my own. I let him continue.

"And my mother, you know she is a widow, lost my father in a mine accident 10 years ago. He was a master miner. Since then, honestly, she has struggled valiantly to afford a decent education for me. You know, Peter, how difficult that was without involvement in Nazi politics? She always begged me to do anything I could to stay alive, to be able to help her with her life when the war was over, just anything I could to stay in the hospital. Well, she lost out in the end. I wanted to leave; I couldn't stand it any longer. Man, would I like to reverse things now!"

He fell silent again and we were sitting there in the early evening, contemplating our past, commiserating with each other about our bad luck.

"Kalle, I don't know if you care to listen to my wishful thinking or not, but I also did things, many things that I would do differently now, if I had the chance to do them all over again. Every time I was in a hospital I tried as hard as I could to prolong my rehab as long as I could, all the time thinking that I would make it until the war was over. I never dreamed that I would be in a spot like this. Each and every time I was a victim to some overzealous inspector. You know, one of those assholes that marred the home front. These sons of bitches probably had to fill a quota or something. They were afraid that they would be sent to the *'Ostfront,'* or they may have even been 'true disciples' of our departed *"Führer,'* Nazi party members. Anyway, they considered me *KV* every time, those bastards. I've been in many comfortable rehabs and a lot of good and bad hospitals together with both willing nurses and not so willing ones. But somehow I wasn't successful. I didn't manage to drag out my recuperation long enough. I still remember my rehab in Cortina D'Ampezzo. Heaven, I'm telling you, heaven, but it didn't last."

The night dragged on and I went on. "My God, Kalle, did I ever tell you about that little Viennese girl who taught me how to walk again after I caught that bullet in my hip? She was really great and such a darling. She taught me a few other things as well. I even proposed to her, but she just laughed, kissed me and told me that she didn't want to become a young widow. Smart girl, I wonder where she might be right now?"

After commiserating silently with myself for a little while, I continued delving into my self-inflicted sorrow.

"And at home, in Berlin, I had a hot thing going. With all the bombs falling, I seldom found the time to go into the cellar or to listen to the falling bombs. I was too busy screwing my brains out. And I'm telling you, I should've done it more often."

We sat there, two young men, 21 years old, sharing our misery. We were both lost in our thoughts of the past and what might have been "if," without being able to change a damn thing.

"Did you listen to that old guy the other day that was with *Wenk's* army that hapless general, commandeered to relieve Berlin after the

Russians were already all over the city? He saw the destruction in Berlin, the rapes, and the devastation. He said his entire family died during the last few days. I wonder what happened to my stepmother."

We finally fell asleep with heavy dreams and frightening nightmares.

The next morning we woke up to total pandemonium. We heard shouting from every corner of the encampment. Shots were being fired rapidly, mostly pistols from the sound of it, but they strangely sounded like firecrackers exploding at a New Year's Eve celebration. Several people were yelling, "The Russians, the Russians are here."

"The Amis turned us over to the Russians!"

"The Amis have all disappeared without a trace, simply vanished, those conniving bastards."

"They are going to rape us," screamed Helga, our nearest neighbor.

I jumped up from my blanket but stayed low behind our car, not daring to get into the line of anybody's pistol shots. With shots ringing all around us, there was no telling where a bullet might be coming from.

What was happening? Who was in control of the camp, the Russians or the Czechs or the Americans? For the moment it was impossible to get any orientation.

I turned to look at the car, which Horst and Helga occupied and saw, to my utter consternation and horror, how Horst wrapped his arms around Helga and gave her what seemed to be a long kiss. Then he raised his *Lugar* behind her back and shot Helga and then shoved the pistol into his mouth and blew his brains out.

"Kalle, Kalle, did you see that," I shouted. But Kalle could not respond, he had seen it and had become violently ill.

All around us we saw similar scenes, shootings, men running with their wives and children toward the wooded area with their side arms drawn. Some soldiers had apparently hidden their pistols successfully from the Americans.

It appeared, from what we could make out that some Russian soldiers had entered the camp and had caused this panic with their feared battle cry, *"Komm Frau."* (Come Mrs.).

Some of them grabbed woman dragging them along with clear intentions. The interference of a Russian officer came too late and was only performed halfheartedly anyway. Panic struck everybody, civilians and soldiers alike.

We heard shots being fired from the wooded area in the back of the camp and could only assume that the suicides continued.

Only efforts by some German soldiers got things under control. Strangely enough, few officers were among them. The performance of the German officers had been singularly disappointing. It was too little and too late to control the 400 captives, whatever the soldiers tried. At least a hundred men, their wives, children or girlfriends, had killed themselves.

Where were the American soldiers? They had gone, disappeared, and had not cared.

On the 12th of February 1945, as part of the accord at Yalta, President Roosevelt had made a deal with Stalin. Stalin's army was to keep all German soldiers who had fought on the eastern front. The Russians made sure that it was kept. The armies that in the end had fought against them disappeared in the gulag.

Now the Russians used the first quiet moment to order everybody to pick up their bare necessities. They herded us away from our cars and onto the road.

"Rasberaitje pa piat!" (Assemble five in a row) they ordered. *"Dawai, dawai"* (Let's go, let's go), *bistraeh, bistraeh* (quickly, quickly).

We did as we were told, and they marched us off towards the town of *Pisek.* Guards were placed every few yards alongside each column. Little was spoken. Everybody was left in deep shock, totally drained of any emotion and of any initiative to resist.

Our world, my world, had come to an end. The old Nazi slogan *"Sieg, oder Bolschewistische Versklavung"* (victory or Bolshevik slavery) had come true.

I wondered whether I would ever get chance to return to the United States and to talk to Lieutenant Snyder, even if I did, what would I tell him?

As we marched through Pisek and beyond, the soldiers slowly began talking to each other again. Hundreds of Czech civilians were

standing on the sidewalks jeering and shouting curses and obscenities at the hated former occupation forces. It was obvious what they
would have done to us without our new 'protectors,' the victorious
Russian Army.

"Kalle, I don't know were we're going, but I believe the final
destination will be east of the Ural Mountains," I said to my friend.
I didn't get an answer. I didn't have to.

We were totally traumatized, almost oblivious to the brutal reality of our situation, not yet fully aware of what it really meant to
be a prisoner of war, what it meant to be part of a defeated army and
country that had ceased to exist, what it meant to have no more rights
in any sense of the imagination. Not to have your own country or any
neutral arbiter to stand behind. With every step further down the road
the realization slowly set in.

The efforts of the entire world had brought Germany to its
knees. Not only that, no, she had been obliterated. We were about to
find out what that signified to all of us.

All over central Europe thousands of columns, millions of
marching German civilians, refugees and captured soldiers, were either fleeing from areas they were forced to leave or were herded into
captivity. Victorious countries claimed to be the new owners of their
occupied farms, homes or cities, or—like us—were being led as prisoners of war toward unknown destinations.

All in all, more than 20 million people were on the move.
Among the eastern provinces East Prussia had fallen to the vengeful
victors. The Russian army occupied part of East Prussia and the
Poles laid claim to Danzig, Pomerania, Silesia and part of Brandenburg, and were seeking revenge as well. The Germans would pay
dearly for the recklessness and the brutality of the Nazis and their
glorious 'Führer.'

For us, the POWs, the worst part was still to come.

We were marching along a road that led us south from Pisek
through the otherwise peaceful looking Czech countryside in the direction of Budweiss (Budewice).

The dense woods along the road were crowded with Russian
troops. All they wanted was to relieve us of everything we possessed.

Boots, watches, gold rings, wallets, belts and whatever else they considered of any value. And since they had next to nothing in their communist paradise, everything was of value to them.

Strangely enough, the Russian guards were our protectors. They had the responsibility of delivering us to our next destination with nobody missing. We had been fastidiously counted dozens of times, and we would find out that this routine of counting would be repeated, from now on, several times a day.

At the first brief stop Kalle and I pulled our long shafted boots off our feet, took a knife and cut the shafts off. Now the boots looked mutilated and ugly. We hoped that in that condition none of the Russian marauders would want them. After all, we had to have shoes to walk. It was a wise decision, because subsequent raids left many soldiers with bare feet, or only with the shoes from the Russian soldiers who had exchanged theirs in turn. We were fortunate enough to keep our severed boots.

We hid our valuables, like my pocketknife and Kalle his watch, on our bodies. The guards continued to defend us from their fellow soldiers as well as they could, shooting into the air, yelling threats at those who tried to invade the column and to wrestle us to the ground. Every few miles a new group of soldiers came running out of the woods to try the same game.

After walking a distance of about 30 miles we arrived late in the evening in *Neu Biestritz*. We bivouacked in a wooded area with a sizable lake in the middle. The lake was too big to swim across. We pitched tents provided by the Russians. To our greatest surprise there was food. Everybody got a mess kit full of hot, yellow pea soup and some ghastly wet and sour tasting black bread. It was the first warm meal we had in about two weeks and our introduction to Russian bread.

The minute we arrived in the forest of *Neu Bistritz* the prisoners formed groups. Kalle, Toni and I joined a group of guys from an artillery battalion, about 25 men, who were led by Captain Frank Gross, their former commanding officer. He had lots of curly hair, an unruly mustache and a loud mouth. By that I mean he talked a lot.

He tried to impress us immediately with stories about the many vehicles he had driven in the German army. His spiel was, "I drove everything from a motorcycle to the *'Tiger panzer'* (a 50-ton tank, the biggest in the German arsenal). Big deal! Who wanted to know at this time in the game what he had driven?

Everybody ignored him because we had other worries, obviously.

There was another guy in the group, whom Kalle and I liked immediately. His name was Arthur. He was relatively short, with blond wavy hair, a ruddy complexion and a *Westphalian* accent. Sergeant Arthur Otto was Arthur's full name and rank. He seemed to be our kind of guy, and we arranged our sleeping places to be in the same tent as his.

Coming from Silesia, his artillery unit had also raced across Czechoslovakia before the armistice, thinking they would be safe once they reached the demarcation line, along the Moldavia and the American occupied area, before the ninth of May. Like us, they had had experienced no casualties on the way. The Americans had stopped them shortly after crossing the Moldavia. Then, the same routine followed as with us. One bright morning Russians surrounded them.

During the day we speculated incessantly what the Russians intended to do with us, where would they take us and what would be our final destination? The new guys weren't any smarter than we were when it came to answers.

More surprises were revealed as the next morning dawned. Our captors assembled the German officers, Captain Gross included, for a meeting. The Russian officer, the commandant, told them, with the help of an interpreter that everybody who attempted to escape, like swimming across the lake, would be shot immediately. The interpreter also informed them that we would be shipped ultimately to the Crimean Peninsula, to help with *the grape harvest.* Whom were they kidding? He went on to say that anybody who spread rumors to the contrary would also be shot. Furthermore they told the officers that, since the glorious and victorious Russian army had liberated us from a brutal dictatorship, they would now help us to have *bolshe kulturny,* have more culture, and to be clean and free of lice. As a first step everybody in the camp would immediately shave, completely from head to toe and help others to do the same. Beginning tomorrow morning the procedure would begin. At noon tomorrow the completion of this procedure had to be reported by the German officers to the Russian camp commander. He explained that all hair, wherever it grew, had to be shaved off, our heads, under the arms, pubic hair, everything. We would get the opportunity to disinfect our clothes in the next camp where complete delousing facilities were available.

When the captain assembled us to relay the order many of the soldiers shouted, "We won't do it. We aren't dirty animals. They can do this with their own kind. We don't need it," and so on and so forth.

Well, those of us who had been foot soldiers in Russia knew that lice appear out of nowhere. Lice are a terrible plight, almost impossible to get rid off. I asked, "Does anybody want to get shot because he doesn't want to shave?"

The discussions raged on and on, but in the end, everybody quieted down, and the guys accepted their fate; they had to.

Next morning the procedure began. Of course, to shave in all the possible and impossible places, the guys had to help each other.

How do you shave your back or around your own asshole?

How do you shave around somebody else's asshole?

It was terrible, degrading and demoralizing. Every available razor blade was used up. Without shaving soap, and only regular soap to use, it was painful and sometimes bloody too. We couldn't even crack a smile when we were finished shaving, looking at each other, our baldheads and total nakedness. The captain looked the worst. He was now as bald as the rest of us, but on top of it he looked pitiful without his decorative mustache and his full head of hair. All of a sudden his pointed nose protruded, he had a chiseled chin and didn't look like an officer any more. He was sitting there with his head between his hands, saying nothing any more about the different vehicles he had driven in the army. Finally he got up and announced, "From now on you can call me Frank; we all look the same anyway, and the thing with the army is over."

Well, he was wrong. But with this procedure, whether that was the intention or not, the Russians had broken the last remaining opposition among the POWs.

In the evening we were fed again, same thing, soup and a piece of black bread. It seemed that this would be our diet from now on. As bad as the food was, it was better than a spoonful of raisins.

After three days in *Neu-Bistritz* we assembled again, the same way, five in a row, 20 rows, in columns of 100 men. Our march through southern Czechoslovakia continued for 10 hours until everybody was exhausted. We had covered about 40 miles; I felt as if my damaged leg would fall off. We arrived at an old *Luftwaffe* base with a functional airfield and barracks, the works. Painted across the sides of the barracks and hangars, sure enough, there were the slogans of the last days of the Nazi's war. We read in big, white letters, lest anybody should forget or not be aware of the final prophecy of the great *Führer* and his propaganda minister *Dr. Joseph Goebbels.*

"Sieg oder Bolschewistische Versklavung."

We were near *Iglau,* the last stop before being loaded into boxcars. Our little group tried to stay together, the guys from Captain Grosse's artillery unit and our three-some from the Kübel.

Toni, Arthur, Kalle and I put our things into the furthest corner of the barracks assigned to us.

"It's always good to have your back against the wall," Arthur philosophized. "We might as well start with the right habits while the shit is climbing."

The barracks were not the most desirable lodgings. What we saw made us wonder, how low the *Führer's Luftwaffe* and their men had fallen, to live in these crummy quarters. Metal bunks, lousy sanitary facilities and none of the comforts of life we had always associated with *Hermann's* flying circus. (*General Field Marschall Hermann Göring,* who committed suicide during the *Nürnberg* trials.)

The few days since the Russians had been in control of the place had not helped any. All light fixtures and switches, door handles and water faucets had been removed, or to put it more accurately, had been ripped out of the walls. Apparently there wasn't anything the Russians couldn't use at home in their workers' paradise. What remained for us, as beds were crude wooden boards resting on metal frame cots. But it was dry inside, and we were protected from thievery and marauding Czechs. My guess was that we wouldn't stay for long.

* * * *

You might probably wonder what was going on with Olga, my mother, while all this was happening. The last time I had heard from her, she had left Switzerland to go to Berlin.

Would she finally regret her decision to come back to Germany, to be closer to her son, leaving the safety of Zurich, having her friends where she had experienced such a wonderful time?

It was the second time that she had made it safely through a war in Europe. But was Berlin the right place to pick for the last days of World War II? Even though she managed to stay away from the worst experiences of the war, with intermissions in Switzerland from 1939 to 1945, she had now chosen a city nobody in his right mind would have wanted to be at the end of the war.

While she had been unable to do anything for her son during the war, her *friends* had protected her from the Nazis. Of course, she had always tried to be near her son and she felt that that alone had been of help to him. She knew that it would have helped much more, if she had chosen earlier on to remain in the safety and freedom of the United States of America. But she had done right after the original mistake had been made and Peter always appreciated his mother's presence.

As Peter was marching on the roads of Czechoslovakia he was thinking constantly of her, and she knew it. She knew that she was his hope of ever making it back from wherever he was going. In his mind she was his only advocate to get out of the mess he was in.

Olga was in trouble, deep trouble. She intensely regretted having left the safety of Zurich. Her decision to return to Berlin looked more foolish every day. The closing days of the war in Berlin were rough, not only because of the daily air raids and falling bombs. Neither food nor potable water nor electricity was available for more than two hours of the day. All resemblance of order had broken down. She had to watch constantly that roaming *Gastarbeiter* (guest workers, or better, slave workers) from occupied countries did not steal the shoes off her feet, or rip the clothes off her body while she was on the street searching for food. These poor people were in dire need of anything they could get their hands on, and the German police were nowhere to be seen.

The bombardment by the heavy artillery of the attacking Russian armies, and the exploding shells was getting closer every day. It was of no help to listen to the radio, which reported ridiculous stories of an army, led by a *General Wenck,* coming from the south to rescue Berlin, to push the Russians back to where they had come from.

What a ridiculous story was that supposed to be? Who was going to believe that? What non-existent armies were coming from where?

At night, when it was relatively quiet and the electricity was switched on, Olga tuned to the BBC news, which to her was the only source to report the truth. There were no German armies any more to resist the Russians. It would only be days or even hours before the victorious Russians would storm into the city. Olga had heard enough stories of the conduct of the Russians, based upon word of mouth, and she believed them. Surely enough there would be large scale raping, if nothing worse. She didn't want to be one of the unfortunate victims so she started sewing a large American flag on her old and trusted manual Singer sewing machine. She intended to pin it onto the outside of her door as soon as the last Germans were gone. The flag, she hoped, would be recognized by the Russians and deter them from doing any harm to her.

The bombing by the Allied Air Forces finally stopped on the morning of the 6th of May. The BBC reported that Berlin had fallen to the victorious Russian army and that the remnants of the German forces had capitulated.

All Olga could hear now, from the inside of the relative safety in her apartment, was small arms fire. She pinned the flag with the stars and stripes on the outside of her door, hoping her plan would work to caution the Russian soldiers and indicating also that all the Nazis were gone. The downside was that if one of the old Nazi diehards discovered the flag, God forbid, the consequences would be worse than what she had to fear from the Russians.

The next day there was violent banging on the door, and Olga, thoroughly frightened, opened carefully. Several Russian soldiers stood in front of her. From the looks of it an officer with a one star epaulette, barked, *"We Amerikanski?"*

"Yes, I am American," Olga, replied smiling as happy as she could.

"Documenti yest?" was the curt and instant reply.

Olga understood that to mean that he wanted to see a document, her passport, which she already held in her hands and gave to him.

She was terribly afraid that the officer would take the passport and disappear, but nothing of the sort happened. The lieutenant, as he turned out to be, took the American passport, opened it and acted as if he could read it, while the other soldiers looked on.

"Ladna, charascho," (Okay, good) he said and returned the precious document.

Then he spoke to the soldiers and apparently gave some orders, where upon two of them entered the apartment and sat down in the living room making themselves comfortable.

Olga tried to find out from the lieutenant what all that meant, but only got the answer, *"Charascho, charascho, Americanski, njet ficky, ficky."* Which meant in a mixture of Russian and German: "Good, good, you are an American; we won't fuck you."

The answer was brutal but straightforward. Olga was relieved to hear it. Her idea with the American flag had worked. Several more times there were knocks on the door, usually with rifle butts, but her two protectors opened the door and told the would be intruders, in no uncertain terms, to get lost.

A few days later the BBC reported that the Allies had finalized an agreement with the Russians. They would turn the province of *Thüringen* over to them and get a four-power status for the city of Berlin in exchange. This meant that the Americans, the British, French and the Russians, each, would be responsible for a sector of the city. Olga was crossing her fingers that this would happen soon and that she would be in the American sector. Initially she was surprised, but the two Russian soldiers were behaving very decently. They even shared some of their rations of warm food with Olga. It was a terrible grub, but warm, and to Olga it was better than nothing. After a few days the soldiers came 'home' with some vegetables and meat and Olga cooked a meal for all of them, American style, the two soldiers were delighted.

There were also a few strange experiences with these guys who obviously didn't know city dwellings. One day they became greatly excited and agitated. It took Olga some time to find out the reason. She finally discovered the cause for their excitement. The soldiers had put a few sausages into the water of the toilet bowl, apparently, as she understood from the discussion and excited gesturing, to cool them. The idea was okay, until one of them pulled the lever of the water reservoir and everything in the bowl was washed down and beyond. Olga tried desperately to explain, with her hands and with words, where it all went. But they were upset and raced to the floor below to retrieve the sausages. They couldn't understand how the system worked and what the bowl was for. Olga tried to explain, as best as she could what a WC was all about. She had noticed during the preceding days that the two Russians always went downstairs to visit the little garden in the back of the apartment house to do their business. The problem was only resolved after the lieutenant came for an inspection. Apparently he was from a big city in Russia and explained the workings of a WC to his men.

They left almost as suddenly as they had appeared, said good-bye: *"Doswidanja"* (See you again) and were gone.

The following day two American GIs stood in front of the door, it was still decorated with Olga's handmade flag, and also asked to see her passport. Olga was so happy to see her countrymen. She hugged both of them and cried and cried. Now everything would be all right. She would find her son and see to it that he could return to the USA. She was wrong, even though she got to know the US Commandant of the American Sector of Berlin, General Lucius Clay, personally. Even though she worked for him for over six months, there was nothing she could find out about Peter and to where he had disappeared.

"There is absolutely no information from the Russians about prisoners. They are very uncommunicative about almost everything. Most of our sessions consist of us asking questions without ever getting any answers," General Clay told her. "I don't know how this is going to continue. It is almost as if they want to pick a fight with us or chase us out of the city."

8

TRANSPORT RUSSIAN STYLE

The worst stress for us was the uncertainty of our situation. Germany was gone, had disappeared as a nation, as a country. It had no legal representation in any international organization. Germany had placed itself outside of the community of nations. What would be our fate? Would we ever return to the civilized world? Or would we disappear in the incomprehensible depth of the USSR, in Siberia, Mongolia or in one of its Gulags? We had absolutely no idea what would happen, and, in our state of mind, were unable to even imagine what the Russians would do with us.

Where were they taking us?

The war was over. Why were we prisoners?

Our lives had disintegrated, and we didn't know when or how we would be able to put them back together again. That is the way we felt.

Why were they keeping us? We couldn't get rid of the nagging questions. What were the Russians going to do with us? Where would we finally end up?

Nobody in their right minds could believe the story about picking grapes on the Crimea. It almost sounded like your mother telling you that, if you endured the dentist's drilling, there'd be a beautiful princess waiting for you at home. Too unreal to be true!

It was suicidal to discuss these thoughts openly. Speaking to comrades in small groups, a few of our fellow prisoners had voiced their doubts. Wouldn't you know they'd disappeared promptly? Where to? We didn't know. Who had overheard them? Who had told Ivan? We didn't know that either. Since the prisoners were from dozens of different units, they didn't feel particularly attached to each other, and no one could be trusted.

By this time nobody even wanted to know more morbid details. The rumors circulating were unbelievable. With every passing day we became increasingly aware that we were prisoners, period. When I say prisoners I leave out "of war," because "prisoners of war" have their country to lean on and international conventions to protect them. Germany was gone. We could only guess how much the Red Cross would do for us, or should I say—might be willing to do for us. The Russians have a descriptive word for people like us. They call them *"Zaklutschorny,"* locked up people. Anyway, the Russians had meant what they were saying and had not been bashful about acting on it.

At night when it was dark, and we were unable to sleep, awake with our thoughts and worries. Kalle and I talked about our doubts, whispering the rumors of the day into each other's ear.

"Kalle, they want something from us, that's for sure," I volunteered. "They don't keep hundreds of thousands of prisoners for the same reason, as they would have during the war. Then they didn't want us to fight any more. Now, that story is over. If they keep us now, it's because they want us to do something, and it's not picking grapes on the Crimea. I guess that they want us to do reconstruction work. Enough has been destroyed in their backyard to keep us busy for a long time."

"You might be right," Kalle answered, as quietly as I had spoken to him. "But . . . what of this couple in *Pisek,* my God. I can still see him without his head, bleeding like a pig, and his brains blown all over the cab of the car. What if he was right and the Amis have an extension of the shooting in mind? Consider that my friend!"

"Okay, Okay," I replied. "If that's the case, mind you, it's just a thought. Then it didn't make sense that they turned us over to the Russians. Don't you think that was foolish if they were planning anything like that? On the other hand, continuing your train of thought, Kalle, it wouldn't have been the first time that prisoners were turned around to fight for a new cause. I could name half a dozen occasions in history when this happened. Look at what the Germans did when they created the Vlassov army."

"Don't even mention those poor bastards," Arthur piped in equally quiet from where he was lying on the other side of me. "Can you imagine what the Russians are doing to them right now? Few people know that the SS planned to use about 500,000 Ukrainians, as *'volunteers'* for the cause of liberating their home country from the Soviets. They put them into SS uniforms. The name of the unit, written on a ribbon on the lower left arm of each uniform was, 'SS Division Vlassov.' I don't know why they agreed to this deal in the first place, whether they were proud of it, hated the Bolsheviks that much, or maybe life as SS men appeared to be more attractive to them than the likelihood to dying of hunger in a prison camp. Yes, as soldiers, they had plenty to eat too."

Arthur had mentioned one of the sorrier episodes of the war.

The Germans, after they had suffered tremendous casualties, had recruited young men from most of the nations they had conquered, or, to be exact, had applied pressure to the appointed figureheads, to provide able-bodied recruits for their elite divisions.

Among the foreign legionnaires helping the Germans was the "Blue Division" from Spain, courtesy of one dictator to another. Generalissimo Franco had been pressured by Hitler to pay off his debts from the civil war in Spain (1936–39). The German "Division Condor" had helped Franco's air force at the time, had transported him and his troops from Morocco to the continent when everything seemed to be lost and had decisively intervened on his behalf for the remainder of the Spanish Civil War.

There was also a Flemish SS Division, recruited from disgruntled Flemish nationals in Belgium as well as a Croat SS Division made up of young Croats who wanted to leave the Serbian conglomerate of nations. Another one came from Norway with the help of Premier Quisling and another one was recruited from the Baltic States.

These unfortunate young men from the Ukraine, who hated communism, were the sons of *kulaks* who Stalin had obliterated by the millions in the 1930's. They had a particularly bad ax to grind.

The Germans had been ruthlessly clever to exploit this hatred. Under the leadership of a former Soviet General, *Andrei Andreyevich Vlassov,* the Germans recruited them straight out of prisoner of war camps. The men had little choice in the matter. The SS would enter a POW camp and ask for volunteers. The first one to refuse to volunteer was shot on the spot. The rest preferred the service in the German Army "as volunteers" rather than share the fate of the victim, or being starved to death. The SS trained them. When the training was over the weapons were taken away from them. They heard nothing but promises for two years. That was it. The Germans, in the final analysis, did not have the temerity to arm these men; and they were afraid to turn them lose against the Russians. They never could have been certain whether or not they would turn around and shoot their former captors, especially after they became aware of the deportation of the younger female population of the Ukraine to Germany.

What would happen to them now?

Typically, Stalin considered all of them traitors. Vlassov was later hanged and his severed head displayed in the center of Moscow's Red Square. All defecting officers were executed, and hundreds of thousands of his men were sent to the Siberian gulag to work in forced labor camps.

"You said it, Arthur, we didn't trust the Vlassov army with weapons, and quite rightly so. I can't see the Russians trusting us. Besides, the whole idea is idiotic and can only be conceived by the frightened mind of a prisoner." Toni injected quietly.

"Until you know for certain, don't count it out," Kalle replied stubbornly.

Any argument by somebody else that put the least bit of doubt into Kalle's theory was rejected outright.

"I tell you what," I contributed. "To my mind we can rule out two things: We won't pick grapes on the Crimea, and we won't find ourselves in Russian uniforms. Maybe I'm a pessimist and don't believe in Santa Claus, but that's the way it is."

As time wore on it was of little satisfaction to me that I happened to be right, on both counts.

Kalle turned away from me, he was angry, and that was the end of our whispering for one night.

At noon of the next day, after the obligatory soup and the sour black bread had been eaten, Kalle came back from one of his "fact finding" excursions with a smile on his face.

"You know, Peter, I just found out that we have 100 men in this camp from a special unit, which was assembled by the German army to get their meals from a special kitchen with a dietary food plan, and they had no front line duty. And do you know why? Because they were all diagnosed with ulcers. Can you imagine that? Ulcers!"

"Who, for Christ's sake, would have the nerve to do that?" I wondered out loud.

"Just the other day you and I talked about missed opportunities," he continued, "How about an ulcer? Now comes the best part. For the last two weeks they have been eating this sour, wet Russian bread and pea soup. Green pea soup, with an ulcer?! Just about the worst you can eat if you have an ulcer. On top of it, they ate this wet, black bread! You know what happened to their stomachs? Nothing!! This unit must have consisted of the largest gathering of hypochondriacs on the face of the earth."

We all had to laugh about that. It was the first time since *Pisek* that anyone of us had heard the other one laugh. Kalle had more news as well, another rumor.

"Peter, listen to this! I have it straight from the horse's mouth. We are going to Romania to rebuild the oil refinery in *Ploesti*. Now, don't tell me that also sound unreasonable. Or maybe you can come up with another hair-brained, logical explanation. We all know that the Amis bombed *Ploesti* to smithereens, and we know that oil is a valuable commodity. The Russians need it like anybody else does. To get us there on the railroad will be a straight line going south. We pass through Austria, past Vienna, then through Hungary and on to Romania. We will know for sure, as soon as we are loaded into railroad cars and the train starts moving. We just have to look at the sun to determine the general direction. Going south from here means Vienna, and then my prediction is true. If the train starts towards the east in the direction of Poland, it means Siberia, and then I am wrong. What do you say?"

What could I say? It was as good as any other stupid story in circulation. The only logical reason for somebody to dream up a story like that was that *Ploesti* was located in Romania and not in Siberia, and nobody even wanted to think "Siberia" much less mention the word.

"Kalle, as always, you are a genius!" I replied with slight sarcasm in my voice. "Do you also know when the loading and the departure will take place? I don't have anything against this camp, but I would like to know when we leave its luxurious quarters."

"No idea," he said, not catching the drift of my question. "But soon, that's for sure."

Arthur listened to our exchange and threw a quizzical glance in my direction, "If you two can't start a rumor, you aren't feeling well, are you?" he remarked.

"I'll tell you what we have to watch out for. Have you noticed that the Ivan is making a strenuous effort to detect and break up the units that arrived here together, you know, all in one piece, officers, noncoms, and everybody close and chummy?"

He looked around questioningly, but nobody knew what he wanted to explain, so he continued.

"Our small gang is an exception because we just met, so to speak. We are from different units and don't seem to know each other for any length of time. They don't like to have a great number of men in one group who know each other or have been in the same unit together or are friends. They either are still afraid of the Germans, or they are knowledgeable about the composition of prisoner transports. If you strain your noggin a little, you will remember that no other nation on earth has as much experience in transporting prisoners as Ivan has. They have transported almost 15 million of his own people to Siberia. Ah, here is that name again! I know you don't like to hear it, but it lurks in the background anyway. Be alert! Keep your eyes and ears open, and don't trust anybody! And one more thing: has anybody noticed by any chance that little by little fellow prisoners have disappeared? Ivan, I believe, is searching out members of SS units who might be hiding among us. They want to take the SS to some other place for special treatment."

"What a strange idea!" I said. "How can they find out whether somebody was in the SS or not? Nobody will tell them, and the guys must have been smart enough to change uniforms, for sure."

"Very easily," Arthur shot back. "They take their shirts off, raise the left arm, and there it is right under the left armpit, a perfect ID. Our *Führer* was so concerned about the well being of his elite soldiers that he ordered every member of the SS to have a tattoo of the individual's blood group engraved under the left armpit. Just a simple O, A, or B, indelibly embedded under the arm does it. Whatever the blood type of the individual, it's the best identification now. After that, in case of critical injuries, blood could be administered immediately without need for lengthy tests. Or blood could be taken from one soldier as well to help a wounded comrade."

Arthur was a shrewd cookie. Most of the time he was quiet, but he was always observant, and, as he had previously reminded us, always with his back to the wall. None of us had known the story of the tattoos before. What an effective way to ID somebody. We were hit with a new surprise everyday and never a pleasant one.

Ivan wanted to show to us what culture really was. In just a few days they built a *delousing building* to make sure that everyone of the dirty prisoners had the opportunity to be free of lice. Looking at some of the people in our barracks and the way they were itching and scratching, it didn't seem to be such a bad idea to me.

We had all shaved from head to toe anyway. The items that needed cleaning, and I mean cleaning badly, were our uniforms and underwear. Ever since we left Silesia, almost three weeks ago, nobody in our group had had an opportunity to take our clothes off, and they hadn't been too clean before then. The other guys were not any better off. We had been working, marching, sleeping and sweating for weeks with few chances to undress or to clean our clothes and ourselves.

The following day we went to the delousing establishment in groups of forty. We had to undress completely. Our clothes were hung on hangers, and the hangers in turn on rods, which were moved into a large, tightly sealed chamber of about 500 square feet. The doors were closed, and the chamber was filled with forced dry air, heated to 90 degrees centigrade. All lice and their eggs died at that temperature. We paraded nakedly into a large room where we found buckets of hot water and a piece of gray soap for each of us. It was wonderful; we needed that.

Coming back to the barrack, we felt like new.

That night there was a commotion at the door. Several Russian soldiers rushed inside and grabbed the twenty guys who slept close to the entrance. It looked like a random action until the next morning when we learned more about it.

The men, or at least some of them, had talked and bragged about their experiences during the war. Those unfathomable idiots! Apparently they had come from questionable units, maybe SS, or Panzer divisions, or even Vlassov. Bingo! They were gone.

"You see," said Arthur, "it's like I said. Keep your mouths shut and keep your back to the wall, always. And beware of the walls! They have ears, you know!"

"*Dawai, dawai,*" let's go, let's go. "*Rasberaitje pa pjat,*" (get in line five in a row). The Russians guards yelled.

It was four o'clock in the morning and still pitch dark outside. We quickly grabbed our things and ran outside. We were being pushed and harassed more than was necessary by the yelling soldiers.

Every night before bedding down, we had packed our belongings to be ready at an instant. Arthur had warned us, "You always have to be one step ahead of these bastards; you'll never know what Ivan has in store for you."

We assembled, as usual, five in a row and were marched to a railway siding nearby. A long line of boxcars was waiting for us. The cars were barely visible in the upcoming morning light. They were 20-ton boxcars, German rail stock, with roofs.

Forty POWs were commandeered into each boxcar. Without much ceremony we climbed through the sliding doors. The interior had been altered slightly. As we entered the boxcar we saw elevated platforms had been installed on the right and left side of the entrance. They were about five feet off the floor and six feet deep, reaching to the rear wall of the car so that the boxcars had an upper and a lower level on both sides of the doors. They were spacious enough to tightly accommodate forty people. Our little group quickly took possession of the upper and lower left side, just to be together and not in front of the doors. The floor was bare with no straw, and, in spite of the open windows, the car smelled strongly of feces and urine.

Each boxcar was routinely equipped with two small windows, about one by three feet in size on each side of the car. The windows had been left open for fresh air but were protected with barbed wire from the outside. Furthermore, our captors had cut a hole of about five inches in diameter into the floor near one of the two sliding doors. A pipe with a small funnel on top had been stuck into the hole as the toilet—for forty men!

"Now you can watch where we're going, south or east, and then we can make bets where our final destination will be," Kalle told me as the train started to move.

My emotional condition was such that I had absolutely no interest in making bets about anything. To me it was clear where we were going. You could call me anything you wanted, and my gut feeling during this war had seldom misled me.

As the countryside went by the moving train mile after mile passed and with it passed one opportunity after another to escape. For the first time since becoming a prisoner the thought of escaping went through my mind. Soon we would be entering Austria. Austria was an entirely different story from Czechoslovakia, and the Austrians were not Czechs. I didn't know how the Austrians felt about the Germans, especially now that the Russians occupied them. But one thing was for sure; they would not murder us.

None of my buddies seemed to be thinking what I was thinking. Everybody was totally occupied with Kalle's guessing game. I kept my mouth shut, and let my imagination play its own games.

How could I get out of this boxcar? Was the barbed wire, which covered the window like openings from the outside, fastened tightly? How fast was this train going anyway?

I pushed myself towards the window on the upper shelf and looked out at the passing countryside. The train went pretty fast as far as I could determine. But then since it was a long freight train, it would probably slow down going uphill.

Maybe I would get a chance to get out of the boxcar for some water or food? This would give me an opportunity to examine more closely how the doors' locking mechanism worked and how they were secured.

I would also find out how the barbed wire at the window was fastened.

"Look!" shouted Kalle. "We are going due south. Vienna it is and not Siberia."

There are occasions in life when you can talk yourself into believing anything you want to believe, and for Kalle this was such an occasion. The whole boxcar cheered his observation. He was proud and happy and not worried out of his wits any more.

It must have been about 10 A.M. when the train gradually slowed down and finally came to a halt. There was a lot of commotion. We could hear the guards shouting and running back and forth on the outside of our boxcar. One of them started to work the latch on the door, and soon enough it was opened a crack. A Russian voice shouted into the car, *"Dawai, adna choloweg suda!"*

One of our men must have been from Upper Silesia where a lot of Polish is spoken. He understood some Russian and said, "He wants one of us to come to the door."

I got up and asked the soldier who had interpreted to come with me. I wanted him to help me understand what the Russian soldier was saying. We went to the door and looked at the soldier, who was very young and obviously very unsure, afraid or apprehensive. Pointing his Kalaschnikow at us he shouted.

"Adna, tolko adna, ja scajietje!"

Our interpreter translated, "He wants only one of us to come; he is obviously afraid of two of us."

"Tell him you are the interpreter and ask him what he wants," I told him.

"Ja tolko perevotchick," (I am only translating) the soldier told the Russian, while I pushed myself to the door.

Backing further away from the door, the Russian proceeded to tell our interpreter that one man and one man only was supposed to come outside to follow him to get some drinking water for all of us. He had two pails standing next to him.

I pointed at myself and pushed the door open a little wider. The Russian stepped back, raised the Kalaschnikov and yelled with a red face, *"Dawai, dawai!"* let's go, let's go!

This much I understood by this time. In the last camp I had been listening for several days to their commands and had tried to pick up every word I could. My thoughts were that since our association with the Russians was definitely not going to be over soon it was better for me to learn to understand what they were saying. Spending time in the Ukraine in 1943, I had been able to pick up a few isolated words of this difficult language. Back then we had always wanted something from the civilians, and there had been girls that we wanted to talk to.

I climbed down from the boxcar, picked up the two pails and looked at the soldier questioningly.

"Tuda!" he shouted, pointing with his machine pistol towards the front of the train.

To fetch water was a concerted project for all boxcars. One prisoner from every car was outside of the cars by now, marching with the guards alongside the train to go to the front. The locomotive was also replenished with water. We were going to get our water from the same source. Each of us filled the two pails and back we went towards our individual boxcars.

During this first outing up and down the length of the train, I had plenty of time to look at the door latches and also to see how the windows were secured. The barbed wire that covered them did not seem to be too tightly secured. The latches on the doors could only be opened from the outside. The doors were held to the side of the boxcar by two rails, which ran alongside the entire length of the car, one on top and one on the bottom. The rollers of the doors on the top and the bottom were placed in these rails. Okay, I thought, I could unfasten or cut the barbed wire, then slide carefully out of the window and lower myself to stand on the rail at the bottom while holding on to the top rail and the window opening. After climbing out of the car, I could carefully move towards the middle of the car holding on to the top rail with my left hand and then try to open the latch of the door with my free right hand. My next thoughts were about the soldiers who guarded the transport. Where were they positioned?

As I have mentioned before, Ivan was an expert when it came to transporting prisoners. Every six cars throughout the length of the train a little balcony had been cleverly installed in the space between two cars. The balcony did not protrude too far off the side of the train, but far enough so that a guard could stand on it, stick his head out and check up and down the length of the train to see if everything was all right. Those jailors had thought of everything.

I climbed back into the boxcar. The guys were happy to get some fresh water to fill their flasks.

"When are they going to let us go to the latrine? I cannot possible use this small hole," one of the soldiers from the other side of the boxcar complained, sounding rather anxious.

"Please let the interpreter ask the guard while the train is standing still."

We tried to get the attention of the guard, and, after a while, he arrived at the door yelling, *"Za sto?"* (What's up?)

Our interpreter explained the problem whereupon the guard started to laugh hysterically. As soon as he had recovered sufficiently to talk again, he replied by saying something that didn't sound very friendly. Actually it was a chain of violent curses. The Russian language is full of them. We discovered much later that the Russians working men love to use them at every possible and impossible opportunity. After those curses he looked at us piercingly and gave a brief and curt explanation. As our interpreter explained to us, from now on the pipe with the funnel on top was our only toilet, and we'd better get used to it.

The men became very upset. Some even started to cry. They couldn't possibly relieve themselves in front of everybody at such close quarters and into this small hole. And they weren't talking about crapping through the hole, no, they couldn't pee either; it just didn't work. Everybody was too close by, one man lying a foot away from the opening to the right, another man a foot to the left of the hole. A few developed terrible bladder pains and didn't know how to relax their sphincters.

At this point let us not forget that not all of the prisoners were battle-hardened soldiers used to deprivations near the front lines and in the foxholes. Many of them had spent the war in relative comfort a few miles to the rear of the action while watching the supplies flow past. Theirs had been the motto, "Comrade, you shoot, while I get the food."

The guys couldn't pee, and they couldn't shit either. The place near the door and especially the door with the pipe became a war zone. The stench, yelling and complaining were excruciating.

In retrospect our group was lucky to have picked the area as far away from the door as possible. The prisoners learned little by little what they were permitted to do and what had to be done. There were no more dumb excuses, no more special diets, no more subterfuges or special connections, and no more crying on somebody's shoulder.

The thing with the pipe and the funnel gradually straightened itself out, and the prisoners learned to do their thing.

Time was growing short, and I finally made up my mind to talk to Arthur and Kalle about my escape plans. I thought that the plan was good and that they would jump onto the bandwagon. I was sure of it. I was getting increasingly nervous about our situation and had nightmares every night. In my dreams the word "Siberia" was flashing in front of my eyes. I couldn't let this go any further. Austria is a small country, and the train, even this slow freight train, would pass through in no time. We would enter an area completely unsafe, that is, if we were to make a clean getaway. I had to tell them about my observations about the doors and the windows and also about my intentions to escape. I just couldn't envision trying to escape alone. Nor could I have managed to slide out of that narrow window all by myself, not without the help of somebody inside the car, holding me while I was groping with my feet for the rail below.

But the Russians, as I have said repeatedly, had a wealth of experience when it came to transporting prisoners. Shortly before the train started to roll again the door was opened abruptly. A Russian officer and an official interpreter stood below facing the opening.

"Listen everybody and listen good," the interpreter shouted. "The officer in charge of the transport has a message for you."

The officer spoke at length and then the interpreter translated.

"I need three men, officers if possible, who will be responsible for this boxcar and will organize the distribution of food and water, and other necessities. I need some volunteers."

Captain Gross reluctantly raised his arm, and two other sergeants volunteered also. The officer wrote down their names, and then came the pay-off.

"These three men are responsible for the aforementioned chores. Also, this boxcar by the official count holds forty prisoners. If anyone of these forty prisoners disappears during the course of this transport, I will order one of you shot immediately, one of you for every one missing. Has everybody understood?"

There was dead silence. The door was closed, and we were left aghast—especially me.

How could I talk to Kalle and Arthur about my escape plans now? I kicked the situation around and around in my aching head and came to the logical conclusion that even *if* somebody disappeared from the car, the Russian officer would not be crazy or dumb enough to shoot one more prisoner. Though his intimidation sounded gruesome and threatening to the three concerned, what about him? That would leave him, the commanding and responsible officer, with even more prisoners missing than the ones that had escaped and even fewer to turn over to his superiors at our final destination. One thing had become crystal clear during the last few weeks. The continuous and repeated counting of the prisoners—some times rather frantically—meant only one thing; the number of prisoners had to be accurate or someone would suffer dire consequences. That was the only logical conclusion. I was convinced of it, and our three supposed watchdogs had nothing to fear.

The shock accompanying this announcement had not fully abated, when the transport started to move again, and the noise of the rumbling boxcars and the click clack of the wheels gave me a chance to confide my thoughts to Kalle without being overheard by any of the others.

"Are you out of your blinking mind?" he hissed into my ear, "Do you want to kill those three? If this maniac gets really mad, he might kill some of us too."

"Now, Kalle, keep your voice down. We do not want to advertise our discussion to everybody in the car. Don't you understand? He will kill nobody except those who are trying to make a getaway. He is much too afraid of the consequences for himself. I wouldn't want to be in his shoes if he does not deliver the same number of prisoners at our destination that he took over in the beginning."

"All right. And if you are wrong, what then? You are off and running through Austria, and these guys each have a bullet through their heads."

Kalle was really excited now and angry too.

"No way! Count me out on this one."

I was not finished arguing my point. After all, I couldn't pull this off without the help of others, and I was sure that my life depended on this decision.

"Kalle," I whispered, breathing heavily. "Now, listen to me. Believe me, if anybody else loses his life because of what I want to do, the entire plan is no good to me. But, I don't plan to leave alone. You and Arthur, I have not uttered a word to him until now, and Toni and maybe a few others have to come along. Consider for a moment what will happen to us if Ivan continues to string us along a few miles at a time with more of his fantastic stories about picking grapes or repairing pipe lines at Ploesti, and in the end we wind up in Siberia? Do you want to tell yourself again like the other day when we were talking to each other about the things that we failed to do, 'that I should have done, or why didn't I do it?' This time it won't do you any good, and only God knows at this moment if we'll survive this ordeal and if any one of us will ever return."

"No!" Kalle said. "And this is final. These are your comrades. You don't put them in jeopardy to gain a personal advantage. You're among friends here, and when you're among friends, all difficulties are easier to bear. Don't do anything foolish, Peter; you'll have to live with it for the rest of your life."

Many, many times afterwards I wished that I had been more persuasive with Kalle and more egotistic myself. Maybe, I would've died during the escape attempt, maybe. But I would've saved myself untold agonies, and Kalle would still be alive. He didn't realize that the word "comrade" and what it had meant during the war was dead, stone dead. It would soon be replaced in German vernacular with the word *"Kumpel,"* which has no meaning of trust and friendship like the word comrade portrayed. Distrust of the guy next to you and narrow egotism would become ubiquitous in the prison camps of the Gulag.

Idiot that I was, I gave up my attempts to solicit Kalle's support. Now I tried to explain to Arthur what I wanted to do and what I had explained to Kalle before. He was all for my plan, but when I related Kalle's misgivings to him, he became doubtful.

"I don't see it quite his way, Peter, but these are such strong feelings. I don't think you'll overcome them. One thing is sure; you can't get out of this boxcar without creating a commotion not even at night. You'll need a number of accomplices to help you and who are willing to remain behind, or else convince half of the men in this boxcar to join you in your escape."

"Arthur," I replied excitedly, thinking that I had at least convinced him, "we will cut the barbed wire, which covers the window then I'll climb out. I'll hang with my hands from the upper rail of the door with my feet holding my weight on the lower rail; I'll slowly make it to the end of the door and pull up the lever to unlock the door. Hopefully the guard will not have discovered me by then; otherwise, I'll have to drop off the train and make a run for it. The door will be unlocked. I'll knock twice, and you'll have to slide the door open from the inside. Holding on to the rails on the outside of the boxcar with my hands doesn't leave me with enough strength to open the door by myself. After the door is open, everybody is on his own. Those who want to come with us, jump; the others stay. My bet is, that a good number will jump."

"Oh, Peter, don't be naïve. The three guys whose lives are supposedly at stake will start yelling the minute they think something is afoul. The guards will come running over the roofs of the wagons, and that'll be the end. No, without the cooperation of those three, it won't work."

"Make a suggestion," I said. "I'm game for anything except sitting here and letting fate take its course."

We turned it over for quite a while, and got Kalle involved again. Nothing, I couldn't even manage to convince Arthur.

The captain, whom we finally turned to—sooner or later we would have had to talk to him anyway—wanted to throw me out off the boxcar immediately. He was another one of our strategic thinking officers and with real courage too. He should've been the one convincing the others that my theory about the continuous counting of the prisoners was correct, but he didn't see it, he was too dense, probably out of fear for his own life.

I, the biggest idiot of them all, abandoned my plan for the sake of my "comrades."

We were now on the train for four days. The daily routine for us consisted of going to the front of the train and getting food from the kitchen car. I tried to be on this detail as often as I could to stretch my legs, to get out of the boxcar, and to give my mind a rest from the repetitive subjects being tossed back and forth by the prisoners. It also gave me a chance to listen to the guards talking and to associate their words with their deeds. I picked up a few Russian phrases here and there and little by little improved my vocabulary. I always came back to the crowded, depressing and smelly car refreshed and animated.

The train was frequently put on side rails to let military transports pass us. Ninety percent of these transports came from the west filled with Russian troops on their way home. Often the trains were composed of German passenger wagons with happily smiling Russian soldiers inside. We could easily look into the compartments since they passed us very slowly. The compartments were loaded with all kinds of loot; furnishings, clothes, or sewing machines taken from apartments in Germany or Austria. The soldiers had strung lace curtains onto the compartment windows for decoration. It looked hideous. Many times they leaned out of the cars shouting obscenities at us. One particular sentence got our guys very upset.

"Matja domoi charascho ficky, ficky!" (Your wives at home fucked well!) It was appalling and some of the prisoners were crying uncontrollably.

Slowly but surely we made our way through Austria, passing through the city of Vienna and later in the general direction of Hungary. After two more days we crossed the Hungarian border. At every stop we saw Gypsies dancing around the trains occupied with Russian soldiers. The Gypsies played their violins, entertaining to get some cigarettes or food. They constantly played a tune called *Katjuscha*. That song must have been a hit tune with the Russians because they loved to hear it and danced to it. We must have heard it until it came out of our ears.

Many years later I heard this pretty song played by an excellent Cossack band. It evoked memories and I cringed; every hair on my body stood up, and I got goose pimples from the vivid pictures flashing through my mind, as I thought of the summer of 1945, traveling through Hungary on a train filled with POWs.

We did not appreciate at the time how fortunate we had been with the seasonal temperatures of an early summer. We never froze or sweat, and we had enough drinking water. By the standards that the German army had set with the transport of prisoners the Soviets treated us well.

It took us three days of slow travel to pass through Hungary until we entered Romania. We had been cramped up in our car for too long.

"See," Kalle said triumphantly, having become rather quiet after our difference of opinion and his idiotic rejection of my escape plan, "as I have told you all along, it's going to be *Ploesti.*"

I didn't comment. It did not matter any more.

The train came to a stop north of *Ploesti,* which is roughly 40 miles north of Bucharest; we were close to a large freight rail facility. As far as I could determine from the surroundings, as I was walking toward the front of the train for our noontime food and water supply, it was the place where the European rail met the Russian rail system with a wider gauge. The big 50-ton Russian boxcars were standing there in the yard for everybody to see. This must be the rerouting place I thought, *"This is the place where they will load us into Russian boxcars."*

Our guards led us to a hastily erected camp. Of course, it had a bathhouse and the usual delousing facility, which we were going to use, hopefully. When we arrived, at least two thousand prisoners were already in the camp. Arthur and I got busy trying to find out what was going on and, if possible, where we would be going from here. By accident, "The world is a peanut shell," I met the master sergeant I had served with in Italy twelve months ago.

I remembered him fondly, a great guy. We had been getting along fine. He took over Asta, my German shepherd when they would not allow her on the ship. I still got angry when I thought about it. Now I was happy to see his face, and I approached him, "Hello, Master Sergeant, do you remember me?"

"I'll be damned; Peter, man, am I glad to see you." He gave me a bear hug. "Stop this Master Sergeant shit. The military is done for, and my name is Fritz, as you know."

I was just approaching twenty, and Fritz to me was an old guy, at least thirty years old. In Italy he had been good to me, to Karl, and, let's not forget, to Asta. It had not been his fault that he had to order us to go up to that stupid church in *Iesi*. The older soldiers in the German army in general were kind of aloof from the youngsters, especially when they had rank. Fritz Losanski had behaved differently, and he was special to me.

"Tell me, Fritz, the first thought that enters my head when I see you is Asta. Whatever happened to my dog?"

"Not that he could help you now, Peter, but I must tell you, Asta died a soldier's dog's death. A grenade hit him. To be more precise, it was a large splinter from a grenade that hit him. It happened about three months after you left on the ship. Asta had been with us all this time even though she seemed somewhat unhappy without you and Karl, probably missing both of you, the faithful animal. We were a little further up north on our retreat through Italy and came under heavy fire. I ducked into the cellar of a farmhouse. Usually Asta knew what to do and followed us. But this time I didn't see her and assumed she had gone with somebody else. When the bombardment stopped, and I came out, she was lying there right at the entrance to the shelter; she was dead. She had a large hole in her flank. The guys were heartbroken and insisted that we bury her, which we did. Sorry, Peter, that I don't have any better news."

I was sad to hear that Asta had died and the way she had died. Even though my memory of her had faded, considering the circumstances and all the things that had happened to me since then, I was trying to retrace the time. Had it been really only 13 months ago? To me it seemed more like ten years since they had carried me onto that hospital ship in the harbor of *Ancona* where I had to say goodbye to Asta.

"Thanks for the info, Fritz. For a while I missed Karl and Asta something awful, especially at the hospital in *Cortina*. It was a lonely feeling you know. They operated on me and wired my jaw. Asta would have been a good companion to have around. I was not worried about her, because I knew that with you she was in good hands. So many things have happened since. Okay, it's not the time to be sentimental. But what brought you to this terrible place, Fritz? And do you know any of Ivan's plans?" He chuckled and replied, "Well, first of all, to tell you about my adventures, I caught a piece of metal in Italy shortly after Asta died not too bad, just a flesh wound in the thigh. The injury earned me a trip to a hospital in Germany where I stayed until I was transferred to our old outfit in a town west of *Guben*. I was surprised at the time not to find you there, but they told me that you had been transferred to the *Armee Corps*. You can imagine the rest for yourself because the end of the war was the same for all of us. I am sure that you know the old saying *wer schreibt, der bleibt* (Those who do the paperwork remain alive). When the issue came up, I volunteered to do the paperwork for the Russians. The little Polish I know helps me to understand their language enough to know what they want and to do the work. In school I had learned the Cyrillic alphabet, which helps. For some unknown reason they want to keep a record of all the prisoners passing through this camp. So far my efforts to do that have been a dismal failure. They expected me to write all the names on pages of old newspaper and with a broken pencil. Can you believe it? Now they have promised better writing material. One thing I can tell you for certain, I am not going to travel any further for the time being. And, as a bonus, the Russian camp commander promised me an immediate release after this camp is dissolved."

"Not any further, Fritz?" I interrupted him with my mouth wide open. "Where do you think everybody is going? Do you have any idea? I mean, if you know you have to tell me."

"To tell you the truth, Peter, I don't know. Ivan keeps mum about it. I have seen many transports leaving, but I don't know where they are headed. They tell me that they don't know either. I tend to believe it; none of them ever seems to know anything or want to know anything. It's worse than our *Barras* (slang expression for the German army). But I have a suggestion if you want to stay with me, to help me assemble and write these records so to speak I think I can swing it with the Commander. You only need to learn how to speak a few words of Russian about as quickly as you learned Italian. And the Cyrillic alphabet shouldn't be too difficult for you. I still remember when we were stationed in *Rimini* and all the girls called you, *el piccolo biondo*. I'll never forget that, you little wise guy." We both laughed in memory of the good wine and pretty girls in *Rimini* on the Adriatic Sea.

"Fritz," I replied after he had made his proposal, "I'll make up my mind quickly. Just let me discuss it for a minute with my buddies, okay?"

We said good-bye, and I returned to my group. At first I sat down on the stoop of our barracks and tried to clear my mind.

Should I follow Fritz's invitation and let Kalle, Arthur, Toni and the others go wherever the transport was going without me? I considered that we had grown accustomed to each other, and, in spite of our disagreement about my plans for an escape from the train, I felt comfortable with them. Staying with them could mean picking grapes on the Crimea or slaving in a coalmine in Siberia. On the other hand, staying with Fritz could mean the same thing. In the end it was purely and simply a question of making a decision all by myself, for myself, and without leaning on somebody else for moral support. Besides, I knew I was not going to ask anybody what their opinion was in the matter.

After I had made that decision I had to live with it. I had learned something important for the rest of my life. In retrospect—20/20 hindsight—I made the wrong decision. One thing was for sure, what I had learned in the long run was that it is a grave mistake to cling to others when your own life is at stake.

Fritz, just as he had told me, returned to Berlin after the camp had outlived its usefulness. The Russian commander kept his word and released him. Years later I met him in Berlin where he told me his story, and I told him my odyssey.

In the processing camp at *Ploesti* I felt like a seasoned infantryman with all the wartime experiences one could possibly have, like a grown, wise old man. In reality I had entered a vastly different world, and I was young, unpolished and insecure. It was true that nobody could or would have helped me with the decision I had to make. Consequently I did the next best thing, I held on to an apparent security. I relied on "comrades," on "friends." As I said, I have learned my lesson, have become more cynical, as far as reliance on other people is concerned, and, as a result, lonelier for the rest of my life.

My decision was made. I went inside to tell the others about Fritz and his proposal. I embellished it and finished with a grand finale, "Of course, I am going to stay with you. I want to be with my friends."

Their answer was disappointing, kind of a let down. "What else could you have done?" one said, and so on and so forth.

I went to tell Fritz and explained my reasons to him. He smiled and said, "You'll learn, Peter, and it'll hurt. When things have cooled down and maybe when we are all back home, let's try to see each other again. Take a look in the telephone book there are not too many Losanskis in Berlin. You'll find me. Good bye, my young friend, I wish you the best of luck."

We embraced and parted each to his personal destiny.

The Russians kept us in the temporary camp just long enough to assemble enough rolling stock for our transport. One early morning, after we had been at Ploesti for one week, at five o'clock, a train with empty boxcars pulled in to the siding next to the camp. About 20 prisoners were commandeered to clean out the cars, which by their appearance had served as a prisoner transport before, and to put fresh straw on the floors. Essentially, with the exception that these cars were larger 50-ton boxcars, he configuration inside was the same. Two platforms, one on the right and one on the left, were inside the boxcars. The famous hole with a pipe stuck into it was near the door. Barbed wire had been nailed to the outside of the four narrow windows to prevent anybody from escaping.

Two days later we were ordered to assemble, were counted leaving the camp, walked over to the rail siding, were counted again and ordered to climb into the waiting boxcars. The customary "*dawai, dawai*" by the guards accompanied this process. Nothing in this language seemed to be without it, and, of course, with the obligatory curse words added.

Sixty prisoners went into each boxcar; it was a tight fit. Our group tried to get the lower left corner of our boxcar. Since we were about 20 *Kumpel* by now, we had enough muscle to make room exactly were we wanted to be. The Russians had succeeded cleverly in mixing up the units of prisoners thoroughly. There were no more friendships or old alliances left. This suited their purpose like a glove. They even included two boxcars with Hungarian officer aspirants to complete the mixture. This configuration of prisoners would not cause anyone to gang up to oppose anything. No, they were submissive, and many times they would rather quarrel with each other about petty details than think of an uprising, like when we were entering the new boxcar for the next leg of our rail saga to reach the *grape picking area of the Crimea.* I couldn't hear it any more but my friends were clinging to this mirage. And groups of two or three prisoners staked out their corners. We were, on the bottom under the upper level, nicely protected from whatever might happen during the journey. Since the subject of a possible escape had been put to rest, it was no need to be on the top level near the window.

In front of the train was the kitchen car with two huge metal kettles inside. It was intended to be the sole source for cooking. For some reason the Russians picked Toni and two others to cook and to sleep in the kitchen car too. It was a stroke of luck for Toni and also for our group.

"Toni," I said, before he left with his belongings toward his new assignment, "Don't forget who your friends are. I will try to see you often. After all, I have to learn Russian quickly, and we'll have to stay in touch."

"You'll do that," Toni replied. "As you know, I speak a little Russian from my wartime exposure and from the Polish dialect we all learned in East Prussia. That's how I made the Russians aware of my talents as a gourmet cook. A little bit of lingo can only help where we are going. There is always something and somebody to interpret and you don't want to be with the peasants, do you? Now, let me go to prepare the next meal for these 1,300 hungry men. It'll be delicious, you bet."

He laughed dryly blinking an eye at me and disappeared toward the front of the train, the obligatory guard trailing behind.

We settled down, stashing our few belongings as pillows under our heads and waited for the train to start moving, curious as ever to discover which direction it would take. At first there was an eerie quiet among the men, but after some time, speculation about our destination resumed. Where were we going to go? I had heard so many theories that my head was spinning, but my own thoughts steered me only in one direction. No matter how much I ached to yell it out loud in frustration, I kept my mouth shut. I had to live with these men, and they could get extremely agitated if their pie in the sky was shot down in flames. I knew that only one guy in the entire car agreed with me, and that was Arthur.

During the war it had always been the same story. The vast majority of soldiers never wanted to face a bitter truth, no matter what the situation was. I was one of the younger ones and had only joined in 1942, when, after three years of war, the first signs of the impending disaster became clearly visible. I also had a different background through the exposure to my mother's circle of people, my time in America and my education in two countries. But 1942 had been well into the war for the rest of Germans, and they should have known by then. Let's not forget the wake-up calls they had received. The African campaign had crumbled; the famous *Generalfeldmarschall v. Rommel* could not bluff his way through the desert any more. Stalingrad was surrounded in 1942 and was about to fall. America had entered the war, gradually finding its footing by landing on the African continent, and the great *Führer* had exposed his true strategic talents more than once. Yet everybody feverishly believed the propaganda stories about secret weapons being developed that would accomplish the impossible hat trick.

Now, finally, in captivity, and on our way to an unknown destination even the last stubborn political holdout understood what had happened and how they had been duped and misled. The first stories of the existence of huge concentration camps for the opponents of the regime were openly making the rounds in the boxcar. And, as odd as it may sound, after so many years had passed under permanent control by the Nazi party, it was only now, in the boxcar, on our way to Siberia that the average guy grasped that the regime of Hitler's goons had prohibited any personal freedom, free speech and brutally suppressed the country. It was over, and the soldiers finally accepted that they had been lied to continuously.

Throughout the war the *Landser*'s (the common soldier) mind had been inventive, especially when he had to grapple with excuses and explanations for everything that happened to him, around him and for every misfortune that befell his country. I started to realize, when I thought back to those times during the war in late 1942, that it was probably the only way for him not to become insane.

Even now the unbelievable inventions of Hitler's propaganda machine roamed through the soldiers minds like a Fata Morgana. The second most popular theme of the soldier's daily reminiscing in the boxcar centered around the weapon systems the German scientists supposedly had developed, but had never really deployed, the so-called *Wunderwaffen* (wonder-weapons). These *Wunderwaffen* had been talked about constantly during the latter part of the war after things were going south. The broadcasts of the Nazi propaganda machine were full of them, promising sudden, vast superiority over the enemy on a daily basis, painting an alluring picture for the suffering population and the outmatched soldiers, thus creating dreams about an impossible final victory. At first it had been the V1, then the V2 (V = Vergeltungswaffe = retaliation weapon). These were the two rockets that were shot rather aimlessly at the British Isles, terrorizing the civilian population but never with any strategic results for the outcome of the war.

In the boxcar, on their way to God only knows where, the men exchanged their *"personal knowledge"* of such weapons, of hundreds of new fighter jets standing on the ground without fuel, fabulous super-sized 50-ton tanks that had been held back for whatever reason, mostly sabotaged by the home-front. They exchanged views of whatever sounded plausible to members of a defeated country.

Listening to these stories, I had to think of my mother. In situations like these she was always prepared with an appropriate saying. I could hear her now, "The truth is very seldom a comfort, my son."

It was not until the beginning of June, and after the first few days of our transport, as we went from Romania through southern Russia, that everybody became terribly subdued. The small windows closed with barbed wire were our only contact to the world, permitting only a limited view of the countryside.

We had all been in Russia during the war, but those had been different circumstances. Now as we crossed the border clearly recognizable by heavy military fortifications, the difference between the Rumanian countryside and its orderly villages and plowed fields and Russia was dramatic. The villages in southern Russia could have been just as rich and prosperous. The crops were good and the climate favorable. But, no, they looked dismal, disorganized, dilapidated, piss poor and grimy. It did not get any better as the train traversed deeper and deeper into the Soviet Empire. What would it look like further to the east, if we were really going all the way to Siberia?

Whenever the train stopped, I volunteered to be on the food detail. To go to the front of the train, to move about in the fresh air gave me a chance to get out of the boxcar, talk to Toni and to hear the latest scuttlebutt. Toni, of course, heard the gossip on the train from everybody and also had additional input from the Russian guards. By the way, they ate the same food as we did. It was more important for me to talk to Toni than to listen to the wishful phantasms of my fellow prisoners.

"You know, Peter," he said one day as I was getting the daily rations for our 20 guys, "I don't like what I hear, or let's rather say what I don't hear. The Russian guards are very uncommunicative. Whenever I asked one of them, they are trying to make me believe that they don't know a thing and *that* I cannot believe. On the other hand I don't understand what they have to hide? We are not going any place. No matter what the final destination might be. Or do you think a single soul on this train will start to revolt because we might be going to Siberia? I don't believe it, do you?"

"No way, Toni. Everybody is so sullen, dispirited and distraught; they won't do a thing, besides it would be useless. The Russians have us by the balls; they know it, and everybody on this train knows it."

We left it at that. The guys behind me in line were pushing me to get going, and the guards were getting restless because we had been talking too long. I took the two canisters with the soup and hung the cloth sack filled with dried bread around my shoulders and went back to my boxcar, the guard trailing closely behind me. Inside the boxcar the stench was nauseating, and the straw looked filthier by the day.

For the last couple of days the food was getting worse. Every day we ate yellow pea soup and dried black bread. The bread was as hard as a rock, so hard, as a matter of fact, that you had to suck it, wet it with spittle or pour water over it before being able to get your teeth into it and chew it. The Russians must have dried it very slowly in ovens to render it almost imperishable. Almost, because we frequently detected mold on the outside, which we simply scraped off. The adjustment to this quality of food came only gradually. Never before had any one of us lived on such a frugal diet. The surprising thing was that the guards, the members of the victorious Russian army, ate the same as we did and seemed to enjoy it. I guess they were happy and content that they did not have to do any cooking.

To pass the time of endless boredom and the ratata-ratata of the wheels of the boxcar we played with an old deck of cards, which was so old and had passed through so many hands that it hardly displayed the pictures and designations any more and was also frayed at the edges. But it helped us pass the time and helped us avoid thinking about where we were going. The gamblers among the prisoners insisted that the scores were kept accurately on tiny pieces of paper to make sure that debts could be paid later on.

As I mentioned before, many small illusions were kept alive. Paid with what? It was one of the make believe stories, even though one might laugh about the gullibility of the prisoners today.

The Geneva Convention does not only have rules for the feeding of prisoners of war but also for their treatment down to the last detail. If prisoners do any work at all, they are supposed to get paid— as if the Germans had ever paid a dime to any of their Russian prisoners, or to the captives of other nations. Therefore, the guys were gambling for the money, which the Russians would pay them eventually for grape picking on the Crimea. These were two idiotic deductions. What a joke!

As our transport slowly traversed the Russia mainland, first Moldavia and then the Ukraine, we became convinced that our train, loaded with nothing but prisoners of war, must have had a very low priority among all the trains in the system. We were constantly side-tracked while other trains sped by in both directions. Many of the tracks in Russia, at least the ones we traveled on, were single rail lines. There was no way that another train could get by us other than with ours waiting on a siding. The civilians at the stations stared at us but not, in as unfriendly or hostile way as we could have expected. They were simply curious.

There was absolutely no doubt whatsoever where we were going; we were on our way east, straight east all the way to Siberia. Kalle did not talk about the subject any more. He sat sullenly in his spot all by himself, did not play cards, nor participate in the conversations. I couldn't understand him or his motives any more. He could have easily said:

"Sorry to have been so insistent, Peter, you were right. We're going to Siberia after all."

But admitting that he had been wrong with a subject so vital to us was more than he could bear. He and I didn't discuss the issue any more; we kind of drifted apart. I was keeping my mind occupied with the things I considered more important for my survival. For example, by learning Russian at every opportunity I got. I had taken Toni's advice and was preparing myself for the future.

After two and a half weeks of the same routine the train crossed the Ural Mountains and was descending east on its way into Siberia. The scenery had changed. The contour was plain and, if that was possible at all, more desolate than before. The train stations were only shacks; the villages that one could see nearby were poor. Most noticeable any agricultural activities appeared to have ceased a long time ago. The next largest city, according to what the guards were saying, would be *Nowosibirsk*. Two days later, soon after we had passed *Nowosibirsk* the train turned south, away from the *Trans Siberian* main line; we arrived at the *Kuszbas* and the city of *Stalinsk*. (Today it is called *Kemorowo*.)

One morning the doors flew open, and the guards yelled, *"Dawai,dawai!* Get out of the train; assemble five abreast and let's have all interpreters or those who can speak Russian up front."

I raised my hand and said, *"Ponjumaj pa Ruski"* (I understand Russian) and that was it. I had identified myself as an interpreter and, for the time being, the guards accepted me as one.

We had arrived at our final destination not knowing when we would leave again or what destiny held in store for us. Many of us would stay forever.

9

WITHOUT THE CIVILIANS WE WOULD HAVE ALL BEEN DEAD

From their behavior and from what I could detect they were saying to each other, the guards were also strangers to these parts of Russia, and they were almost as concerned about what was going to happen to them as we were. Having grown up as children of the Stalin era and having lived through the deportations of millions of their countrymen they knew the old saying. "Once you are in Siberia, you are stuck in Siberia; it's hard to get away."

First, however, they had to obey their orders. Deliver the prisoners to their final destination with nobody missing.

"Rasberaitje pa piat." The old battle cry of all Russian guards, "Assemble five in a row. *Dawai, dawai.*"

The prisoners had spent the last fourteen days since leaving *Ploesti* in a filthy boxcar. Many of them had not moved out of the car during the entire trip. They got up slowly and unsteadily and gathered their belongings. My earlier decision to make the daily trip to the front of the train to gather the supplies proved to be right. My legs were still strong and nimble, and I easily jumped to the ground from the boxcar. To keep up his strength, Arthur had exercised on a regular basis and was also in much better shape than most of the men were.

My first job as an interpreter was to translate this simple order to the guys in our boxcar and to see that it was understood. The columns of POWs finally got organized, five in a row, twenty rows deep, one hundred men per column. The march through the Siberian city of *Stalinsk* began with one guard in front, and one in the back of each column. They did not worry about anybody running away any more. Where would we be running?

The railroad siding was located near the edge of the city. We saw a huge steel mill in the distance with five coke ovens steadily belching white steam.

Of the two thousand men on the train twelve hundred started to march in one direction while the other eight hundred stayed behind.

Later we learned that these eight hundred went to a camp directly in the town, the so-called "city camp."

Our contingent of twelve hundred marched through the town of Stalinsk past dreary looking shacks, a few small houses and large construction sites. Few people were walking on the road and only once in a while did a truck pass by leaving large clouds of dust behind.

Stalinsk, as the town was called as long as Stalin was alive, is located on the Tom River, a tributary of the Ob River, about two hundred miles south east of *Nowosibirsk,* roughly five hundred miles northwest of the Mongolian Republic and four thousand miles distant from Moscow. Its population at the time of our arrival was about 150,000, most of them were prisoners. *Stalinsk* was also the most easterly point of a famous strategic rail supply line that stretched between *Magnitogorsk* west of the Ural Mountains and the *Kusbasz* region to the east where *Stalinsk* is located. Struggling in the twenties and thirties to achieve industrial independence, the Soviets had built several iron ore processing plants to bolster their steel making capacity. American engineering, money and know-how had helped to build these huge complexes at each end of the line. Thus, long trains, loaded with the iron ore from *Magnitogorsk* supplied the ore to the steel mills at the *Kusbasz* region 2000 miles away. On the return trips they carried the coal from the *Kusbasz* to supply the mills at *Magnitogorsk.*

We continued marching through deserted streets. Only a few people were walking home from exhausting shifts at their places of work. None of them seemed to be interested as the German POWs passed.

In my capacity as an interpreter I had used my influence with the guards to position our group in the first four rows of the first of twelve columns of one hundred prisoners. This way we did not have to swallow the dust of preceding columns which was stirred up by hundreds of shoveling feet, and we were better able to observe where we were going and what was ahead. Even though *Stalinsk* was an industrial town, the streets were mostly dirt roads, bone dry and dusty from the June heat. It was early in the morning, and already it was at least eighty-five degrees.

After we marched for twenty minutes, passing only a few civilians on the street, I turned to my friend, "Hey, Arthur isn't that strange; I would have expected some heckling from the civilians, you know, similar to what we experienced on the roads in Czechoslovakia. After all, the Germans were the enemy, despised all over Russia for what they did to the population during the war. What do we get? Not even a peep, not even a stare."

"Well, if you wonder why, look a little to your left and to your right and beyond this road. You can see work gangs. They don't appear to me as if they are working voluntarily. And over there, can you see? There is a prison camp—four towers, wooden fences, barbed wire, the works. And over there you can see two more of the same. I have yet to see a child on these streets."

"What a drab place," was Toni's comment. Kalle grunted disgustedly.

They were right. If the whole town looked like what we had seen so far, it was nothing but a gigantic prison camp.

As time wore on, our first impression was confirmed. *Stalinsk* had a civilian population, which lived outside of the camps in shaky looking barracks and run-down apartment buildings, but at least forty percent of its people were confined behind fences and watchtowers.

We continued marching through the town past building sites, houses, barracks and factories. The building sites were buzzing with activity. Two miles further down the road we approached a river, a very dirty river. The water on our side of it was dark black, like ink. The water seemed to be coming from the cooling towers of the steel mills, cooling water, needed for the steel processing. We couldn't see a bridge up or downstream. As a matter of fact the river seemed to be the border of the town. A large ferry was waiting for us on the riverbank to take us across. Five hundred yards away on the other side, in the haze of an early morning river, we could make out a few single, old, weathered wooden blockhouses. Otherwise there was nothing in the distance but steeply rising gray hills with little vegetation, which survived the fumes.

The ferry was large enough to transport two hundred people at a time. It was riding back and forth across the river on a wire suspended over the water for about four hundred yards and fastened on each side of the river to heavy embedded concrete pillars. Two ferrymen worked the ferry with a manual pulley, which was attached to a second much thinner wire, which pulled it slowly across the lazily moving river. After coming across safely, each contingent of two hundred prisoners got off the ferry with relief. We waited until all twelve hundred men had made it and were led a few hundred yards further away from the river, toward a solitary, rusty railroad track. An equally ancient looking steam engine with a huge belching smoke stack, which must have dated back to 1920, with fifteen flatbed cars in tow was waiting for us.

"Look at that thing. I hope they don't want to transport us on these contraptions. We'll all fall off," Kalle observed unbelieving.

Just then the guard came and told me to tell the men that one column of one hundred POWs had to get on each flat bed.

A hundred men should fit onto a 20-ton flatbed? I could not believe my ears and looked at him questioningly.

"*Bistray* [Be quick]. I think you are an interpreter," he yelled at me and made no bones about his impatience. He waved his Kalaschnikov threateningly.

I translated his command and the prisoners, complaining and cursing loudly, started to climb aboard. We barely fit. We squeezed together and stood shoulder to shoulder all the way to the edge of the platform, and we strained to hold onto each other.

"There is nothing to hold onto. What if this asshole shakes a little? We're all going to fall off?"

"We'll fall off like dominoes. The Russians, these fuckers are crazy. They want to kill us before we even get to where we are going."

Those and more comments came from all sides.

Frankly, the guards did not give a shit. They knew that we would fit onto the cars, and they knew it would work without anybody falling off in spite of our complaints. In any case, we noticed that our old guards, after the appropriate signing of paperwork, turned us over to a new set of guards, but not before we were counted one more time by both sets of guards. The new guards were all clad in blue instead of the customary greenish-brown army type uniforms. "My" guard, the one with us since departing *Ploesti,* turned around, waved briefly at me with a happy smile on his face and headed toward the ferry. He was eager to get back as quickly as possible to the rest of his buddies.

The new gang yelled at us to get going quickly and without any further obstruction of their orders. *Bistray! Bistray! Dawai! Dawai!*

It worked; we climbed onto the flat beds, and nobody fell off. Not a single prisoner fell off the flat beds.

Naturally, our complaining continued unabated and grew even louder as the train started with considerable jerking. To make it worse, the wagons were loosely attached to each other. The play between couplings was enormous and we held on to each other as best as we could, not knowing that from now on this would be our mode of transportation to and from work every morning and every night.

The ride was short. The rusty, crooked-looking rails had been nailed onto roughly shaped tree trunks and then placed onto the rocky surface of a gently sloping hillside on our right. To our left stretched a flat valley all the way to the Tom River, which disappeared between the hills in the far distance as if it had dropped off the earth. As far as the eye could see was field after field covered with large white cabbage plants.

After six miles of a rocky trip the track ended abruptly in the middle of nowhere. The lonely engineer in the cab of the ancient engine blew the whistle and sent a blast of white steam into the humid summer air. The train stopped, and we were told to get off. *Bistray!*

From where the train had stopped, somewhat elevated on the slope, we could see a prison complex three hundred yards down a narrow dirt road, placed in the middle of a wide expanse of nothing surrounded by white cabbage as far as the eye could see, nothing to the right or the left except endless fields of cabbage. A mile away, back in the direction we had come, the silhouette of a small village was perched upon the green fields. The camp looked like the ones we had noticed during our first glimpses while marching through the city. Four towers stood, one on each corner, hammered together with raw wood each one had a wooden ladder for the guards to climb. Solid wooden fences connected the towers. Three rows of barbed wire were on top of them. We couldn't look inside the camp; the fences were too high for that. We only saw the rooftops of a few barracks peeking over the edge of the fence.

Arthur, never far away from me, came up close and murmured the first words we exchanged since we had climbed onto the flatbeds. We had been too stunned by the experiences of the last few hours to talk.

"If this is our new home then I have only one thing I wish to know. When are we going to leave?

It was not funny, only *Galgenhumor* (humor of the gallows), and he was swallowing tears as he said it. We were thousands of miles from what we called civilization; here we were confronted with the prison that seemed to be our new home, a prison camp in the middle of Siberia surrounded by an ocean of white cabbage.

Most of the prisoners minds and feelings were too anesthetized to realize the apparent finality of this location, and I didn't know what they were thinking, but Arthur and I longed to get back home, desperately so, and we couldn't think of anything else. We were devastated.

Around the camp, hugging the wooden fence tightly was a strip of meticulously raked sand about twenty feet wide. We guessed that it was prepared to detect footprints of escaping prisoners or to keep out or discourage any possible trespassers.

"*Pa piat, pa piat*" (five, five). The guards shouted their litany as we jumped off the train to assemble and to march a few hundred yards toward the camp. We were ordered to sit down and wait alongside the wooden fence.

It was a scorching hot summer day in the middle of June, and we had little water left from the supply we received the night before still on the train.

"Peter, why don't you ask this blue guy where we can get some water?" One of the fellows asked me to do my job.

I tried to get up, but the guard shouted angrily for me to sit down and to stay down. It was no use arguing with these guys. They did not look as if they were in a mood to discuss anything with us.

The heat was getting worse as the day wore on and must have reached ninety degrees or more. We were still sitting on the ground in front of the camp without any shade. To make matters worse, the guards once again began to search every one for valuables. They were young paramilitary soldiers from the local area and had not had a chance to get a pick of the loot so far and didn't want to lose their last opportunity to get a watch, jewelry or some other trinket—invaluable to a poor guard in the workers' paradise—before we disappeared inside the stockade. They probably knew that their guard duty was temporary and that they'd have to turn us over to a new set of guards as soon as we disappeared in the camp. For them it was now or never.

Slowly one by one, we had to get up and raise our hands to be patted down thoroughly. What could they possibly find after dozens of their fellow soldiers from the camps of *Pisek* to *Ploesti* and on to *Stalinsk* had searched us? But how could they have known? The disappointment showed in their faces and the lack of success didn't make them any happier.

At about 2 P.M., after what seemed for us like an endless time in the blazing heat, a small cart appeared from the direction of the village, loaded down with a huge barrel, which as it turned out was filled with fresh, cool water. A very small, tired and meek looking horse pulled this barrel on wooden wheels. A local farm hand, a *kolchos* worker, was sitting on top of the barrel with a bored expression on his face, continuously beating the little horse with a stick without any visible results.

A few prisoners made an attempt to get up to jump onto the wagon to get some water but were promptly chased back by guards who, surprisingly, made a determined effort to explain to me—to tell all the others—that this water was not safe to drink. It would have to be boiled first. The contents of the barrel, which splashed over the rim with each turn of the wheels, looked clean enough to us, but the guards wouldn't let us get near it. The cart disappeared through the two entrance gates, which had swung open slowly as if moved by an invisible hand. Soon another guard yelled, "dawai, dawai," to get a few prisoners to help with unloading of water inside the camp. An announcement was made that we would have to wait until the water was boiled on a special brick stove erected just for this purpose. Considering the quantity of water to be heated to a boiling point, it would be at least another hour until we would get any water to quench our thirst. After another hour of indeterminable waiting, the guards led the first column of prisoners into the camp, counting very carefully, row by row as we passed inside, *raz, dwa, tre, tshatery* (one, two, three, four). We were escorted passed the "water kitchen," where each prisoner was able to get a cup of warm water. It was the biggest tease we had ever seen.

The same *kolchos* worker reappeared again with the water barrel after another hour and the whole process was repeated. By now, almost six hours after climbing off the train, two to three hundred prisoners were inside the camp without any guards to control them, or to hold them back. And they were thirsty, very thirsty. As soon as the next load of water rolled through the gate, they rushed to the small vehicle, jumped on top of the cart and refilled their canteens with refreshingly cool virgin water. Fighting for the water became fierce. Even the few sensible men among the prisoners could not hold the others back or wanted to stay behind. Only a few waited for the water to be boiled; the others did not give a damn. Arthur and I were among them.

Theo and two more were commandeered to a barrack in the corner of the camp. The barrack looked like the others but housed the kitchen and the supply rooms. It had windows, which were protected by rusty crossbars. We hoped that Theo and the others were going to cook our soup for the evening.

Slowly all the prisoners entered the camp during the late afternoon, had their fight with the water and were squatting down in a large square in the middle of the camp. All we wanted to know was when they would let us out of the sun and into the barracks.

First, the camp commander in a blue uniform addressed us.

He climbed on a barrel so that we could see and hear him better and began, "I want all officers, German or Hungarian, to step forward. You will face your fellow prisoners, and they will select their spokesmen from you."

As the officer started to speak, I begged off the translator's job because I was way over my head with the limited vocabulary I had acquired thus far. That was a dumb mistake because it was the end of my interpreting job and most certainly the end of any perks that would have come with it. Two guys who were from one of the Baltic and one from Upper Silesia took over. Both were speaking excellent Russian, and I wondered where had they been up to now.

A hundred Hungarian and nine German officers obeyed the order of the commander. We were totally surprised. What was this? Where did all the Hungarians officers come from so suddenly? When they had climbed on the train near *Ploesti,* they had been simple officer aspirants.

As soon as the officers were lined up in front, the German prisoners yelled promptly and loudly, "We don't want any German officers," they shouted agitatedly and repeatedly. "We want Hungarians."

"For the last six years we had enough of German officers! They harassed, tormented and lied to us for six years!"

It was not a single protest by a single man but an outburst. Shouts were coming from all directions and from a growing number of prisoners, who expressed their objections, intermingled with cusswords. The same reverberated from all corners of the assembled group of eleven hundred German prisoners. Our little group—which so far had managed to stay together—was silent. We did not share the intense dislike the average *Landser* showed for his superiors. Since the camp commander did not show any reaction, the shouting continued unabated.

"We want Hungarian not German officers!"

The Hungarians had joined our transport when we left the camp in *Ploesti.* One hundred twenty of them had come aboard led by an old colonel, the head of an officer's academy, where they came from. The academy had been in southern Hungary, and the Russian army had scooped them up during the final days of the war and had taken them to *Ploesti.* During the long trip to Siberia, this colonel had promoted most of the officer aspirants without rank, quite astutely, to lieutenants. Not knowing what the Russians would do and how they would apply the Geneva conventions, he promoted them to the lowest rank of officer to spare them from hard work and to get better food rations for officers as agreed upon under the Geneva Convention. In the long run his scheme didn't work out the way he had planned because the camp administration didn't give a hoot about the Geneva Convention or who was an officer or not. They fed them the same, treated them the same and let them work as hard as anybody else. At this point, for reasons the camp commandant did not share with us, he said that he wanted a spokesman for each group of fifty POWs.

Our group and one other from the entire lot of eleven hundred German POWs chose a German officer as spokesman. We picked our captain, and I must say that he was loyal to his men as long as he lasted in his assignment. He didn't try to use us, exploit us, or to gain any undue advantages for himself. In any quarrel with our captors he took our side.

At first the Hungarians didn't know what to do with their unexpected popularity and power, but they caught on quickly, prompted by the colonel and a few other hot shots in their own group.

Following this vote of no confidence, the prisoners were divided into groups of fifty, assigned a Hungarian officer and led away into the barracks. The assembly grew smaller and smaller as everybody gradually disappeared inside.

As we were sitting in the assembly place we looked around to get a picture of the layout of the camp. We saw ten buildings eight of them ordinary barracks. Two were built like Quonset huts with half round roofs of a perfect half arch with only two or three windows on the front and back. Inside the Quonset huts were wooden plank-bed structures, stretching from one end of the building to the other. There were two tiers on the right and left side where the arches descended and the height was limited. The middle of the hut, separated by an aisle from the lower structures on both sides, had four tiers. Each was four feet from the next and stretching the entire length of the hut.

The other eight barracks were conventionally built similar to the barracks we had seen before in military installations. As we found out later, they were single room construction, with no separating walls and large enough for about one hundred double tier wrought iron cots. No matter what the configuration of the barracks our captors put two hundred men into each of the barracks. One barrack was reserved for the kitchen and eating hall and another for the sick ward and administration. Two barracks stayed empty.

In one corner of the camp was a latrine building about sixty feet long and open on both ends with no doors. Inside, to the right and left of a gangway stretched a row of wooden boards the entire length of the building. Each board was a foot from the next just wide enough to squat on without falling into the pit. The pits below the boards were ten feet deep.

There was another small building in the camp, which we couldn't identify at first. Later it turned out to be the delousing facility. No matter where you went in Russia there were lice, and we had plenty of them in Siberia.

The elected spokesmen, together with their German and Hungarian interpreters, were called to the eating hall to receive instructions. Meanwhile the rest of us shoved and pushed around inside the barracks for the best positions on the naked planks.

Our group ended up in a Quonset hut. It was hot as an oven by the time we entered it. The two tier plank-beds on both sides—where the ceiling was lower—were already occupied. Inside the hut it was dark. We had only two windows in the front and the back. The sun had been shining on the tarpaper roof all day long and had done a job. Our group was separated in the 'free for all' for the best sleeping positions in the middle section. I was lucky to get a place on the middle tier. As we discovered later the ground level was drafty and moist on rainy days. The middle tier was okay; at least I wouldn't have to climb up high when I returned at night dead-tired from a day's work. The upper tiers, number three and four, could only be reached by climbing up wooden rungs that were nailed onto the support pillars like on the mast of a sailing ship. The climb was arduous. The higher you were, the hotter it was, almost unbearably so.

When everybody finally found a spot, we realized that with two hundred prisoners in the hut, the sleeping place for each person was so narrow that we could only lie down sideways. Arthur found a spot six guys down from where I was also on the middle tier, Kalle and the others were scattered about. At that moment it really didn't matter, at least not to me. The lack of feeling that had overcome me was not only disorienting, but also totally demoralized me. I'll never in my life forget the first night in a Siberian prison camp.

We finally had reached the end of the road, and what an end it was. Was this where we would have to live from now on? It dawned on everybody, even Kalle, that there were no grapes to be picked in Siberia.

From this day on, the fighting started. Everybody looked out for himself most of the time. Comradeship had gone out the window a long time ago; now it became downright ugly. At the end of our first day at the *kolchos* camp—as the prisoners called it—the hunger grew. Would we be getting anything to eat today and when? Had the Russians brought us here to let us starve to death?

When the Captain came back from the meeting at the eating hall, he informed us that everybody would receive warm soup three times a day, 800 g (about 29 oz) of dry bread and a small portion of *Kascha*. What was *Kascha* (similar to grits)? A schedule for each barrack was announced. We were told when to go to the eating hall for soup and when to pick up the bread. For the purpose of collecting and dividing the bread rations, groups of ten men were formed. That sounded easy enough but in reality it was difficult. Hunger, real hunger, turns people into animals, and we would see quite a bit of it.

Each bread group was encouraged to build a scale. The scale would help us to divide the bread loaves in to ten equal parts, one for each member of the group. The captain told us that we'd receive the first bread rations the next morning.

And then there was the water! The prisoners didn't want to believe that the water was full of bacteria and had to be boiled to render it potable. It certainly tasted all right. The minute a full water cart entered the camp it was overrun by hordes of soldiers. They climbed on top to scoop fresh, deliciously cold water out of the opening. I was no better than the rest of them and drank it also. Eventually it did the same thing to me as it did to all the others who couldn't discipline themselves to contain their thirst.

The soup that we received on our first visit to the eating hall was a huge shock. It was boiled water with a spoonful of millet on the bottom. It contained chunks of crudely cut sauerkraut. We found just enough millet in the soup to give the water a different color but not enough to make a difference in the taste, nourishment or consistency of the watery concoction. We ate, rather drank the soup as quickly as we could and went back to our sleeping places.

During the night, trying to sleep on the hard wooden boards, the space was so narrow that turning around, from side to side, was only possible if ten or fifteen guys turned at the same time. Everybody was grunting, cursing and pushing without any consideration for the neighbor to the right or left. It was awful, humiliating, and demoralizing. Besides, it was impossible to sleep.

The fight for the bread rations the next morning was predictable and only a few levelheaded men saved the day. The soup was of the same watery consistency as the night before, crudely cut sauerkraut with millet cooked in water.

At six o'clock all prisoners were assembled near the front gate. After the obligatory counting we marched through it and proceeded up the small hill in complete silence. It was three hundred yards to the train for our first trip to an unknown work place in the city of *Stalinsk*.

Arthur and I and some others from our group stood together on the flat bed, but nobody was talking. The train returned along the same route it had come from *Stalinsk* the previous day. It couldn't have gone any other way. We got off, marched a few hundred yards to the ferry and were divided into groups of two hundred POWs. After crossing the river each group marched to different work assignments in the city.

Our group had only a short walk toward a huge sawmill called DOZ 2.

The sawmill had been built near the river for practical reasons. The trees to be processed at the mill came floating downstream on the Tom River from the wilderness of the Altai mountain range to the south for hundreds of miles. Our first assignment was to pull trees out of the water with the help of steel hooks attached to ten feet long poles and to move them onto chain driven, continuously moving pulleys. DOZ 2 was a huge sawmill with seven large, steam driven mechanical saws of up to six blades each. It was the only plant cutting wood for the construction activities in the city of *Stalinsk*. The mill provided framing wood, boards of various sizes and whatever else you can possibly think of needed for construction. The prisoners had to do all primitive work such as pulling trees from the water, cleaning up waste-wood from the mechanical saws, loading flatbeds and cleaning up everywhere else. Mountains of trim, of edgings, as they were spewed out by the mill, were loaded onto rail cars. Boards were loaded onto an endless procession of trucks. To me it seemed as if everything had to be done with great haste. All the while the *Natchalniks* screamed and cursed at us continuously.

"*Dawai, dawai, bistray, jibit twoiyou matj.*" (Let's go. Let's go, quickly. Fuck your mother.)

We were introduced to a new curse that the Russians lace their language with constantly. I am not exaggerating, the Russian language, especially the workingman's language is full of curses. Only a nation of prisoners and deportees can develop such an elaborate vocabulary of condemnation and use it like a singsong, continuously and without interruption.

On our first day at work the prisoners were dumb enough to listen to the *Natchalniks* and did their best to satisfy their demands. They were still under the erroneous impression that hard work might improve their lots. Nobody had yet learned to work slower to conserve energy.

At noontime we were permitted one half hour of rest. We sat down, had a piece of dry, soggy bread and received another mess kit full of watery sauerkraut soup and a spoonful of *Kascha,* and then, *dawai, dawai!* The demands for faster and faster work continued.

The extent of our predicament grew. As I said, at the beginning we mistakenly thought that faster and faster work would get us something, more food, better treatment or living conditions, whatever.

Some of the men had gone to the latrine five or six times as the first day of work in Siberia came to a end, and we also experienced severe stomach cramps. Nobody realized that this was the first sign of a looming disaster.

Arthur was one of the first to realize how serious the Russian's warning had been. It caused him to break the silence between us. They had told us repeatedly, do not drink water that has not been boiled.

"You know, Peter," he blurted out, "everybody who drank the water including you and me seems to be shitting into a bottle. Dysentery is rampant. We'd better listen to them from now on. They know their water, the river and where it is coming from. Let's do it even if it means being thirsty most of the day."

"Easier said than done," I replied quietly. "But you are right. Let's go to the sick ward—if they have one in the camp—and find out what the medics say about this and if they have any medication to treat it."

At night we went to the barracks, which had been assigned to the medic and found out that he knew nothing about dysentery, or the water and had no medication whatsoever for anything. His only advice was, "Do not drink or eat anything for three days and then, maybe then, with a little bit of luck the dysentery will go by itself."

Under the circumstances we had no choice but to ignore his advice, because it was not only unbearably hot, but we were also hungry as wolves.

During the night there was a continuous traffic to the latrine from all barracks. Together with our dysentery we experienced severe stomach cramps. All this commotion together with our tight sleeping places didn't allow us much sleep.

It was not only because we were getting up continuously, running to the latrine, it was the moaning and complaining that was heard from all corners of the Quonset. The guys didn't go five or six times to the john as they did during the day, it was more like fifteen or twenty times, and we didn't do any better.

On top of it, to worsen the condition in the barracks even more, the smokers had managed to obtain some Russian tobacco called *maxorka*. It smelled like burned rags and the air inside became sticky. Once more we were lucky that we didn't sleep on the top level where the air soon became not breathable.

At 5:30 A.M. the next morning we were chased out of the barracks.

"Get your soup, receive your bread rations, divide the portions and assemble at the gate. *Bistray, bistray.*"

Without going into an hourly description of our miseries and the suffering, let me assure you that during the following days the work at DOZ 2 escalated and demands became more exhausting as we grew progressively weaker. Slow work by the prisoners held up the production of the mill. The *Natchalniks* grew increasingly impatient. They talked to the guards to get us going, which was all we needed in our condition. During lunch break, several days later, while we were eating the usual water soup, *Kascha* and bread, Arthur came to talk to me.

"Peter, we have to pull ourselves together. I can only tell you that I've made my decision. Like the medic suggested, I won't drink any water for three days and I won't eat any soup or bread. Otherwise I'm going to die for sure and as dismal as our situation is and as hopeless, I believe it's too early to throw in the towel and to give up. *Reiss Dich zusammen*. [Pull yourself together.] We have to make that decision, and we have to make it now before we lose our last bit of strength and energy. You always tell me about your mother and going home to the USA and seeing this asshole lieutenant in Batavia. Pull yourself together. Join me. Together we'll make it, or we'll both croak, and you can kiss America good-bye and your mother too."

I knew it would be hell; I was so fucking hungry I could hardly think of anything but food. I wasn't sure that I would make it, but he was right, there was no alternative.

"I don't know whether I can do it, Arthur, but I agree with what you said. Let's try."

At noontime we gave our watery soup to some of our buddies and saved the bread for the time when we could eat again. We didn't drink anything. But the dysentery continued throughout the afternoon and the night just the same. I went to the john ten times and Arthur nine. We managed to climb onto the flatbed in the morning, dragged our feet during the day and did our chores as slowly as the cursing *Natchalniks* permitted. We encouraged each other to hold out and not to weaken in our resolve.

I don't know how we did it, but we lasted through the three days, weakening considerably. The lack of any fluids was plain torture. In the end the medic had been right. At the end of the second day the dysentery decreased and finally stopped altogether. It was a great relief for both of us to see the first results and not to spend the night and most of the day running to the john, managing to pull our pants down in time, so as not to shit down on our legs like so many of others did and dirty ourselves without a chance to clean up. Though getting up in the morning was still painful, almost impossible, we started to feel better.

The watery shit from the perpetually worsening diarrhea, which the guys couldn't hold any longer started to drip from above through the cracks between the wooden boards during the night. Many men had grown too weak to get up. But they had to smoke, of course, and they exchanged the last bit of life saving solid food—the bread rations—against *maxorka,* the only tobacco like substance available in Siberia. There were always civilians at work who would gladly supply the prisoners with *maxorka* in exchange for bread. Bread was still rationed in the Soviet Union at the time and we discovered to our great surprise that our daily rations of bread were larger than those of the civilians.

The stench and the filth in the barracks at night became excruciating. Some men in our Quonset hut had grown too weak to face another day at work and they thought that they couldn't get up in the morning. They didn't know what it meant in the eyes of our Russian captors to be too weak for work, but they would find out soon enough.

That was when the Hungarian officers demonstrated that it was their time, finally, to get back at the Germans. True to the obligation they had assumed when they took over as leaders of German POW contingents they climbed up on the benches, second, third or fourth tier and threatened to throw the guys down below. One of the Hungarian officers, named Calman, was a particularly objectionable, brutal character. As a Hungarian his appearance was atypical. Usually Hungarians have a darker skin and dark hair. Calman had light blond hair, blue eyes and a fair skin, like he was from Scandinavia. He was dressed in a clean, new uniform and wore polished leather boots. God knows how he had managed to hold onto them this long. He was extremely conceited and vicious. He strutted through the aisles, slapping the shafts of his boots with a riding whip, yelling; *los los*—the only two German words he knew—which meant the same as the Russian: *Dawai, dawai.*

If the men did not move off the benches fast enough, he would hit the prisoners with his riding whip. As he approached our area the captain stepped up to him and yelled, "Get your ass out of here, you little runt." With the captain being 6'4" and Calman 5'4" there was a natural reaction. Calman didn't like what he saw and heard. He turned around and came back two minutes later with a Russian guard and a Hungarian-Russian interpreter. A quick exchange ensued between the guard, Calman and his interpreter with the captain totally out of sync, unable to participate in either language. The guard turned and yelled at our captain, who still didn't even know what had been said, because he didn't understand Russian or Hungarian. We could easily imagine the set of lies Calman fed the Russian guard. Calman had won the encounter, which started a reign of brutality and terror by the Hungarian officer's contingent.

Meanwhile Olga was in Berlin without money. The manager of my father's business had found his way back from the war to reclaim his job. He had been fortunate enough not to be retained as POW by either side and managed to get in touch with her to let her know that he had to speak to her. She was supposed to come to his office at the Schwarzlose plant. When she got there, he told her with a sad face that the company could no longer provide her with the money stipulated for her in her divorce agreement with my deceased father. There was total chaos everywhere and no business for the company. Olga didn't know what to do. If she wanted to return to the United States, she would have to buy a steam ship ticket but she didn't have money for the fare. In her predicament she remembered her meeting with General Clay a few weeks earlier and decided to try to talk to him. Maybe she could make herself useful. After all she knew Berlin and he did not. In the end she was surprised how friendly and receptive the general was and how easy it had been to see him.

"Hello, Mrs. Schwarzlose. How have you been? What a coincidence that you come to look me up, because I need help from someone I can trust and you, as the former president of the American Women's club, may be the right person.

"But, before we start working together let us come to an agreement about this name of yours, which I always forget and cannot pronounce correctly anyway, may I call you Olgie?"

Olga laughed because it was not the first time this had happened to her and she replied, "Of course, General Clay, I am used to the difficulties my name causes for English-speaking people and 'Olgie' sounds good to me. What kind of work are you talking about, because I am looking for work to make some money. I am stuck in Berlin without funds and would like to make myself useful—for a fee, of course."

"Olgie, you know the city intimately," the General went on. "I need somebody like you and, as I said before, somebody I can trust. I meet Germans every day; they speak English excellently, but I'll never know whether they are telling me the truth or not. If you believe what they are saying, nobody was ever a member of the Nazi party or participated in any of their schemes and activities. Well, I don't give a damn about the individual but sometimes it's important for me to know the God's honest truth in this war-ravaged city and not be told a pack of lies. I tell you, we'll make a deal; that's all I can arrange for you at this time. You'll get all your meals in our officer's mess and a few hundred marks a month to pay for your rent and incidentals. Whenever we get settled with our affairs here in Berlin, and I get my bearings, I'll arrange for your transportation to the USA. How about it?"

"That's a very good offer, General. It's a deal. Since I have nothing to do we can start right now."

General Clay laughed and told her to get into his car, because he had a problem that needed solving right now, and she could help him with it. They went outside, got into the car and drove off to a pretentious looking "Villa" in the *"Westend"* of Berlin. "The house used to belong to a Nazi bigwig," he told her, "an SS officer or rather an SS doctor, with a high rank by the name of Professor *Dr. Karl Gebhardt."* It was located in the direction of *Spandau* near the *Heerstrasse.*

Olga remembered the professor's name well, because during the war it had appeared many times in the newspaper. It was Professor *Dr. Gebhardt,* a surgeon who had worked and operated in a hospital complex seventy miles to the north of Berlin, in *Hohenlychen.* The public and Olga had heard about him because he had made a name for himself with new and daring operating procedures involving knees and hip joints.

Somebody had found a diary with apparently explosive contents in this villa, which during the war had been occupied by Gebhardt and his staff. *Professor Dr. Gebhardt,* or whatever his title in the SS was, had been arrested by the Allies under suspicion of conducting cruel and inhuman experiments with inmates of concentration camps, especially the one in *Ravensbrueck* near *Hohenlychen.* He was currently in jail and was going to be tried by a court, a tribunal for war crimes scheduled to be in Nuremberg, which would deal with the Nazi big wigs. Ironically, shortly before the war ended, the professor cleverly assumed the presidency of the German Red Cross.

Even though there was incriminating evidence against *Professor Gebhardt* much was only circumstantial. General Clay hoped that the diaries would supply the missing link. Olga wasn't allowed to take the diaries home with her. The General was afraid they might be stolen from her or might disappear mysteriously. They had to be kept in a safe at the Headquarters of the US Military in *Dahlem.*

Olga started to translate the next day. It had always been easier for her to translate from German into English rather than the other way around, so she had to stop often because of the horrible activities described in black and white and in the Professor's own handwriting. In this diary he wrote in minute detail how he had used the inmates of the concentration camp Ravensbrueck, near Fuerstenberg in Mecklenburg, to furnish him with limbs for his experiments in his hospital in Hohenlychen, which he tried to graft onto wounded SS men who had lost their legs during the fighting. He expressed and explained in his own words how he had cut off whole legs from healthy inmates at the concentration camp and taken them to be transplanted onto wounded soldiers who had lost theirs. While the amputated man—if he was lucky—continued to live as a cripple, the wounded soldier's immune system regularly rejected the implant, and many died of gangrene or other complications. The diary spoke of other experiments, which he had conducted with the inmates of the concentration camp, to check on the survival chances of the human body after being exposed to severe freezing temperatures. It was a series of gruesome descriptions by a doctor who had sworn the Hippocratic oath.

Olga was nauseated and did her translating as well as she could, but she was happy when General Clay relieved her of the job and handed it over to a court-appointed interpreter.

The diary furnished enough proof for the conviction of *Professor Gebhardt* who was tried and convicted at Nuremberg and subsequently hanged.

After a few months at headquarters, the General alerted Olgie to be on the ready whenever he might call her with the news of an available berth on one of the military transport ships. Olga had convinced herself that if she could do anything at all for Peter, it would be from America.

In Siberia in the factories and on the building sites, which for us was DOZ 2, and wherever else the others were toiling, and also in the camp, the agony of the torturous dysentery among the prisoners continued for days and weeks and even months into the winter of 1945–46. There was only little relief from a medical point of view. The three days "hunger and thirst" had become routine treatment, the only one available. The only difference was that the men who tried this cure could now spend three days in the camp under supervision in the medical building. The medics had a good life, because they got all the soup they could eat and sometimes the bread rations disappeared, too.

One day the dying started. Two older guys, over forty years old, down the bench from where my spot was, didn't get up in the morning. When Calman and his henchmen climbed up to chase them out, he noticed that they had died during the night. He pulled them to the edge of the bench with the help of another Hungarian and simply pushed them over the edge to fall to the ground 18 feet below where they hit the boards like two bags of potatoes. To get out of the barracks we had to step over the dead bodies, since we were too weak to do anything about it.

When we came home in the evening from an exhausting day at the mill the Russians commandeered five guys to the front gate. A horse drawn cart loaded with ten or twelve dead bodies, grossly deformed by rigor mortis, was waiting for them. Arms and legs hung stiffly from under a tarpaulin, which covered the load of dead bodies. It looked gruesome. One guy who and had been commandeered to the burial job was in our hut. He told us later without any visible emotion, he was too tired and weak to feel anything, that they had followed the cart, crossed the rail line and continued to climb up the hill for another five hundred yards, all the way to the top, dug six shallow graves and threw the bodies into them—two to a grave.

Arthur and I had managed to complete our three days of fasting earlier. We felt better even though the amount of food we had not eaten contributed to our weakened condition. Our rations, the regular quantities we were now able to obtain from our own kitchen, didn't do anything to rebuild our strength, but at least we had saved our bread ration from the last three days to fill our empty stomachs and to give us a temporary feeling of being satiated. Our consolation was that the dysentery had stopped, and we didn't shit into a bottle any more.

The conversation among the prisoners centered on food, obviously, and on torturous dysentery. Whenever someone was able to fart the refrain was, "That's the language of men who will live for a long time."

Nobody cared or noticed that the last time we had washed or had been deloused was five months ago in *Ploesti*. We were dirty, we stank and the lice were eating us alive. Who cared?

Every morning we could hear or observe fights surrounding the distribution of the daily bread rations. To be as accurate as possible with the weight allotted to each bread group, Toni cut tiny pieces of bread, which he placed on top of whole loaves until his scale leveled, and the exact weight had been met. So far so good, but these tiny morsels of bread presented a tremendous temptation to the guys who picked up the bread. More than once they were observed on their way back to the barracks as they quickly stuffed these morsels into their mouth. The consequence was a severe beating by the other members of the group.

Arthur and I tried to visit Toni hoping to gain some favors from him, but he was secluded and totally locked up in his bread-cutting room near the kitchen and didn't recognize, or didn't want to recognize, our presence.

Fortunately for us neither Arthur nor I were addicted to nicotine and managed quite well without the *maxorka* that many others craved.

The dying and the corpses were ubiquitous. During one of the following nights when the row of sleeping bodies turned around, I pushed the guy next to me to turn over. He didn't respond and shaking him by his arm I noticed that his body was already cold and stiff. He was dead. He was dead!

The first time it happened to me, it was a shock, but the experience repeated itself several times during the following months. The only realistic thought that crossed my mind rather than sorrow was that we would've more space to sleep during the night and that we might even get a chance to divide the dead guys' bread the following morning. The callousness that embraced us was unbelievable. Come to think about it now, I believe that it was a psychological defense; it kept us from cracking up.

At work everybody tried incessantly to hunt for food, anything to eat, beets, carrots or cabbage, whatever. Arthur talked to me one afternoon with tears in his eyes, because of what he was asking me to do.

"This can't go any further. I am so hungry and so weak I can hardly stand up any more. I'll cover for you here at work, looking busy and finding excuses, and you should make some productive use of your language talents. I have heard some guys talking about begging runs. It appears that the civilians understand the plight of the *zaklutschornys,* you know, us German POWs. Since most of them were in the same shoes when they arrived here in Siberia and know from their own experience what hunger is like, they tend to share their bread rations with hungry prisoners without objection."

I retorted dryly, "If you'd asked me that a month ago I'd have thought that you were crazy. Now I can only hope that you'll cover for me. What're you going to do if they catch me and beat me half to death? I hope that the civilians don't call the police and will have some bread to spare when I knock on their doors."

I sneaked through the dilapidated fence, which surrounded the factory and went on my way. I climbed over another fence and continued down the road, trying to find an apartment complex with people not at work. Luckily I managed to slip away undetected by the guards. Once I was in the building I knocked on the first door on the ground floor. It was my first experience as a beggar and, in spite of the hunger, I felt horrible; it wasn't an easy task. An older woman answered my knocking, opening the door just a crack and quite suspiciously. I made my little speech, which I had carefully prepared and rehearsed.

"Tjotja, daitje minia cusotchka xleba" (Aunt, give me a piece of bread) was my plea spoken haltingly with my heavily accented Russian. The old lady did not show any reaction whatsoever. No matter what she might have been thinking about the prisoner at her doorstep—and our uniforms however lapidated and torn were a dead giveaway—she didn't say a word. She closed the door, and I heard her walking away. I waited fearfully that she might not return. Then, as I already prepared to disappear as quickly as possible, I could hear her footsteps coming back. After a short time the door opened and here she was, sticking her hand through the narrow crack in the door handing me a piece of black bread, obviously simply broken off a larger loaf. I grabbed it with a perfunctory *"spassiba"* (thank you) and beat the hell out of there. The piece of bread weighed about 10 ounces. I felt terribly tempted to sit down in a corner of the entrance and gobble it down. Arthur, however, was just as hungry as I was, and he was covering my tracks. I had to do better than just 10 ounces to satisfy both of us. I tried again at the next door and then the next, covering the entire building systematically. I was not always as lucky as on the first try, and the pieces of bread I received were mostly smaller. Finally, after knocking on six or seven doors I had begged almost a pound of bread and decided not to stretch my luck, hastily beating it back across the street toward DOZ 2. The sleepy guards hadn't noticed my absence; Arthur with his hungry eyes blazing like automobile headlights was happy to see me back.

"Did you get anything? Did it work, Peter? Were you successful? Did they curse you or beat you? Where is it?"

I pulled the pieces from under my jacket, and we wolfed down the bread greedily. It was the harvest of my first begging expedition, and it wouldn't be my last.

The first question any Russian would ask a prisoner was, *"Gitler kaput?"* (Is Hitler done?)

In the Russian alphabet there is no H; every H becomes a G, and they used the word "kaput" thinking it was perfect German. In reality the word had been made-up by German soldiers during the war, thinking it to be a Russian word.

In my case it was a minor *Natchalnik* who directed our work detail at DOZ 2. I simply replied, *"Nisnaju"* (I don't know).

With his question the *Natchalnik* had alluded to the glorious *Führer* who, from all reports in the Russian media, had disappeared in his bunker in Berlin. The Russian propaganda machine preferred to keep it a mystery about whether or not Hitler really died during the last days of the war or had gone into hiding. Who else should know where he had disappeared but the Russians when they conquered Berlin? They arrived first on the scene to examine Hitler's Chancellery, his bunker and his remains.

The *Natchalnik* laughed and replied—like they all did—"You little liar." He exclaimed, "All you Germans of course know where he disappeared to. But to the glorious Russian army it doesn't matter. Soon we will have war with America and then, just as Lenin prophesied, the whole bourgeois clique will be gone, and communism will prevail."

War with America? This was terrible news to me. What an absurd idea? How would we ever get out of Siberia if America became an enemy?

Whatever the truth was, his remarks further deepened my despair and my assessment of the hopelessness of our situation. If there were ever a chance to get out of Siberia it would only be by some initiative of the western nations led by America, at least that is what I believed. If that was at all possible, my gloominess deepened after this latest rumor.

Basic urges like smoking, especially for the soldiers who were addicted to nicotine, were another problem of our miserable lives.

What did one have to do to get tobacco or cigarettes in Siberia? The smokers among the prisoners gradually used up whatever smoking material they had. It had gone up in smoke whether it was real tobacco or some tobacco like stuff that they had obtained from the Russians. But smokers are addicts and, no matter what, they will find what they need to pacify their addictions.

Anyone who wanted to smoke in Siberia needed two things—*Maxorka* and newspaper. *Maxorka* is the name for a crude tobacco cut from a plant in the tobacco family that grows under the most adverse weather conditions in hot or in cold weather, whatever. In Siberia it was important that the plant be able to mature in a short summer and withstand the cold temperatures of early spring. *Maxorka* grows on a sturdy stem that looks like a miniature tobacco plant. The leaves are smaller and leathery in contrast to a real tobacco plant and are only two to four inches long. The plant itself grows about two to three feet tall at maturity.

The inventive residents of Siberia, the Sibiriakis, grew the plant in their back yards and harvested it before the winter became really cold. They dried the entire plant, stem and everything not just the leaves as in the case of normal tobacco. Then they chopped the leaves and also the stems into small pieces the size of large rice kernels. The finished product is dark green and very coarse. The main thing is that it contains nicotine. The second item needed is paper—newspaper. The only use for newspaper in Siberia when I was there was to use it as cigarette paper. Despite the wishes of the authorities nobody seemed to be interested in reading the latest propaganda that the newspaper spread and certainly not the latest Communist Party slogans. Yes, believe me, it is correct—that the news "paper" was used only as cigarette paper!

To fold a newspaper correctly in preparation for cigarette paper was a science, which took the prisoners some time to learn. A page of newspaper was carefully folded back and forth, first lengthwise and then crosswise, into a final pattern of 2×4 inches. Once this pad was completed, one leaf of the folded paper was torn off the pack then the tobacco was placed on it and rolled into a cigarette. It was handled in much the same way as if one used a leaf of cigarette tissue paper. The newspaper was filled with maxorka, rolled into a cigarette, saturated at the edge with saliva and closed. Since saliva dries and loses its stickiness, and since the tobacco was coarse, the two ends of this "cigarette" had to be tightly twisted to prevent the *maxorka* from dribbling out. There was your cigarette. The smoke tasted and smelled like a burning cloth rag. The first time I tried to smoke a *maxorka* cigarette I almost threw up, but, as I said, the main thing was that it contained nicotine, which did the trick for the needy smoker. The civilians would give the prisoners, with whom they worked, *maxorka* every once in awhile, but charity goes only so far. After the charity stopped, the smokers had to sell their bread rations to get money to buy the *maxorka* they craved. The going price for a ten-ounce piece of bread was 200 rubles. The same 200 rubles had to be paid for a *stakan* (normal drinking glass of about 4 ounces) of *maxorka.* Newspaper was also a valuable commodity. *Isvestia* and *Pravda,* the principal daily papers, sold for 25 kopeks (100 kopeks = pennies to a ruble) at the store and were resold as cigarette paper for 5 rubles, twenty times that amount. With nothing to eat to begin with and very little bread, smoking was an expensive habit. Some prisoners sold the last remaining trinket, a pair of prescription glasses, silver coin, or ring they had hidden successfully up to now.

In the absence of paper bags or other wrapping materials throughout Siberia the *stakan* was an omnipresent measuring device. Almost everything on the open markets for produce was sold and priced by *stakan,* flour, sugar, and rice, even Vodka or tobacco. The buyer either poured the tobacco from the *stakan* into his pants pockets, or he had another kind of container, or cloth sack to transport the goods he had bought and wanted to carry away.

Of course *stakan*s varied in size and clever sellers tried to outdo the buyers by buying in a large *stakan* and selling in a small *stakan.*

My begging expeditions were not always successful, and one day I was beaten up terribly by some young Russians who just had been released from the army. I returned to Arthur black and blue in the face—limping worse than ever but happy that nothing was broken—with the firm resolve never to venture away for another begging expedition.

"We have to do something else," Arthur said without being overly appreciative of my injuries. "There is a *stalowaja* [cafeteria] in this place, and everyday at lunch the workmen get their hot soup from there. A *stalowaja* must have supplies, carrots, potatoes, beets, anything. If we can find where they keep that stuff and get our hands on it, then we just have to smuggle it into our camp or find a place here at DOZ where we can cook it somehow."

Arthur was trying to be inventive, but he was not the one who had been beaten, and I was not inclined to try anything else after my last experience. I told him, "You do that, Arthur. You look around for supplies and don't forget to look for some way to cook, roast or fry whatever you find. For the time being you take the lead, okay?"

A few days later Arthur returned from a far away corner of the saw mill where he had been sent to do some cleanup work. He was excited.

"You won't believe it, but I have found the supply shed for the *stalowaja*. Lots of potatoes and turnips are lying around on the ground only protected by a simple wooden fence. I also have found a solution for the cooking. Come on, Peter, your wounds have healed by now, you must have almost forgotten about it, and we are still starving. We have to do something if we want to survive. I also checked the boiler room, you know, the one where the coal boilers are to generate the steam for the engines driving the saws? There are three large boilers, which are covered on top with a fine sandy material probably for insulation. The sandy material is about a foot thick. Six inches down, it is very hot. It was too hot to push my hand any further down. Once we have 'organized' some edibles we'll take our heist—provided, of course, that we're able to pilfer the supply shed— bury the beets or potatoes or whatever in the hot sand on top of the boiler and leave them there until they are baked. After two hours or so we'll return to pick up the finished product. What do you say?"

I was amazed! This buddy of mine surprised me every time. He definitely had a positive attitude, which was more than I could say for myself. He wouldn't give up no matter what happened to us, and that was my blessing.

"Arthur, you are great; yes, I have recuperated, and I'm as hungry as you are. I'll do the stealing, and you can do the cooking."

The stealing from the supply shed turned out to be easier said than done. We weren't the only ones to be hungry in *Stalinsk*. The civilians didn't have much to eat either. Consequently all supplies were well guarded and protected. But we continued our observations with the tenacity of starving people and discovered that the guard of the supply area left his assignment every day to have lunch at the *stalowaja*.

The following day when the guard left his post, I climbed over the fence into the supply area, filled all my pockets with potatoes and made it back safely. Arthur's plan for the cooking worked out perfectly. Slowly but surely the potatoes baked and softened in the hot sand and were edible after three hours.

That evening when we entered the camp, at the gates of the camp where two carts loaded with dead bodies, waiting to be buried. I was not quick enough to disappear around a corner, and the guards caught me and included me in the detail to go up the hill. When we reached the top after an arduous climb over one hundred burial sites confronted us. Assuming two men to a hole that meant two hundred men had already died. How long were the rest of us going to last?

Most bodies we transported up the hill were naked. Rigor mortis had stiffened the limbs, which were sticking out grotesquely in all directions from under the tarpaulin. We had to break arms and legs to fit the bodies into the shallow graves. It was strenuous additional work for us to dig the graves at night after a full day at Doz 2 and without any extra food or even our evening soup. The bodies were skinny, nothing but skin and bones, and two of them fit easily into the holes that we dug, after we straightened the arms and legs.

It was a ghastly, nauseating job, which to this day wakes me up at night in a cold sweat whenever I relive that dreadful experience and remember the waxy feeling of skin and hear the squeaking noise of bodies rubbing against each other.

One hour later I was back in the camp, got my soup from the kitchen, fell on the wooden planks and was asleep instantly with only six hours of night remaining before the beginning of another day filled with: *Dawai, dawai.*

The blue uniformed Russian administrators, guards in charge of the camp were not only crooks—that was to be expected—but they were incompetent crooks, which was really bad. It was amazing that no serious illnesses or infectious diseases had swept the camp so far. We had no chance to wash our clothes or ourselves and the delousing installation was perpetually out of order. As a matter of fact, we had not washed ourselves for over four months. It was now late September. Even though they were in charge, the Hungarians had no interest in changing the procedure. As long as they could provide for their own cleanliness they didn't give a damn about the Germans.

In the evenings after returning to our barracks the prisoners were sitting on their naked cots picking lice off their shirts, sweaters or underpants. Our underwear that used to be white was by now dark gray. It wasn't only dirty but filthy and full of holes.

"God have mercy on us if anyone in this camp should develop typhoid fever," Arthur mumbled under his breath. "We certainly have enough lice to carry the disease."

Finally the fear of a possible catastrophe happening must have convinced the authorities to do something. The delousing establishment was repaired and cranked up, and little by little all prisoners were permitted to take turns washing themselves and delousing their clothes, but only on Sundays. Our jailors didn't want to lose a day of productive work.

Lice have the habit of laying thousands, no millions, of eggs wherever they crawl inside your clothes. They also deposited millions of eggs on the rough, dirty wooden boards where we slept. Only a few days after the delousing had taken place just as many lice tortured us as before. Only people who have been personally exposed and have suffered from lice are able to appreciate what plague lice are. Feeling that something is crawling constantly somewhere on you, on your skin, the constant itching and discomfort is indescribable, and now we were approaching winter, which, in Siberia, starts in early October.

The first signs of beginning winter were clearly noticeable. What would happen to us when it became really cold?

Kalle who always knew even the tiniest piece of scuttlebutt joyfully confided the latest news to us. He had finally started to talk to us again.

"We're going to get winter clothes, padded pants, jackets, which are called *fufaikas,* also felt boots, *valinkis,* and fur coats and gloves. The *Natchalnik* at Osmu 4 told us not to worry. Whether we are civilians or POWs, this is standard gear for all *zaklutschorny* in *Stalinsk.* I presume they don't want to kill us right away but rather slowly as we work ourselves to death."

Arthur and I hoped that his scuttlebutt was true for once even though we couldn't understand Kalle's warped sense of humor, but he was right. It was true. At the beginning of October the weather changed quickly; temperatures dropped to twenty degrees almost over night. We started to freeze at work during the day and continued to freeze at night while sleeping in our unheated barracks with no material provided by our captors to heat the built-in ovens. Most prisoners had no blankets for cover, and only a few had retained their long army coats, which were too thin and worn out to be good for anything.

One evening, rather suddenly like most actions by the administration, we returned from work, were called to assemble near one of the empty barracks and received winter clothing. Every one of us was issued cotton-padded pants, cotton-padded jackets, *valinki,* the felt type boots everybody needs in the winter, a very heavy fur coat and a pair of mittens just as Kalle had predicted. The fur coats were sheepskins turned inside out and proved to be very warm. The weather had been on schedule right to the minute and the Russians were too. The following morning we woke up to a foot of snow.

Loaded down with heavy coats our work at DOZ 2 became even more cumbersome. We discovered a new winter routine—work twenty minutes and warm up for five minutes. *Dawai, za kuritj* (let's smoke), as the Russian workmen called it. Little heated huts were erected all over the lumberyard; they were strategically placed for everybody to get to them quickly. Work details, ten or twenty men, tried to squeeze into a hut at twenty-minute intervals when their turns came to warm up. All men, Russians and Germans alike, had a quick smoke and warmed freezing feet and hands on a small red-hot iron cylindrical stove.

Up to this time I hadn't known what it meant to be cold, I mean really cold. My mother had always maintained that the summer heat in New York was worse than the cold weather in Germany. Her saying was, "When you are hot, there is a limit to what you can take off, but when you are cold you can always put on one more thing."

Well, she had never been in Siberia, because believe you me; at forty degrees below zero, you freeze no matter what you put on. The nights in almost unheated barracks, twenty-five to thirty-one degrees Fahrenheit, covered with a short fur coat and a thin army blanket, were unbearable. With only one small stove in each barrack temperatures at night seldom climbed above twenty-five degrees Fahrenheit even after our captors finally provided us with some heating material. With so may people dead we now had plenty of space, and I tried to get a place near a stove. After succeeding I crawled so close to the stove that I burned my shoulder severely without even waking up. I still carry that burn mark today as a memory of my first winter in Siberia.

The only guy who had a warm place to sleep in the whole camp was a character from Berlin. He slept alone in one of the empty barracks. His name was *"Icke"* (Berlin slang for *'Ich,'* I). I discovered him one day during my search for heating material. He was hidden away in a far corner of his empty barrack.

"My God, what are you doing here?" I asked. "Don't you have to go to work? What a racket!"

Icke got up from his cot, and I noticed that he walked with his body horizontally bent forward, at almost a ninety-degree angle. He walked and looked like Charles Laughton did in the famous movie, "The Hunchback of Notre Dame."

"What's the matter, Icke? You have an old injury? A reminder from the shooting game?" I asked wondering how the Russian captors let him get away with that excuse.

"No, my friend," he responded, "I am the only guy—so far— who fell off this stupid flatbed train-car on our first journey. And now the bastards have diagnosed that I have injured my spine. The Russians have put me in here until I feel better, and until I am able to straighten my back again."

"The Russians have put you here? And don't they come to check on you? Man, you really have it made. Come on, Icke, don't tell me that you can't walk properly?"

"As a matter of fact, I will, and I don't think it's funny, nor do I think that it will become any better 'til we are going home, and I can go and see a specialist."

After our first introduction in his dark and cold barrack I visited Icke often and cooked potatoes on his stove. He had a stove, a stove all for himself. Can you believe it? And he also heated some water to brew black tea. Throughout all turmoil of our captivity and transport to Siberia I had kept hidden a small quantity of black tea in a plastic army issue jar. Whenever dysentery hit me, my black tea was like medicine and healed my stomach and my intestines. I shared some potatoes with Icke, and we traded memories about Berlin.

Icke managed to protect his deal perfectly, and, even though, we suspected a certain amount of showmanship, the Russians never caught on to him.

In the middle of 1946 Olga returned to the USA on a troop transport called "General Lancaster." After Olga arrived in New York, and with the help of her cousin Alma, she had found a place to stay. She continued to search for her son by going directly to the Soviet Consulate in New York. They admitted her all right and a vice consul talked to her at great length, letting her ask all her questions. She had to fill out several questionnaires about her son and was asked to come back a few days later, because as the vice consul assured her, this matter would be treated with the utmost diligence, and the Consulate wanted to make sure that they could give her correct answers.

Upon returning after a couple of weeks, she was ushered into the office of the same official whom she had seen before. By this time he had a happy smile on his face and said, "Please sit down Mrs. Dalzell,"—after returning to the USA Olga had assumed her maiden name again—"We have good news for you. Your son is in a particularly agreeably situated camp in South East Russia where soldiers from Germany are housed and where they help with reconstructing our badly devastated country. For security reasons I cannot tell you where the camp is located, but it is located in a city with a large bread factory and the prisoners get fresh rolls and hot chocolate for breakfast every morning."

My mother looked at him with an angry frown and said, "The Soviet Union certainly must have changed its policies since the time, a few days after the war, when I met their designated and uniformed representatives in Berlin. At that time I had my hands full inventing a way to avoid gang rape. Now you are telling me that you are serving hot chocolate to your prisoners of war? Mr. Vice Consul, what you are telling me I find extremely hard to believe. But one more word, please, before I leave. When will you release these fortunate prisoners of war?"

He was flustered. He didn't know what to say, of course. He didn't know, because at that time the USSR didn't know herself or have any plans to release prisoners of war. Besides the Vice Consul's story was a pack of lies. To pacify her, he told my mother to check with him from time to time. To assure her that he would also do his best to keep her informed. It was a polite brush off, nothing else, and she never went back.

Our discovery of a supply of turnips and potatoes at the DOZ 2 depot as well as my begging routine—which I resumed after my bruises healed, driven by perpetual hunger-pains—put Arthur and me into an enviable position as far as food was concerned. We were hoping that nobody would change our work assignment. We didn't get exactly fat, but we held our own. Having stopped shitting water for the time being, we weren't losing weight any more. We discovered for the umpteenth time, and to our great dismay, that nothing in life is permanent. It is particularly distressing when you live on the edge and even the slightest disturbance can put you over.

The dying of the prisoners continued at a fast rate and reduced the population of the camp dramatically. The original horse drawn cart used to transport the dead bodies up the hill was not big enough any more. Increasing numbers of dead prisoners were lying at the gate every evening when we returned. It was a good thing that the temperatures were below freezing. Many bodies, stacked in a pile, one on top of the other, in the rear of the camp, were sometimes waiting for days until someone transported them up the hill to bury them in the frozen earth. The freezing temperature protected the corpses, and nobody in the camp's administration bothered to look for gravediggers.

Our experiences of every day life taught Arthur and me to keep away from the others. This was not the time to talk to or to trust anybody. The Russian NKWD (Secret Service) had assigned an investigating officer to the camp for the purpose of uncovering members of those units, which had committed war-time atrocities.

Judging by the accent free German he spoke our NKWD officer must have been born in the Volga Republic and had learned to speak German with his mother's milk. In order to get a few more pieces of bread or an extra portion of soup, we knew that some soldiers would invent and tell him the wildest stories. People disappeared and were never heard of again. Arthur and I had no intention of joining their fates.

By the end of February 1946, eight months after our first confinement to this camp, the number of dead POWs had climbed to five hundred ninety-eight. This was almost fifty percent of the original number of twelve hundred. We noticed the first signs the Russians were getting nervous and worried.

The members of our original group from *Pisek* worked in different locations in the city; we had little contact with any of them and hardly ever saw them anymore. Kalle, when I saw him from a distance, was hardly recognizable. He looked as if he weighed less than 100 pounds. Like the rest of us, the captain had been transferred to a work detail after his fight with Calman, and had suddenly died of malnutrition and dehydration.

Our strength wasn't much to talk about either, in spite of the additional food that we scratched for and scraped together. Arthur had me worried because he looked like a ghost. He was emaciated with black rings under his eyes and gray, sickly looking skin. Fortunately we didn't have any mirrors. I didn't want to know what I looked like. If I looked the way I felt, it must have been awful.

Everybody continuously hallucinated about food and told each other stories of wonderful meals they had eaten at home, at Christmas time, during birthday parties and the like. I, for one, remembered distinctly, (and I was positive that my memory was not playing tricks on me) that part of my constant hunger originated from my mother's refusal to let me have second helpings of strawberry pound cake (my favorite) during birthday parties. I could literally see those damned pound cakes, covered with deliciously glistening sweet, red strawberries in front of my face, while saliva was running from both corners of my mouth.

Arthur's memories were different. He didn't care for sweets but had delirious memories of his mother's cooking, especially the meat roulades, which she prepared for the family dinner on Sundays. He was positive that his hunger was caused by his father's insistence that he, the head of the household, was the only person to get two roulades with plenty of mashed potatoes and gravy. We couldn't conceive—and it never came to us—that there was anything strange about these hallucinations. As a matter of fact, several serious fights started in the barracks because others doubted the correctness of these elaborate descriptions.

The soup, which we gobbled down three times a day never changed in its consistency of water, sauerkraut and a little bit of millet. It was at least warm, sometimes even hot. There was no fat in it, no meat; nothing of the kind ever came near it. Now, don't get me wrong. It was not as if the soup—the liquid—was full of sauerkraut or millet, no, it was a quart of hot water with maybe a spoonful of a solid substance on the bottom. In our crazed and starved minds the perversity never stopped. We drank the hot water from the top and saved all solids to put on a piece of our bread, imagining that this would still our hunger more. It didn't! And one spoonful of *Kascha at noon,* this Russian staple, made of millet, was our only solid food. It was absolutely tasteless, without salt or fat or anything else, and couldn't pacify our craving.

Each day the end pieces of bread loaves were given to a different guy when bread rations were divided in the morning. The end piece had a crust and was harder. Thus it was more to chew than a soggy piece from the middle. Everybody in the group observed this procedure with great jealousy. The POWs watched closely that no mistakes were made, and that they didn't miss their turns.

In Stalinsk, bread was the currency for most deals, not only for us, but for the civilian population as well. I never found out whether anybody lived in Stalinsk by his own choice. The majority of inhabitants were prisoners, *zaklutchornies* or former prisoners who had completed their sentences but had been condemned to remain in Siberia for the rest of their lives.

Their enthusiasm for the Russian political commissars who ruled everyday life was minimal, sometimes it was even hostile. Surely there would have been uprisings if it had not been for the hunger. Bread was the controlling factor. The supply of bread was strictly regulated by the authorities and kept everybody at bay. Without it there would be instantaneous starvation. There were no small bakeries in Stalinsk, just one large bread factory surrounded by a high fence, four towers and by guards.

While a loaf of bread cost only five rubles if bought with the daily ration card, the price was one hundred to hundred and fifty rubles on the black market. A few clever traders amongst the soldiers in our camp bought the *maxorca,* which the POWs needed for cigarettes, and then they sold it with a slight surcharge inside the camp either for rubles or bread. Bread ruled everything.

In the beginning of April 1946, the temperature climbed occasionally to thirty degrees. Slowly it became warmer in our part of Siberia.

If you look at a map you'll find that our camp was way up north at 55.2 latitude and 86.05 longitude. To get a better idea about the location, look for Prince Rupert near the Chatham Sound on the southernmost border of Alaska with Canada—that is how far north on the globe *Stalinsk* was located.

Spring in the air was not the only change in our ongoing saga. The Russian Government became concerned because too many prisoners were dying. They sent a commission from Moscow to investigate the conditions in the POW camps all over Siberia. We were figuring that if the death rate in other camps was as bad as it was in ours, the disappearance of millions of German prisoners without any records of who they were, or anything else about them, or how they had disappeared, could look bad for the Soviet Union. Maybe there was a world opinion after all?

Wild scuttlebutt was racing through the camp.

"They are sending us home."

"They are afraid of world opinion."

"They want to increase our rations."

Other outrageous speculations were making the rounds, which could only have been invented by our sick minds. At this time world opinion did not give a damn about the German prisoners in Russia. Whatever the reason was for the commission, it most certainly was not charitable.

When the commission finally arrived, it consisted of a group of doctors in officer uniforms. Some army officers together with administrative personnel were with them to keep them on the straight and narrow. Most likely they were political commissars. Every prisoner in the camp was lined up for a medical evaluation. Not surprising to us it wasn't a medical examination, as we knew it, but an inventory of the physical conditions of the prisoners.

The procedure took place in one of the empty barracks. The Russians didn't talk much and were certainly not discussing anything with the POWs. We had to undress, were weighed; they listened to our heartbeats and our lungs and pinched our rear ends. Our weight had dropped so low that our bottoms were hanging in slack pockets, not round and firm any more like a healthy ass should be. Some rear ends looked particularly slack and limp. Those guys were ordered to stay home from work and were isolated in barracks as "oka." No, not okay, but Russian "oka." We never found out what that abbreviation meant, and it didn't get anybody one iota more food, just rest, lots of rest and staying inside the camp going crazy thinking about nothing but food.

Arthur was pronounced "oka." He could stay in the Quonset from now on, lie on his back on his wooden slat and dream of food. I wasn't as lucky. I had to go to work. My weight had dropped to 115 pounds. I guess they wanted me to continue to work until I was dystrophic. Arthur and I parted, and I promised that I would try to supply him with whatever edible substances I could organize.

For me the summer of 1946 started with a change of work assignment. The cooperation between the camp and DOZ 2, the big lumber mill, had apparently ended. They were sending us now to OSMU 4, a huge construction site in the middle of *Stalinsk*. OSMU 4 was a housing complex, similar to the former *Stalin Allee* in the eastern part of the City of Berlin—if anybody has ever seen that architectural monstrosity—just beyond the *Alexanderplatz*.

The Russians were planning a grandiose thoroughfare in *Stalinsk* and a park, lined with eight-story apartment buildings. The street was laid out with buildings 150 yards apart, with two roads on the sides and with grass and trees in the middle. The outside walls of the buildings were designed to be over three feet thick. Brick walls for apartment buildings and they were three feet thick? The building and its foundation looked more like a fortress than an apartment building. The Russians explained that this was, "To keep out the cold during the winter months."

They had no experience or technology for insulation. Therefore, they perceived that the thickness of the walls would keep out the cold in the winter and conversely the heat in summer. I will talk a little more about these buildings and how they were constructed, but at the time it was not my main concern when we were working in OSMU 4.

My main concern, and really my overriding concern, was that my source of food, potatoes and beets at the *stalowaja* of DOZ 2 was gone, and I was ravenous with hunger and was losing more weight. No more turnips, no more potatoes and the search for a productive "begging-run" would be difficult, because Arthur was not with me any more. I had to look for a new partner to protect my rear while I was scavenging for food.

As luck had it, I was commandeered to a detail of four men in charge of placing windowsills into walls of half-finished buildings. We met a gaunt forty to fifty year old Russian, called David. He was in charge of the job, "the specialist" as the Russians liked to call these people. It was his job to give specific details to me and another guy called Fritz. Fritz was an architect by profession from Frankfurt/Main. He was about fifteen years older than I. He thought that he knew more about what we were doing than David did, and he told him so, kind of talking out loud to the guy in German, as if this Russian would understand German. To our surprise David, the Russian, replied in a clear though harshly accented German. He said that we should be more civil and courteous before coming prematurely to the wrong conclusions about his knowledge and talents. It turned out that David was one of those unfortunate Volga-Germans, deported by Stalin to Siberia at the beginning of World War II.

The Communist dictator had been of the opinion that the whole Volga Republic—over two million people, to be exact—people of

German extraction—in the line of the advancing German army was too dangerous for the safety of his country.

Catherine II, historians gave her a surname, "The Great," had summoned these Germans to her country in about 1763 from the state of Hesse and the Palatinate; 30,623 people followed her invitation. These people fled partly because of the devastation of their farming communities following the Seven-Years War between Fredric II of Prussia and Austria and because of oppression in Hesse. The invitation by Catherine the Great included a promise to live in Russia free and unencumbered, to form an independent republic with no obligation to serve in the Tsar's army and with privileged taxation. They believed her and founded the Volga Republic. The population of the republic grew until in 1897 it was 1,790,439 strong. The reversal of their fate started during the First World War and became tragic, after Stalin issued a decree on September 1, 1941, condemning the Volga Germans to Siberia. The Soviet Government officially reversed this decree in the mid 1960s but the damage was done. The Volga Germans were permitted to return to their original homeland after the Chancellor of West Germany, Helmuth Kohl, struck a deal with Premier Gorbachov in 1989. Over two million descendants took advantage of the opportunity to get out of the communist empire— whether they could speak German or not—and returned to Germany after over 250 years.

David was a kind man, a considerate boss, well educated and cultured. He knew better than most what it meant to be in Siberia. He told us many tales of his own experiences and those of his people. He played along with us and closed his eyes to my begging expeditions, wrote up *nariads* (performance certificates) of 100%, when he damned well knew that we had never accomplished our norm. Fritz worked hard to make up for my absenteeism. I shared bread I collected with him and saved some to take with me to the camp where I visited Arthur at night to supplement his meager rations. My friend was in bad shape, and I feared for him. But outside of being 'oka,' which kept him away from the grueling labor sites, there was little more we could have done.

Fritz became a good friend. He repaid me with a great act of friendship at a time when I needed it the most.

After working with Fritz for a few months, installing windowsills at OSMU 4, he left to join a new work detail consisting of architects and men of an engineering background. They were the lucky ones who worked in an "office."

The winter of 1946–47, at the OSMU 4 construction site, taught me realistically and compellingly that the Russians are most inventive when it comes to accomplishing difficult tasks with either no machine at all or with ingenious improvisations in impossible situations. There was never a question whether things could get done. This "can do" attitude was present with the *Natchalniks* as well as with the lowliest worker.

For instance, it is assumed to be impossible—theoretically—to excavate foundations for buildings in frozen ground at temperatures of twenty to forty degrees below zero. The ground was literally frozen solid as hard as a rock three feet deep. There was no way to get into it with pickaxes or any other manual tools. What did the Russians do?

Every evening the last job before going home was to hammer aluminum rods into the ground. The rods were about three feet long and one inch in diameter. Once they were in place we connected them with crude, naked aluminum wire without any insulation. After that was done the *Natchalnik* connected the entire grid of rods to the local electric power–supply, and I mean power of one thousand volts or more. Electricity, generated by hydroelectric plants was plentiful in Siberia, and the power that surged through the frozen earth during the night thawed and softened it sufficiently and as deeply as the rods penetrated. When we arrived for work the next morning we could see the whole complex steaming, and the ground was as soft as in the spring. The Russians told us to remove the soft earth with the customary, *"dawai, dawai,"* only to repeat the whole process the following day until the excavation was deep enough to put up the scaffolding for the foundations. Any construction specialist in the rest of the world would have thrown up his hands thinking of the expense and the waste of energy.

And then the method to lay bricks in this weather!

Theoretically it would have been impossible to mix mortar in sub-zero temperatures and keep it soft until the bricklayer placed the bricks and let them dry. The water would have frozen and rendered the mortar useless. In this type of weather, building sites in central Europe are closed, but not in Siberia.

The mortar was mixed with boiling water, the bricks were laid before the mortar could cool off and identical aluminum rods, as I have described before—only half as thick—were stuck in the wall in a regular pattern between the bricks as the wall slowly grew. At night the rods were connected to the electricity, and in the morning the mortar had sufficiently dried not to be ruined by the freezing temperatures. The waste of electricity was tremendous, but nobody seemed to care. For the Russians the words "can't do" did not exist. Everything was excused with the overwhelming need to fulfill the current five-year economic plan. We experienced that many times, and each time was a new revelation of their resourcefulness under adversity.

10

THE CITY CAMP

When our transport arrived at the railroad station in *Stalinsk* in June 1945, eight hundred prisoners went to finish construction of the so-called city camp. The camp had been designed to be big enough for two thousand POWs. It was never finished, and now it didn't have to be. Hundreds of prisoners had died. Only around one thousand were left of the original number.

The camp's location in the middle of the city had been designed to accommodate the prisoners as close as possible to their places of work. The trip from the *Kolkhoz camp,* far away in the country, into the city every day was too long and also too costly. The time had come to abandon the *Kolkhoz* camp and to move the prisoners into the city camp. Maybe the Russians hoped that less wear and tear would keep us alive longer. One never knew what was going on in their minds.

For some unknown reason the administrators wanted to keep a small number of prisoners at the *Kolkhoz* camp to work for the *Kolkhoz* and for the little village near by and to keep the camp in operating condition, which would have been difficult without inmates.

On an icy cold morning early in 1947, before we assembled to go to work, everybody was ordered to grab our belongings and to leave nothing behind. At the gate the Russians picked out fifty men at random to step aside and to stay in the camp. I was the only one from all my buddies chosen to stay. Arthur and I were separated. Even though he was still in the "oka" barracks and theoretically did not go to work, he, and the other "oka" men, had to go to the city camp. Everything went so quickly; he was gone before we had a chance to talk or to make arrangements about how to stay in touch.

I had never before met any of the forty-nine men with me now. They'd come from different army units, had been in different boxcars and had been housed in other barracks. We were ordered to pick up our stuff, *bistray,* and move to a regular barracks. Of the two hundred available cots in the barracks we picked a number in the corner of the huge room close to the stove. In order not to miss a day's work we had to go to the gate for our next work assignment immediately after the others had left.

I was terribly upset to be separated from Arthur and for a moment did not know how to get along without his advice and counsel.

But in the end it was a stroke of luck for our group to stay behind at the *Kolkhoz* camp, as we found out soon enough.

Freezing temperatures during the winter—we experienced temperatures as low as 40 degrees below zero—created a challenge for the *kolchos* management to protect and store the harvest, especially the preservation of perishable crops like potatoes, cabbage and turnips. Potatoes and turnips do not remain edible in temperatures below freezing. They become mushy with rot. Only cabbage can be cooked after it defrosts, but it has to be done immediately; otherwise it rots too.

The Russians had devised a system to protect potatoes and beets from spoiling during the winter months. They carted the entire harvest into deep, well protected and slightly heated—about thirty-six to thirty-seven Fahrenheit—bunkers. Each bunker was embedded about twelve feet below the surface and was four hundred and eighty feet wide. A road that led into the bunker descended gradually down into the bunker from both sides. The road was wide enough to permit trucks to drive down through, exiting the other side. The trucks unloaded their cargo into the stalls and departed out the other end. Stalls of twenty by thirty feet in width and length were aligned on both sides of the bunker. During harvesting time these stalls were filled with potatoes, turnips or beets. Two brick stoves were positioned at the end of the bunker to keep the temperature—meticulously controlled by an attendant—at the desired level. In some areas of Siberia the bunkers were constructed of logs. In our area a local stone quarry permitted the *kolkhoz* to choose a more solid construction. The walls were erected of solid granite stone from the quarry that belonged to the *kolchos,* and I mean "solid," about two feet thick.

This was where we came in. We were sent to the stone quarry to break stones for the construction of a new bunker.

We didn't know where we were going when we left the camp. We only saw that the train was gone. Our guards were not very communicative, marching us silently—one guard in front and one in the back of the small column—to the little village where a thrilled member of the Kolkhoz was waiting. The man was in charge of the stone quarry. He was the *Natchalnik*. Only after a lengthy discussion between the camp interpreter and the *Natchalnik* did we find out that our work would be drilling holes in the quarry. Upon completion the holes would be filled with dynamite to blast the quarry, break the stone, and enable them to "harvest" the broken stones.

The *Natchalnik* led us to a tool shed and handed us a supply of chisels of various lengths, hammers of various weights and sizes, and thin rods of different length with flat little scoops at the end. We had no idea what they were supposed to be used for, but one thing was for sure, the old sing song was awaiting us—*"Dawai, dawai, natchinaitje"* (Let's get started).

A low ridge of hills stretched along the valley. They were completely bare of vegetation. I had yet to see a tree since my arrival in *Stalinsk*. The elevation to the crest of the hills was about three hundred feet. We proceeded a few hundred yards into the hills and arrived at the entrance of a stone quarry. One could see that it had been worked previously.

The *Natchalnik*, who walked with an exaggerated swagger of a soldier—he was probably released from active duty only a short while ago—walked ahead into the quarry and started to explain to us what we would have to do. He described the manual drilling process and marked each drilling locations with a red paint spot on the surface of the rocks. He wanted hundred and twenty holes finished before the next blasting. Each hole, he said, had to be six feet deep. We would need chisels of different length and scoops of different length, as the holes grew deeper. He also started talking about our daily norm.

During our work at DOZ 2 we had learned that for every work-process in the Soviet Union there was a norm; a predetermined fixed amount to be accomplished by one man in one day. It didn't matter what the work entailed; the managers of worker's paradise had contrived a method to measure the performance of every process in percentages. If the worker accomplished 100% of the norm, he received his full ration of bread, and in case of the civilians, of pay. If he accomplished less than 100%, a commensurate amount of bread and or pay was deducted. A book, bigger and more voluminous than the bible—the Russians called it *nariad*—contained detailed descriptions of all physical labor, together with the applicable norm. For instance, a different norm applied for digging a hole in soft sand than for digging one into solid earth, or gravel, or frozen ground and so on and so forth. Every year a new *nariad* was published with changed norms or with the addition of new work processes. It was an art to understand a *nariad* and to interpret its contents.

The *Natchalnik* told us that we would have to work in teams of two men, and that the daily norm for a two-man team was to drill five feet deep into the rock.

As we had walked away from the village and deeper into the hills the guys had grown restless. We were getting further and further away from any possibility of organizing extra food, which was vital for us. What interested us was that there were no civilians around and nothing to eat anywhere. Where could we go on our accustomed begging-runs or, in my case, to find potatoes or beets?

Though the group had been thrown together at random we all knew we survived only with the help of compassionate civilians. Now the big question was: were we supposed to drill holes in a stone quarry, hitting a sledge hammer onto chisels all day long with only watery soup to eat, a spoon full of *Kascha* and our meager bread rations?

Our *Natchalnik* must have guessed what we were thinking, or he knew from previous experience what *zakluchornies* craved. He had more news for us.

"Once a week you'll work in the potato bunker. Maybe you'll work there more often depending on the condition of the potatoes and also depending on the quality and quantity of your work in the stone quarry. Occasionally, we'll need you in the bunker near the *kol-*

chos to sort out potatoes," he proclaimed grandiosely, as if he was giving us the British crown jewels.

Our ears perked up. Potato bunker? Sort potatoes? That also meant eating potatoes, stealing them, cooking them, whatever. Visualizing potato-eating orgies we already felt better about the stone quarry.

We didn't comprehend immediately what it meant to drill a hole five feet deep into granite stone in one day, and how many times we would have to swing the hammer to get there.

The *Natchalnik* randomly selected the teams. Thank God none of us knew the guy next to him.

One man in the team had to sit down, hold a short chisel between his feet with both hands, and to make a round hole turn it one quarter of a full turn after each stroke of the hammer. As the hole grew he had to use the scoop to get the stone dust out of the hole. The scooping had to be done after fifty to sixty strokes depending on how forcefully the chisel was hit. Now we knew what the scoops were for. The chisels had a curved blade to chip away at the stone while preventing them from getting stuck in the hole.

The second guy on the team stood in front of the sitting man, swinging a three-pound hammer, hitting the top of the chisel as hard as he could. The chisel had to be hit hard to do any cutting at all because the stone, even though it was not solid granite, was very hard. It took us one hundred strokes with the hammer to drill one-quarter of an inch deep. We took turns hitting and sitting, holding the chisel, and with practice we became accurate hitting the top of the chisel without hitting the hands of the man holding it.

My partner was a lanky Austrian. He told me that he had been a first sergeant in the army—they never give up—by the name of Stepski, Ernst Stepski. Later on, as we got to know each other better, he told me he came from a blue-blooded family in Austria, near Vienna. Before arriving in Siberia, Ernst had never done a solid day's work in his entire life. As first sergeant in a support unit he hadn't been a picture of physical activity either. It showed when he started to swing the hammer. First of all he was skinny as a rail. His biceps looked like a two-inch metal pipe with skin wrapped around, which looked even worse than the rest of us. When it was his turn to swing the heavy tool, he hit my hands and wrists several times. But I noticed that he was at least trying, and, after a little practice, he did all right. He was not strong—the dysentery had weakened him too—and our drilling efforts on the first day resulted in a hole of two feet. Only one team had managed to fulfill eighty percent of the norm.

After Arthur's departure, Ernst turned out to be soothing for my bruised mind. We hit it off together and learned to get along well. But in the beginning I cursed and yelled at him to get his act together. I wasn't going to starve just because he couldn't or wouldn't hit the chisel with the hammer forcefully enough.

"If you want to starve, Ernst, go ahead, but don't do it at my expense. We're going to fulfill our quota, comrade. You can bet your life on that, or I'll trade you off for another hundred pound weakling."

He looked at me with bloodshot eyes that were as droopy as those of a St. Bernard dog, and replied with his inimitable Austrian accent.

"You always try to be the obedient German prick. Why don't you watch me and learn how to survive with less work instead of more. We'll reach our quota, don't you worry." I wasn't sure what to reply but I didn't like his insinuation.

In the evening upon inspecting the quantity of our work, the *Natchalnik* was furious, mad and cursed to high heaven about these lazy mother-fucking German prisoners, and threatened.

"*Nitchevo nyet kartoschki tibia* [No potatoes for you, none]. You have to work harder and not be as lazy as you were in Germany. That's why you lost the war, probably too lazy to fight, *yibit twoiu matj.*"

We trotted home to a strangely empty camp, slowly trying to figure out who the other guys were. We'd been thrown together quite unexpectedly, and I remembered my friend Losanski in Ploesti and his parting words about comrades.

We now slept in a real barrack, not a Quonset, with bunk beds, plenty of space, ate our soup quietly, since we were the only ones left in the entire camp with no Hungarians to harass us.

The work in the stone quarry was as brutally hard on OSMU 2. In the evening we fell onto our hard wooden boards in the bunk beds, dead tired, covered ourselves with dirty and frayed army coats and piled every piece of clothing we had on top.

Learning to live with the vermin of lice and bedbugs was a twenty-four hour fight.

Did you know that bedbugs are extremely clever when it comes to finding their prey? To sanitize the wooden boards of our beds and, to kill the bedbugs, we took each board and quickly pushed it into the door of the stove, one by one. If one did it quickly enough the fire only singed the surface of the board without burning the wood thus killing the bedbugs and the eggs they had deposited. That should have taken care of the problem for a while, or so we thought. We had grossly underestimated our adversary. Bedbugs have survived millions of years and have developed an instinct for finding food. The bedbugs in our barrack had found a home between the cracks in the wooden boards on the floor and on the walls. We only managed to scorch a small number of bedbugs on our bed-boards. The others immediately began to find their way to the iron cots, climbed up the four legs and onward to the boards to feed at night on our tired, mutilated and filthy bodies.

Our next attempt to keep the bedbugs away was an awkward, but ingenious idea. We found empty cans thrown away by the civilians, placed one can under each leg of the bunk bed and filled it with water. Every morning plenty of small, medium and large bedbugs were swimming in the water. We fished them out and squashed them with a vengeance. You might think this would be the end of it. No sir, our bedbugs simply regrouped—it took them about four days—climbed up the walls and reaching the ceiling, crawled to a position above our bunks and dropped onto the sleeping prisoners. We gave up after that, it was impossible to get rid of them.

The work in the quarry became more excruciating—if that was possible—as we went along, because we were getting progressively more emaciated and obviously hungrier. The only food available was food from the camp. Watery soup, *Kascha* and the bread ration were too little to satisfy our metabolism and to sustain us for the hard work without any other supplements.

If we'd been a little less hungry, we might have appreciated the dramatic sight of the quarry as we entered it every morning. It surely had been exploited for quite some time and would have made a good backdrop for a Hollywood movie. The high and ragged walls, the work-gangs—prisoners—shabbily dressed, filthy dirty, constantly cursing, surrounded by walls of stone and swinging hammers.

Our drilling efforts were more successful as we became more accustomed to the hammer and also more skilled and nimble scooping the crushed stone-dust from the holes. As the drilling progressed and the holes became deeper and deeper, the chisels and the scoops we used needed to be longer and longer and more difficult to handle. The little scoop at the end of the rod was only 1/2 inch wide and held only very little dust as it was slowly pulled out of the hole. Scooping the dust out meant a rest period for the hitter but a pain in the neck for the guy with the scoop. On the average we managed to drill four feet a day, one team accomplished the norm of five feet.

Ernst snorted, "Dumb shits, I am an *Edler of Donovan,* a blue-blooded Austrian Count, and nobody is going to push me to swing this hammer any faster. This is slavery in its purest form. Fuck all of you."

"Oh yeah, my blue-blooded Austrian coworker," I shot back. "We'll play it my way, or you'll look for somebody else to fuck around with. Move your ass a little faster or you're a goner."

For some reason Ernst didn't want to change partners and tried a little harder.

Some of the prisoners were still shitting in watery streams and had little strength left. I guess they couldn't leave the water alone or still didn't believe the Russians, or their story about the water. The first guy was found dead in the morning after working a few days in the stone quarry, and a number of the other men became progressively skinnier and skinnier, if that was at all possible.

The *Natchalnik,* the man responsible for the production of the quarry wanted his work done. He had his own quota to fulfill, and he didn't want us to die. Where would that have left him, his norm and the new bunker? He decided to let us work in the potato bunker to still our hunger, in the hope of getting better drilling results during the following days. Of course he knew what would happen in the bunker, but how many potatoes can a man eat, even if he is very hungry? After all, the bunker housed thousands upon thousands of tons of potatoes and beets.

The following day we eagerly walked down into the cavernous bunker and started to sort potatoes with hungry eyes and empty stomachs.

At first we didn't understand the idea of sorting potatoes. The new crop had just arrived. What was there to sort? Wherever we looked; Siberia was different and couldn't be measured by normal standards.

In Siberia, with its transcontinental climate with no interference from a large mass of water, winters are long and summers are short but almost tropical. The hot sun is often interrupted by showers, which made for a high humidity. In the middle of May, shortly after the winter ended and the ground had barely thawed sufficiently for planting, the seed potatoes were put into the ground. Extreme heat and a moist climate had the effect of a hothouse. In only four month the harvest was ready, and the potatoes had to come out of the ground quickly because of the threatening frost. The earth in this part of Siberia is black and extremely fertile. In a short time the potatoes became huge, but many had grown so quickly they developed cavities in the middle, filled with a watery liquid. Those potatoes rot easily if they have water inside, and have to be sorted out before they infest the surrounding fruit. That was our work. We sorted potatoes from one stall into another. What pleasant and easy work that was. The bunker had stoves on each end, which we used to cook potatoes.

It is absolutely amazing how many potatoes fit into the empty stomach of a starved prisoner. I'm talking about boiled potatoes, with skins peeled off after boiling. Under normal circumstances you'll choke after the third one, but not us. My best performance was putting away a full two-gallon pail of pealed potatoes in one sitting.

What we didn't know was that potatoes—when you eat them in our emaciated condition without any protein in our diet—aggravate dysentery even more. In the beginning of our eating orgies in the bunker, we had no idea, and it was a wonderful feeling to have our stomachs filled ready to burst.

We felt better after a day in the bunker. Everybody had a small reserve of potatoes stashed away in the camp, and the POWs hammered away vigorously to fulfill the daily norm of five feet. Most of the teams accomplished the norm, and the *Natchalnik* was happy too.

After a few weeks of the same routine, learning how to handle the equipment, we requested bigger, heavier hammers from the tool shop at the *kolkhos* to hit the chisels harder. We also discovered little tricks to help us extricate the elusive, powdery dust of the crushed stone. We poured a small amount of water into the hole after each drilling cycle—or just peed into the hole because the available water was frozen quickly. The fine dust compacted with the moisture and could be removed easier and faster, in one or two scoops, instead of four or five. We saved time and drilled faster—"stupid Germans" as Ernst said.

In the long run the potatoes didn't do us much good. More guys died. And the rest of us had the runs. But with time our metabolism got used to the different diet, and those who had made it up to now, persevered. Ernst was as stubborn as a mule about his work ethic, and we fought and disagreed continuously on that subject.

After one hundred holes had been completed the *Natchalnik* arrived with a guy who was the *specialist,* the blaster. He came equipped with dynamite, filled the holes, and blasted the quarry while we watched from a safe distance at the entrance of the potato bunker. As soon as the dust had settled, we went back, this time with heavier hammers, to bang away at the broken boulders, which were too large to be handled. The *Natchalnik* also provided primitive wooden stretchers to carry the stones out of the quarry to a site one hundred yards away where we stacked them neatly for later use by the *kolchos,* to build a new bunker.

It was crushing physical labor, but it had kept us away from the city camp, so far. The reports that reached us from there were scary and made us work even harder.

The cycle of drilling, blasting and carrying stones continued throughout the spring and summer. In the mean time it was getting cold again, November 1947, to be exact, and our little group had lost only a few men and was doing okay otherwise. The snow that soon fell made everything slippery in the quarry and climbing over the stones on the ground was dangerous, especially if two guys walked with a heavy stretcher loaded with two hundred pounds of stone.

The situation didn't improve with the presence of a German-Czech national by the name of Adolf Gaida. He was a sadist who had managed to gain the attention of the Russians because he understood the language. As a Slavic language, Czech is somewhat related to Russian. He started to beat the weaker prisoners when they sat down, or, in his eyes, didn't work fast enough. He further punished them by taking food away and using all kinds of other deliberate, distressing brutalities throughout the day. When we went up the hillsite to bury an unfortunate dead prisoner he stood over the grave, pulled out his prick, and, while continuously cursing the bloody Germans, urinated onto the dead bodies. It was disgusting. But as the saying goes, "The Good Lord sees everything." Gaida was taken care of at a later date.

One day, as we returned to the camp, a guard approached me and said, "They tell me you are a *specialist.* You have worked with communication equipment. You must know something about radios, right?"

"I do, what is it all about?"

"A farmer from the village has a radio that needs repairing. He brought it from Germany. He needs some help with it. Do you think you can handle it?"

"Of course," I replied smelling FOOD. "Where is the farmer, and where is the radio?"

The guard apparently had also been promised a reward if he could come up with a *specialist* for radios. He took me to the village, to the house of a *kolkhoz* worker. The whole family greeted us with open arms as we entered the sparsely furnished little house. The wife was looking forward to music from the radio, and the owner was proud that he had stolen the thing from the motherfucking Germans, as he put it. The guard—the poor son-of-a-bitch who was probably just as hungry as I was—sat down and motioned me to do likewise. We were both served large amounts of food. I started protesting, because I wanted to see the radio first, to find out whether I could repair it or not, but the farmer waved me off magnanimously. His wife served *borscht,* the famous Russian soup. I mean the real thing with meat, potatoes, red beets and *kapusta,* also deliciously filled *piroshk*i, sweetened beets and other semi-cooked vegetables. We both ate until we were ready to burst. Finally I insisted that I wanted to see the radio. The farmer took me into the corner of the room were I saw it, thunderstruck; he had connected a simple electric metering device to the net. The little round disk inside the unit was turning and turning, and the small numerals kept counting slowly, just like electric meters do.

In socialist Russia, however, in Siberia, where electricity was only introduced to the to the small communities after the inception of the Soviet Union, electricity had always been free. The concept of installing a meter in each household, to measure the consumption of electricity, was unknown.

I looked at the darn thing and was stunned. The guy had stolen an electric meter, probably ripping it out of the wall in a German house, thinking it was a radio. How was I going to explain, with my limited knowledge of the language, what this useless thing was all about?

"This is no radio," I said watching his face, which suddenly seemed to freeze in great amazement, eyes wide open, and forehead wrinkled, his mouth gaping.

"Za sto? Pa idiot, da? Smatritje, pa idiot charascho!" (What's that? It runs, yes? Look, it runs very well!)

"Running does not mean playing and this is only a meter; it will never play. It only measures electricity, *ponjumaish?"* (Do you understand?) I talked with my hand and feet knowing that this would be crucial.

The discussion went on back and forth and I wasn't making any progress. The guard was getting restless. All three of them kept yelling at me. The wife was the loudest. From all I could understand they kept accusing me of misrepresented my talents, I had eaten the family's food under false pretenses. The guard was afraid he would be guilty of participating in the plot, and both of them started to beat me with their fists and with things they picked up around the house. By the time I finally managed to get out of the door I had received a good thrashing. The guard continued to beat me all the way back to the camp. I was black and blue all over while my stomach was pleasantly filled. I didn't think it had been worth it.

While lying on our cots in the evenings, talking, Ernst and I got to know each other better. We didn't have to make the trip home from the city every night, and we had time to talk before falling asleep. At home in Austria, he told me proudly, he was a nobleman.

After the First World War ended, and Emperor Franz-Joseph I had been deposed by democratic forces, the new Government issued a decree forbidding use of all titles of the old monarchy. In a country like Austria, where the wife of a letter carrier was addressed as "Mrs. Letter Carrier," this was a joke. The people had loved titles, which were a part of local culture, custom and everyday life. Little by little the old titles were used again, but not as openly as before the war and more as a matter of courtesy. Anyway, in Austria Ernst was *"Baron von Stepski Edler auf Donovan."* He explained this in great, suffocating detail to me. I wasn't really interested, but his story helped me for several minutes to keep my mind off food. Ernst was older than I and had been in the war since the very first day. He could never quite drop his Austrian accent, which sounded charming at times but could be nerve wrecking when he applied it with deliberate slowness. It sounded almost like a broad, accentuated southern drawl in a tavern in New Orleans.

Our group of forty-five was now all that was left in the Kolkhos camp. One man all by himself ran the kitchen. The number of guards had been drastically reduced, and if it hadn't been for Adolf Gaida, it would have been okay. He was a devil, that one, a mad devil!

The men started to talk again. I mean not just about food or barking at each other, but really talk. Our discussions turned to home most of the time and evaluated our chances to return to civilized lives.

Ernst had finished school in Austria before the *"Anschluss"* (literally the connection), as Germany's occupation and subsequent confederation with Austria in 1938, had been called. He had seen the good life, plenty of it, before being drafted into the German army at the beginning of the war with Poland in 1939. He told me endless stories of life at the university, beautiful girls, and delicious Austrian food—of course, food had to be mentioned—and I tried to keep up with him by relating my experiences with Marcella. As we talked, sex remained a strangely clinical subject. Our physical condition had improved, but our sex drive hadn't returned, so far.

"If we ever get back home, you'll have to visit with us," he said more than once. "Vienna is the most beautiful city in the world. What wouldn't I give to sit in a *Kaffeehaus* right now?"

"You're getting carried away, my friend." I tried to neutralize his dreams. "I'd be happy with a double ration of dry Russian bread."

"Yes, you would, but then you aren't Viennese." He was relentless in his love for his hometown, but so was everybody else.

I hadn't told him anything about New York, my mother and about America. Arthur was the only one I had confided in. I intended to keep it that way, especially in the presence of continued claims by our captors that war with America was imminent. I didn't want to become a preferred target of the NKWD.

The construction of the barracks in the camp was ingenious for the climatic conditions in Siberia. The structure was raised three feet off the ground, on stilts, with a skirt of wooden boards covering the raised foundation. This created an air cushion under the barracks, which cooled the air inside the building in the hot summer, and conversely protected us, from the terrible cold in the winter. Generation of prisoners before us had used the space under the floorboards as a garbage dump. They'd cut trap doors into the floors of the barrack and had thrown everything down below. Potato peels, vegetable remnants etc., too lazy to carry them to the latrine or the garbage dump. The food remnants had attracted rats. Many rats! Big rats! GIGANTIC rats! As a matter of fact, none of us had ever seen rats of this size before, almost as big as little dachshunds. They were ferocious too.

Our jailors never let us sleep in complete darkness. They always had a few naked light bulbs lit at night, and we saw the beasts scurrying about trying to find something to eat in the middle of the night.

That alone wouldn't have been too bad, but one night they nibbled on the ear of a sleeping prisoner. With half an ear missing when he woke up, the guy had been too weak from exhaustion and too tired from work to even notice anything until the next morning. He was still bleeding badly when we got up. Our one and only remaining medic had to keep him in the camp until he stopped the bleeding. Gaida was furious about the lost hours. He wanted to please the Russians by finishing our drilling assignment quickly. He thought about this mishap for a couple of days, turned it over in his demented mind and then developed a plan.

A few nights later when it was dark outside, he put a metal washing basin on the floor, turned it upside down, tilted it 45 degrees and propped it up with a wooden stick on one side. Then he placed a small piece of bread under it. He tied a string to the wooden stick, which held up the basin. The string was long enough for him to hold it in his hand while lying on his cot. He stayed awake until the rats started to investigate their nightly hunting grounds. The very second the first rat crawled under the metal basin to get at the piece of bread he pulled the string. The wooden stick gave way, the basin fell flat to the floor, and the rat was trapped underneath.

A few of us woke up from the noise and ruckus and watched him as he proceeded with his scheme. That evening he had brought a piece of wood shaped like a fork with him. Now with the rat caught he proceeded to pound the basin with a metal rod, which produced a continuous ringing sound like of a dull bell. He went on beating for a while, banging away at the basin until he suddenly lifted it up. The rat sat totally motionless and dumbfounded from the continuous noise ringing in its head.

Gaida quickly pinned the rat to the ground with his wooden fork and tied its feet with the help of another guy. Now the rat was helpless, struggling and squeaking. Gaida also had found tar in the tool shop at the *kolkhoz,* which they used to insulate the roofs in the little village to protect them from rain. The two guys took the rat, spread its hind legs and filled its asshole with tar, as much as they could press into it. The tar worked like cork and would most effectively prevent the rat from emptying its bowels. After the job was finished they untied the strings from the rat's feet, and it ran away disappearing quickly into some hole, not knowing what was going to happen.

The following evening, when we returned from work, we heard terrible shrieking and squeaking noises. Gaida was laughing cruelly. The rat probably exploded and the other rats, having witnessed the agony of the animal, disappeared to live someplace else. What a sick mind this guy had! We wondered what he'd been doing during the war. But he was right as far as the rats were concerned. It was the end of the rats in our barracks.

The administration finally decided that they should take precautions against an outbreak of infectious diseases and began to inoculate the POWs. The first injection, which was jammed into my back right underneath the shoulder blade, was typhoid vaccine. It was our own medic who gave us the inoculations. He did it rather brutally with a needle large enough for a horse, but he excused himself and explained that the Russians hadn't supplied a thinner needle. He only had one needle for all of us and did a hasty sterilization job, dumping the used needle briefly into a pot of boiling water. Everything was fine at first, but a day or two later I developed a sizable swelling at the location of the injection, and the medic diagnosed it nonchalantly as an abscess. The needle hadn't been sterile after all, and he was sorry that he could only do his job with the equipment furnished. That was a lot of bullshit as far as I was concerned; he had been too lazy to perform a more thorough sterilizing job.

The swelling continued to grow and hurt terribly. A doctor who came once a month from the main camp for routine cases, decided to cut and drain the abscess. He warned me beforehand that the pain would be severe. He didn't have any painkillers to help me.

"Put a large piece of cloth into your mouth, bite down on it and grab the legs of the table," he advised me. Then he told me to bend over the edge of a normal table for the procedure.

"I'll try to be as quick as I can, provide you manage to lie still."

What were my choices? The pain had become intolerable, I couldn't go to work, my food rations had been drastically reduced, and all I wanted was to get rid of the abscess and the pain.

I must admit that I'm quite timorous of pain, especially when I have to lie down, not seeing what is going on, and knowing that somebody is going to cut into me any second. To be truthful, the piercing pain of the two quick cuts was excruciating and totally justified my pusillanimous, cowardly behavior.

The doctor yelled, because the puss that squirted from the boil hit him in the face, and I almost fainted when he inserted a drainage tube, pushing it under my skin from one cut to the other. He explained to the medic how to treat the wound in the succeeding days and left. I had to rest for one day in the barracks, and Ernst commiserated with me when the gang came back from work in the evening.

Gaida cursed me, called me a malingerer and promised to award me with preferential treatment the minute I returned to the quarry. In short, I was fucked all the way around.

One experience after another in prison taught me that nothing in life is impossible and the word "can't do" is a myth and the opposite is axiomatic.

I survived Gaida's vengeance and kept going with the help of the potato bunker, Fritze's compassion and—strangely enough—with the help of the *Natchalnik* of the *kolchos* who had taken a liking to me and pulled me aside for special jobs. I don't know what did it, because the guy never showed any particular emotion. Maybe he liked the fact that I seemed to understand him and was able to answer his questions with my limited vocabulary, whatever; when he had something special to do he walked into the stone quarry and yelled,

"Petja idi suda," (Peter, come here) much to the annoyance of my friend Gaida.

On one such occasion he came with a little horse and buggy. It was the cart used for transporting small loads of just about anything. The buggy looked more like a small flatbed more commonly used to carry fruit from the field during harvest time. The horse was the usual tired, small beast with an unkempt coat and with many scars on his sides from all the beatings it had received during its lifetime. I climbed aboard without asking questions and the *Natchalnik* didn't volunteer any information either. We drove for two hours, deep into the hills past the camp until he stopped the cart and jumped off, took two shovels and told me to come along. Fifty yards further he came to a halt. It was in the middle of a small clearing, on the bank of a small hill, and he showed me how to scrape the topsoil off the rocky underground. We scraped until we hit a hard, black and stony looking substance, like black rock. The *Natchalnik* took a broom and brushed the loose soil away until I could clearly see the pitch-black rock, or so I thought. He looked at me, smiled and said, *"Anthracite."* He took a few pieces of the rock coal, piled them neatly on top of each other over a piece of paper and lit a match to light the paper.

The rock on top of the paper started to burn almost immediately. It was the purest, highest concentrate anthracite I have ever seen. He'd found it only ten inches under the surface!

I stood there with my mouth open and didn't know what to say. That was Siberia for you.

The *Natchalnik* seemed to be proud of his treasure and explained that he had taken me—the prisoner of war—with him because he didn't want anybody in his village to know where the coal was. He continued his speech with a raised finger, "Petja, if you know what's good for you, you'd better keep your mouth shut."

I congratulated him on his find and assured him that I wouldn't divulge the location of his treasure to anybody; I never did. He let me work with a pickaxe and a shovel for a while, while he sat on the ground and smoked a cigarette until I had loaded enough coal onto the buggy. We climbed aboard and were back at the quarry just before dark after another two-hour ride. The only guy who wanted to know what had transpired was Gaida. I told him a story about working for the *Natchalnik* in his house and he didn't ask anything else.

Our visits to the potato bunker where we gorged ourselves with cooked potatoes and smoked beets were few and far between and barely kept us going with enough food. Some of the POWs were still weak as the dysentery reappeared sporadically.

The sugar beets were the delicatessen delights in the bunker. You really can't do much with a raw sugar beet, I mean like cooking it or cutting it up or so. The beet is too large, too hard and takes forever to soften if you try to cook it and, as we concluded after a while, cooking the beets just wasn't worth it. That is until one of the guys came up with the idea of hanging a sugar beet in the chimney of the stove in the bunker. We left it there for the whole day and inspected it shortly before our shift was over. What do you know? The beet had become kind of rubbery, almost as soft and juicy as a pear. We could peel it and cut it like butter. It tasted—to us—sweet like a piece of candy. Well, it was sweet, we could swallow it, it filled our stomachs and it agreed with our digestions.

Many times in my life it took me a long time to learn my lesson. Things often took a turn for the worse because I had a big mouth when I should've kept it closed. Too many times I tried to show people how clever I was or, on other occasions, that I was not afraid to speak my mind, that I had an opinion, or knew things better.

The top guy among the Germans POWs in both camps and a trusted lieutenant to the Russians was a Silesian-Polish guy by the name of Hans Schwartz. He was the coordinator for all job assignments for the POWs in the *Kolchos* and the city camp. On the occasions of his visits to our camp he tried to indoctrinate us and rambled on about the formation of an AntiFa (Anti-fascist) organization, which had been established in Moscow by former General Field Marshall Paulus, the ill fated commander of the German 6th army. Three hundred twenty thousand of his men were annihilated in *Stalingrad,* but he lived in relative comfort in Moscow.

Schwartz explained to us the tremendous service we could provide to the World Socialist Revolution if we'd become active in this organization, and thereby demonstrate to our benevolent captors we were Germans who in our hearts didn't participate in the crimes promulgated and committed by the Nazi rulers. True as many of the things were, his presentation was pompous and reminded me of many propaganda sessions in years gone by, by the very same people he was placating.

I, the dumb shit, had to open my big mouth!

Of course, I knew better! Well, I should've kept my mouth shut, because it didn't take long until Schwartz lost his patience with my unsolicited comments. He didn't do anything spectacular. No, he just informed me and two other guys, who had been on Gaida's shit list that we were being transferred to the city camp the following day, just like that. I was stunned. Too late it dawned on me how stupid I had been, and that my ordeal had just begun.

I said good-bye to Ernst, my blue-blooded Austrian friend, as I called him when we were alone and walked to the train. The train was still the only transport into the city.

It was early spring of 1948 and the continuous scuttlebutt, originating most of the time in the latrine of the camp, was fomenting dreams about our future. There was no future. It was a bleeding agony from morning 'til night, and my idiotic behavior was the reason I landed where I certainly didn't want to be, right in hell's kitchen.

The city campsite included a barrack for "oka" people; Arthur had left it a few weeks ago as they told me. He was back at work.

The sight of the guys in the "oka" barrack was pathetic. In comparison to them I looked like a prize boxer. I'd managed to keep the dysentery under control in the *kolchos* camp. I'd worked hard all winter supported by plenty of potatoes and beets from the bunker; In comparison I had slummed.

The city camp continued to have a high attrition rate. The prisoners were dying and, although POWs from other camps in the area were arriving every month, the total number had shrunk to eight hundred fifty.

I looked for Arthur but with the limited time in the evenings after work it took me several days until I finally located him. He was weak and skinny like all the others, but had found a good working place in a huge garage for *kolchos* trucks. The trucks, which were serviced in the garage during the night, rolled out to their assignments in the morning, and the prisoners had to clean up the area were they'd parked.

We hadn't seen each other for several months, and the change in his demeanor was visible. Even this mentally strong man was gradually affected by the constant, persistent, debilitating hunger, the deprivations and the hard physical work.

"Peter, am I happy to see you!" he exclaimed, breaking into a sick looking grin, which seemed to split his skull sideways.

Arthur, as I'd remembered him, always had a ruddy complexion, red skin and shining blue eyes, now the skin was sallow and the eyes looked dull.

"You certainly look good. Watch out for yourself; it doesn't take much down here to get you down. This truck job is not the worst location. Often trucks have a few potatoes left on the platform, and at other times drivers bring some edibles from their trips. These guys are great and understand what it means to be a *zaklutschorny*. Where do you work and why in Hell's name did you come here? I mean this is the home of the Devil?"

"OSMU-2, at the cement factory," I answered. "We're pouring concrete for stepping stones for buildings at Osmu-4. It's tough especially without supplements. So far I haven't found another begging-run, and the guards at our place are mean and strict."

"Don't try to break any records. Work as slow as you can it conserves energy," was his advice before he trundled off to his barrack without turning around. From the way he walked I could see that every step was an effort.

Fighting for survival accelerated to another dimension. At one time part of the rations for us consisted of a flat, flounder-like fish with a white and black striped skin. To keep the fish from spoiling they were stored in wooden barrels in a saline solution. We called them zebra fish. Our cooks didn't have an idea about how to cut the fish into portions for every prisoner. Maybe they were too lazy to bother. Who knows? Anyway, they threw the fish into boiling soup for want of a better solution and cooked them until they disintegrated. You know what a flounder looks like? It has lots of little bones in fins surrounding the body. As I said, the cooks threw the fish into the sauerkraut soup. The fish disintegrated in the hot cooking water, and all big and little bones swimming around loosely in the soup pierced the sauerkraut. Eating the soup was like trying to eat strings of barbed wire. You should've seen the riot that broke out. We wanted to hang and quarter the fat cats in the kitchen. The Russians sent some of the cooks to work, and new personnel were assigned to the cooking, which didn't make the food any better, wholesome or more plentiful.

The cement factory was a pitiless place. It was too far from the next housing complex and we didn't have a chance to go begging. We had to walk a thousand yards across an open field to get away from that place. Even the sleepiest guard could've spotted a lonely figure trying to sneak away. It just didn't work. I was losing weight, and on top of it, the dysentery struck again, I didn't have the energy anymore to treat it with "three days of hunger and thirst." I didn't lose weight slowly; I lost it rapidly. I ran to the john all night long and felt like croaking. Once more my thinking about food assumed paranoid dimensions.

At this time the prisoners didn't talk anymore. In the evening the barracks were filled with an eerie silence. All you could hear throughout the night were shuffling noises from tired feet on their way to the latrine.

Weeks went by, and I don't remember anymore how I survived, (what I call today *"my time in hell"*). I only remember that one day I fainted at work, and a guard kicked me with the butt of his gun to get me going again.

In the camp I saw some guys eating raw salt, washing it down with water. Everybody believed that the salt would cause the body to retain water. Any doctor knows today about it and tells you to avoid food with high sodium chloride content. The guys were speculating that the dropsy would gain them a trip home, not caring, or giving a damn that they ruined their health in the process. I didn't join them in this nonsense, because in spite of everything; I still strongly believed that we'd go home. I didn't want to be a cripple for the rest of my life.

When the next commission from Moscow arrived it went through the usual ass pinching procedure, and I was declared "oka". Nobody was sent home because of the dropsy, not this time anyway.

The period of rest in the "oka" barrack helped me regain some strength, even though I started to suffer from something similar to dropsy. My legs filled with water, and the water kept rising in my body until I had trouble breathing, and it happened without eating salt like the others had done.

During a check up in the "oka" barrack the medic told me that they had a new medicine for my condition, a diuretic, appropriately named *Deuritin*. It would help me to shed the excess water fast, he said. I took the pills and started to pee like a hydrant, going to the latrine twenty to twenty-five times a day. In a few days I lost thirty pounds. Now I *really* looked like a scarecrow.

The kitchen of the camp was the only place with a scale and I took the opportunity to weigh myself one day, while attempting to visit Toni in the hope of getting an extra portion of soup from him. The scale read 79 pounds (36 Kilo). It was my low point, the absolute bottom, and I didn't get any extra soup from Toni. He wouldn't even see me.

Olga had busied herself finding a job after arriving in New York. Alma put her up with some friends, until she found a place of her own and told her that it was difficult if not impossible to find any work without a vocation.

"Didn't you do anything in Europe all those years? I mean what did you do to keep yourself busy?"

What could Olga tell her? That she played bridge rather well? That she had been president of the American Women's Club? Should she tell Alma how much time and effort it had taken to avoid the Nazis and to stay out of jail? How to get enough food and stay warm? No, instead she replied, "You've been living here all your life, Alma. What would you do if you were in my shoes? I didn't learn anything. Trying to go to college now would take too long, and cost money that I don't have. Tell me, what can I do or learn to do to make a living?"

After a few days she called Olga and asked her to come to her house to meet an old friend of hers whom she knew from her school days and who was working as a head nurse in a hospital in Brooklyn.

Olga met Catherine Mann, the head nurse—a registered nurse—of a hospital on Herkimer Street in Brooklyn. You know how it is in life when you meet people. Some people you dislike immediately. The majority you meet and forget, and in a few isolated instances you immediately form a bond. Catherine and Olga saw each other for the first time and liked each other instantly.

"You're in a tough spot, Olga, but if you don't fear working I think I can and will help you. I'll put you up in a small room in the hospital. You'll join the nurses training program and become a practical nurse. During this time you can eat and sleep at the hospital, and we'll pay you ten dollars a week. If you pass your final exam I'll help you to get a job in the hospital."

Olga agreed, moved into a tiny room, which was twenty-one by nine feet, had a bed, a closet and running cold and warm water. As I said before, my mother was a practical woman and knew when she had her back to the wall.

Catherine and Olga developed a close friendship, which lasted for the rest of their lives.

11

THE BLUE ONE, A FRIEND

Just about that time I ran across Fritz, the architect with whom I'd worked at OSMU 4, putting up windowsills. After the architectural assignment folded, he'd managed to get a cushy job in the office of the administration of the camp. He was in good shape, but when he looked at me his forehead wrinkled with worry and concern.

"You don't look too well, Peter. I wish I could do something for you." He continued after a few moments as if he had just thought of something. "Do you think you could work if I get you a job with enough to eat? I mean really hard work. Some guys I've sent to this place I'm talking about didn't make it. I know you're on "oka" relief, but we could change that easily enough."

Was he kidding me? All I could think of day and night was eating, and I was sure that if I could get enough to eat I could work again like an ox.

"Fritz, what are you talking about? Do I look that bad? You remember how we slaved together over those windowsills at OSMU 4? I could work like that again, but I can't do it on camp food alone. And Fritz, if you send me any place at all or especially if you've got a good job available, think of Arthur and us as a team. He doesn't look good either. If you can, do something for him too. He is my friend. Maybe you can help both of us. Where is this fabulous job you're talking about? "

"Let me think about it," he said slowly turning around to leave. "I'll talk to you again in a few days. And one more thing; keep your mouth shut about our discussion and your things packed and ready at all times."

I went back to the "oka" barrack, packed my things immediately and waited, hoping and praying a little, too.

Three days later, at the end of the summer of 1947, we'd just finished our watery breakfast containing four leaves of rotten sauerkraut and ten kernels of millet together with the morning ration of soaking wet bread, Fritz entered the barrack. He looked around and came straight to me. "Get your things and come along." He turned and walked quickly away.

I grabbed my bundle and followed him out of the barrack as fast as I could without saying a word. We walked towards the gates of the camp, still not speaking to each other. A truck with the engine running was waiting in front of the closed gate. I looked up at the platform of the truck and saw Arthur standing on the rear end looking lost and rather curious. Fritz went to the truck, talked to the guard who was sitting with the driver in the cab and handed him some papers. He turned and looked at me with a smile.

"If you can make it, get up on the truck now." Coming close, he whispered into my ear, "You two are going to the bread factory, hard work, but plenty of bread. Let me know how you're doing."

He gave me a push from behind as I struggled to step on the truck's rear tire and up to the platform. I turned to wave to him, knowing that he didn't want me to say a word about his act of kindness. He must've had his reasons. I was so elated I was speechless anyway.

The truck passed through the gate and drove for about twenty minutes, before we arrived at the bread factory, a large compound on the edge of town. During the trip Arthur and I said 'hello' and were sitting behind the cabin of the truck to prevent falling off the moving and shaking vehicle.

"How did we get this lucky, Peter?" Arthur asked. "I didn't know what hit me when they told me this morning not go to work. Then Fritz came and told me without further explanation to come along. Do you know anything about this?"

"You know, Arthur, Fritz and I worked together at OSMU 4. That was the time you were in 'oka' up in the *kolchos* camp. I went on my begging trips with Fritz's help and that of the Volga German, David. I told you about him. Fritz, of course, always participated in my spoils. He probably feels grateful about my help and wants to reciprocate. When he approached me a few days ago, I asked him not to forget you, but he didn't say yes or no and didn't tell me what this was all about or where we were going. He only said it would be hard work, and that I should try not to disappoint him. Let's see how much bread we'll get. Eating as much bread as I want sounds like a dream, no matter how hard they want us to work."

Entering the gates of the bread factory was an experience like entering the portals of heaven; it was a moral boost for our bruised souls.

"Sto, nyet paxetje, nyet pashla nitchewo nyet kackda" (Stop, you can't go nowhere no place).

The guard watching the gate was asserting his authority. He looked as if he was from Uzbekistan, brown skin, slightly slanted eyes, and lots of pockmarks. He spoke an accented and grammatically incorrect Russian, which is often heard in the Siberian melting pot of languages, dialects, and races. What he had just said was an example of a Russian triple negative.

The good part was that the man with the slanted eyes and the scarred face at the guardhouse had the audacity to stop a military truck with two soldiers in the cab. His instructions were not to let anybody who didn't belong get past the gate. With a deliberate aura of authority he slowly walked to the driver's window of the truck. He questioned the soldiers who explained to him—rather flippantly—that they had to deliver us to wherever we were supposed to go, to let the truck pass immediately without further ado. After all, they implied, they represented the government.

The guard barked abruptly, *"yubbani wrod, iditje na chui* (Fuck your mouth and go to hell)."

"Those are two POWs." The soldier in the cab pointed toward us on the back of the truck and continued, "We've got to deliver them to a safe location so they can't escape. Don't you understand?"

"Yes, of course, I understand. But I don't understand what you two hungry thieves want to do in the bread factory except try to steal bread. The fact is you're supposed to deliver two POWs to the gate, and we'll take responsibility for them from here on. That's all. Now, let them climb off your truck and back up. We'll see they get to where they're supposed to go. There's no further need for you two to remain."

No matter how hard the two guys tried to get inside the compound, the guard wouldn't let them pass. For Arthur and me, two broken down, demoralized prisoners, it was a revelation. We wouldn't see any of these obnoxious, dumb and "wet behind the ears" assholes anymore, not as long as we worked in the bread factory, anyway.

I've talked so much about bread because it's easy to understand why it was the most valuable commodity for everybody in *Stalinsk*, civilians and prisoners alike. The bread factory was protected like Fort Knox with an eight-foot high wooden fence and with guarded watchtowers on every one of its six corners. The fence and towers were higher and better protected with barbed wire than the prison camps. The large complex was at least four times the size of our camp. We could see several storage buildings, a rail siding with separate entrance gates, a powerhouse, and a huge factory building.

We discovered that the factory ran in three shifts, day and night to manufacture bread for the population of *Stalinsk*.

Turning to the right side as we entered the factory, only fifty yards away from the guardhouse and hugging the fence on one side, we saw a small house, the house for prisoners and our home to be.

After sending the soldiers on their way, the guard took us to this house. He talked continuously as we covered the short distance. He was easy to understand because his language skills and his grammar were not much better than mine.

"These idiots, they should know better. They have nothing to say in here. You two look terrible. Haven't they fed you? You'll like it here. Just do your work and don't steal. Everybody steals in Russia, especially bread. I warn you right now, beware. We watch the place and check out everybody who comes and goes, and we don't miss a trick. Your buddies are doing fine work, and we appreciate them. Just watch yourself and you'll be okay. Hey, one more thing, you're the experts. *Gitler kaput?*"

"If we knew, we'd tell you for sure," Arthur replied.

With that last warning and the redundant question about Hitler's fate he dropped us in front of the house and returned to his guardhouse.

As we entered a single room of about forty-five by thirty-five feet confronted us with two small windows on the factory side and a stove with a big hearth in the middle. Wooden bunk beds were lined up alongside the walls, doubled up and spaced around the room the way we knew it from the camp. Between the beds and the stove was a long, crudely carpentered, wooden table with benches on each side. Only one small window was on the far side, the outside wall of the factory. The room was in no way luxurious, but by comparison it was clean, comfortable and large enough for the occupants.

The delicious odor of soup hit our nostrils. A big iron pot was cooking on the stove. A round-faced man, almost totally bald, stood in front of it, stirring. He turned and smiled at us.

"You must be the two new ones. There's so much work, the group isn't large enough any more. I'm the cook, and my name is Pinkepank but just call me Pinke. What are your names?"

"This is Peter, and I'm Arthur, Pinke. I must tell you we're both deliriously happy to join you. I've never smelled such a wonderful soup during all my time at the camp. Will we be able to sample it today, or are we only included in your rations as of tomorrow?"

As he said that, Arthur looked longingly at the soup as if he could devour it with his eyes if he only stared at it long enough.

"Let me give you some quick advice before the rest of the gang gets back for lunch," Pinke replied, smiling happily. "Yes, I cooked all this expecting two hungry guys like you." He chuckled. "You'll get some soup and a piece of bread, too, whether you're included in today's rations or not. The guys will expect you to start working today right after lunch and work hard. Don't expect any mercy because of your physical condition, but we've enough food, more than you can eat. Arthur, I think they want you to run the coal cart; it's a horse and buggy operation. You've got to take care of the horse, feed it, and be responsible for the transport of coal from the rail siding to the boiler house to see that the factory is supplied with enough coal to keep the power plant running at all times. Peter, you'll work as a *grushik,* carrying sacks of flour from boxcars into the warehouse. That's what the other guys are doing most of the time. The way you look to me right now the sacks weigh more than you do. Don't complain. Don't try to find excuses. Just try to survive. The guys will accept you after a while, and then you'll have it made. Try not to disappoint them."

He looked around the room. "Your two cots are over there near the door. They're new and without lice. Do you have any lice?"

"No, not that we've noticed," both of us answered at the same time. "The last delousing at the camp was a week ago, but we'll see."

"Good, let me have your mess kits. You can taste the soup and tell me if you like it. One more thing, you have a chance to wash yourself regularly. Use it."

We probably smelled like pigs.

We'd entered the gates of heaven. There was good food, plenty of it and bread, too, impossible for us to imagine only that very morning. Pinke filled our mess kits with thick, delicious soup full of potatoes, millet and *kapusta.* We sat on the bench gulping it down without saying another word not caring that it was extremely hot. To us it was like home cooking, and I wondered where Pinke had gotten the supplies. We saw real vegetables swimming in the soup and tasted onions as well.

"Pinke, fabulous! Simply fabulous! Even if you throw us out tomorrow, this soup was worth the experience," I said, and Arthur added some comments of his own. "Let's hope we'll be able to do the work."

"The leader of this group is a former sergeant of the German *Wehrmacht,*" Pinke explained. "His name is Kurt Prange, he's okay, a regular guy. The one with the biggest mouth who always wants to run things and tell everybody what to do is Hans Wehrhahn. He's a typical *Rheinländer,* a *Kölsche Jeck,* (from Cologne) but not as bad as he may seem in the beginning. You're the new ones. Humor him."

Pinke had just finished his sentence when the door flew open, and twelve guys stormed into the little room. All of them looked like pictures of health, muscular and ready for anything. A guy with a reddish round face, thick lips, relatively short blond hair, protruding eyes, and a short neck introduced himself.

"I'm Kurt. They put me in charge, and for all it's worth, I'm responsible for what goes on in this commando and that includes you two. I work like everybody else, and I'll tell you later what you have to do. Now, for everybody's benefit, what are your names?"

"I'm Arthur, and this is Peter," Arthur said. "We're happy to be here."

One by one Kurt introduced us to the others who were regular guys and seemed to be nice until it was Hans's turn.

"My name is Hans. My God, you look like two corpses who jumped out of the death cart. How do you expect to do this work? The sacks you'll have to carry weigh seventy-five to eighty-five kilos [hundred sixty-five to hundred eighty-five pounds] that must be almost twice as much what you weigh. Kurt, I think we should ask for two other guys. These dystrophic looking figures will just eat our soup and bread and expect us to do their work for them."

Arthur and I had been looking at each other while this guy was throwing his weight around. What a pontificating prick! We were about to respond almost simultaneously when Kurt lifted his hand to stop us and turned to Hans.

"I didn't know you had taken over, Hans. Since when are you sitting on such a high horse? I remember when we arrived in this paradise we didn't look any different than Arthur and Peter look now. Shut up and let me decide what this commando will do or not do."

Turning to us he smiled, "Welcome. We only have thirty minutes until our lunch break is over. Arthur, you'll run the coal cart. Pinke will show you where to go and help you with the horse and the other details; it used to be his job before we made him the cook. Peter, you'll join us unloading a few boxcars loaded with flour, which arrived this morning. It costs money every minute they stand on the siding of the factory. It's going to be rough on you, but stay close to me, and I'll show you a few tricks on how to handle a sack of flour without you breaking into two pieces, okay?"

I can't say that Kurt and I ever became close friends, but he was straightforward and fair and didn't allow any bullshit from anybody.

Lunch was over much too soon. I felt as if I never had eaten as much or as well in my entire life. It didn't make me any stronger right away, but it gave me the confidence to know that I would manage the work, no matter what.

As soon as I started lifting and carrying sacks I was in dire need of all that confidence, because the other guys were literally running with the heavy sacks on their backs and were so well practiced handling these monsters that they didn't even need their hands to hold them on their shoulders. Two men lifted a sack and placed it onto the shoulder, and it was, standing upright without any assistance, as if it had grown there. It looked almost artistic. I was struggling. My knees wanted to buckle, and my old war injury and the bullet in my hip were hurting like hell. I was doubling over horizontally as I walked with a sack lying on my back. I was stumbling along, almost falling to the floor, fighting my weak knees to reach the storage building. Getting into the building and climbing on top of the stack of sacks took all my energy. Was I actually supposed to climb up on three sacks? I couldn't make it. Kurt came to my rescue and directed me to throw my sack on the floor as the first of a new pile. I saw stars in front of my eyes, and only the thought of food and bread gave me the strength I no longer possessed.

The end of the shift came as a blessing. I stumbled home toward our little house. The others were way ahead of me, walking loosely and with a quick gait. At that moment, as I passed close to the factory, a door opened and an elderly Russian woman stuck her head out. She waved and called out to me.

"*Woyenna plenny, idi suda.* [Prisoner of war, come here] Mother of God, you must've just arrived. You look awful. Come inside. I have something for you."

She pulled me through the door and handed me a bag full of small pieces of broken bread. She also handed me a metal baking form partly filled with what looked like bubbling, liquid dough.

"Here drink it. It's *droge,* liquid yeast. It tastes sweet, with a little flour mixed in. It's good for you and will make you strong quickly."

I started to drink the thick and creamy substance, a little sour, bubbly and also sweet. I thanked the woman, trying to smile and took the bag with bread and left.

Black bread, in a Russian bread factory, is not baked from kneaded dough, as we know it, but rather "cooked" from liquid dough, it is poured from huge mixing vats into metal forms. Consequently the baked bread is moist and sticky. A limited quantity of liquid yeast is added to the dough, which the Russians called *"droge."* The metal forms were stacked inside the factory by the thousands. The workers, mostly women, had to wipe the inside of each metal form with an oily piece of cloth and place it on a conveyor belt to be filled with dough. Sometimes they didn't do an adequate job with the oily cloth and the bread stuck to the form when others tried to knock out the hot loaf as it came out of the oven. If the bread stuck to the form and broke up they couldn't take it to the market. Most of the broken pieces of bread were worked back into the next batch of dough. Some of the broken bread was taken home by the workers or given to a friend, like the woman had given to me.

The *droge* was potent stuff, almost like a power diet. Every day after work my *sponsor* called me inside the back door and gave me a good portion of the stuff to drink. She also always gave me pieces of broken bread to take home with me. She continued to do so until one day, after about three weeks, she looked at me and remarked, "You look all right now, much better. How do you feel"?

"Otchen xarascho, ja xarascho, bolsche spassibo tibia" (Very good, I am fine. Thank you very much). I replied full of gratitude to my benefactress.

She was an older woman and seemed to have been in the war as a soldier like a lot of the Russian women had been. Yet she had shown a kindness and compassion toward one of her former enemies, which was awesome. As I've said before, "Without the civilians we'd all be dead."

I now looked like a picture of health, a little blown up if you'd asked me, but definitely not dystrophic any more. Believe it or not, stepping on the scale in the warehouse, it displayed seventy-two kilos (hundred seventy-five pounds). I'd gained over sixty-five pounds in three weeks. I didn't check whether my body had absorbed too much water again or not. I really didn't give a damn. What mattered was that I was feeling fine, that I could do my work without any further harassment by my friend Hans, and that the world encouraged me to smile again.

Arthur had gone through a similar process, looking healthy and smiling every once in a while. The boiler room supervisor no longer bothered him about the supply of coal. He provided enough coal with his cart to keep the factory going and that was it. The guy was happy with Arthur's work.

We were content, and Arthur and I started to worry about the next possible calamity. Instead, we received an astonishing piece of news with the next transport of supplies from the camp.

As we came back from work, Pinke greeted us with a big smile at the door of our little house. He was so exited he could hardly stand still.

"Guess what happened!" he yelled to us from afar. "We can write home. We can tell the world that we're alive. They're not going to sweep us under the carpet anymore." He was beside himself and showed it.

The Russians, in collaboration with the International Red Cross, had come to an agreement whereby every prisoner could write a postcard with no more than twenty-five words—including the address of the recipient—to inform relatives in Germany that he was still alive. They even supplied a standard postcard to every one of us. The postcards would have to be written the very next day and delivered to the camp immediately. The return address was provided to us as:

> *Stammlager* 624
> Administration POW
> UdSSR

Of course, we had no writing utensils and contrived mixing a charcoal colored liquid from powdered coal and water and cut pieces of wood, which we split in the front to work as a quill. After a long and heated discussion about what to write with our twenty-five words, the group picked me to compose a message, which would tell the essentials to our families in Germany. The quality of our writing looked more like the accomplishments of a group of analphabetic imbeciles than anything else, but the main thing was that our address and that of the addressee were legible.

After long deliberation with myself, because I didn't know where my mother was or how the people in Berlin had weathered the final days of the war, I wrote to a cousin of mine on my father's side.

She lived in *Kaiserslautern* near the French border. My first attempt to compose the proper message on a piece of newspaper went like this: Frau Erna Hausmann, I wrote. Then eliminated the "Frau" right away to save one of the precious twenty-five words. I tried again:

> Erna Hausmann
> Hauptstrasse 25
> Kaiserslautern/ Pfalz
> Deutschland
> I am alive and well. Inform everybody.
> Pass on my address:
> Stammlager 624
> Administration POW
> UdSSR
> Peter Schwarzlose

The text fit exactly on the backside of the postcard with the address on the front. In the end we had all worked together, polishing the text of this important message, and everybody wrote the same. The postcards went to the camp the next day. We couldn't sleep until late into the night; the excitement and the implications for all of us were overwhelming.

"Now the world knows," Arthur said to me. "Now we will return. I'm positive. This is the happiest day of my life. What do you think, Peter?"

First of all I must admit I was still speechless and close to tears. Where for over two years there had not been a sliver of hope, suddenly there was hope. My mother would know I was alive. No matter where she was, she would receive my message. She could investigate what could be done and hopefully help in finding a solution.

In the end she couldn't do a single thing.

The first Chancellor of the newly created Federal Republic of Germany, Dr. Konrad Adenauer, went to see the Dictator in Moscow to plead our cases. He did everything he could for us. During a state visit to Moscow he left Stalin in the dark as to whether the new Republic of Germany would join the Western Alliance until Stalin committed himself to the return of the POWs and issued orders to release them. The deal was more complicated than I describe it, but Konrad Adenauer finally made the deal.

Arthur and I often discussed what we'd do if our job at the bread factory was discontinued, and we had to return to the camp, thinking of facing the many deprivations and scarcities of camp culture again.

"I totally agree with you, Arthur," I said one evening, as we walked about the compound of the factory where nobody could overhear us. "We'll hang in from now on, no matter what. We won't go through another cycle of starvation, so help me God. But we have to establish some backing in the camp, though, and organize our group into something more cohesive, more effective, just in case the Russians decide to send us back to the camp before they send us home. In general prisoners are egotistic, only willing to look out for themselves. Beware how they'll react if we have to go back to the camp and the going gets rough."

"You have a perceptive mind, my friend. That's my opinion, too," Arthur said. "If we should be sent back to the camp, this whole group needs to stick together to hold onto our health and new found strength. What do you propose we do?"

"First, Arthur, you'll have to involve the voice of authority in our plans and that's Kurt," I replied. "I'll tell you the details in a minute. But you'll have to be the guy to sell him on this plan. Being the youngest of the group I'm not the best person to be considered an authority among our friends. You, as a former sergeant, like Kurt, had more rank in the army than I as a simple corporal. Don't object. That's the way it is. It certainly plays a part in the back of their minds even if you are laughing. Now here's my plan. First, we establish a fund. I mean money, a sort of war chest to help the group overcome hard times. We have to get everybody involved in contributing to this fund. I suggest that Kurt be the custodian.

"Secondly, should we ever have to go back to the camp, we'll have to take care beforehand to have some clout within our administration. That would mean, for instance, that our group would be housed and work together as one group and not be fragmented again like they did with us at the beginning of our captivity. Remember *Budweiss?*

"Thirdly, let's agree never to discuss the details of, or any changes in, our plan in the presence of the others. Whatever we discuss remains between the two of us, okay? You are the man, the tactician, right? If we need to talk, we'll take a walk in the evening or use other opportunities when we're alone. How about it? What do you think about my concept so far?"

Arthur looked at me and chuckled, shaking his head. "Peter, you never cease to amaze me. You look like sweet sixteen. Your beard is just begining to grow, but you behave like an old veteran of the war and talk like a sixty year old. Where do you get these brainstorms? But, yes, seriously, I like your plan. How do you propose to get money?"

Shortly after we arrived at the bread factory, Arthur and I began to wonder where the onions, the special vegetables, and other food items had come from.

Then one night, after about two weeks in the factory, we were awakened by a knock on the outside window of our house.

The wall of the house was positioned flush with the fence of the factory. It was actually part of it. A window was cut into the outside wall, one foot wide and one foot high. It was secured with a double crossed iron bar. The iron was as thick as a finger and served to prevent us from escaping or to prohibit intrusions from the outside by potential thieves.

That night somebody knocked at the window. Kurt jumped out of his bed, and Pinke hurried toward our supply of bread to grab a few loaves. Kurt whispered to the rest of us, "It's the Black Hand. I'll see how many loaves he wants this time and how much he wants to pay."

He opened the window silently. The hinges miraculously were well greased. As the window opened, a hand with a crude black glove reached through between the iron bars. Four fingers of the hand were raised.

"Pinke, he wants four loaves." Kurt whispered, and Pinke hurried to give Kurt the bread.

"Pa tchom?" (How much?) Kurt whispered through the window, and the Black Hand reappeared with a hundred-ruble note.

"Ladna, xarascho" (okay, good) Kurt whispered and pushed the four loaves through the opening, receiving four hundred ruble notes in return.

The window closed. Arthur and I noticed that everybody in the room was wide-awake. Pinke took the money and said, "Kurt, you'd better explain to Arthur and Peter what we just did. We don't want any wild speculations disturbing their sleep."

Kurt came over to our cots near the door and whispered—you never knew who could be spying on us from the outside—"that's the Black Hand. He suddenly appeared at this window, shortly after our arrival, offering to buy bread."

From that day on the POWs had saved whole loaves supplied by the camp for the Black Hand. They had eaten the broken bread instead, swiped almost daily from the factory. The money was the source of funds to buy vegetables and a little fat and sugar from the market outside. Kurt wanted to know whether or not we also agreed to these transactions, because they weren't without danger and whether or not Pinke should treat our bread rations the same way. Of course, we agreed. We participated in the spoils handsomely.

I asked Kurt how the Black Hand managed to get so close to the outside window of our little house without being detected by the guards. The bread factory—like all the other fenced off compounds—had a well-raked safety zone around its parameter.

"Sometime when we are outside, Peter, you can make an inconspicuous pass by our window and look for yourself. You'll notice there's a cinder block lying exactly underneath our window close to the wall. We assume that the Black Hand put it there to cover the width of the raked ground with a wooden board, which rests on top of the cinder block. He puts one end on the stone and walks safely across the raked area. Smart guy! He avoids touching the ground with his feet. When I say this, I have to admit I assume he does, because I've never seen him or tried to investigate it more closely. I'm happy the way it's working. So, don't to talk to anybody about it, okay?"

Of course, I agreed. I wasn't idiotic enough to jeopardize a good deal when I saw one.

"Have you counted how many loaves we've sold since we arrived two months ago?" I said to Arthur in response to his question about the money. "I think the whole operation can be run more efficiently, and I think that after talking to Kurt you should take control of it. We can still continue to live in royal splendor but be able to accumulate money for the purpose I explained to you. Do you agree?"

"I do completely, and I'll talk to Kurt the next chance I get, promise."

These two had their discussion, very secretly, very privately, and Kurt, who was no dummy, talked to the others. One by one he pulled them into the boat. Hans, of course, tried to be difficult but acquiesced in the end.

Just because we had enough food didn't mean our lives were easy. To be a *grushik* is hard work. You either carried the sacks from the boxcar into the warehouse or lifted them from the ground to place them onto the shoulders of the *grushik*. Twelve to sixteen *grushiks*— and some Russians always joined us in our work—carried them into the warehouse. A boxcar contained 700 to 800 sacks of flour depending on the weight of the sacks and how well they were stacked. Look at it this way, lifting 700 sacks in rapid succession is almost impossible even if one is trained, practiced, and strong. The two 'lifters' were exchanged two or three times during the unloading of a boxcar. Running with the sacks and climbing up five or six sacks— the height to which the sacks were stacked—with a heavy load on your back is hard work too. Usually we unloaded a boxcar in two and a half hours and changed assignments frequently.

The Russian economy had not weathered the war well. How could it? Too much money was in circulation, and during the war the printing presses had worked around the clock with the result that inflation was rampant. In the beginning of 1948 the Soviets deflated the value of the ruble ten to one without any advance notice to their population. They issued new paper money with a different design.

We were lucky this happened at the beginning of our "war chest." Kurt had a hard time exchanging the old rubles we had accumulated against new rubles. He took a ten percent loss, paying a commission to the guy who went to the bank for us. It was the Uzbek guard from the gate. From now on the Black Hand offered ten rubles for one loaf, which was fine with us. All prices for supplies changed similarly.

The *Natchalnik* in charge of the entire factory was a tall man of about forty years. You didn't see many tall people in *Stalinsk*. I'm six feet tall, and on occasion when I walked through the town, people would turn around, because to them I was tall. The *Natchalnik,* the "Blue One," as we called him, because he was always dressed in solid blue, like a uniform, was about six foot six. He was an imposing figure by any stretch of the imagination. At times he came to check on our work, usually yelling *"bistray, bistray"* (faster, faster), because the next boxcar was waiting outside the rail gate. The fee paid per boxcar, while standing on the siding of the factory, was high, and he wanted to save money. When he appeared, everybody ran a few steps faster. This wasn't only the case with us prisoners. The Russian *grushiks* were intimidated by his presence as well. He had an intelligent face, penetrating eyes, and a protruding chin. One could easily see he was used to exercising authority.

It was evening and already pitch dark when somebody knocked loudly at the door of our house. I went to answer it.

Mind you, our little house was old. It must have been built before the factory was constructed. It had a small door made for small people and to keep the cold out in the winter. My own six feet barely fit through without bending my head, but I did so as a precaution anyway because the height of the inside door was only six foot two.

That evening, as I opened the door, the doorframe was filled with this blue giant. He appeared to be even bigger because he wore a *fufeika* loosely draped around his shoulders.

"Ponjumaish pa Russki?" (Do you understand Russian?) He barked at me, and I replied immediately, *"Da, ponjumaiu."*

He barely opened the *fufeika,* which hung around his shoulders, revealing two loaves of bread hidden under it. "Here, sell 'em for me. I know you can do it. I'll return in a few days to pick up the money. Eight rubles per loaf, okay?" He turned without giving me a chance to reply and walked off.

I stood there totally aghast. How did he know that we sold bread? I turned and saw the rest of the group looking at me equally stunned. Everybody wanted to know what the *Natchalnik* had said. I told them.

After a minute Arthur opened his mouth. "Come to think of it, this house probably has been occupied by generations of prisoners before we arrived on the scene. The Black Hand knew it, and now we know the *Natchalnik* knows it, too. I think he means what he said. Personally, I believe he has no way to smuggle bread out of the factory even if he wants to. *Natchalnik* or not, money is something we all need and never have enough. Even a *Natchalnik* needs it. Who knows what he wants to buy with his sixteen new rubles, but who cares. Let's sell the bread for him, and we'll have a powerful friend."

"That's what you think," Hans objected vigorously. "What if he only wants to test us only to return later with a command of soldiers to arrest us and throw us in jail?"

"Oh, yes?" Arthur cut in. "Are you going to give his bread back to him when he returns and risk that he sends all of us back to the camp because we're too stupid and inept? Did you see the way he came here with the bread hidden under his *fufeika?* Is that the demeanor of a man who wants to test you? No my friend, he needs *mula, diengi,* money. He wants to use us because he knows we are POWs and will keep our mouths shut."

Arthur was getting agitated, and I was grateful he had spoken before I blew my stack. The discussion between the men raged on for several more minutes until Kurt finally decided to step in.

"We are going to sell the bread for the *Natchalnik,* and that's final."

Kurt was often a little pompous for my taste, but I must say he upheld his authority and knew when to use it.

After a few days and at the usual time, after the onset of darkness, the Black Hand knocked at the little window, and the deal was consummated. The bad part was that he only wanted four loaves. On the other hand, we were able to net two rubles on each of the two loaves we sold for the *Natchalnik.*

True to his promise the "Blue One" reappeared a few nights later and asked for "Petja," me. I went to the door, which was totally filled by his frame. He stretched out his hand towards me without saying a word. I gave him sixteen new rubles. He turned without looking at me, and left. This procedure repeated itself every few weeks, and nobody objected any more.

Life continued to be good to us. We had enough to eat, better food than ever before during the last three years, and we were strong enough to do whatever was asked of us.

The factory was an interesting place to be, not only because we had enough to eat. On one assignment a Russian had taken me inside the building to work with him on something or other. I looked around in the dark, fifty-foot high warehouse, and I wondered why the ceiling was not painted white like everything else. I asked the guy, and he just laughed.

"It's white, but it's covered with millions of cockroaches. Of course, you can't see them from down here, but they're there. Believe you me. They are everywhere. It's impossible to get rid of them without poison. Poison in a bread factory is worse than cockroaches, don't you agree? What do you do with cockroaches in the bread factories in Germany?"

To satisfy his curiosity and to tell him the truth I would have had to go through a long explanation about bakeries in Germany, the private sector, the retail scene, and all. I didn't like doing that. I had learned from previous occasions it was best to agree with them and skirt the issue about how different life was in the Soviet Union.

I replied, "We handle it the same way. It seems to be practical." The subject was closed.

Now I knew why the metal forms for the bread were passed over a red-hot iron plate before reentering the manufacturing process—to kill the cockroaches before they were baked together with the bread. As the metal forms passed over the red-hot metal, they became very hot. The cockroaches jumped out, landed on the glowing plate and disintegrated with a puff. I've mentioned before that the Russians had a practical solution for everything. This was not exactly a hygienic method, but it served the purpose of getting rid of the vermin.

Usually the guards at the entrance of the factory let us pass unmolested to go to the open-air market, which was only a few hundred yards from the factory. As we passed, they made sure we weren't smuggling any bread. Everybody passing the gate—and that included the *Natchalnik*—was patted down while their arms were raised horizontally. The guards went down both arms, the side of the body, the back, between the legs, and down to the floor with practiced motions. After that a short command followed, "Idi" (Go).

Every once in a while some idiot thought he might fool those guys. No way. And prison was not worth a loaf of bread.

With the money that came through the little window, we went to the market to buy our supplies and to improve the quality of our diet. At times the camp would supply the weirdest items, and we didn't question any more why the food in the camp had always been so bad. With one of the deliveries from the camp, we received as part of our rations a sack with thinly sliced, dried potatoes. They looked grayish brown, were not peeled, and smelled awful, almost rotten.

None of us wanted to eat them. We were too spoiled, and Pinke suggested we throw them away.

"How do you want me to cook this stuff? I can't even clean it properly, and it'll spoil the taste of anything else in the soup."

"Wait a minute." Hans piped in with a big grin on his stupid face. "Our big mouth here, Mr. Know-it-all, will solve the problem." He was pointing at me. "I'm sure Peter can take the sack to the market and sell the potato slices to the Russians, let's say forty *Kopek* [Hundred *kopek* to a ruble] *stacan.* What do you say?"

The shouting and laughing were overpowering.

"Yes, that'll bolster our reserve fund." Or, "He's the right man. He'll turn a profit on anything," and similar stupid wisecracks.

Nobody asked me, and I could hardly object. Finally I relented, took the sack, went to the gate and asked permission to leave. They let me pass after examining the sack thoroughly. I passed to go to the bazaar, sat down, opened my sack of sliced potatoes, put a *stacan* on top and waited. I didn't know what to say. I had observed during previous visits that the civilians didn't talk much, just sat there, or waited until somebody asked for the price. That's what I did.

The first Russian who came by walked past me, looked at the sliced potatoes, turned around, and asked, "How much?"

"Tchatiernazed Kopeke stacan" (forty Kopek a glass), I said.

"Okay, five *stacan,"* the guy said. I measured well, poured the merchandise into a cloth bag, which he had pulled from his pants and held open for me. He paid me two rubles. It didn't take three minutes before people surrounded me, practically ripping the stuff out of my hands. At forty *Kopekes stacan,* business was good, and I went home with a pile of money after only twenty minutes.

That same evening the Uzbek guard from the gate came to our house, almost laughing his head off as he entered the door. They always liked to come to sample our soup.

"Petja, you scoundrel, what did you do? You sold sliced, dried potatoes to these poor people pretending they were sliced, dried apples, you smart little sob. *Yibit twoyu matj* [Fuck your mother]. How did you manage to do it? I mean, what did you tell them? Everybody could see they were potatoes."

My fellow prisoners started to laugh. When I had come home with the money, they had wondered how I'd sold this awful looking stuff so quickly, and I couldn't even explain it myself.

"Didn't I tell you he can sell the tits off a nun if he has to?" Hans yelled boisterously.

Now I started to protest. "I never said anything about apples. I never said anything at all about the product! The first guy came, looked at the slices, and asked for the price. I told him forty *Kopekes,* and he bought five *stacan.* After that it was a riot. They couldn't get the stuff out of the sack fast enough."

The guard laughed. "It's too late now anyway, Petja, but I suggest you don't go outside for the next few weeks. If any one of the buyers recognizes your face, they'll beat you severely, believe me."

I had nothing against it. I didn't like the market anyway.

It was in April 1948 with the winter almost gone when the "Blue One" knocked on our door, pointed at me and barked, "Petja, *idi,"* turned and walked away. He wanted me to follow him, which I quickly did with a woozy feeling in my stomach. What did the guy want from me this time? I followed him all the way to his office. I'd never been in the administrative building before. It looked grandiose but needed paint everywhere. His office was as impressive as I'd imagined Mr. Rockefeller's office to be rather than the office of a *Natchalnik* in charge of a Siberian bread factory.

He flopped down on a big leather armchair, threw his legs on the desk in front of him and barked, "Sit down, Petja. I've got to talk to you. I know you're an intelligent man. You're the only one of these dumb prisoners who speaks enough of our beautiful language to converse with me intelligently. Now, Petja, you'll interrupt me if you don't understand anything I say, all right?"

"I have understood you so far, *Natchalnik,* but please try to speak slowly. I don't know all the vocabulary you're using."

"*Ladna, charascho,* I'm having a problem right now. You can help me solve it. Our factory has been offered a wonderful opportunity to buy a large quantity of high-grade flour at a greatly reduced price. I'd like to take advantage of it. Now, here's my idea. I'll put you in charge of a purchasing expedition, traveling up north past *Nowosibirsk* with a truck and a driver, to a *sovchos* [State operated agricultural complex] that we do business with to execute the deal. It involves twenty boxcars of flour, about one thousand tons, maybe a little more. At times—even though we live in the Soviet Union— there are differences in prices depending on a situation, the season, the harvest, and the people involved. My old friend, Boris Ivanovitch, at the *sovchos* offered us a fabulous deal." I was trying to respond, but he lifted his hand to stop me before I opened my mouth.

"If I send a team of my own people or some Russian blokes with a team recommended by the main administration, I wouldn't get twenty boxcars but only nineteen. They'd tell me a cock-and-bull story about the disappearance of the twentieth boxcar, but when the dust settles, they'll have stolen a whole boxcar of flour. It always happens that way. I know it, believe me." He stared at me intently as if trying to hypnotize me and continued.

"Now the way I'm figuring, you prisoners aren't angels, but your advantage is that you're afraid to get into trouble because all of you want to get home eventually, and you have no connections here in Siberia to strike such a deal. Maybe you'll steal one sack of flour. That's okay as long as I share in the profits, but otherwise you're too timid to endanger your return to your mama and papa or whoever is waiting for you back home.

"I also know you people normally don't speak Russian, and I couldn't send just anybody who doesn't understand what's going on around him. That would be foolish, wouldn't it? In your case it's different. You speak Russian well enough to conduct the little transaction

I have in mind. And what's also important is that, from what I have observed, you're good with figures and fast on your feet. I loved the deal with the dried potato slices you sold at the market."

He laughed uproariously and slapped his thighs, and I wondered what else he knew about us prisoners and about me. When he calmed down, he looked at me seriously again, piercingly.

"I'm fully aware you're a *woyenna plenny* [POW] and I shouldn't endanger you in any way, or let you get caught outside of our factory. I'll see to it that you're properly protected and that nobody will know you have gone on this mission, I promise."

I was about to interrupt him again when he lifted his hand once more to shut me up.

"Now, Petja, before you answer hastily or form a final opinion, I'd like to remind you that I'm a prudent businessman. I know how to enforce and to finalize what I have planned. In this case, I'm sorry to inform you that if you choose to refuse my proposal, I'll make sure you return to the camp with the next supply truck." He tilted his chair back, pulled his boots from the table with a bang. He leaned forward and wrinkled his forehead saying, "Now you know the whole story. What do you say?"

I looked down at my shoes for a few seconds then looked up at him and smiled. "When do I go?"

The "Blue One" tilted his head back and laughed a throaty laugh, got up from the table, came around to my side, and embraced me with a bear hug. "Petja, you are my favorite prisoner of war. I've not misjudged you. I want you to be my friend. There are only a few people in this world who have a perceptive mind, can recognize an opportunity and seize upon it immediately. You are one of them. I am Nikolai Nikolajewitch, and we are friends."

I must admit I didn't understand his message as fluently as I'm telling it now, but Nikolai Nikolajewitch had taken great pains to speak slowly, to make sure I understood what he wanted to tell me, and had watched me closely for affirmations. What could I have said? His proposal was straight forward and his threat, too.

He became a true friend and was there to prove it when I needed him.

When I came back, the guys couldn't believe what I told them and made many suggestions.

"Don't try to run away. You'll never make it—it's too far." This came from Hans the idiot, who couldn't conceive one original thought by himself.

"Watch out that nobody sees you. Some damned guard might want to pin another medal on his chest."

"How're you going to negotiate? They'll know and hear immediately that you're no Russian. You have an accent." (The story of my life.)

Arthur looked at me, smiled, and nodded his head. He knew I would handle it, and he trusted my judgment.

Many more comments were made, most of them similar to those that had crossed my mind while sitting in front of Nikolai Nikolajewitch, the *Natchalnik* of the bread factory and my new friend.

I didn't have a choice, and if you don't have a choice, you'll do what you have to do and make it work. That much I'd learned by then.

When we started off, I couldn't understand why we took the old ZIS (*Zavoda Imenina Stalin* = factory named Stalin) truck that had seen better days, to go as far as *Novosibirsk* and a few miles further to the northwest in the direction of the Urals. We could just as well have taken the railroad and would have arrived at our destination much faster and more conveniently. And on our way back, we wouldn't have had to worry about that stupid truck breaking down. Nikolai Nikolajewitch wanted us to take the truck, and he didn't bother to explain to me the minor details of the mission. He trusted my judgment, and he probably feared I might chicken out in the end and was happy I'd decided to go. He even assured me he had excellent papers for me and that nobody would bother me. The longer I thought about this adventure of a prisoner of war gallivanting around in an old truck through the endless expanses of the Siberian countryside, the crazier it became.

"Don't worry where you have to go, Petja, or ask for a map. You just go where this gangster, Vanja, is taking you," he said when we parted, handing me a thick envelope. "Give this to my friend Boris Ivanovitch at the *sovchos* after the loading of the flour has been completed to *your* satisfaction, *ladna?!*"

Those were his final instructions, and I intended to follow them. The alternative had not been appealing to me. I considered this trip might even turn out to be fun.

The designated driver, Vanja, was a pleasant, talkative, permanently hungry guy. He was young with a typical Russian haircut—very short in the back and on top, with long hair in front, tousled in wild curls and sticking out from under a cap, which he was constantly pushing forward until it was resting almost on the tip of his nose. With the hair and the cap I wondered how he'd see where he was going. If he wasn't smoking, he ate roasted *sjemitchki* (sunflower seeds), which he carried in his bottomless pants pockets. He was always on the lookout for food and girls. The description of a chain smoker fitted him to a T. He smoked *maxorka* wrapped in newspaper all day without interruption. But he knew his assignment; he knew where we were going, and he found his way unerringly.

With mostly bumpy dirt roads to travel on, it took us the better part of two days of continuous slow driving to cover a few hundred miles. At night we slept in the community house of a small *kolchos*. Vanja seemed to know them all. They were not very comfortable but clean. My head was sore from permanently bumping on the metal roof of the cabin and the violent shaking of the truck as it negotiated the obstacle course of worn out roads.

In contrast to the condition of roads in the former Soviet Union, the railroad network was well maintained and ubiquitously present in every little town. At that time, real roads, covered with macadam or concrete were nonexistent. For comparison of size, the former USSR stretched over twelve lines of longitude and over seven time zones. It's more than twice as wide as the United States.

Before we left, Nikolai Nikolajewitch had provided clothes for me less conspicuous than our usual POW garb. Ordinarily we wore a combination of bits and pieces of torn and leftover German uniform parts and typical Government Issue prison clothes and a typical German military cap with a visor. The new clothes were old but distinctly Russian, typical of what most civilians were wearing—in short, inconspicuous and ordinary. With the outfit came a wrinkled cap that was of particular attraction to me. The cap of a young Russian male is his fashion statement. It was worn with great pride and attempt at individualism. I'd always wanted a cap like that and decided to ask the "Blue One" if I could keep mine after the job was done.

Leaving the area of *Stalinsk,* well known for the many political prisoner and POW camps, we were stopped repeatedly. Vanja's valid papers and my falsified ones were checked diligently. I don't have to stress that I kept my mouth shut and didn't volunteer to strike up a conversation with the policemen.

I had never entertained the thought of trying to escape from Siberia, not only on account of the distance from *Stalinsk* to the center of Europe—over 4,000 miles—but also because of my physical condition. There were many other reasons as well, and the most important was that deep down in my heart I'd never given up hope that our captors would let us go back sooner or later. During my entire time in Siberia I remember only one successful escape. The prisoner left his place of work, turned south, and made it on foot across the Altai and the Himalayas all the way to India. At least that's what we had heard, but we had no way finding out whether it was true or not.

Driving in the truck with Vanja, I observed how deeply the net of police surveillance covered and penetrated the entire country. If one patrol didn't catch the fugitive, the next one would be more successful for sure. I had no intention of testing this net.

If I had known the ramifications and hazards of this trip beforehand, I wouldn't have agreed to it. Every time an official police patrol waved us to a stop, I started sweating as in a sauna, all the while looking as nonchalant as I could. Crazy or not so crazy thoughts raced through my mind about what they'd do with me, or to me, after they discovered who was hiding behind those inconspicuous looking clothes.

But the good Lord was watching over me one more time and protected my charade.

Taking a look at Siberia from a truck taught me that it was a much more beautiful countryside than I had assumed. As we passed by I could see many little brooks and streams, beautiful old forests, and gently rolling hills. It reminded me of a trip to upstate New York traveling toward Elmira near the Finger Lakes.

A *sovchos* is a state-owned agricultural complex, much larger than a *kolkhoz,* which is like a commune owned by the village, consisting of the usual array of rundown buildings, rusted grain silos, and broken-down farm machinery one would be confronted with everywhere in Russia, not only in Siberia. An equally dismal looking, tiny village was close by. But it had a rail siding, and, believe it or not, when we arrived we saw twenty empty boxcars ready and waiting for our shipment.

After meeting Boris Ivanovitch, the *Natchalnik* who had been fully clued in, by Nikolai Nikolajewitch, Vanja and I had our hands full to supervise the counting and loading of fifteen thousand sacks of flour. We were counting the sacks, as they were loaded into each boxcar, supervising the closing of each car and its certification and sealing. The *sovchos* men were quick, worked hard, and completed the job in only three days. Now was the time to hand over the envelope Nikolai Nikolajewitch had given to me for his business partner. Everything was completed to *my* satisfaction. I asked him to step aside and pulled it out of my *fufika,* where I had hidden it carefully during all this time, never taking the jacket off, not even while sleeping.

Boris Ivanowitch opened the envelope, read the letter, and examined the contents. It must have pleased the *Natchalnik,* because he laughed.

"That old devil. He is always ready to strike a deal, *ladna.* Petja, you're a good man. It was a pleasure meeting you, the *woyenna plenny.* In his letter Nikolai Nikolajewitch speaks highly of you. Let's all go and have a celebration and drink to the completion of the deal. I think after this hard work everybody descrves it."

People like to party, and the *Sibiriakis* are no different in that respect. Vanja and I and the people from the *sovchos* organized the food and the drinks, and the women started to cook all kinds of little Russian specialties. There was fabulous *borscht,* deep-fried *piroschkis,* and plenty of freshly baked white and dark bread, and to top it off, the *Natchalnik* provided a few bottles of vodka. Somebody wheeled in a barrel of home made *kvas* (a beer made from bread and sugar), and the party started.

The community hall of the *sovchos* where the party took place was as drab on the inside as it was on the outside, with the exception of the usual slogans and banners that decorated the walls. However, the people were great, and the atmosphere was gregarious and friendly with lots of laughter and plenty of jokes I didn't understand flying back and forth. Working with them, and now eating and drinking, enjoying their hospitality, made it difficult for me to hide my true identity.

"Germanski, da?" the fellow next to me asked quite pleasantly. When I nodded, he continued, "Good, don't worry about it. This is Siberia, and everybody here has a past, good, bad or indifferent. Very few want to be here except the native *sibiriakis,* and there aren't many of them." And then it came, the stereotypical question every Russian had to ask. "Gitler kaput?" With the inability to pronounce an H, to say Hitler, he repeated what hundreds of Russians had asked before him, is Hitler dead?

That kind of talk I heard from all sides, men and women alike, all evening. Many of them made an effort to tell me how they felt towards me, the POW. It was a wonderful display of sympathy and understanding, which warmed my heart and made me grateful and mindful again that, as was said repeatedly, "Without the civilians, the prisoners would all be dead."

As the evening wore on and after many glasses of *kvas* and a few *stacan* of vodka, a young girl across the wooden table started to flirt with me. After two years as a prisoner, after all the hardships I had suffered, and after my physical breakdowns, it was the first time I had looked at a girl with the eyes of a man.

The girl was a typical peasant woman with a full, round, shining face and high cheekbones, bespeaking her Slavic heritage. Her head was covered with the obligatory white scarf, a little blond hair peeking out. And she could laugh and have fun like the best of them. Above the table where we were sitting, chatting away, I could see a fully cut white blouse, which was tied at the neck, but revealed well-proportioned breasts underneath. She seemed to be full of life and fun and ready to live up to the moment. I laughed at her and was just starting to warm to the occasion when I realized Vanja had seen us. He raised one eyebrow imperceptibly and shook his head ever so slightly. I guess he wanted to tell me, "Don't get into trouble." He didn't really have to warn me, as good as the girl's attentions made me feel, I was longing to get back to the safety of the factory all in one piece. I wasn't going to endanger my safety or violate the trust that Nikolai Nikolajewitch had placed in me.

Somewhat uneasily we staggered back to the truck after the evening came to an end. Vanja took me to the front of the vehicle and busied himself with the hood of the engine. He raised it ever so slightly to allow me to peek under it. I could clearly see a sack of flour fitted tightly on top of the engine.

"My God, Vanja," I stuttered, "where did you get that from. Did anybody see you?"

"Are you kidding? They put it there for us; I didn't do a thing. Why do you think Nikolai Nikolajewitch wanted us to take the truck? The *sovchos* was happy that we came, and they wanted to show us their appreciation. We'll sell it on our way home, and everybody gets one third. Nikolai Nikolajewitch, you and I, *ladna? Xarascho?*"

Three hundred new rubles for each one of us, the way I figured it from the going price for a sack of flour on the open market. Not bad. Now all that was left to decide was whether we'd send the train off in the morning by itself, or whether I'd accompany the precious freight. Vanja suggested he should take the truck, sell the flour on the black market on his way, and that I should ride with the engineer in his compartment making sure the train didn't have any "unscheduled" stops on the way.

The engineer wasn't happy with the surveillance. I guess he'd counted his chickens before they were hatched. I made sure our purchases arrived all in one piece, so to speak.

Would anybody ever believe my story? I was wondering to myself on the way back. In the middle of Siberia I, the *woyenna plenny,* had acted as the purchasing agent for a bread factory.

Nikolai Nikolajewitch was happy when we arrived with all twenty boxcars. My buddies were happy about the three hundred rubles, which gave a welcome boost to our war chest, and I breathed a sigh of relief when the gates of the railroad siding closed behind me. I'd returned safely behind a fence.

By the way, Nikolai Nikolajewitch let me keep the cap.

"We're coming to point two of my plan," I said to Arthur as we walked around outside of the house. "We haven't done anything so far to endear ourselves to the administration of the camp, and that's very important. We haven't polished any apples, nor have we done anything to make new friends. You have to talk to Kurt to move his ass. He has to do something in this direction. I think it would be best if he and I go to the camp before the next delivery of supplies is due and spread some good will. What I'm talking about, of course, is bread. A few loaves of bread distributed judiciously among the proper people will go a long way when the time comes."

Arthur agreed, and a week later Kurt and I were on our way to the camp with a truck, courtesy of Nikolai Nikolajewitch. I had told him about my plan, and he had replied, "By all means do it. Nothing is more effective than to grease a man's palm, and none of us knows what the future holds, especially if you're a prisoner of war."

When we arrived at the camp, I went immediately to see Fritz. In my estimation he would be the best contact to help us with our plan, and he was the most deserving one, too. Many things in the lives of the prisoners were decided by the German administration inside the camp, and he was at the center of it.

He was happy to see me in excellent health. As a matter of fact he couldn't get over how well I looked. After we exchanged all the customary pleasantries, I opened my *fufika* and pulled a loaf of bread from under it, and put it on the table in front of him. He took one quick look and let it disappear into a drawer without blinking an eye.

"Fritz," I said, "do you know how long we're going to stay at the bread factory?" He only shrugged his shoulders, looking at me with a question mark in his eyes and I went on. "Of course, one never knows, and it's always best to be prepared. I'd like to ask you to do us a favor."

"Shoot."

"As soon as you hear anything of a possible recall to the camp, could you organize it so all of us from the bread factory will be housed together in one corner of a barrack, and that we'll all go to the same place of work? We'll be eternally grateful and will show our appreciation."

"I think I can help you with that, and I'm looking forward to your next visit. Don't stay away that long again."

I understood his message loud and clear, as he had understood mine. Living in that bloody camp, he was hungry as a bear and had few opportunities to get any food over and beyond his normal rations.

Before I left, there was one more thing I wanted to ask of Fritz. "Have you ever heard of Ernst Stepski? To use his full name in civilian life, Ernst von Stepski Edler von Donovan. He's Austrian. I worked with him in the stone quarry at the *Kolchos* camp. Is he still around?"

"You know the Austrians have concluded a separate peace treaty with the Russians, don't you? The so called *Staatsvertrag.*" He looked at me with raised eyebrows, and I shook my head. "Well, they did. Shortly thereafter orders came from Moscow to assemble all Austrians for a trip back home. Two weeks later they left. With them in the same transport were 30 Germans who had the dropsy and were in such miserable shape we don't know whether they made it or not. Your old friend, Kalle, was among them. He looked like a corpse when he left. Don't ask me what happened to them. We haven't heard a word."

I left Fritz's office and stood in front of the barrack contemplating my fate. I had not been so unlucky, after all. I never found out what happened to those two.

Kurt talked to a few of his friends, and when we left we were all squared away. From now on we made regular trips to the camp, every two weeks, to pick up our supplies, and made everybody happy with our edible presents.

At the end of June 1948 the door of our little house opened, and Nikolai Nikolajewitch stood in front of it with a sad face. He almost looked as if he was ready to cry. He wanted to talk to me.

"Petja, the POW's administration is too greedy. They have increased the charges for your work by over 22%. By now *woyenna plenny* are 40% more expensive than our own people. My administration isn't going to go along with these increases any longer. I'm telling you now, because if we're unable to negotiate a better deal, we'll have to let you go back to the camp. I'm going to miss you, all of you, and particularly you, my friend. You've been the best workers we've ever had." He spat out one of these drastic curses. *"Yibit twoiu bocha matj,* if only I could do something about it," he said then turned and left.

I translated that for the others, and we sat in silence and total consternation.

Our arrival in the camp at the end of July 1948 didn't cause a ruffle. Nobody noticed us except the guys in the third barracks near the entrance who were being reshuffled to make room for us. Our contacts did what they had promised to do.

12

BACK AT THE CITY CAMP

The Russians delivered one further proof that they had recognized our existence. Every prisoner received two pounds of sugar.

The Geneva Convention, among other things, stipulated that prisoners of war receive a daily ration of seventeen grams of sugar (about seven ounces). We hadn't seen sugar since we were taken prisoner, almost three years ago, or thousand days without any sugar. It would have been too much to expect thirty-eight pounds of sugar to make up for this omission. It was a miracle that we received any sugar at all. But, too much of a good thing can be a bad thing, and that is what happened to the sugar. Eating that much sugar causes diarrhea. The POWs had too little protein in their system and on top of it they were terribly hungry. Some ate the sugar in one or two sittings. That's intolerable for your digestion if you are undernourished. We, the ex-bread factory *grushiks,* were better organized. We sweetened our *kascha,* put a little sugar on our bread and made the two pounds last for over two weeks. In short, we tried to behave sensibly and were disciplined.

At work we had also established begging routines to keep us in bread. If bread became scarce, we dipped into our war chest and bought some on the open market.

The injury to my mouth, during the war in Italy, not only smashed my jaw, but also seriously damaged many of my teeth. It started to show. The thin wires, which had been tied temporarily around the base of each tooth, aggravated the decay further. They had served as anchors for the rubber bands that kept the jaw closed. All this had been done in the hospital at *Cortina D'Ampezzo* where they'd fed me a diet of sweet vanilla and chocolate soup. The sweet stuff damaged the enamel on my teeth. Last but not least, during the last two years of the war I had other things to worry about than going to the dentist, and I don't have to explain that prison camps in Siberia don't have dentists. On top of all that—for lack of a toothbrush and toothpaste, or soap—I hadn't brushed my teeth for the last three years. During the first days of our captivity knowledgeable Russian soldiers had taken all toothbrushes from us. My teeth were hurting now, hurting badly. Of course, there was no aspirin, no painkillers of any kind. Eating sugar had reminded me, quite painfully, of my infirmity.

Always full of surprises, the Russians announced one day that anybody who wanted to visit a dentist should report to the administration. They'd set up an appointment to see a local dentist. I was one of the first to accept that offer.

A week later a guard from the camp chaperoned us into town to visit the office of a nice and capable female dentist. She was about forty years old and looked very efficient. The office was clean as a whistle, and the assistant wore a spotless white smock. When my turn came, I was directed to an old-fashioned dentist chair—she called it a *"stuhl,"* another word acquired from the German language—and told me to open my mouth. After a preliminary examination she explained in great detail to her assistant the elaborate work done to my teeth and to my jaw. Then she addressed me—speaking slowly using both of her hands—explaining how many holes I had in my teeth. I answered in halting Russian and surprised her by asking to fix as many holes as possible in one sitting. I did this because I was doubtful how many more times the camp would allow us to return.

She was an excellent dentist and did a great job. Under the prevailing method practiced by dentists, she drilled all teeth needing treatment and filled holes with temporary fillings to be finished during my next sitting, which was set for two weeks hence.

So far so good. After a short while the pain of the teeth she treated was killing me. As I had suspected, the camp administration decided to cancel all future visits to the dentist. I was left with temporary fillings in my mouth. I could only wait until they fell out, some sooner, some later. Once the temporary fillings were gone the root canals were without protection and decayed further. Soon the nerves in the decaying teeth were fully exposed.

"Why don't you pull out the nerves yourself?"

This was from Hans, the asshole.

"Are you out of your mind?" I replied. "Do you know how an exposed nerve hurts without touching it? And you suggest to me that I pull them out by myself? How'd you do that anyway?"

"Oh, I don't know, but if the tooth hurts as much as you tell me—mind you I never had a toothache in my entire life, so I don't know—I'd do something about it. Do you want to wait until they ship us back home? That may take a few more years, you know?" He laughed one of his dirty laughs probably thinking he had been funny.

"The guy is an absolute moron," was Arthur's opinion about Hans. "He's probably looking forward to the day when you'll actually do it, because the pain will be unbearable. He wants to watch you squirm. But seriously, what're you going to do about it?"

I looked at Arthur with my swollen cheeks and said,

"He's such an idiot, but he got me thinking. I've always tried to watch people doing mechanical things. I watched the dentist in *Cortina D'Ampezzo* closely when he worked on a root canal, removing the nerve from one of my teeth, of course, with adequate anesthesia. But nevertheless it was an interesting procedure. After opening the root canal, he took a very fine drill head, a needle with a wide twist, which was like a drill for drilling holes into the ground to excavate soil. He held it between two fingers and slowly screwed it into the cavity. After the drill entrapped the nerve he extracted it carefully. When it came out the nerve was pinkish and a little ragged on the end. The procedure hurt severely in spite of the anesthesia. I couldn't imagine doing it to myself without any painkiller."

"Well," he said, "since the seed has been planted in your brain, you tell me when the pain becomes unbearable. In the meantime I'll look around for a precision-tool maker. He might come up with an idea how to make the drill you're talking about."

I was far from even thinking about this procedure or about performing it by myself. But, when it comes to a persistent, permanent and excruciating toothache, time can be persuasive.

It was in the middle of August 1948, shortly after my twenty-fourth birthday, when I couldn't take it any longer. I couldn't sleep any more. I was seeing stars in front of my eyes, and I had all I could do not to moan constantly. Arthur took me to the precision-tool maker whom he had located in the meantime. He was from *Baden-Württemberg* from the *Black Forest,* spoke with a heavy dialect that was thick enough to cut with a knife. He was hard to understand, as he drawled, hardly opening his mouth. But he understood what I wanted and knew his profession. The hardest part was to get a needle thin enough, made from the right material, not cast-iron; to forge and twist the drill I'd been talking about, and hardening it properly. I didn't want to run the danger of breaking the drill off inside of my tooth. He finally located a piece that suited our needs. The people who worked as automobile mechanics in the city had found it. They told me it was the needle from a disassembled carburetor. His only condition for helping was—aside from half a loaf of bread for his work—that he didn't have to watch what I needed to do.

When it finally came to the point of no return, the only person willing to help and to assist me was Arthur. I sat down on a bench with the fragment of a mirror in front of me, took a deep breath, and started to attack the worst offender in my mouth.

Even though I know that the greatest blessing for mankind, according to the Greek mythology—next to the ability to hope—is the ability to forget, I don't think I'll ever forget the intolerable, mind-boggling, unimaginable pain caused by the extraction of a nerve from my tooth. At one time I whimpered so loudly that other guys in the barracks started complaining.

Arthur's tears of sympathy were flowing almost as fast as mine were. He told me later he almost ran away because he couldn't watch it any longer. Unbelievable as it may sound I got the nerves out—all of them. After a period of further pain and recuperation, I felt like a newborn baby. The broken teeth continued to rot and small pieces were breaking off eventually, but the pain was gone.

Several months since we'd written our postcards—over half a year to be exact, and several of the prisoners had received post cards in return—when the NKVD officer of the camp, a Volga German, called me to his office, and told me with a very serious demeanor, almost white in his face, to sit down.

"Tell me what your family has been up to? I mean what's your father's business?"

I explained and he almost immediately interrupted.

"Don't tell me any bullshit, you mother fucking asshole. Lying will not help you and from the way it looks, I'll recommend that you be removed at once from this friendly camp to a serious correctional facility."

I was terrified. His demeanor and obvious anger hit me right in the gut. This man wasn't kidding, something must have happened. I didn't have to wait long to find out; he pushed a postcard across the table, which was addressed to me and was written by my relative to whom I had sent my postcard. It read:

> Dear Peter, we were certainly happy to hear from you and to hear you are healthy and not dystrophic like most of the *Heimkehrer* [returning prisoners] coming home from Russia these days . . .

> *"This idiot! How could he write such a letter to Russia, to a prison camp where I was at the mercy of the officials who would censor his stupid, imbecilic criticism of the Soviet Union?"* But it got worse.

> We are all fine and we've informed everybody where you are. You'll be pleased to hear that the factory is doing a *Bombengeschäft*.
> All the best Herbert und Erna

The word *Bombengeschäft* in German is a colloquialism meaning business is very good. It is derived from the perception that selling bombs must be a good business. But for the NKWD officer it translated literally to: *"a business with bombs."* I tried to explain this to him. "It's only an expression to describe how well business is going and not a description of what business you are involved in."

The NKWD officer, who had been assigned to the POW camp, because of his background as a Volga German, spoke German well, but the words, the expressions, and the jargon he knew and used were antiquated. The Volga Germans had left their home country two hundred years ago. He'd never heard the word *"Bombengeschäft"* and couldn't conceptualize what I tried to explain and didn't want to believe me.

It flashed through my mind that I'd better be careful what I said next. If I'd come across as a patronizing wise guy, I'd be gone in no time. I don't think he'd have given me a second chance to explain the expression, *"Bombengeschäft."*

I looked up and said with a troubled and deadly serious face. "Isn't it terrible what the damned Nazis have done to the beautiful German language? In their perverted desire to push the German people to fight this terrible war, terrorizing their neighbors, they have even introduced word creations like this."

"What do you mean? Explain," he shot back. It always got them when the Nazis came into play.

"Outwardly it sounds as if this second cousin of mine, who is answering my postcard, or my own family, is in the business of making bombs. Nothing could be further from the truth. Hitler and his clique continuously confronted the population with similar word fabrications."—I was using strong words.—"This one just means that business is going great, it's explosive, gigantic, that's all. But if you find this implausible, I'd think that you might want to check my interpretation with someone more trust-worthy than me. May I suggest the head of the camp's ANTIFA, Jahn Lutter?"

Lutter wasn't my type, but he was a 100% communist. In this case he was the best I could think of. I didn't believe he'd do any damage. He'd have to support my interpretation of *Bombengeschäft*—that was if the NKWD officer went along with my suggestion to consult with him, to confirm what I'd said.

"I'll do that right now, before you tell me any more nonsense. Guard!" he shouted, "put this prisoner in a cell."

The cell was a dark, moist, dirty little room ten by five feet with nothing on what to sit or lie down on. In one corner was a pail to do what you had to do. It stank of urine and feces. I waited for two days without food or water, gradually filling the pail, sitting on the floor, walking three steps in one direction and three in the other, thinking fearful thoughts. I was not sleeping much. A small, solitary window was high on the wall. It was closed. I tried as hard as I could to think positively. But more and more I got the impression that they'd forgotten all about me. On the third day the door suddenly opened, the guard stuck his head inside and ordered, "Idi" (Go).

I stumbled into the light and back to our barracks, fell on my bed and trembled uncontrollably. A hairsbreath from getting lost in the Gulag had saved me.

From that date on that relative was on my priority shit list.

The Soviets had abolished capitalism but had never created incentives for its citizens to replace the lures of capitalism with anything to motivate them to work to their fullest capabilities and to stay true to the principles of Marxism-Leninism. The official theory, *"The Soviet Union is practicing socialism on its way to communism"* didn't fool anybody. The official interpretation and vision of communism, as it might be achieved some day in the distant future was that no money was needed for the exchange of goods. Everybody would have enough of everything. That's a tall order, and nobody knew how that was going to be accomplished. However, the party logicians insisted on the predictions of Marx-Leninism.

We know that the dream of ownership, ownership of just anything, of private property, cannot be replaced by socialist incentives, no matter how contrived the schemes were, and how hard the *aparatchniks* tried to indoctrinate the people.

In every town and small hamlet and on almost every building in *Stalinsk* one could observe billboards with pictures of the most productive, the most inventive, or the most faithful communist workers in the city and the country. It was a gigantic farce. In our experience the workers did what they had to do and not a damn thing more. At the factories or construction sites, or in the coal and ore mines, wherever they worked, they stole everything that wasn't nailed to the ground, either to sell it, or—because there was nothing to buy anywhere—to use it at home. Many times it was a simple product like paint. There was no quality paint to buy anywhere, not in the Soviet Union, not in any other socialist country.

The one and only satirical magazine published in the country, *"Krokodile,"* printed a joke describing the situation very aptly. The question they'd put to the readers went like this, "If the Soviet Union should occupy the Sahara Desert, what would happen next? Answer: For the first five years nothing and then they'd run out of sand."

People who visited Moscow or Leningrad in the late forties may have seen some stores and *magazines,* but in many of the smaller cities there were few retail stores. What for? There was nothing to buy.

The POWs learned quickly how the system worked. When the city camp was built the kitchen was constructed from the most rudimentary and primitive material, wooden floors, cheap iron vats to cook the soup, *kascha,* or potatoes, to be stirred by hand with wooden paddles. A single water faucet graced the corner of the kitchen. In other words, there was nothing. Our cooks didn't like it and asked prisoners for many items to improve the surroundings and equipment, such as tiles, in order to improve the appearance, the efficiency and cleanliness of the kitchen. The prisoners in their quest for food became creative smuggling these items into the camp, sometimes one tile at a time. They could do this most effectively during the winter. The heavy fur coats, *fufeikas* and *valinki* provided additional hiding places. The payment for everything was food—soup to be exact. For everything they needed the kitchen guys were willing to pay with an extra mess kit of soup or two, and sooner or later they got what they wanted.

Three years later a commission from Moscow arrived to check on the kitchen's cleanliness. They were amazed and stunned when they entered the kitchen. What they saw almost blew their minds as they were confronted with a facility that was fully tiled, floors and walls, the vats were copper lined and small electrical motors had been installed to move the mixers. Water faucets were on top of every vat. The shelves were made of hard wood, and various electrical gadgets were hanging from the walls. The prisoners had stolen everything—for a price.

This is a small example of how communism had corrupted peoples' behavior. Mind you, we were well-guarded prisoners, checked almost every time on our return from work as we passed the gate. One can easily imagine how the private sector worked. It didn't bother anybody that the penalties for stealing "from the people" were severe like five, ten, or even twenty years of hard labor; people took their chances anyway.

The pressure to whip up productivity to fulfill the five-year plan was enormous, and the inventiveness of the Soviet propaganda to create some enthusiasm among its population was astounding. Somewhere in the Ukraine—at least that was the official version of the story—a Russian miner had declared he would demonstrate how much could be accomplished with the proper energy and dedication during one day of the year, and how much one *should* accomplish during one working day to honor *"the victorious Soviet Union."* During this one day the miner exceeded his norm—the amount of coal to be extracted from the mine by one man in one day—by 350%. My figures may not be accurate, but the drift of the story is clear. This man's name was *Stachanov.* To follow his example a nationwide "Stachanov-day" was initiated and religiously celebrated every year by every worker on every work site all over the Soviet Union. The workers hated that day but had no choice but to follow the Government's *suggestion* during this 'one' day.

The East German satellites, always the most obedient, found a man to do the same in some uranium mine in Saxony. His name was *Heinecke.* The ANTIFA group in Moscow distributed this information to all prison camps, and we were encouraged to follow *Heinecke's* example. As Churchill had so aptly characterized, "They're either at your feet or at your throat."

In September 1948 our brigade—the Russians liked that name "brigade"—had conceived a plan to break all records, on *Stachanov* celebration day, for the number of bricks put down by one man in one single day.

I had checked the *nariad* about the matter carefully. It didn't say anything how many people could serve and assist this one bricklayer as helpers, as long as he physically put the bricks down, one on top of the other, with his own hands. We had the right man to do the job. In our brigade was a bricklayer from Berlin. His name was Horst Josewski. Horst was big and strong and was willing to be the front man for the *woyenna plennies (POWs)* on *Stachanow* day. The timing was perfect. The end-wall of a building was going up at OSMU 4. It had no windows, no doors. It was a straight wall. To make it even more appealing the wall had a thickness of three feet. When we discussed the matter with the *Natchalnik* of OSMU 4, he was all for it and supported what we wanted to do. Of course he did, it would be a feather in his cap as well. The scene was set.

Days in advance we took care of all the preparations. We had enough bricks on hand. Two railroad flatcars loaded with bricks were standing at the siding nearby, and we had our own mortar-mixer and made sure that nobody was interfering.

At 6:30 A.M. sharp on the appointed day Horst started slapping the bricks down, supported by twelve people who did everything for him, except lay the bricks. The mortar was poured where Horst directed it. A sufficient supply of bricks was always at his side, and Horst worked like a devil laying a total of 50,000 bricks in one single day. Granted, he went a little overtime. But what the heck! It was an incredible feat, which had never been accomplished before and has never been repeated since. Horst managed to continuously pick up bricks during an eight-hour day to build a solid wall at a speed of almost 1.8 bricks per second. Everybody was dead on his feet at the end of the day, especially Horst Josewski. The members of the Brigade each received one loaf of bread from the camp as a reward. As a reward it was a joke, but we knew that before and said *"nitchewo."*

September 1948 was almost over. The group from the bread factory was still in good shape, but our accumulated reserves were shrinking rapidly, no matter how much we scrimped, tried to supplement and went on begging-runs; we were hungry and the next winter was nearing rapidly.

13

IN THE STONE QUARRY

O n most Sundays we had a day's rest. I was on my way to our barrack when I ran into Fritz. Trying to strike up a conversation and also to kid him a little, I said, "The last time we met unexpectedly you threatened me with a very hard job, and then you sent Arthur and me to the bread factory. Do you have another hard job like that for us? I mean a job where they need real men not softies, but where we can also develop our own initiatives?"

"This is quite a coincidence, Peter, and you may think that I am making this up," he replied with a serious face. "I'm on my way, trying to put a detail together for a job site that nobody wants, and which has such a terrible reputation, even the administration of the camp doesn't want to accept the assignment. They're afraid too many POWs will die. By the way, they are concerned about the dying. They don't want that to happen any more if they can avoid it. The jobsite, OSMU 11, pays good money to the camp. It's six miles from the camp, has no guards, no fences, has its own barrack and its own kitchen. We'll have to send a cook also. You're on your own. What I'm talking about is the artificial stone quarry to the west of the city where they dispose of the slag from the furnaces. You can see the little engines in the background over there." He pointed toward the horizon. "They break stones from an eight hundred degree hot iron ore slag. The end result is road-surfacing material. OSMU 11 supplies all road sites in *Stalinsk* with surfacing material. They call it *macadam.*"

As a place of work that didn't sound very exciting to me. You can't eat tar or stones, but, on the other hand, it spelled freedom all over and a chance to run our own lives again. We were still strong enough not to fear the hard work.

"Fritz, can you hold your decision for just five minutes?" I blurted out. "I'll call an immediate meeting of our group, and I'll be back in no time with a decision, okay?"

"Go. There's nothing in such a hurry that it can't wait for five minutes. You know where to find me and take your time, Peter."

I ran back to our barrack as fast as I could, where I found Arthur and Kurt and the others, and told them what Fritz had explained to me.

"I don't know what you think, but no work can be so hard that we can't manage it as long as we're free, without fences and guards and can arrange to supplement our food supply."

"I totally agree with you," was Arthur's instant reply and Kurt also vehemently nodded his assent.

"Our money is almost gone, and we can't live on camp food alone," was his convincing statement. "Go for it Peter. We'll never hold it against you, even if it doesn't work out."

I went back to see Fritz and told him to include all of us for the new detail going to the stone quarry of OSMU 11. The camp sent forty-five men, including Pinkepank whom we had suggested as the cook.

The designated leader of our command was a man called Ossipenko. He was a brash, young guy of twenty-one whom the Russians most likely favored because his Russian was flawless and also because his father had used his influence with them. Father and son Ossipenko had been in the camp since the beginning. Nobody had seen them on the transport from *Ploesti* and people 'in the know' suspected them to be planted by the NKWD. Arthur and I had talked about them at times and came to the conclusion that they were most likely *Vlassow,* trying to hide in our midst to gain information, pass it on to the NKWD, to please them and then to be set free someday. The basis for our conjecture was remarks both of them made about their time in Germany and their intimate knowledge of the area around Stuttgart.

It didn't matter to us who the leader was. Somebody had to do the job, and the younger Ossipenko wasn't intelligent enough to do any real damage.

OSMU 11 was at the southern edge of town. On a clear day we could see a range of hills in the distance, and that is exactly where it was. Among the prisoners OSMU 11 had a bad reputation and was the most feared "Slave Labor Assignment". Everybody assured us that we wouldn't live long on OSMU 11, but nobody we talked to had ever worked there. Where did all this knowledge come from?

"It is a death sentence to be transferred to OSMU 11" was the common opinion.

Our "war council" decided that freedom from supervision by the guards and from the confinement of the camp would leave it up to us to shape our destiny. We'd find out soon enough whether it was a slave labor site, an abomination, or a blessing beyond belief.

For us armed with the right attitude, it turned out to be the latter. Work? We didn't fear work. Being *grushiks* in the bread factory had been hard work, but we'd thrived on it, and the new guys who joined us now and hadn't been with us at the bread factory believed what we said, knew our reputation and followed our lead.

After a twenty minute ride on the back of two trucks, driving through parts of the city, past construction sites, shacks, past the walls of the steel mill which we'd never seen before, looking just as drab as any steel mill in the rest of the world, we arrived at OSMU 11. We jumped off, unloaded our things together with a week's supply of food and looked around. The two obligatory, morose guards climbed back onto the truck and disappeared in a cloud of dust without looking back.

We stood in front of a large, old and dirty barrack, which hadn't been painted since it was built. On the street side it had several French windows that had never been cleaned. Across a dirt road from the building was a small, steam-generated powerhouse, topped by a precariously rickety, rusty metal chimney, rising thirty feet into the sky, belching dirty smoke. Behind the powerhouse was a single rail line that came to a dead end in the back of the barrack. Dominating the scenery in the background, stuck against a steeply rising hillside of the pit-heap was a *macadam* processing plant. It consisted of a stone crusher and several mixing drums, which turned and tumbled its content of stone and tar with incredible noise. On the side were a tar mixer, a large, square tar pit and two loading docks to accommodate trucks. Behind the barrack were a tool shed and a workshop and further down, on a field beyond, the outhouse.

Everything was covered with a thick layer of dust. The noise from the plant was deafening. The *Natchalnik*—he looked more like the lowliest worker in the bread factory rather than the "Blue One" whom we had respected so much—tried to beat the noise by yelling at Ossipenko.

"So, you want to work at OSMU 11?" It was a question, which was almost a rebuttal like "how dare you!"

"We need good workers. The camp promised us you are the best. We'll pay you good money. You must be good because you're very expensive. The *zakluchornies* before you weren't worth a damn. They were always hungry, always complaining about the work and lazy as hell."

He rubbed his stubbly, dirty beard scanning the prisoners suspiciously one by one and continued, *"Ladna,* why don't you send a few men inside the barrack right now to clean up the pigsty the others left behind after I threw them out? After that I'll show you your assignments and explain what you'll have to accomplish to fulfill the norm."

I perked up my ears; this was my forte he was talking about. I would have to get busy reading up in the *nariad* about the various norms concerning artificial stone breaking, handling of materials and other incidentals.

Ossipenko took off with the *Natchalnik* as most of the others did, but Pinkepank and a few more stayed behind to clean our quarters. The barrack certainly was large enough for forty-five men. The *Natchalnik* had described it correctly, filthy like a pigsty beyond belief.

Inside we found four rooms and a small kitchen. One room was really small, but it would be large enough for Ossipenko. The big room in the middle could easily sleep thirty guys in double bunk beds. The third room was adequate for fifteen people in double beds. It was taken over by us, the hard core. The remaining room, right at the entrance, with a door to the kitchen and a disbursement window could be equipped with a long table and a few benches. This way we wouldn't have to eat sitting on our beds. The kitchen was another matter entirely. Pinke was wringing his hands about the filth. The hardened residue of food stuck to everything hadn't been cleaned off in ages. And then the ancient stove and the smell! There were no utensils, not even large vats for cooking, or any spoons or ladles, nothing.

"What have I done to deserve this?" he wailed in mock complaint, wringing his hands, looking at the ceiling and blinking an eye at me. In reality he was as happy as all of us were. We had escaped the camp.

It took us the remainder of the day to clean up the place, clean the boards of the beds, which seemed to be thoroughly infested with lice and bed bugs. We carried the boards across the street to the boiler room, opened the furnace and pushed them into the opening, right over the red hot coal, once or twice, to give them a quick burn out, just scorching it slightly to kill the vermin sticking to it.

We white washed the walls with chalk provided by some friendly workers of the macadam plant, which the bed bugs hate. We then cleaned the windows and put the kitchen and the stove in working order. After we finished, the place looked almost presentable. Pinke had managed to borrow some utensils from the neighbors to cook our soup for the evening.

Ossipenko called everybody to assemble in front of the barrack, to instruct us on what the *Natchalnik* had said and what he expected from us:

One man would be assigned to the kitchen; that was Pinkepank.

One man would run the powerhouse with a Russian. Our man was a friendly looking, hefty guy called Bertram.

Four men—in two shifts of two—took over the workshop to work as carpenters, mechanics and toolmakers. (Their first assignment was to make some utensils for Pinke.)

Four men—in two shifts—would work in the tar pit feeding the mixing drums.

Four teams of eight men each would work the hot slag-stone pits on top of the plateau, to break up the solidified slag, reducing the big pieces with heavy hammers to handling size, and then transporting them with field lorries to a site above the stone cracker, to toss the stones down the hill.

Four men—in two shifts of two—would feed the stone cracker with the stones, continuously providing the plant with gravel for the *macadam* operation.

The Russians handled the plant, the mixing of the stones with tar, and the loading of the trucks. Because that was—as it turned out later on—that was where extra money could be made. They left to the prisoners all those areas where problems with the chain of supplies could develop.

As we got involved with the work on a day-to-day basis, the configuration changed slightly. The *Natchalnik*—who was seldom around anyway—had given Ossipenko those numbers to get us going and left the execution to us.

We learned a lot from workers at the plant during the succeeding weeks. They were great pals, and as time wore on, they learned a few things from us, too. Our happiest time in Siberia—if it was at all possible to describe any time in Siberia as happy—had begun.

I might add that we immediately protected our claim. Whenever people from the camp came to inspect the site, we complained bitterly about the inhuman work, the dirt, the brutality of our coworkers and so on and so forth. We didn't listen to their comments about our apparent good health.

At 5:00 the next morning we got up, ate our soup and went to work. The men went to their respective assignments, but first we went to the tool shed to receive our tools. With the help of a Russian who told us what we needed, they handed us several heavy, ten pound hammers, six extra long crow bars, six pick-axes, shovels, several pincer-like metal contraptions, to pick up hot stones, thick gloves and also a pair of shoes each with thick wooden soles and a rough linen cover. The linen cover was crudely nailed to the soles. All shoes were used, obviously. We were told that we wouldn't be able to walk on the hot slag stones without them. The wooden soles wore off easily on the razor sharp surface of the slag stones and needed to be replaced regularly by our tool shop.

Two Russians were waiting for us to lead us to the stone pit above to explain the assignments in detail.

We followed our man up the side of the pit-heap, walking on a well-traveled path to the top hundred and twenty feet above the valley. As we turned around we were confronted with a panoramic view of the entire city of *Stalinsk* and its surroundings. We could see all the way to the Tom River and could even make out the rising steam of the old engine, which had taken us to the *kolkhos* camp after our arrival. The engine stood in the far distance billowing white clouds towards the blue sky. A cloud of dust hung over most of the work-sites. It looked like a filthy city, which it was.

Unbelievable! Fifteen years of pouring slag had created this huge plateau. The eight rails traversing the plateau were each for a different purpose. One rail stopped next to a concrete basin of gigantic dimensions, located above the *macadam* plant, always filled with water, with a huge crane hovering over its side. The basin must have been at least ninety feet deep.

A second rail passing the basin reached all the way to the area were we stood at the top of the plateau with a third rail parallel to it, used by a small crane-on-wheels.

Four rails were reserved solely for the trains to transport slag to the far end of the plateau, which was about a mile or two away. Every twenty minutes a train with six to eight *kofshays* (that's what the Russians called the rail cars carrying conical shaped containers filled with hot liquid slag) passed by at full speed, pulled by *Ohrenstein & Koppel* steam engines, furiously belching clouds of white steam into the sky.

We stood there, getting used to our new work place and its surroundings, while our guide was in a hurry to finish his instructions and get back to his own work.

"Listen, *towarishi* [comrades]—I'm only here to explain things to you, I have my own job to do, let's not stand around wasting my time, okay? The entire valley that you see in front of you is fertile. If summer in Siberia lasted a month or two longer, we would have an agricultural paradise. One thing is missing though—stones. With the exception of a few small stone quarries, which belong to the *kolchos* across the river, there isn't a stone to be found for miles [We knew that one, we had worked there]. That's the reason why the city has established this site as an artificial stone quarry. We need stones to build roads, and we also use the slag for insulation material, which is put between walls of buildings to protect them against the freezing temperature in the winter and the heat in the summer. The concrete basin you see over there is filled with water. When the red-hot slag is poured into the cold water the shock breaks it down into a frizzy material, which is ideal for the insulating job. You have nothing to do with this operation.

"Alongside this rail track you see eight shallow holes, about three to four feet deep, twenty-five feet wide and forty to fifty feet long. These holes are big enough to accommodate the load of one or two *kofshays* filled with red-hot slag. Whenever we need a 'filling,' the *Natchalnik* calls the iron ore mill, and they divert the next train, which you have seen racing up and down on the plateau, to our siding. It will slowly pull up to a hole, and one of our engineers activates the little crane to tilt a *kofshay,* emptying the contents into one of the holes. After two days the slag has cooled down sufficiently for you to start your work. During the cooling process the chemicals and whatever else has been added to the ore during the melting process, slowly rise to the top to form a hard, light and porous, almost foamy looking crust. It can be peeled off easily, piece-by-piece, with pickaxes and thrown aside with shovels. That's the first step of your work. Just throw the stuff over the hill in the back of the holes and leave it.

"After that you wait two more days until the stones cool further causing them to contract. That'll develop small cracks. During that time the slag has become cold enough for you to walk on with your wooden shoes. Start working from the edge toward the middle, find the cracks, ram the crowbars into them pushing the pieces apart, turning them sideways, and then use the hammers to hit the stones to break the pieces into manageable sizes. Everything is very hot, and you'll have to watch the flying chips of slag when the hammer hits the stone. Don't burn yourself. You'll see the glow of the cooling stone in the early morning before the sun comes up. At that time the stones are about eight hundred degrees centigrade, so, I can only emphasize again; watch out. When the stones are small enough to be handled with the pincers, you'll pick them up—careful they are still very hot—carry, or throw them up to the edge of the hole and load them on to the lorries, using the gloves or the pincers."

He pointed to three beaten up lorries standing on a narrow gauge rail between the big rails. Three lorries had been attached to each other to form a train.

"You'll push the lorries down the rail toward the plant directly to the point above the cracker. You'll empty the lorries to feed the cracker, and that's it. You're done, that's the whole process. Only experience will teach you how to handle the crowbar and the hammer, where to hit the stone to split it, and how to handle the pincer. Watch the glowing heat. I can't repeat that often enough. Keep the stones coming, because if we don't have enough material at the plant everybody is unhappy, and we'll start screaming, the plant will stop producing material, trucks will stop loading, road-building in the city will stop, and a lot of people become angry and won't be able to fulfill the norm, and you know what that means?"

He looked around with a serious face, his eyebrows raised to see whether we had understood. "Don't let that happen and you are in good shape. And now, *towarishii* you are standing in front of two holes waiting to be worked. Let's go!"

He turned, left us standing near the holes and disappeared down the hill.

In later years I participated in many elaborate meetings, listening to well-prepared presentations from pontificating managers, Americans, Europeans, and whomever else, and listened to descriptions of industrial processes. This man, a laborer, in a stone quarry of OSMU 11, in the depth of Siberia, had offered the facts concisely and clearly with the fewest words possible. He presented nothing but the facts. He knew exactly what was going on, and he put the required results right on the line.

After he'd left we stood there dumbfounded and started to debate where to start first and what to do next. Our surroundings looked like the surface of the moon, full of craters, it certainly was hot enough.

"Let's see how much of a reserve we have at the cracker," some-one suggested. We walked hundred and fifty yards to the spot right above the cracker and looked down the eighty-five degree embank-ment to check on the reserves for the plant.

Nothing! We saw an empty hillside and a deserted stone-cracker. Not a fucking stone on the entire hill. The plant was stand-ing still, and several trucks were waiting in line to be loaded. Kurt adroitly sized up the situation and directed us, "Everybody back to the first and second hole, they're uncovered and ready to be broken. We'll get the mother-fucking macadam plant going within the hour, or we'll go back to the camp."

There wasn't a word of dissent from anybody. We raced toward the first hole, grabbed the crowbars and the hammers, pushed, pulled, hammered and slugged, carried the stones to the lorries with the pincers, rushed the lorries to the top of the hill above the cracker, dumped the load, and yelled for the men below to get going and feed the cracker. The Russians couldn't believe it. The plant had stones and started to operate within thirty minutes.

It never stopped again as long as we worked and broke stones on OSMU 11.

The job, especially in the heat, was a hustle. We weren't laugh-ing, but we weren't hurting either. We caught on to the tricks of the business, how and where to hit the stones with the hammer, to hit them right on an invisible seam to break them apart, to swing the pin-cers, clenching the glowing rocks securely and with the least possi-ble strain to our backs, pushing the lorries down hill without derailment, and we managed to keep the hill uncluttered by falling stones, letting them tumble down all the way to the cracker. We be-came experts. Once we had worked up a reserve of stones, uphill from the cracker, we settled into an acceptable working routine to keep stones coming and busied ourselves with the most important thing—bread.

The area around OSMU 11 was new to us. We had to find our way around in a new part of town, establishing a supply line to a number of begging areas, to find enough bread for our hungry stom-achs without bothering the civilians unduly. Since the *macadam* factory was at the edge and away from the city, we had to walk further to get to the next housing development and to find sympathetic locals. But that is a minor problem if one is hungry enough, and we didn't have belligerent guards to worry about.

Working the hot stones had another advantage. The winter at the construction sites had been an abomination for the prisoners, especially in 1945, '46 and '47 with temperatures ranging to below 40 degrees. At OSMU 11 the winter had lost its terror. Now we had "built in heating" at the stone quarry. The snow melted all by itself as it fell onto the hot stones; our fingers never froze. Neither cold feet nor the snow, which had to be pushed aside to operate the lorries, bothered us anymore.

The feeling to be at OSMU 11 was exhilarating. The Russian workers at the plant appreciated our efforts, because they made more money on the side than ever before. Even if they didn't, they were at least able to fulfill their quotas, which was supremely important for everybody in the worker's paradise, and had enough to eat for themselves and for their families.

We developed a daily working routine, changed our schedules as needed, and scheduled the shifts at the stone cracker and the tar pit to work around the clock. The *Natchalnik* knew a good thing when he saw one and never interfered or bothered us.

We improved our tools with the help of our carpenters and mechanics and employed the best equipment possible.

The men, who hadn't been with us at the bread factory, caught on to the spirit and were doing great. As the cold season approached, we adjusted to a Siberian winter at the stone quarry.

The work was hard and demanding, but we were happy being free, having enough to eat, not tortured by an empty stomach, feeling gnawing hunger, or being harassed by camp officials or the ever-present chicanery of the guards.

The questions, constantly repeated by our civilian co-workers, by the people we met begging for bread and just about everybody, *"Scoro domoi pajechit?"* (Are you going home soon?) were a thorn in our side, because we were obviously as curious as they were how much longer we would remain in Siberia. There was no word from anybody, and we preferred not to think about it—even though dreaming was permitted. More and more often at night one could hear discussions between the men.

"Do you think they'll send us home soon? We'll have a New Year coming soon, 1949, what do you think?"

Nobody had an answer, and the Russians weren't talking. Scuttlebutt passed from man to man and was often believed and plausible especially when it reached outlandish proportions.

Processing *macadam* needed stones and tar, plenty of it. The winter arrived early in 1948 and with it the usual temperatures of twenty, thirty and forty below freezing. The tar, stored in an open pit alongside the plant, froze like everything else. The tar pit was hundred twenty feet long and sixty feet wide with about a foot or two of tar in it. It was constantly replenished by tank wagons that pulled alongside the pit. Steam lines from our plant heated the wagons. The tank wagon slowly discharged its black, sticky load from a valve. During the summer the tar flowed nicely by gravity all by itself, simply emptying into the pit. Later we scooped out the tar, with ordinary pails, into a processing container, heated it with steam until it became watery and ready to be poured into the churning mixing drums containing the stones. The mixture was mixed thoroughly and dumped onto the trucks that ferried the material to a road-site somewhere in the city of *Stalinsk.*

The fact that the tar froze in the winter was nothing new to the Russians, but we couldn't believe and couldn't accept the way they dealt with the problem. They hacked away at the frozen stuff with pickaxes, hammers and wedges to gradually and laboriously separate small chunks of frozen tar. They threw them by hand into the processing container to be melted by steam from Bert's steam powerhouse. That's the way they'd done it for years and never thought anything about it. It was stupid work, hard work and dirty work. One cubic yard of frozen tar was the established norm for two men for one day. That was so little that the *Natchalnik* wanted to employ a second team of two men to supply the plant with an adequate amount of tar for a continuous operation. These two men would've had to leave the stone breaking team. We had our hands full breaking enough stone for the plant as it was. We couldn't spare two guys, and why should we? We had to come up with an answer and the Russians, with whom we talked, were absolutely of no help. It was Arthur who had a revolutionary idea.

In the past years, at various building sites in the city, we had marveled at a clever double-winch, which was ubiquitous on all construction sites. I'll call it a "double-winch," because it had two drums loaded with a steel cable running side by side. Both drums were securely fastened on a wooden bloc. Each drum could be operated separately with a handle to break the drum, either pulling or releasing a steel cable. Usually the machine was employed to level a field of dirt, or to fill in a pit with dirt, or to push around whatever needed to be leveled or flattened. The Russians lacked heavy earth-moving equipment, mechanical plows, or Caterpillars, to push large quantities of earth around.

The winch worked as follows. A long wire cable was wound around one drum of the *lebiotka* (the Russian name for the winch) with the other end connected to the second drum. If you'd let the cable run out to its full length, it formed a loop. A scraper was attached to one side of the loop. At the far end the loop was fed through a pulley that was fastened to an iron rod in the ground holding the rope stretched out across the area to be leveled. The rope ran back and forth through the pulley. The two electrically operated drums of the *lebiotka* were used alternately winding it up on one, or releasing the cable on the other. This dragged the scraper back and forth across the field to be leveled. It was a simple system, because the *lebiotka* needed only one operator to move the two handles. Fortunately some of us were blessed with inventive talent, and Arthur was one of them.

"You know," he said, standing in front of the tar pit at the end of our shift, with five or six of us nearby, deliberating how to solve the problem with the frozen tar, "have you ever thought of using a *lebiotka?*"

"A *lebiotka?* What do you want to do with that dumb machine?" Hans, as usual, had spoken without thinking.

"Why don't you let the man finish his thoughts? He looks to me as if he is coming down with something," Kurt interrupted. "I've seen this wrinkled forehead on other occasions, and it has always produced something noteworthy."

He was right. Arthur looked as if he was in the final stages of being pregnant with an idea of some consequence.

"Do you think we can produce a *lebiotka* from somewhere and a simple, old fashioned plow? One of those that used to be pulled by horses, to break the ground when there were still horses around?"

"That sounds mysterious, Arthur. Before you keep us in suspense for much longer, why don't you tell us what you're thinking, besides it's getting too cold to stand around here," I prodded him.

"I have an idea," Arthur continued staring at the tar pit without paying attention to my interruption. "If the *lebiotka* I'm looking for is powerful enough, it'll work. What we'll do is this: We'll place the *lebiotka* on this side of the tar pit and secure it. The rod to hold the rope-pulley is jammed into the ground on the other side. Then, instead of attaching a scraper to the rope, we'll attach the plow. Next, we'll dig a hole into the frozen tar on the far side of the pit. The hole has to be a foot and a half deep and large enough to accommodate the plow. One man steps down to hold and to guide it just like a farmer does on the field, and then we'll let the *lebiotka* do the rest of the job pulling the plow through the tar breaking and splintering the stuff with greater ease than we'll ever be able to do with the present method. How about it?"

Everybody seemed to understand immediately. The enthusiasm of the group was tremendous.

"You are a genius, Arthur!"

"You are the greatest!"

"You should be an inventor!"

The comments of admiration came from everyone, even from Hans. Kurt directed a few guys to find a *lebiotka* and somebody else to locate an old and abandoned plow. The *Natchalnik* who had observed all our talking suspiciously, but not understanding a word, started to curse us. "You shouldn't spend endless time in useless chatter while the factory is idle. Grab some tools to produce tar," he interrupted, jumping and down getting really excited. Ossipenko finally managed to explain our plan and the *Natchalnik*—still with the face of a nonbeliever—stood aside to watch us.

It took us some time to locate a *lebiotka,* to convince the owners to part with it and to transport the thing, which must have weighed at least a ton, to our tar pit. Another day passed to do all that, and the *Natchalnik* was nearly ready to call the camp to have us all transported back to do something useful, as he put it.

Finally everything was installed and the magic moment came: Would the *lebiotka* be strong enough to pull the plow through the tar?

"Come over here, Arthur, you're the inventor, you've got to start the *lebiotka,*" Kurt called out to him.

Everybody not working at the moment stood at the edge of the tar pit. What was going to happen?

"Oh, don't make such a fuss about it, it'll work," Arthur mumbled. "But okay, if you want me to, I'll cut the ribbon." He walked to the pulleys and threw the lever for the electricity.

The *lebiotka* came to life and Arthur grabbed the two handles of the machines.

"Hold the plow steady. I'll pull slowly to give you time to adjust," he called out to the man in the pit who was holding the plow upright while the machine tightened the cable. "Now I'm going to give it a tug." The cable attached to the plow vibrated with the tension the *lebiotka* applied.

"Don't fool around, give it a real pull."

"Break the fucking tar already," Hans yelled.

As usual there were plenty of smart remarks from everybody, but Arthur was not deterred and continued to increase the pressure gradually. All of a sudden the plow jerked forward and the tar splintered and parted like magic.

It worked like a charm. The *Natchalnik* couldn't believe his eyes as piles upon piles of splintering tar accumulated on the side of the plow, which tore through the tar like butter. It was enough tar to feed the mixer for days to come.

The men were yelling and shouting excitedly, and even our Russian co-workers got caught up in the excitement and were cheering us on.

I tried immediately to figure out what percent of the old daily norm had been exceeded in just one hour. It was stupendous and no attempt by the *Natchalnik* to belittle our invention was making an impression on us. No matter how hard he tried to avoid paying a huge premium for the new work process, we stood our ground.

We had enough tar. The Russian workers at the plant, who all lived in the neighborhood of the plant, impressed by what we were doing, came to visit us with requests to solve little problems, to be fixed in their *semliankas*. The POWs were in. The consequence was that our diet improved steadily. We had plenty of vegetables, potatoes, onions and even garlic, and most of the time Pinke concocted fabulous soups. It was almost as good as being in the bread factory.

What always bothered us during the four years of captivity was the dirt. Wherever we'd worked or had lived, vegetated I'd say, the inability to wash ourselves on a regular basis, to wash our clothes at least every once in a while, to avoid being invaded by lice, had a demoralizing effect. I'm not talking about the luxury of brushing our teeth, which we hadn't done in years. That had even bothered us in the bread factory. We knew the Russians didn't like it either. Some of them came from larger cities, further to the west—if not from Moscow—and knew the comforts of plenty of hot water. They were in *Stalinsk* as punishment, or had made their way via some Godforsaken prison camp. They knew about saunas with plenty of warm water and soap.

Kurt, Arthur and I walked home one day in May of 1949, coming from a bread-begging expedition into the city, meeting up accidentally about a mile from our quarters at the beginning of our plateau, lady luck shone upon us one more time.

Leaving the last dwellings of the city, the slagheap gradually started to rise in front of us growing higher and higher. Here where nobody lived, at the edge of the plateau, the slagheap served as dumping ground for everything an industrial city wanted to dispose of. Everything would soon be covered by slag anyway.

As we were walking alongside the edge of the rising plateau I saw a large, square, black steel tub, an industrial container for liquids, lying upside down, below. The walls of the black monstrosity were about two feet high. The tub was approximately nine feet long and five feet wide. I stopped cold in my tracks. I'd been struck by a gigantic idea.

"Hold everything, Arthur, Kurt. Do you see that metal container?" I pointed to it with an outstretched hand.

"Of course," was their reply. "What about that damned tub? Do you want to start a scrap metal business?" And they continued walking, they were tired, they were on their way home to the barracks without paying attention to me.

"Hold it, hold it my friends!" I called after them. "Listen to this. For the longest time we suffer from filth. How about taking a nice hot shower after work?" That stopped them immediately, still not knowing what I was driving at.

"What're you talking about? What does this metal tub has to do with a shower?" They'd stopped though and slowly sauntered back as I started to outline my idea, which had come to me in a flash. I explained, "We'll drag this tub back to our barracks. I mean we'll get enough people to drag it back to the barracks. Then we'll erect two single T girders adjacent to the powerhouse about four feet apart and seven feet off the ground right next to the wall, both in rectangular fashion. They'll do fine as support beams. We'll heave the tub on top and connect a water supply to it. We have one in the powerhouse. Then we connect a steam pipe into the tub. We have plenty of steam in the powerhouse, too. Affix two showerheads underneath the tub, add two valves for hot and cold water and build a fence with a door around the whole thing and: *voila!* We'll have a hot and cold shower. How'd you like it?"

"Kurt," Arthur exclaimed, waving his finger at him, "I've told you many times. Watch this guy! If you let his brain alone for only two seconds, he'll come up with a big one. In all honesty, Peter, congratulations, this is a fabulous idea. I'm not a mechanic, there're some in our group who can handle the construction, but it shouldn't be too difficult to handle. Let's drag this tub over to the barrack tonight before it disappears. Nobody needs to know or needs to question what we're doing."

Arthur was rubbing his hands in anticipation, already thinking of his first hot shower. Kurt laughed and giggled almost deliriously, probably dreaming of all the showers he'd take after over four years of not having any.

"Can you imagine?" he yelled into the sticky, smelling air, "I won't smell of sweat any more, I won't itch, and I can wash my hair under running hot water, I'll have to go begging for a piece of soap, whoa, we'll live like normal people."

I looked at him, at us, and had to agree with him. The appearance of this group of unshaven, dirty looking prisoners—under normal circumstances—would be revolting. Transporting the tub wasn't as easy as I had visualized. But what the heck! It was the idea that counted. The moaning and groaning from the men who dragged the tub and from our mechanic who fixed the pipes, the steam connection and the handles, only prolonged the execution of the project a little. Two weeks later we had the first shower and Kurt, Arthur and I initiated it, deliciously washing, soaping and singing dissonantly, standing under the streaming hot water, completely clean, for the first time since captivity, boisterously laughing like young men do in a moment like this.

If nothing else had done it, the shower put us on the map. The Russian workers at the plant used it from now on at the end of their shift. The *Natchalnik* did too. And since everybody left a little something for the "inventors," we didn't have to go begging as often any more.

We came up with other little "inventions" as well by installing central heating in our barracks. Yes, with the help of boundless steam from the boiler across the road. A pipe was put down under the road leading into the barrack, and a radiator was installed in every room. The Russians thought we'd lost our marbles, never satisfied, always changing, always complaining.

But . . . But we had no news about going home. Nobody knew a thing, no matter how many times we were questioned by our co-workers, *"Scoro domoi pajechitje?"* (Are you going home soon?)

The civilians were mostly living in *semljankas* (literally: earthen homes, built from earth) around the plant. They had many jobs for us to do, especially helping to work the little patches of land awarded to every Russian as a private enclave, to raise vegetables or potatoes. The men would go with the civilians and dig, plant and care for the gardens and received meals in return or raw vegetables or potatoes.

Our mechanic, Karl, came running to get me one day just after I'd returned from my shift in the quarry.

"Peter, you have to help me," he said. "There's an older Russian in my shop and he's all exited about something he wants me to do, but you know, I don't speak the language. Please come before he disappears again."

We walked to the shop behind the barrack where an older man stood, waiting patiently for us.

"Drastruitje (Good day)," I said. "My name is Petja, how can I help?"

"*Ladna,* nice to meet you, Petja, my name is Igor Ivanovitch and I hope that one of you guys can speak some Russian, otherwise we'll be standing here until tomorrow," the old guy replied.

He was talking excitedly with his hands and feet trying to explain his problem, speaking a dialect that I had a hard time understanding. I stopped him and asked to repeat everything slowly, and we finally came to the meat of the matter.

He and his wife had built a *semljanka* three years ago, right after the war, not far from our barrack, as a matter of fact, about a ten minutes walk from our place. Wisely enough somebody had inserted a pipe in the middle of the little hut, deep enough into the ground to access water. But the pipe had never been fitted with a pump. There were no pumps available shortly after the war. He wanted water, though, to save his wife the work of lugging pail after pail from far away. Then water could be pumped out of the ground under the *simljanka.* He'd finally acquired a manual pump, at great expense. Now he needed somebody to cut a thread to the end of the pipe, to fit the pump. The fitting had to be tight enough so that it wouldn't leak under pressure.

I translated to Karl and emphasized, "Karl, if you accept the job, do it well. We want more people to come to ask for our services."

Karl, who smiled broadly at the old man as his only means of communicating, responded, "Of course, I can do it, I cut threads all the time onto all kinds of pipes at the plant during my regular work. They ruin a piece of machinery every day, and I have to refit it and hook it up again. Why shouldn't I be able to do that for the old man, especially if it involves some chow? But, Peter, you'll have to come along in case there is something to translate, okay?"

I turned to the old man and said, "He can do it. What'll you pay him for his work?"

"Pail of potatoes," was his immediate reply. He had his plan laid out very well.

Karl was happy, the old man was happy, and we fixed a time around five in the afternoon when Karl's shift would end, and Igor's wife would be home also.

We left with our tools at the appointed time and walked over a dam, which was four hundred yards from our barrack.

The Russians had displayed their talent to be practical with engineering problems once more. What did they do to build a new dam for the railroad? They placed ties on the naked ground, fastened rails on top, so that a train could traverse slowly but safely. Then they pushed a number of cars filled with dirt over the rails, emptied the dirt on both sides until the end of the ties were covered with dirt. Then they came with powerful but primitive hydraulic lifters, similar to a jack one uses to lift up the car to change a tire, placed the jack under the ties in the middle between the rails, and lifted the rails until the end of the ties broke through the dirt and rested again on top of it. The process was repeated many times as the dam gradually grew higher and higher, always leaving a cavity, a ditch between the rails.

Well, Karl and I climbed over the dam, which by now was about twenty feet high and still growing. We slid down on the other side and continued our way passing an assembly of *simljankas,* each of them built of different materials, of different shapes, of different sizes and on varying plots. There was no pattern to it, no planning. We couldn't detect any paint on the outside of the *simljankas* anywhere—maybe some whitewash on the walls here and there. After walking a few hundred yards further, we saw Igor waving to us from the distance.

He was a small man but his wife, Alexandra, who stood by his side, was almost five inches smaller than he was. She was tiny, had a completely wrinkled face and hands, like people have who have worked in the sun all their lives, a scarf tightly wrapped around her head, routinely tugged in on the sides of her face, to protect her fore-head. She looked at us, her eyes darting back and forth. She gave us the once over, so to speak, and seemed to be satisfied with her evaluation. After a short greeting she said. *"Dawai, natchinaitje,"* meaning, "Let's get started."

Karl got busy inside the *semlianka* with the pipe, which was in a very awkward position. He had a hard time cutting a thread around the end of the pipe with little space to move. He was cursing under his breath. It seemed that whichever way he turned there was always a wall or a corner in the way. He called me after a while to help. We finished our work. Now came the tantalizing part. Would the pump have enough suction to bring up water? Most importantly, was there a well underneath the house at all? Did the pipe go deep enough into the ground?

I guess Igor was even more apprehensive than we were, and I told Karl again, "Be very careful with what you are doing. Don't disappoint the guy, whatever you do. It would mean trouble all the way." I vividly remembered my experience with the radio at the *kolchos,* a few years ago.

"Don't you worry, if the old pump is any good, it'll work. That pump must be at least a hundred years old. Where do they find these things?"

At first Karl started pumping very slowly, just a few strokes to test the pump for suction and then, feeling the rising of the water in the pipe, turned to the old man and said,

"You want to break it in?"

After my translation the old man smiled and went into the corner, looked at his wife, grabbed the pump and gave it a few slow, deliberate strokes. Eureka! Immediately a strong jet of crystal clear water shot out. The pump was working.

Babuschka Alexandra was the happiest person in the room because she wouldn't have to go to the distant, communal well any more to lug pails full of water back to the house.

Babuschka—I'd decided to call the old lady *Babuschka,* because she looked like a grandmother—fixed wonderful borscht, and we ate with gusto.

We were still eating when the door opened, and a pretty woman of about thirty entered the *semlianka*. Her head was covered by the same kind of scarf *Babuschka* wore covering most of her face, but I could clearly see two big, brown eyes surveying the situation in the room, and I could recognize without a doubt—even under the scarf—that she was young and good looking.

"Galina, these are the *woyenna plennies* we were talking about. Remember, it was about the pump. They came immediately and fixed it. We have water in the house now. Isn't that marvelous, Galina?"

Her name was Galina. I introduced us, "This is Karl and I'm Petja."

We exchanged a quick smile and a few words of greeting.

Galina had rented a tiny room in the back of the house from the old couple, which provided additional income to them.

Before we left, *Babuschka* and I made another date to visit again, to help her with the planting of the seed-potatoes for the coming season on their plot on top of the hill.

"We'll have to do it on a Sunday, Petja, on your day off, because it'll take a whole day, *ladna?*"

I agreed. She gave Karl a pail of potatoes for his work, which made him happy. He was grateful for what I'd done to get him the job and the extra food, and we went home talking about two nice old people and also about the pretty woman we had met.

"It's really strange, I can look at a woman again and feel my member twitch a little," Karl confided to me. "For a long time, during these last four years, I thought that would never happen again. Now I feel more and more often that it's high time to go home to demonstrate to my wife that I'm alive. Peter, I can't tell you how grateful I am that you guys took me with you to the "Slave Labor Site." I was afraid, at first, and I didn't know what to expect, but you guys from the bread factory were so sure of this, it was catching. Now we only have to go home. Man do I want to go home, especially after seeing this woman, Galina; she sure is pretty this one."

I had similar feelings and for the first time in a long time, I thought about Celli and Susi too.

Babuschka and I met sometime later when the weather was warming up and went on a strenuous walk up the mountain, way up to the top of it. From our plateau of artificial slag the natural grown mountains rose another six hundred feet to the top, a location where many civilians had their tiny plots. I was totally out of breath by the time we had reached the crest. The old lady was laughing at me. We worked hard for several hours, turning over the soil of her plot with a simple spade, planting the potatoes for the coming season, and returning at sundown.

At the onset of summer—in late May 1949—the heat of the slag convinced us it would be better to change our working hours. From now on we began working at four in the morning and finished at twelve. The stones were hot enough without the sun beating down on us. The added advantage with the new schedule was that we had more time for little jobs to do for the civilians in the afternoon, since our regular workday ended early.

When Babuschka and I returned from our digging expedition and entered the *semlianka* Igor was already there, and Galina stuck her face through the door of her room.

"Petja, nice to see you again. I've a little problem with the locks of some cabinets at the *stalowaja* [cafeteria] where I work. Could you come tomorrow and take a look at it?"

"Be glad to, Galina. But tell me a little more about the job. I'll need some tools and I don't want to bring the wrong ones."

She explained that the doors of some cabinets didn't close properly and she also wanted to have something installed to lock the doors because she experienced a considerable amount of theft. We fixed a time, and she went back into her room.

"She's a nice woman," *Babuschka* said. "She's with us for almost a year and is very quiet and pleasant to have around. We think she was 'ordered' to *Stalinsk* by the NKWD. She was married in Moscow and has left three little girls behind. Something must have gone wrong between her and her husband. In Moscow, the easiest way to get rid of a wife is to complain to the NKWD about her political reliability, and she's gone in no time, especially if the complainer is a member of the party. Don't tell her that I told you. She doesn't seem to know anybody here in *Stalinsk,* which suits us fine. All we need is some jerk to come in here, to check up on us. Again, Petja, please don't say anything to her. All we want is to live in peace. That's all we want, really."

An additional benefit from our outing had been that we'd talked quite a bit, and *Babuschka* and I had become friendly with each other.

The following day I took Karl's little toolbox, having promised him to return everything intact and cut him in on any spoils from the job. I went in the direction Galina had described to me, to find the *stalowaja,* and arrived just before closing time. Galina waited for me at the door, and led me to the back to the storage facilities. The repair of the cabinet doors was simple, and I was able to secure the doors, as she had wanted. Afterwards she invited me for a mug of hot tea and a dry, sweet piece of cake, man oh, man, "a piece of cake"! The last time I'd eaten a piece of cake was almost four years earlier. We started talking. She really was a nice woman, and I began to like her.

"Do you have any plans for now, Galina? I mean do you still have to go places, or are you finished working?" I asked.

"No, I'm finished," she said. "I'm going home. Alexandra sometimes fixes a soup and shares it with me. I don't do much after work. To go into the city is quite a trip, and I don't have a bicycle. I don't like to use the trolley, because too many men will try touching and bothering me. Sometimes I walk up the mountain after work and look down on the city. It gives me a chance to contemplate, and it gives me peace."

She was talking to me totally relaxed, and though I'm writing down this conversation freely, as if my Russian and my recollection were perfect, and as if I could easily understand every word she said, that wasn't so. My grammar was bad. My accent was very noticeable and my vocabulary was limited. It was surprising to me that this young woman talked to me, the POW, so openly.

"I never thought of going up to the mountain, that's a great idea," I replied. "Do you want to go now? Maybe I can come with you? I mean, I'd like to, and I couldn't think of anything more enjoyable than to be in your company."

What was the matter with me? I was falling all over myself and almost bit my tongue, but I made a concerted effort to express myself better.

"That's a wonderful idea, Petja," she said, and a bright smile lit up her face. "I didn't know how to ask you, I mean, how do you ask a former enemy of your country," she laughed again, "a prisoner of war, to go for a walk? I just want to say, I'm not afraid of you, not at all, as a matter of fact, I feel secure in your presence. You aren't like the other guys. They always undress me with their eyes, you know. That's why I'm always clad like a mummy; it keeps the 'stares' away."

That was a mouthful. It was the first woman I'd talked to since becoming a prisoner four years ago with the exception of the elderly dentist. I blushed. I blushed!

Galina blushed too, grabbed her *fufika* and led the way. It was the first time in my life that I'd gone on a date with a pretty woman and a toolbox. My friendship with Galina had begun.

I haven't written much about the propaganda and other political efforts by our jailors, trying to make communists out of the former Nazi enemies. Actually it was always present in our daily lives. We were surrounded by red banners, strung over buildings and nailed to every available wall space in town, on every work site and every wall in the camp.

"Support The Victorious Peace-Loving Soviet Union, The Champion Of All Workers."

"Welcome To The Defenders Of Freedom And Equality."

"The Day Of The World Revolution Is Near."

"Marx-Engels And The Steadfast Stalin Will Save The World From Capitalism."

"Proletarians Of All Countries Unite."

I could go on and on about the slogans we saw every day. There was one saving grace. Most of us couldn't read Cyrillic, especially when we first came to *Stalinsk;* but the repetitive slogans had given me a chance to improve my knowledge of the foreign alphabet and to slowly acquire a better understanding of it.

To make sure that the meaning of political messages didn't escape the prisoner's dulled minds, the Soviets employed the ANTIFA as mediator in the process to educate us about advantages of Communism and Socialism.

In case of OSMU 11, the representative of the ANTIFA was a seasoned German communist. He was forty years old, had been an

active member of the German Communist Party under Ernst Thael-
mann, the head of the German KP (Communist Party) and of the
youth movement, before Hitler assumed power and put Thaelman
into Nazi concentration camps where he died in the early forties.

The ANTIFA guy at OSMU 11 was from *Chemnitz,* in the State of
Saxony, the hotbed of communism in Germany since 1918. He spoke this
terrible Saxon-German dialect. He, believe it or not, I've forgotten his
name—talking about a Freudian slip—had it in for me. He must have
heard about my background. To him I was the capitalist offspring of a family who owned a factory and "exploited" workers. That was his interpretation. Whenever he started to rant and rave during his presentations
against people like me Arthur stood up, objected, took my side and complained about his prejudices. No dice! The guy wanted my skin. This went
on for several months as the summer of 1949 and it was intolerable.

In the stone quarry. (author front row right)

He must have overdone it, or Arthur and I had friends on OSMU 11 that we didn't know about. Anyway, one day in the afternoon shortly after we came back from work, we noticed a dark blue limousine; a ZIS special had pulled up to our barracks. I hadn't seen it because I was inside. One of the men from the bread factory stormed into the room and yelled, "Petja, the *'Blue One'* is outside. What do you think he wants?"

I couldn't believe what I heard. My friend, *Nikolai Nikolajewitch,* had come to OSMU 11? Unbelievable! Why did he come to this place? And why didn't he call me to come out to see him?

I ran outside and saw the familiar figure, clad in blue, as always. What was he doing here? He was standing in front of our man from the ANTIFA. He towered over the guy and was thrusting his finger at him, jabbing it into the man's chest. He spoke loudly and the guys who knew him shrank away from the scene while Ossipenko was translating.

"I don't know who you are," he said. "You mother fucking little shit-faced prisoner, but I'm hearing that you're giving my friend Petja a hard time. You're threatening him with severe consequences. Is that right? Now, my little friend," constantly jabbing his finger into the man's chest, "let me tell you. No, I'll make a promise to you. Should Petja have any troubles at the camp, should his repatriation to Germany be delayed in any way, I'll make sure that you'll never see the light of day again, and forget about going home to the God-forsaken hut from which you probably came. Mind you, I've been a member of the Communist Party for twenty years and before that of the *Comsomolsk* [the youth movement of the Communist Party]. I am a declared 'Hero of the Soviet Union' during the war of the Fatherland against barbarians like you. I am a member of the Communist Party's City Council of *Stalinsk* and an honorary member of every communist organization in this town that you can think of. I, *Nikolai Nikolajewitch,* can assure you, I have influence! Remember *that* before you say another word against my friend Petja."

He looked piercingly at the guy, still stabbing him in the chest, turned around and, seeing me, imperceptibly blinked his left eye, got into his car and drove off. I never saw the "Blue One" again, but if you want a definition of the word "friend," it was *Nikolai Nikolajewitch,* the Russian *Natchalnik* from the bread factory in *Stalinsk.*

It's rare to bestow friendship; it's even harder to prove it when it needs to be proven. I was fortunate to have had friends in Siberia, Arthur and Nikolai Nikolajewitch and. . . . let me continue.

The ANTIFA man from *Chemnitz* never bothered me again. He knew how his party worked. He wasn't going to mess with a high official. Upon returning to Germany, East Germany that is, he assumed an important position with the government of the DDR (*Deutsche Demokratische Republik*) until he was later purged and disappeared unceremoniously.

My friendship with Galina deepened slowly but gradually. In the evenings I would pick her up at the *stalowaja* to walk her home. We had always lots to talk about. I, with my terrible Russian and she teaching me patiently, was correcting me, having a laughing fit whenever I mispronounced one of these difficult, long Russian words. I asked her if she'd mind being seen with a German POW, but she only shrugged her shoulders.

"What more can they do to me? My fellow workers and the *Natchalnik* don't mind what I'm doing with my spare time. Everybody is kind of busy with his own problems. Some day I'll tell you my story, and you'll understand."

I was happy the way things were and wasn't going to do anything to rock the boat or to ask dumb questions.

As the weather became warmer and warmer, it enabled us to walk through the bleak countryside as late in the evening as we wanted to. I don't know what we'd have done in December, or January. Alexandra and Igor smiled when I brought her home and didn't object to us standing in front of the *semlianka,* watching the sun go down and the moon coming up. We talked and talked, and with Galina's help and instructions I became more fluent in this difficult language.

Galina was at least two inches smaller than I. She was thirty-one, as she confided to me with a worried face, and in her own words . . . "much too old for you." She had thick brown hair, which she tied back in a bun had absolutely smashingly, huge, brown eyes and a cute small mouth, which could smile like sunshine. Her nose was turned-up nicely, just enough to look daring and bold. One can appreciate by my description that I was falling in love.

I never forgot, though, that I was a POW. I could be severely punished if I took any liberties. Fraternization was definitely out for both sides. By now we knew each other for about a month. One night we were standing near the *semlianka,* watching a big bright moon come up over the horizon when I couldn't contain my feelings any longer. I turned around, took her into my arms and kissed her. She must've been waiting for my move because she didn't object, but returned my kiss and put her arms around my neck to hold me close. We kissed and kissed until we were both out of breath.

"Petja, I didn't know the Germans could kiss like that. Let's try it again."

Galina's position in the *stalowaja* had advantages for me that I hadn't considered when I met her. Every few days she had a small present for me, like small pieces of meat, some strange looking dark brown oleo, which nevertheless tasted wonderful (I called it "monkey fat"), always something edible to make me happy. I was in seventh heaven, almost. We had not yet consummated our love affair and I was feeling my blood churning. I mean, she was thirty-one, and I was twenty-six and what do you do if you are in love?

"No," Galina said firmly when I made one of my efforts to make love to her on the little couch in her room that served as her bed. "No, Petja, not until you bring me a certification from the camp doctor that you're free of syphilis."

I stared at her in disbelief.

"I don't know why you think I may have syphilis. Where should I've infected myself? I'm a prisoner for the last four years, most of the time too weak to stand up, much less do anything else. Where should I've caught a venereal disease like syphilis? If I did, I certainly would've noticed it before now. Why do you think that I have syphilis, Galina? What do you think a camp doctor would do if I'd ask for a Wasserman test? He'd know immediately that I've something going with a Russian civilian. He would pull me back to the camp and throw me in jail for breaking the iron rule against fraternization." I certainly asked her a lot of questions, but she'd upset me.

"Petja, listen to me. Joseph Vissarionowitch Stalin, the chairman of the Communist Party, in his never ending wisdom decided a few years ago that this disease should be wiped out. By now he has almost succeeded, only very few cases are reported these days. Do you know how he did it? In the Soviet Union everybody who is diagnosed with syphilis is executed immediately. This way the disease doesn't spread, and the unfortunate victim doesn't have to be treated at great expense to the state. His treatment is cheap. It only costs a bullet. Stalin initiated and executed drastic measures, and it's effective."

"My God," I blurted, "what a terrible thing to do. Isn't there another method to cure the disease? I'm not too familiar with it, but somebody said the other day that an English scientist has come up with a cure or a new medicine."

"I know, I have heard about it too, but it'll take a long time before the Russian medical system will approve it, and that wouldn't help us now."

She was stubborn and stuck to her guns, no certification, and no sex.

I was frustrated beyond belief. In the bread factory and at OSMU 11 I hadn't only regained my strength and was feeling strong and healthy, but my sex drive had returned with a vengeance.

It was a few weeks, many kisses and heated petting sessions later, when one evening I was waiting in her little room for Galina to come home. The two old people always let me into the house, treating me almost like a son, and made no objections to my friendship with Galina. I must have fallen asleep on her bed, because I didn't realize that Galina had come into the room and was sitting at the edge of the bed, until I felt somebody trying to stick something into my mouth. I opened my eyes but Galina immediately murmured, "Keep you eyes closed, Petja, and taste what I've "requisitioned" for you at the *stalowaja.*"

I opened my mouth and tried to discover with my taste buds what was put into it. At first, I couldn't believe what I thought it was. Was this really a chocolate covered cream filled praline I tasted? To me, "the man with the sweet tooth," the sensation was extraordinary. I kept my eyes shut and my mouth open, and Galina continued to feed delicious pralines into my mouth. She must have noticed the bliss on my face, because I heard her chuckle happily. As I kept my eyes closed I heard herself busying with something and recognized she was lying down next to me.

"If you had one delicacy, you might as well have another one; let's make love Petja, *lubya moya* [my love], and damn the consequences."

That's what we did. She enjoyed it as much as I did, and nobody caught syphilis either.

It must have been a few days later. Arthur and I had just finished our shower when he started to talk to me. No, he didn't talk. He started to stutter. It was almost comical, and I laughed and said,

"Do you have anything in your mouth? It almost sounds as if you're eating a hot potato?"

"Asshole, nothing of the kind. I just wanted to tell you that I have a girlfriend, *Natasha* is her name. I feel guilty because of my wife back home, but at the same time I am deliriously happy. I'd almost forgotten how wonderful it feels to get laid. The only thing is, she is terribly afraid of the syphilis and wants me to get a certificate from the camp to assure her that I'm healthy."

I burst out laughing and told him about Galina's worries whereupon we both had a good laugh together.

"I didn't know you were chasing the ladies, Arthur. Where'd you meet her anyway?"

"Oh, I was helping an old lady planting her crops when she asked me if I could help her neighbor also. She introduced me; she was young and good looking; and one thing led to another. I wouldn't want to stay here in Siberia, but life is certainly more pleasant with a little love."

Natascha, Galina, Arthur and I became adventurous and brazen. The women organized civilian clothes for us to blend in with the locals. We wore the typical caps as the *Sibiriakis* do. I still cherished wearing the one that Nikolai Nikolajewitch had given me after I returned from *Novosibirsk*. We shaved our hair at the neckline like the Russians did, practiced the Russian swagger, a kind of boisterous, swaying walk every young man learns in the army, and went into town together, to stroll up and down the main drag where everybody went on Sunday afternoons. We listened to outdoor concerts in the park, ate ice cream, or saw a movie—compliments of the girls—we didn't understand a word. In short, we were audacious as hell. Love and women can easily turn a man into a fool. We were well on our way. Fortunately for us the Good Lord was protecting us, and we didn't get caught, though we had a few close calls, especially when we ran into the old lady Arthur had worked for digging potatoes. But dressed as we were, she wasn't sure where she had seen us. We disappeared in a hurry, the two women running after us laughing their heads off.

Amongst ourselves at work, or taking a walk after work, we spoke about these two amazing women, and commiserated with each other about our overriding desire to return home. We were developing split personalities.

Galina and I often talked about our lives prior to our relationship, about the war, about America and Germany, and she finally confided in me and spoke of her previous life in Moscow. It was an emotional nightmare for her to talk about her three little girls whom she had to leave with her husband. After listening to her story I understood why.

In 1937 she'd married at a very young age, an engineer who had a good job with the city government. He was almost fifteen years older than she and a trusted member of the Communist Party. When they'd met, she'd admired his mature looks, his position and his intelligence. It turned out that he wasn't only a self-centered man, as she discovered, but also had strange sexual preferences which she disliked. Galina didn't elaborate. The couple grew progressively apart after the third girl was born, and they hardly spoke. Her husband had girl friends and didn't try to hide it from her.

One day, at four o'clock in the morning, there was a knock at the door and two uniformed members of the state security police (NKWD) told her to get dressed, and took her along. Her husband ostensibly didn't know what was going on. The NKWD took her to the *Ljubjanka* prison, interrogated her for several hours, and accused her of activities against the State and against the Communist Party. She allegedly had made "derogatory" remarks about Joseph Vissarionowitch Stalin.

She was put on a transport to *Stalinsk* and never saw her children or her husband again. She never got to the bottom of it but assumed her husband had engineered the whole affair, to get rid of her, because she had accused him of extramarital affairs. She hadn't anticipated his cunning and brutal reaction just to have his freedom to do whatever he pleased.

"You know, Peter, there must be thousands of woman in Siberia experiencing the same fate as I. Husbands simply used their good standing with the Party to send their wives to the Gulag. I don't know what will happen to me, but I don't anticipate returning to Moscow to see my children again as long as this monster is alive."

Now I had heard the story the two old people had hinted at earlier. I couldn't help Galina except to listen to her and to take her into my arms to console her. What was going to happen to her after I left?

The summer passed and September 1949 arrived. I had been in the Gulag now for fifty-one months. Persistent questioning by the Russians—"*Scoro domoi pajechitje?*" (Are you going home soon?)—couldn't pacify our longing to depart Siberia for one second, or convince our suspicious minds to believe the day of our departure was any closer. All we could think and dream about was to leave Siberia for good and return to civilization. The postcards we'd written home over a year ago remained the strongest proof our hopes were justified. They'd strengthened our belief the Russians couldn't and wouldn't sweep us under the rug, or retain us in their Siberian Archipelago Gulag forever. We also heard through radio broadcasts, observed by the camp's ANTIFA officials, that a new Socialist German Government had been installed in the Russian occupied zone of Germany. The Western Nations intended to do the same in the west. As soon as a nation called Germany existed again, we reasoned with ourselves, we would've legal representation, and there would be hope for our return.

Okay, *ladna, nitchewo,* it doesn't matter; don't think about it, it's easier to bear that way. I said to myself. To some degree we made peace with the way we were living, with the monotonous food, with the deprivations of every day life. But on the other hand, how could we forget where we came from? What life was all about on the other side of the iron curtain and what we were missing? During many sleepless nights I thought of my mother and where she might be at the moment, whether she'd survived the war, had returned to the USA, and whether I'd ever see her again?

At OSMU 11 the scourge of hunger, that dreadful, disabling and demoralizing need, had disappeared. After years of low protein foods, our metabolism had adjusted to the Russian diet; our system extracted all it needed to do our strenuous work in the stone quarry from the food we got. Finally we had enough to eat. The supplies from the camp, the generous help from the civilians, our own organizational skills and the rewards for extra work assignments kept us in "fodder." No matter how you slice it, our life as POWs had become bearable. There was nobody dying any more. We were no longer in danger of starving to death as so many of our fellow prisoners in the second half of 1945 and throughout 1946 and 1947. Our fraternization with the civilians, especially the ones we worked with during the day, had gone far beyond the official Soviet party line. Arthur and I had progressed the furthest in this regard. We had girlfriends.

Galina and I were lovers and used every opportunity to meet, to be with each other, to make love, to enjoy each other's company and to philosophize endlessly about life. I think Galina was much more aware of the frailty of our relationship and its continuation on borrowed time. The day I would leave would come sooner or later.

Galina came home from work one evening and was all excited.

"Petja, we have an invitation to a wedding celebration. The son of the *Natchalnik* of the cement factory and one of my coworkers will tie the knot. With so many people attending, and with the father in such exalted position, I'm sure the celebration will be absolutely wonderful. There'll be good food and lots to drink. The father of the bride is wealthy and can afford a sumptuous wedding. But the best thing is that they picked a Saturday to wed and to celebrate. This way we know that we can enjoy two days of fun, and we won't miss a beat at work. How about it? Will you come? Will you go with me? You know how much I care about you. I don't mind the stupid regulations about fraternization with *wojenna plennies.*"

Why should I object? I felt proud and comfortable in her presence. She never teased me about my linguistic limitations and my inability to master difficult Russian grammar. Whenever I was making a fool of myself in the presence of others, she jumped to my rescue. Going to the wedding was okay as far as I was concerned. It would be my first occasion—as a POW—to take part in such an event.

The reception was supposed to be held about one mile from our barracks in one of the regular houses not far from where Galina was living. Under the Communist regime all churches had been demolished or converted into garages or workshops. The communist regime officially considered religious ceremonies a criminal act. Conversely, one could find an Icon with a picture of the mother Mary or Jesus Christ in almost every house in Russia. Sometimes in blatant blasphemy the pictures showed Jesus with the facial features of Stalin. Most people went about worshipping uninhibitedly and the authorities closed their eyes apparently.

I was told that all weddings took place in the presence of a "pope," a Russian Orthodox priest who was quite busy exercising his various duties in the community. He lived on the donations he received. Galina explained to me how the community of Orthodox Christians supported the pope with money and food.

Of course, I told Arthur and Ossipenko that I was invited to a wedding. They had to know where I was. Ossipenko had no objections.

That Saturday I cleaned and scrubbed in our marvelous shower, and went to Galina's place to meet with *Babuschka* Alexandra and her husband Ivan.

These two nice people who had introduced me to Galina in the first place had become a little jealous about our relationship, asking inquisitively, "Where're you two going? What will you be doing? You know, Petja, you shouldn't be seen with a Russian girl, don't you Petja?"

To show curiosity in other people's affairs was highly unusual for Russians. The less one knew the better it was. People didn't want to get involved. Their motto was, what you don't know you can't be held responsible for.

I became worried about what they might do with their knowledge. What would happen if they reported me to the police or to the camp administration? I knew them well I thought, but could or should I trust them completely, or anybody else for that matter? I loved my relative freedom, and I was in love with Galina and didn't want her to get hurt, because of some stupidity of mine.

That evening, as I always did until Galina arrived, I chatted a little with them, to keep them happy, and I helped them with their evening chores, chopped some wood and got water from the well—polishing apples if you want to know the truth.

Galina came back from work, and we went into her cubicle, closed the door and kissed, happy to be together again after a long hard day's at work. We didn't start anything more serious because the party was coming up, and we had to get going. Our good-bye from the two old people was friendly.

When we arrived at the wedding, the pope was just beginning with the ceremony. A makeshift altar on one end of the main room was covered with a red cloth to hide an old table underneath. The organizers of the affair had built candelabra on top with the Icon of the house hanging in the corner nearby. The couple was standing holding hands in front of the table. They were dressed in normal working clothes—nobody in *Stalinsk* who belonged to the working class had more than one or two sets of clothes. The bride had white flowers woven into her hair and the groom was wearing a brand new blue cap tilted proudly way back on his neck with curly locks falling over his forehead.

The priest was reciting something from an old Bible, which I didn't understand. Most of what he said was spoken too quickly or mumbled, and when I tried to question Galina, she whispered into my ear, "Shhh, I'll explain everything later. Keep quiet and don't interrupt the ceremony."

The ceremony lasted an eternity. The Russian Orthodox Church executes the longest and most drawn out wedding ceremony I've ever witnessed or listened to.

When it was finally over Galina and the other girls had shed a few tears, the groom kissed the bride, and everybody congratulated both of them. The groom gave me a wink and said, "Hey, Petja, you're next. Maybe some day, Galina and you'll follow in our footsteps, how about it? I don't think our government will ever let you return home; you Germans are much too efficient. What would they do without you?"

I must've paled visibly, because Galina asked me if the thought of getting hitched to her was such a terrible idea.

"No, Galina, you know how I feel about you, it's the thought of spending the rest of my life in Siberia that frightens me. It would be much better if you'd inquire, without raising any suspicion, how your chances are of immigrating to the United States. I assure you my mother and you would love each other at first sight, and English is not such a difficult language to learn. I'll see if I can get an entry permit for you to come to the USA when we're released."

"You're sweet, Petja, but you're also naïve. I'm, through the never-ending mercy of the NKWD, a *zaklutschorny* out on bail. I'll never be able to leave Siberia, not even to visit one of my daughters in Moscow. Do you think they'd let me go to the country of Russia's worst enemy? Petja, by the grace of the Almighty, we'll both enjoy a brief and I might say very happy interlude in our lives. Every minute we see each other is 'happiness' and a blessing for me. I don't want to think of the time thereafter. Be quiet; let's go and get something to eat and to drink."

Her statement was brutally truthful and closer to reality than my fantasies were. That's what you learn to do after you've accepted that your alternatives are zero.

We rejoined the others, ate *blini* and *piroschki,* a wonderful *calbassa,* and I tasted excellent *borscht,* likes I'd never eaten before. The *kvass* we drank was home made, foamy and potent. The father of the groom raised his glass to toast the happy couple. To join him every member of the party had received one *stacan* of vodka.

The glasses we used at this wedding celebration were the typical *stacan* made from thick glass, hardly breakable. At the cost of ten new rubles per *stacan* vodka was a real luxury, a sign of the stature of the father of the groom.

Drinking plenty of vodka and kvass helped to improve the mood of the party rapidly. I was introduced to everybody as the POW friend of Galina. Most of the guests were friendly to me, the German prisoner of war. This wasn't necessarily the case at work or when we met the same individuals in town. During these occasions, when others could observe their behavior, some of them were even rude. An exaggerated fear of the authorities dictated people's behavior.

While offering me a *papyrossi,* an expensive, branded cigarette made from real tobacco, one of the guests satisfied my curiosity.

"See, Petja, this city and Siberia, as such, are not typical for Russia. You can look at *Stalinsk* as a gigantic prison camp. All, or let's say most of us, are being watched constantly. It takes only a wink of an eye by one of the NKWD watchdogs, and we're thrown back behind bars. You of all people should know what *that* means. And let me tell you one more thing if you think your POW prison camps are bad, you haven't seen anything. Some of the camps for our own people in this town bar the description. The German prisoners may not see the Red Cross and may believe it doesn't even exist, but believe you me the Red Cross watches over you with great attentiveness all the way from Moscow. The graft in our camps, in contrast to your situation, is beyond belief, and nobody speaks on our behalf, which means that food and bread is even scarcer than in the POW installations. I know what I'm talking about, I've been there."

I had heard rumors to that effect but never as directly and strongly expressed as at that moment by a former inmate. What I did remember well—how could I ever forget—were the first eight months in *Stalinsk* in 1945, at the *kolchos* camp, when the graft of the administrative officials and the dysentery had almost killed all of us.

Galina saved me from getting into further details with this guest. When Russians drink alcohol they get funny at times. Depending on the character of the individual they could switch from exuberant friendliness to outright and extreme dislike. Galina didn't want me to get into any trouble if she could avoid it. She had embraced a very risky experiment anyway by taking me to the wedding with her, so why stretch it?

The party continued through the night and everybody consumed Kvass, plenty of it. I must admit that I was beginning to feel it. Galina lifted her hand, wiggled a finger in a mock reprimand and said.

"Watch it Petja, we don't want to see you get drunk. The others could start having their fun with you, and you wouldn't like it."

Somebody had put pillows on the floor and a small group of us, about eight guys and girls, sat down in a corner of the crowded *semlijanka,* talking and eating and drinking. It was a good feeling to be sitting on the floor. That way nobody realized how much alcohol I had consumed.

If I had never experienced it, I wouldn't have believed what Russians had told me many times before. Only Russians can become totally intoxicated and drink themselves sober again. You had to keep on drinking long enough, so they'd said. Well, I was on my way to try that prescription.

A few native Sibiriakis, but also people from other corners of the former Soviet Union were among the group and, of course, I the POW. As night wore on everybody wanted to tell everybody else what a rough deal he'd received, and how they'd been screwed in more senses than one. I didn't talk, I'd learned my lesson, Galina was watching me, and she knew my story anyway.

The women especially were swimming in tears as they relived memories of children left behind, of rape and hard labor in camps around the *Altai* region of southern Siberia. The guards in most camps are brutal. I didn't need to add my own memories to make all of us feel sorry for ourselves, a feeling, which increased dramatically as the drinking continued and grew in intensity.

I must've fallen asleep for a short time, because Galina shook me gently to wake me up. It was three o'clock in the morning; it would be getting light soon. Some of the guests had gone home already and others were sleeping in the corners. Galina held a glass of *kvass* in front of me and said, "Come on, drink up, Petja, it'll sober you. I don't want you to go home in your present condition. It would be bad, real bad, if you get picked up accidentally by a patrol from the militia."

I gave her a kiss, she was such an angel, and did as she told me. Kissing everybody on cheeks and mouths we said good-bye to the others, and started on our short trip home. I took Galina to her place. She refused to let me come inside for a "night cap" but rather admonished me to go home without any detours. I had no intention to detour, it was late, and I was tired and drunk.

14

GOING HOME

O n my way home I had to cross the railroad dam under construction with a single rail on top. The construction was creative, indeed, but not if one is drunk and stumbles home, skip jumping from one tie to the next as fast as possible.

All of a sudden I missed a step, and fell into the space between two ties. I thought I'd been pretty good thus far in negotiating the obstacle course. Under normal circumstances I would've climbed out, cursed myself for my clumsiness, and continued on my way. But I was drunk, it was still dark, and I was giggling and laughing and having a hell of time sorting things out while hanging with my legs between two ties, my stomach lying on one tie, sticking my head between the next two ties trying to pull up my legs, which of course was impossible. Well, in the end I managed to get myself disentangled somehow and climbed back on top. I continued on my way across the ties, sliding down on my rear end on the other side of the dam and was about six hundred yards from home smiling happily and remembering the wonderful celebration, all the nice people and my drunken silliness. To make it short, I felt no pain as I took a short cut stumbling across the field toward our barrack, until I slid into something soft and wet. At first I didn't realized what had happened until it suddenly dawned on me and rendered me completely sober, instantly. I woke up to reality fast.

Forty to fifty prisoners lived in our barracks, and before us there had been others. As I've explained, we did "our business" in outhouses. The prisoners had dug holes into the ground, about eight feet deep and six feet wide; wide enough to put a double seated out-house on top of it. An outhouse to sit in was luxurious in comparison to squatting on two boards inside the camp's latrine. The outhouse was located seventy to eighty yards from our barrack, to keep the smell away. As soon as one hole was filled all the way to the top we'd dig another hole near by and move the outhouse to the new hole. The old hole remained were it was. To stop the exuding stench; a thin layer of earth was thrown on top of the old hole. The system worked perfectly, nobody else walked over the field anyway and—while I was sober—I knew were the old holes were.

To be exact it worked very well until that early morning when I was coming home pleasantly drunk from my wedding party. In my drunken stupor I'd strayed off the well-known path, taken a short cut, and slid into one of the discarded holes filled to the brim with shit, old shit.

I immediately stretched out both arms, to grasp the edges of the hole to hold on for dear life. The thought of drowning in excrement had sobered me rapidly.

Slowly, carefully I tried to raise myself out of the shit. There was nothing to step onto on the sides of the hole, and the more I struggled the deeper I sank. The sides of the pit were smooth and slippery, and didn't support my groping feet. I was panic-stricken, pressed my lips together and breathed only through the nose. Then I tilted my head backward and yelled, "HELP," as loud as I could. Our barracks were only 70 yards away and somebody should have heard me, though the noise of the macadam plant was drowning all sounds.

To this day I believe that under normal circumstances I would've drowned in my own and everybody else's excrement. It was five o'clock, Sunday morning, and everybody was still asleep, normally. But this was a special day. During the night something totally unforeseen had occurred. As so often before, the dear Lord had been holding his hand over me, one more time.

THE RUSSIANS HAD DECIDED TO SEND US HOME.

This most unbelievable event came overnight! The one thing that had been foremost in our minds, and in our dreams for over four and one half years had actually happened. We'd go home, we'd return to the other side of the iron curtain, we'd escape Siberia, and we'd rejoin civilization as free men!

I don't expect that anybody who has never been in Siberia will understand what the POWs felt upon hearing the unbelievable news.

Once the Russian had made their decision the machinery of bureaucracy went into high gear. They had to gather the prisoners into holding camps, to check the POWs over one more time, do some final interrogation, weed out a few more hidden SS men, or survivors from the Vlassow army, the Balts etc., etc., etc.

At 4.30 A.M. on a Sunday, early in September 1949 four Russian guards from the camp arrived at our barrack, woke up everybody, and started to do what they'd been doing daily for more than four years—counting.

And then the unbelievable nightmare happened. One guy was missing! They counted again and again, and every time the count came up short.

The missing person was struggling not to drown in the shit.

The men in our little commando were panic-stricken. By now everybody knew what this sudden visit by the guards meant. They were being counted to GO HOME. What would happen now? One prisoner was missing! Where did he disappear?

Would they all have to stay in Siberia because of one missing prisoner?

Would their transport be delayed?

Arthur, who knew exactly where I had been during the night, persuaded the others and the Russian soldiers to start looking for me at once.

Since I was yelling my head off only seventy yards from the barracks, while sinking slowly deeper and deeper into the stinking mess, it didn't take them very long to find me. When I heard them coming I tried to yell even louder. Rushing over to help me the first guy almost fell into the hole with me.

It took four guys to pull me out, two guys pulling my arms and another two holding on to the first two. Everybody backed off when I was finally lying next to the hole, the stench was overpowering.

"Get into the shower, quickly," Arthur yelled. "We'll all start throwing up if you don't clean this shit off. You have to throw away the clothes you are wearing. Don't even bother to clean them. You better get undressed right here and throw everything into the hole, you can run over to the shower as you are, and I'll collect some bits and pieces of clothing for you from the others in the meantime."

Our shower came in handy. No, it was a blessing. I showered and washed and scrubbed and showered, standing under the hot water for an eternity, cleaning every inch of my body to get rid of the awful smell.

As soon as I was ready the Russian guards commandeered us to the trucks and drove to a camp at the edge of town, which we had never seen before. It was weird to be in a camp again, surrounded by watchtowers and fences. At the stone quarry we had grown accustomed to the open space and to our freedom.

Arthur and I stayed together in spite of the awful smell I continued to radiate and tried to find out what was going on. It turned out that the proposed schedule for the preparation of our transport was exceptionally brief, considering what we were used to.

We'd stay two more weeks in the camp they told us, to complete all the checking and assembly of the transport and were due to arrive in *Frankfurt/Oder* after only two weeks on the Trans Siberian railroad, crossing Russia from east to west. To be in *Frankfurt/Oder* in four weeks sounded unbelievable to us!

"Arthur, do you really trust these conniving bastards?" I asked. "Are they trying again to pacify us, as they did four and a half years ago when they brought us here? Where do they want to ship us this time?"

"I can understand your suspicions, Peter, but I believe that this time we're going home. They couldn't ship us to a worse place than Siberia, and by now we're docile prisoners. Why should they make up stories now? But let me tell you one more thing. Watch it, Peter before we're finally loaded into boxcars they'll pluck the last remnants of undesirables out of our midst, to stay right here. I wouldn't be surprised if some heretofore unknown members of the SS will be discovered before then."

"Okay, I sincerely hope that you're right. You've got a point. It's just that I'm extremely nervous and suspicious. Considering the aforementioned group, which might be staying here when we leave, I've got a few names in mind. You know all these people from the former Baltic states as well as I do? Why would they let them go? The way they figure a man's nationality they're Russians by now anyway."

During our time in the staging camp food rations were as plentiful as they hadn't been for years, and nobody in the camp was going to work either. The bread was lighter and dry, and the *kascha* was cooked with a little bit of fat. When we saw that we knew we were really going home.

Galina was constantly on my mind. I had to let her know what was going on, I couldn't simply disappear. In the end I managed to convince the Russian administration I had to return to the stone quarry. I had to finish some accounting for our work in progress I explained, when we were leaving rather abruptly. They'd been very appreciative all along that I'd done the *nariad* calculations for them. They hated paper work. Otherwise, I argued, they wouldn't be able to collect any money for our work. Money, as everywhere, was the final argument even in the socialist system. After the administrator gave me a *propusk* (Pass), I went across town to see our old *Natchalnik* at the stone quarry to straighten things out. That was my excuse, in reality and most of all I wanted to see and talk to Galina.

As I entered the *stalowaja* where she worked I saw her from afar, standing behind the counter at the other end of the large dining hall, dishing out food to the workers. I was forty yards away at the entrance of the eating hall, she couldn't have seen me; but the minute I saw her, and looked at her, she lifted her head and looked in my direction with her big brown eyes, a smile crossing her face. I went to where she was working. She interrupted what she was doing to come to the side of the counter. Before I could open my mouth to say something she squeezed my hand and said, "Petja, I know everything. The release of the German POWs is the talk of the town. Petja, I'm so happy for you, but . . ." tears were welling up in her eyes, "I'm so sad for us, I'll never see you again in my entire life. Go, Petja. Go with God; greet America and your mother from me. Be happy and don't come back to see me again."

She gave me a hug and a quick kiss, turned around and disappeared into the kitchen.

Her prediction was correct. We never saw each other or heard from each other again. *Galina Dimitrewna Xerimnik*—she was the third friend I found in Siberia.

Upon returning to the staging camp I hurried to see Arthur to tell him about meeting Galina, and how miserable I felt leaving her, and leaving her most of all—as I firmly believed—forever. He had a similar experience with Natasha, his girl. We both sympathized and felt awful. But no matter how both of us suffered emotionally about leaving these two wonderful women, the joys of leaving Siberia, and leaving it alive and healthy, was overwhelming and let us forget everything else.

The Russian prison authorities and the NKWD were busy avoiding allowing anybody with a "past" slip through their net. They kept us for another ten days for further examination. They wanted to make sure punishment would be assured for the guilty parties. Most of all they were searching for SS men.

"I wouldn't be surprised if they'd pick the two Ossipenkos. They always said they were from Baden-Baden, but they speak perfect Russian and very bad German as far as I can judge, they are Vlasso,." Arthur whispered to me. "And then there is this guy who was so chummy with all the guards. He was always busy doing things in the office of the administration and the ANTIFA. I wonder where he learned his Russian, and I'm curious to know the questions they're going to ask him, now that they don't need him any more?"

Arthur was right. These people disappeared very quickly. But it wasn't only these few obvious people. Painstakingly and systematically the Russians examined everybody. There wasn't the slightest scar under, or on top of a left arm, which escaped their attention. They diligently investigated whatever could appear to be a trace of a removed tattoo, a scar or a blemish, always searching for the SS men's blood group identifications.

When I earlier related my experiences in the *kolchos* stone quarry I mentioned a man called Adolf Gaida, the guy who peed into the graves of soldiers during burial. I said at the time, "The dear Lord

sees everything." Well, he did. We heard that Adolf Gaida had belonged to a special unit the Russians wanted. He stayed behind with
a few others.

Our group from the stone quarry had a particularly hard time
during the examinations. Most of us had scars and burns from flying
hot stone chips. Mind you, from red hot glowing stone chips. These
chips of slag flew around with explosive force while we were hitting
the hot stones with our heavy hammers to break them up into smaller
movable pieces. They stuck to the sweaty surface of the skin burning it immediately.

The scar on my left arm from the injury in Italy was very noticeable. It drew their attention. This one, like other scars, caused intensive
questioning and several witnesses were asked to testify about their past.
Strangely enough, many so-called good friends and old buddies suffered sudden bouts of amnesia. Only Arthur was a true friend and swore
to the authenticity of my injury. (He hadn't been with me in Italy.)

On our last day in the prison camp, the Russians hit us with one
final act of intimidation. An NKWD officer, together with an interpreter, called us into a meeting room single file. Each one of us received a sheet of paper to sign a written statement. I don't remember
exactly what it said, but the wording was very straightforward and
simple. It went about like this:

PLEDGE

The glorious and victorious Soviet Union has
graciously decided to release me from captivity,
where she kept me for four and one half years,
because of the many atrocities I committed in
the name of the fascist Nazi hordes devastating
our motherland and murdering our citizens.
On this day, the 26th of September 1949, I swear
I will never again raise a weapon against the
glorious Soviet Union or any of her Allies. I am
aware a 25 year prison term will be
automatically imposed if I violate this pledge.

Signature

Arthur, who stood next to me whispered into my ear, "Peter, I know your reaction, for heavens sake, don't start an argument now. We don't have to tell them that we haven't committed any atrocities. It won't solve anything; it'll only keep us for further investigations. Just sign the bloody thing and get the hell out of here."

I did what he told me. I would've done so anyway, even without his well-intended interference. I was pig-headed, but I wasn't stupid.

On the following day we marched to the same railyard where we had disembarked four and a half years previously, and climbed into boxcars on our way to Frankfurt/Oder. It was on a sunny afternoon when finally and without further delays, fifty men each were ordered into 50-ton boxcars, not one hundred men as on our trip to Siberia. Can anybody imagine how we felt, climbing into that car and seeing it rolling in a westerly direction?

This time it was more comfortable, for sure. We had plenty of straw to sleep on and open car doors at all times. We were permitted to leave the train, to relieve ourselves whenever it stopped and we felt like it. This time we didn't have to try to aim through a pipe in the floor and were treated like free people, almost, if that's at all possible in a country where even the citizens are prisoners.

On our way east, shortly after the end of the war in 1945, the POW transport had stopped continuously to wait for other rail traffic to pass us by. Not this time, the transport leader seemed to be in a hurry. We were approaching the Polish border after only ten days.

Crossing the border was quite an episode. Heavy fortifications were everywhere. Several multiple lines of barbed wire and dragon's teeth were positioned, on both sides of the railroad; also trenches and artillery positions, without guns though, and there were personnel bunkers. Whom were the Russians fighting now? Or was it just their natural paranoia?

The train was at its most western destination on the Russian rail gauge. It would have to continue on European gauge tracks from now on. All boxcars, steam engines and other rolling stock changed.

Our train rolled onto a dead end track and stopped. We stood on a siding, on one edge of a field two hundred yards wide, separated in the middle by a low, wooden fence. The fence had only one gate and on the other side of the gate stood another train with twice the number of 20-ton boxcars as our train had.

In front of the gate, on our side, were several tables and next to each table were two chairs. Several men in white smocks were walking around. We didn't know why they would wear a white smock, but the men looked almost like doctors. The doors of our boxcars were open, crowded with POWs eager to know what this was all about. A tremendous curiosity was evident everywhere. What could this set up mean? Was this a last minute surprise by our jailors?

An officer appeared from behind our train together with an interpreter. Both carried megaphones with an amplifier.

The officer made a short speech in Russian. He spoke with a heavy Ukrainian accent; I didn't understand a word. The interpreter interrupted him intermittently to translate to us.

"*Woijenna plennies,*" now from the interpreter. "You'll leave your train to get on the train over there. You'll take all your possessions with you. Don't leave anything behind in the boxcars. Pass these tables in a single file, starting from over here with the first car behind the engine. You'll totally undress and the doctors will examine you from head to toe, including your rectum. Anything hidden anywhere will be taken from you. You're not allowed to take any pictures, list of names or dog tags, other than your own with you. No more than one hundred rubles per person will be permitted to leave the Soviet Union, no precious metals or stones either."

There was dead silence form the prisoners, not a word of protest and no comments. The first car started to disembark. The men walked over to the tables where they undressed completely. The doctors made spot checks of their rectum—all this in front of the watching prisoners—using rubber gloves. They cleaned the gloves in a soapy solution after every examination, while leaving them on their hands.

Fortunately the checks were far and few between. Our car was in the middle of the train. The eight or ten so-called doctors seemed to have tired of their work by the time our turn came. But, would you believe it; they'd found two or thrce guys with hidden pouches. How could anybody be so dumb? The guys were taken away and we didn't see them again.

Everybody also finally passed the gate and climbed aboard the other train. Late in the afternoon, after yet another humiliating experience, it departed the field.

As we entered Poland the landscape changed. The fields were plowed and farmers worked everywhere. The comparison with the Russian landscape was noticeable. Whenever the train stopped Polish children kept approaching, yelling, *"Soldat, hast Du Brot?"* (Soldier do you have any bread?)

At first the men were very upset. After all, Poland was one of the victors in the last war and an ally of the Russians. If the Poles didn't have any bread how would conditions be at home in Germany with their children?

During the sessions by the ANTIFA we'd always been told, no, had been religiously indoctrinated how the Russian people, together with the new, peace loving, East German Socialist party the SED, (Social Unity Party of Germany) were struggling to rebuild the economy of the country, this was in plain contrast to the three Western Zones of Germany, American, British and French, which were being exploited by capitalistic forces, the true enemy of the working class.

In communist dialectic we had interpreted this to mean that the East was starving and the West had everything.

What we saw now looked really bad. After many more stops and another hundred to hundred fifty miles travel from east to west through the Polish countryside, we discovered, to the relief of the worrying fathers on our train that the begging children needed the bread to feed their tame rabbits, and not because they were hungry.

On October 7, 1949 we arrived in *Frankfurt/Oder* in the DDR (Deutsche Demokratische Republik = German Democratic Republic). The train crossed the border without much fanfare, we only noticed because it crossed the Oder River. Soon it rolled slowly into the middle of a large camp, which was protected by barbed wire fences. German Red Cross nurses waved flowers shouting greetings to us. A banner was strung between two wooden poles reading.

"Willkommen Ihr Heimkehrer aus der siegreichen UdSSR" (Welcome returnees from the victorious Soviet Union). It lacked any warmth and realism. It was a truly stilted performance. Organized enthusiasm, typically communistic horseshit we thought—in total silence.

We were assigned barracks, received warm soup and a piece of bread and of course more instructions.

Those of us able to write in Cyrillic letters were asked to volunteer for registration duty. I volunteered and took Arthur with me to help with sharpening pencils. We recorded everybody's name, both in German and Russian, together with the man's final destination. At the end of the day the names were handed to a German radio station to be announced during a nightly national broadcast at 8 P.M.

Later on we discovered that everybody in Germany listened to these broadcasts. During the end of 1949 and the beginning of 1950 the Russians released over two million prisoners of war. It was the fervent hope for millions of widows and mothers to hear the one name they were waiting for. Over two million other German soldiers taken prisoner would never be heard of again.

We were sitting in an office, decorated with pictures of Wilhelm Piek and Otto Grotewohl—the two East German henchmen appointed by Stalin as heads of the SED—and recorded the names of everybody who passed before us. A man from the stone quarry whom Arthur and I knew well stood in front of us.

"Horst Schimanski, I am going home to *Duttweiler.*" We looked at him and laughed.

"That's not your name, Hans. What's the matter with you? Do you want to pull our leg?" Arthur said, and I started to write his real name.

"No, no, no, Peter, Arthur, I'm not Hans Schmidt anymore, and I'll never return to my old home either. During the darkest days in *Stalinsk* when we didn't believe that any of us would ever return home again, a few buddies' and I were sitting together contemplating this very moment. Mind you, we never truly imagined this moment would ever come. You know how it was, everybody was dreaming. We decided that it would be foolish to return to our wives who'd cheated on us during the entire war while we were risking our lives for them. Only God knows what they are doing now. We thought this would be a wonderful opportunity to disappear and to start a new life.

Well, it is! And that's what I'm going to do right now. Nobody knows who died in *Stalinsk* and who survived. This is the cheapest divorce I could ever have. Come on fellows don't give me away. It's no skin of your backs anyway. I know ten guys on this train alone who will do what I'm doing now."

Arthur and I laughed and consented. What did we care? The thought had never occurred to us.

At the end of the day Icke came by to register. My mouth fell wide open. The guy walked ramrod straight. "Icke, you scoundrel," Arthur and I exclaimed in unison, "did you already see a specialist?" All three of us laughed, and Icke enjoyed it the most.

Every former POW received *"einen Entlassungsschein"* (a Certificate of Release), a document, which we needed to register at our local city hall. This document, the German official told us pompously, would enable us to collect compensation from the Government for the time we'd spent in Siberia as soldiers of the German *Wehrmacht* without pay. The guys were jubilant and quickly multiplied the number of days in Siberia with the last pay they'd received in the army and came up with princely sums. Now, they thought, they'd receive start up capital to begin a new life, to buy new clothes and necessities.

The next morning we stepped into a regular passenger train for the short trip to Berlin. From Frankfurt/Oder it is just thirty miles to Berlin. Propaganda! The Government didn't want us to climb out of boxcars, to greet our loved ones.

The only station in the middle of the City of Berlin and in the Eastern Sector, which hadn't been totally destroyed by bombs and fighting, was *Bahnhof Friedrichstrasse*. The train slowly rolled into the station. The platform was crowded with women and men and a few children, but mostly old people.

I gave Arthur a big last hug as the train stopped. One more time we promised each other to keep in touch, no matter what. I got off the train to take a look around and immediately hid behind a newspaper kiosk to find out if anyone had come to pick me up. Sure enough there she stood nobody but her.

Celli had listened—like all the other German women—to the radio broadcast with names of returning prisoners and had come to pick me up. I pulled myself together, suddenly caught up in my own emotions. I stepped out from behind the Kiosk and started walking toward her. She was easily recognizable with her blond hair, dressed to the nines, quite differently from the drab appearance of most people on the platform. She couldn't see me in the ebbing crowd of men. We all looked the same in our prison garb. Suddenly she must have recognized me. I saw her throwing up her arms as if she wanted to embrace me. Even though I couldn't hear anything in the noise of a train station, I saw her lips form the word "Peter."

She pushed her way through the crowd to where I was standing with my wooden box, gave me a big kiss and a hug, and immediately backed away wrinkling her nose.

"What's that smell? Do you have to go to the bathroom?"

I still smelled from my fall into the latrine, and though the men on the train had not complained it must've been terrible to an unsuspecting person. I laughed and pulled her with me down the stairs from the station toward the street.

"I'll explain later," I said, "but it's not what you're thinking, Celli, all I want to do right now is to go home. Let's find some transportation."

Celli hadn't missed a beat. Around the corner from the exit a taxi was waiting for us with a typical Berlin cab driver at the wheel. Celli directed him to leave the Russian sector on the shortest route possible, and we were on our way.

Suddenly it came to me—the reality of the situation was so enormous I couldn't say a word. Celli kept jabbering away at a mile a minute without any response from me. I sat there staring through the windshield in front of me, hypnotized as the taxi drove the short stretch along *Friedrichstrasse* approaching *Unter den Linden* where the driver turned right to traverse the last half-mile towards the Brandenburg Gate.

There it was, looming in front of me. The construction was larger than the windshield of the cab; *THE* symbol of the most western point of the Russian Empire was within my reach. If the taxi drove through it, if we'd make it without interference, if nothing went wrong at the last second, I'd be free, free after the most unimaginable four and a half years in any man's existence. I was leaning over the front seat to see better, my head next to the driver, staring at the huge gate, and suddenly my tears started to flow like never before in my life. I was choking uncontrollably. The gate embraced us and we passed through arriving in the western sector of the divided city.

Nobody said a word, Celli and the driver were caught up in the moment and I didn't hear and see anything.

Just in time, before we reached Celli's home, I recovered my composure.

Can anybody believe it? I had made it! Against all odds, I had made it!

I had suffered like Job and had lost seven of my formative years but with God's help I survived. My tears that day at the Brandenburg gate were not only tears of relief and happiness at being free at last but were shed also for the one million seven hundred thousand of my compatriots who did not return. God had plans for me as I began a new life at the age of twenty-five.

5 days after returning from Siberia

Epilogue

I will tell you the rest of my story in a subsequent book but let me give you a brief overview of what happened with the rest of my life.

My relationship with my stepmother ended soon after my return from Siberia. I obtained a visitor's visa with the help of my mother and joined her in the United States of America.

My friend Arthur returned to his wife and his home in Westphalia, they had two children. He died in 1999.

I do not know what happened to Galina and I didn't think it to be advisable to return to Stalinsk (Kemerowo).

The Schwarzlose Cosmetic Company limped along for a few more years and was sold to a competitor.

With the help of many friends I stayed in the USA for a total of nine months while traveling extensively. All in all I saw forty states. During this time I visited with Lieutenant Snyder and made peace with him. I had to return to Germany to obtain an immigration visa to enter the United States and become a citizen.

I worked odd jobs in New York City and took courses at Columbia University.

My first full time job in New York was with Revlon Inc.

In 1955 I was informed that my stepmother committed suicide in Berlin.

I married twice and have one daughter with my first wife and two grandchildren.

In 1958, I joined Avon Products Inc. Learning of my background the company sent me to Germany to build a direct selling organization.

I remained at Avon for fifteen years as general manager of the German organization with more than ninety thousand independent saleswomen.

After a short period with Tandy Radio Shack and Wrigley Inc., I started my own marketing company, distributing our own brand of gummy bears.

In 1985 at the age of 92 my mother, Olga, died.

After eight successful years I sold the gummy bear business to my partners to retire.

In 1990, however, Mary Kay Ash asked me to lead her German company, which I did until 1995 when I finally ended my business career.

*Peter with his mother at the Schwarzlose
family reunion in West Salem, Ill. 1950*

Acknowledgments

I would like to extend my gratitude to everybody who helped, supported and guided me to put my story together:

Dick Gray, a good friend and golf partner on Hilton Head Island, who suggested with great tact and kindness that my English was less than perfect. He spent a lot of time editing the entire book.

Kathryn Wall, a writer of several wonderful low country novels, who helped me to recognize translated German words and terminologies and also introduced me to George Trask of Coastal Villages Press, who did more than just to turn a manuscript into a book.

Elizabeth Tierney did a painstaking job of correcting my punctuation and eliminating redundancies and adjectives where they were not needed.

My friend David Smith gave me a final boost. He convinced me to go the extra mile with his encouraging comments, corrections and creative suggestions.

I would like to thank many people, too numerous to mention here, who listened to my tales, showed interest, and encouraged me to write about them. Most of all I thank my wife, Monika, who was always ready to listen, to make suggestions and to offer words of encouragement.

I don't need to mention again my friend Arthur, or my Russian angel Galina, or my mother Olga. They are watching me and are cheering me on. Without them I wouldn't be here.

My wife Monika and I would like to thank all the people on Hilton Head Island for their warmhearted welcome and sincere friendship.

About the author

Peter Schwarzlose was born in Berlin, Germany. His mother was American, and his father was German. He grew up during a tumultuous time in history. He served in the German army and was a prisoner of war in the Siberian gulag. He has personally witnessed most of the events described in this book.

Educated in Germany and in America, he spent his business career in his father's company in Berlin and as an executive with American companies in the United States and in Europe. He is now retired on Hilton Head Island, South Carolina.

Ordering Gulag

Ordering additional copies of GULAG is easy.

Go to www.gulagmemoirs.com and follow instructions.

Or send check for $24.95 + $4.05 for shipping to:

Peter Schwarzlose
22 Lighthouse Road #493
Hilton Head Island, SC 29928